Masked Performance

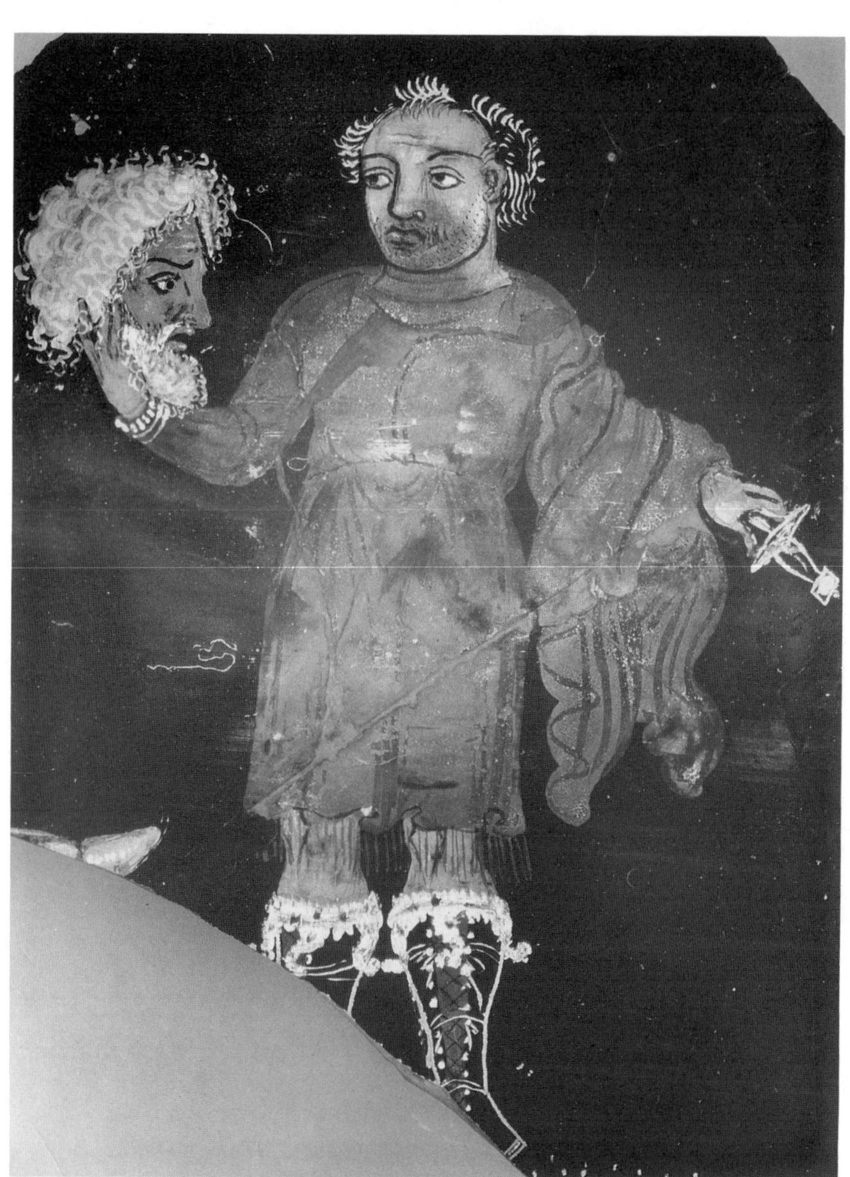

Masked Performance

The Play of Self and Other in Ritual and Theatre

John Emigh

University of Pennsylvania Press

Philadelphia

Printed in the United States of America

Library of Congress Cataloging-in-Publication Data

Emigh, John.
Masked performance : the play of self and other in ritual and theatre / John Emigh.
p. cm.
Includes bibliographical references and index.
ISBN 0-8122-3058-2 (cloth : alk. paper). — ISBN 0-8122-1336-X (pbk. : alk. paper)
1. Masks. 2. Theater—Indonesia. 3. Theater—India. 4. Theater—Papua New Guinea. I. Title.
PN2071.M37E44 1996
792'.095—dc20 96-17690
CIP

Frontispiece. A vase fragment from the fourth century BC depicts a Greek actor regarding a tragic mask (Photo: Karl Öhrlein: by permission of Martin von Wagner Museum of Würzburg University, Würzburg, Germany)

Cover: Ancestral Mai mask dancing: Mindimbit, Sepik River, Papua New Guinea, 1974. (Photo: author)

For Ullie

Contents

Illustrations ix

Acknowledgments xiii

Introduction xvii

1. Playing and Masking: Observations on Masked Performance in Papua New Guinea and Beyond 1

2. Dealing with the Demonic: Strategies of Containment in Hindu Iconography and Performance 35

3. Playing with the Past: Visitation and Illusion in the Mask Theatre of Bali 105

4. *Jelantik Goes to Blambangan*: A Topeng Pajegan Performance
I Nyoman Kakul 157

5. The Domains of Topeng 171

6. A Joker in the Deck: Hajari Bhand of Rajasthan
Written with Ulrike Emigh 207

7. A Capacity for Wonder
Interview conducted by James Schevill 244

8. Conclusion 275

Appendix: A List of Basic Questions That Might Be Asked About Performances 293

References 301

Index 321

Illustrations

All photos are by the author unless otherwise specified

Figures

1. Iatmul Mai Mask, Sepik River, Papua New Guinea. xxii
2. Tau-tau figures, Tanatoraja, Sulawesi. 4
3. Tau-tau of a queen, Kete Village, Tanatoraja. 5
4. Carved wooden water buffalo head, Kete Village. 6
5. Demonstration of si galegale puppet, Samosir, Sumatra. 9
6. "Mudmen," Highlands, Papua New Guinea. 12
7. Musicians, New Ireland high school graduation. 15
8. Making Uramot Baining mendaska mask, New Britain, Papua New Guinea. 16
9. Mendaska mask modeled by its maker. 18
10. Kirtimukha stone relief, Uluwatu, Bali. 36
11. Kirtimukha, Mukhtaswara, Bhubaneswar, Orissa. 38
12. Kirtimukha, Prambanan, Java. 39
13. Bhoma as Kirtimukha, Pura Kehen, Bangli, Bali. 40
14. Face of Narasimha as Kirtimukha, Bhubaneswar, Orissa. 42
15–18. Papier-mâché Narasimha masks, Ganjam, Orissa. 44
19. Narasimhi mask, Aiho, Malda, West Bengal. 47
20. Shri Arjun Satapathy offering puja to Narasimha mask, Baulagaon, Ganjam, Orissa. 48
21. Ganesha gives his blessings. 51
22. Hiranyakashipu in performance. 53
23. Boy actor playing Prahlada. 54
24. Entranced Narasimha performer being restrained. 58
25. Barong Ket, Jimbaran, Bali. 62
26. Rangda mask being restored, Singapadu, Bali. 63
27. Rangda's daughter, Rarong, being attacked by "keris dancers," Batubulan, Bali. 65

28. Rangda, Rarong, and the Barong Ket honored together, Pejeng, Bali. 68
29. Rangda mask as pamurtian for Wisnu, Sanur, Bali. 69
30. Entrance to Goa Gajah, Pejeng, Bali. 71
31. Representation of proportionate attention to body parts by human brain's motor cortex. 72
32. First impressions of Rangda by Aaron Emigh, age 4. 73
33. Eleventh-century stone relief, Kutri, Bali. 82
34. Early twentieth-century temple painting of Durga killing Mahisasura, Jayapur, Koraput, Orissa. 83
35. Mask of the Birdcatcher of danda nata, Ganjuguda, Phulbani, Orissa. 86
36. Kali mask, gambhira performance, Aiho, West Bengal. 87
37. Shakti mask, Takurani temple, Behrampur, Ganjam, Orissa. 88
38. Large processional mask used to honor Shakti, Chikiti, Ganjam, Orissa. 92
39. Prabhats and giant kings and queens, Holi, Borokadanda, Ganjam, Orissa. 94
40. Gable mask guarding spirit house, Angoram, Sepik River. 97
41. I Nyoman Kakul, Batuan, Gianyar, Bali. 106
42–44. Kakul before his performance, Tusan, Klungkung, Bali. 109
45. Cremation sarcophagus paraded prior to Kakul's performance. 110
46. Kakul saying mantras while preparing to perform. 112
47. Prayers, Balinese odalan. Mas, Gianyar, Bali. 114
48. Kakul teaching his granddaughter to dance. 117
49. Masks of I Ketut Kantor, Kakul's son. 119
50. Kakul as Patih Lepang. 121
51. Kakul as Pasung Grisgris. 122
52. Kakul as I Gusti Dauh Bale Agung. 124
53. Ida Bagus Alit as tua, Sangeh, Bali. 126
54. Kakul as Penasar Kelihan. 128
55. Kakul as Penasar Cenikan. 133
56. Another performer as Penasar Cenikan, Batuan, Bali. 135
57. Kakul as Patih Jelantik. 138
58. Kakul as Dalem Blambangan. 139
59. Kakul as Si Mata Mata. 141
60. Kakul as Desak Made Rai. 144
61. Kakul as Culcul. 145
62. Statue of historical king in image of a Balinese dancer. 146
63. Kakul as Sidha Karya. 149
64. Priest preparing offering at topeng pajegan performance, Gelgel, Klungkung, Bali. 152
65. Sidha Karya presenting the offering, Tusan. 169

66. Nested domains of drama, script, theatre, and performance (R. Schechner). 173
67–68. Pages from Kakul's notebooks. 178
69. Expanded model of the domains of topeng. 185
70. Diagram of audience attention to domains as directed by Kakul's performance. 188
71. Diagram of Kakul's engagement of domains. 190
72. Transformative cycle involving nature, art, and offering. 191
73. Hajari Bhand, Chittorgarh, Rajasthan, India. 208
74. Hajari Bhand making up to play the Pagal. 209
75. Hajari Bhand putting on the costume of a Muslim Fakir. 219
76. Hajari Bhand as a Police Inspector. 220
77. Hajari Bhand as a Bania. 226
78. Hajari Bhand as a Doctor. 230
79. Hajari Bhand in the mask of Hanuman at Diwali. 231
80. Hajari Bhand as Shiva. 232
81. Hajari Bhand as Majnun, hero of a Persian romance. 234
82. Hajari Bhand as an aging Kanjari thief and prostitute. 235
83. Hajari Bhand as a Nakhti. 237
84. Author as a roguish bondres character. 250
85. Puppets designed by Bernice Bronson for the Looking Glass Theatre Production of *Tjupak.* 256
86. Author as Dalem Bedahulu. 258
87. Author, I Made Bandem, and I Wayan Suweca in topeng production. 260
88. Red Riding Shawl. 263
89. The Wolf. 264
90. Grandmother. 265
91. Mosca and Voltore, *Volpone.* 269
92. Author as Penasar Cenikan. 272
93. Brothers Mai exiting after a performance. 290

Color Plates (follow p. 152)

I. Ancestral Mai masks, Papua New Guinea.
II. Bhoma head at cremation, Gianyar, Bali.
III. Narasimha in a *Prahlada Nataka* performance, Kamagunda, Ganjam, Orissa.
IV. Rangda and her daughter, Rarong, Batuan, Bali.
V. Ida Bagus Alit, full topeng costume, Sangeh, Bali.
VI. I Nyoman Kakul as Dalem Baturenggong, Tusan, Klungkung, Bali.
VII. Hajari Bhand as a Gaduliya. Chittorgarh, Rajasthan.
VIII. Opening scene of *Caucasian Chalk Circle.*

Acknowledgments

I owe so much to so many over such a wide geographical field that I have chosen to list most acknowledgments separately in the appropriate notes for each chapter. I have tried to make sure that scholars and artists to whom I owe the greatest intellectual debts are acknowledged in the body of the text; still, I have inevitably slighted many whose works and words have affected my thinking and writing. Some debts need to be acknowledged at the outset.

The journals and other publications where the articles recycled here first appeared are listed in each chapter; I am grateful for their editors' permission to reprint and revise the work. I also wish to thank the various photographers whose work I have used for their generous cooperation, and the W. H. Freeman and Company for permission to reprint the diagram pertaining to the somatosensory cortex. Grateful acknowledgment is made to the Graduate School of Brown University and the family of Lee Strasberg—Anna, Adam, and David—who made it possible to print the color plates and photographs in this volume. Strasberg's love of Asian theatre, and his appreciation for the theatricality and truthfulness of its many masks, are a little known aspect of his own search for the vital links between person and character that took him in a very different direction.

Over the years, my students at Brown University have challenged me to state clearly what otherwise would remain a far murkier set of thoughts and experiences. Their names are too numerous to set down, but I am fortunate to have had to explain this material to young people with keen minds and little tolerance for nonsense; I thank them for the opportunity, and for their often helpful comments. My colleagues at Brown have also contributed a great deal to the thinking that has gone into this book, challenging and supporting lines of inquiry. Among those who have, knowingly or unknowingly, helped this project along are Lina Fruzzetti, Bill Beeman, and Robert Jay (Anthropology), Nancy Dunbar, Jim Barnhill, George Bass, Birje Patil, Shelley Wyant, Don Wilmeth, John Lucas, Spencer Golub, Lowery Marshall, Elmo Terry-Morgan, Julie Standberg, and Michelle Bach-

Coulibaly (Theatre, Speech, and Dance), Shep Shapiro, Jim Koetting, Andy Toth, and Carol Babiracki (Music), Anani Dzidzienyo and Rhett Jones (Afro-American Studies), Jim Schevill, Edwin Honig, Mark Spilka, Keith Waldrop, Paula Vogel, Tori Haring-Smith, David Savran, and Susan Slyomovics (English and Comparative Literature), Donna Wulff, David Pingree and Robert Hueckstedt (South Asian Studies), and, in conversations begun more recently, Sheila Blumstein, Jerry Daniels, Michael Paradiso, Jerome Sanes, James Anderson, Phil Lieberman, James McIlwain, and Bill Warren (Cognitive and Neurosciences). Pamela Pion and Antigone Trimis performed vital tasks in readying this manuscript and constructing its initial index, for which they have my gratitude and affection. I also wish to thank Patricia Smith, Ridley Hammer, Alison Anderson, and their associates at the University of Pennsylvania Press for their faith, patience, and hard work in readying this text for publication, and Laura Moss Gottlieb for creating the index.

My colleagues in the Association for Asian Performance have been invaluable as a source of wisdom and encouragement. Carol Sorgenfrei, Kathy Foley, Judy Mitoma, Fritz deBoer, Ron Jenkins, Phillip Zarrilli, Farley Richmond, Jim Brandon, Richard Frasca, William Sun, Paul Barstow, Roger Long, Tevie Pourchot, Rakesh Solomon, Andrew Tsubaki, Mike Pedretti, and Leonard Pronko come to mind among those who may see their traces in these pages. Outside that sphere, Richard Schechner, Laurence Senelick, Herbert Blau, Moni Adams, Elinor Fuchs, Joe Roach, Robert Wessing, Eberhard Fischer, Sally Banes, Amrit Singh, Rachel Cooper, Rucina Ballinger, Richard Wallis, Joan Erdman, Rhonda Blair, Lynn Kremer Babcock, Pete and Judy Becker, Dragan Klaic, Martin Banham, Jean-Marie Pradière, Eugenio Barba, Larry Reed, Shelly Wyant, Eileen Blumenthal, and Karine Schomer have all shared ideas and experiences with me on many of the subjects addressed below; so, too, have Peter Schumann, Carlo Mazzoni-Clementi, Fred Curchak, Islene Pinder, Bunny Bronson, Erminio Pinque, Leonard Pitt, Anna Deavere Smith, and Kate Bornstein; we have not always agreed, but I have never walked away from any of these friends without feeling richer or wiser. It is my loss if I have not used their counsel to best advantage. I only met Victor Turner once, but, he, too, deserves my special thanks for opening up possibilities for rethinking the significance of events I had witnessed.

My children, first Aaron and Rebecca Emigh and now Eric Emigh, and my grandchildren, Jaama and Toby Moynihan, have been a source of wonder, inspiration, and often whatever wisdom I have managed while working through these ideas on and off the stage. Allison Erikson, Farida Khan, Hannah Pitterman, and Amy Catlin shared many of the experiences that have gone into the writing of this book. They have my heartfelt gratitude for the times when their companionship encouraged and sustained me. The greatest debt of this kind, though, is to my wife, Ullie Emigh, who shared motorcycle rides on non-existent roads, traveled all night in packed buses and trains to performances that sometimes never took place, patiently worked through chapters with me, and without whom this book and a great deal else that I treasure would not exist.

The most substantial debt of all is to the people and performers of New Guinea, Bali, Orissa, Rajasthan, and several other locales that figure less prominently in this narrative, but were none-the-less important to its genesis. Dhiren Dash, I Wayan Suweca, I Nyoman Wenten, I Made Bandem, I Nyoman Sumandhi, I Ketut Kantor, I Wayan Dibia, I Nyoman Catra, I Gusti Windia, Desak Laksmi Suarti, Ibu Masih, Suresh Awasthi, Kapila Vatsyayan, Shyamanand and Chetna Jalan, Durgadas Mukhapadhyay, Kedarnath Sahoo, Sanjukta and Raghunath Panigrahi, K. S. Dora, Pashupati Mahato, Komal Kothari, Simanchalam Patra, Biswa Bihari Khadanga, Chandrabhanu Pattanayak, Lepan Lea, and, of course, Hajari Bhand and I Nyoman Kakul deserve particular thanks. The mistakes are all my own, but this is their book no less than mine.

Finally, I owe an enormous debt to my parents, Eugene and Katherine Emigh, and to my sister, Peg Emigh. They taught me to be curious, encouraged me to use my imagination, allowed me to journey far away, provided a home to which I might always return, and told me to tell the truth as best I know it.

Introduction

The studies that follow deal with various performing traditions—mostly in Asia, and especially in Bali—that rely on masks and masking for their expressive power and imaginative life. Some of these studies are primarily descriptive, some primarily theoretical, and others an attempt to bear witness to my own experiences. I did not set out to write a book about masked traditions in other parts of the world, but rather to understand theatre better, and to make better theatre. In the process of observing and participating—taking notes and lessons, performing and seeking out other performers, directing, giving workshops, teaching, writing, and mulling over all of these experiences—I have come to regard the relationship of the mask to its wearer as a paradigm for the relationships between self and other (and self and self) that lie at the heart of theatrical process. I also have encountered performative traditions that have challenged me over and over to rethink the possibilities inherent in theatrical circumstances. The chapters that follow discuss some of these traditions in depth and offer a range of observations on the dynamics and significance of their enactments.

First, though, to provide a point of entrance for readers of these essays (and at the risk of being tedious), I wish to recount a few anecdotes that illustrate the concerns and experiences which have prompted and sustained my research and writing about masked performances:

Twenty years ago, on a grassy field by the Sepik River in Papua New Guinea, a huge, haystack-like figure, fitted out with a magnificent mask that was carved of wood, decorated with cowrie shells, natural dyes, and the tusks of a boar, and festooned with flowers poised himself in front of a log. Having paid a small fee for the privilege, I crouched before him, excited and nervous, my newly purchased camera in hand, getting ready to take a portrait of this magnificent creation. Suddenly the masked figure leapt over the log directly toward me, bellowing and hooting as he came. I scrambled back to give space, while all around me the assembled villagers of Mindimbit burst out in uncontrollable laughter. I had happened on this performance quite by accident in my wanderings up the river, and as yet understood very little of its significance; surely, in my zeal to document what I little knew, I had disturbed a ceremony of importance to these people—perhaps a vital ritual. After the performance, embarrassed and ashamed, I sought out the dancer who had animated the haystack and struggled to apologize in barely acquired Pidgin English. As the gist of my apology became clear to him, he broke into a great, huge grin, and said that, on the contrary, the spirit (*masalai*) of the mask—called to earth from the wilder and more powerful time of the ancestors—had enjoyed my presence immensely, and so had all his neighbors. Laughter again rippled through the improvised changing room.

A few years later, in Providence, Rhode Island, where I live, I went to see the production of a new play, *Arthur Rimbaud's in Town*. Since a student of mine was acting in the production, I knew something of its history. The Moroccan actor who played the title role—Ismail Abou El-Kanater—had at one time dropped out of the production, only to rejoin a few days later. His performance was superb by any standard and, having spent some time as a musician in Morocco many years ago, I sought him out afterward to compliment him. "Yes," he said, "this time Rimbaud really enjoyed himself. It took a while for me—for Rimbaud—to accept the script. But now he has, and he's up there having a fine time." The actor smiled, rolled his eyes, and shook his head in bemused wonderment.

More recently, in Shrewsbury, Massachusetts, after performing a one-man show involving a series of masked characters, I came through the curtain—for the first time without a mask—to take my final bows. "Why is he so tired," a woman in the front row whispered (loudly, so I could hear) to the woman beside her, "all he's done is send out all those other people." I took the remark as a compliment and laughed, but any actor knows there is more than a grain of truth in her jest. At a certain stage in the process of acting, usually when all is going well, it is hard to know what credit one can take for the "rightness" of a character's words or actions. It wasn't "you" performing them.

These three anecdotes all involve ironic play with the identity of the performer and the performed. In so far as they are jests, they play with perception and experience, converting epistemological dis-ease into a field for humor and paradox. Frequently used as a symbol for theatre, the mask calls attention to the often ambiguous play between self and other involved in its alchemical procedures. The unworn mask begins as something clearly set apart: an inert and disembodied other. The actor confronting the mask is nakedly and pathetically himself (or, increasingly, herself). For the actor, the otherness of the mask becomes both the obstacle and the goal. He or she must redefine the sense of self in order to wear the other's face and be true to it in spirit, thought, and action. This work is approached through a process of play (though work and play are frequently synonyms in theatrical jargon): the actor plays with the mask as if it were his or her own face, allowing the suggested life of the mask to play upon and to reshape the actor's imaginative sense of self. An actor facing a text with new words to speak—as Hamlet, for example—has a similar task. Initially set apart, the text must be appropriated, owned.

This ontological juggling of self and other within a field marked by ambiguity and paradox is characteristic of theatre, but not unique to it. Compare the zen student pondering the relationship of archer to target at the moment that the bow is released:

> "Do you understand," the master asked me one day after a particularly good shot, "what I mean by 'It shoots, It hits' "?
>
> "I'm afraid I don't understand anything at all," I answered, "even the simplest things have got in a muddle. Is it 'I' who draw the bow, or is it the bow that draws me into the state of highest tension? Do 'I' hit the goal or does the goal hit me? Is 'it' spiritual when seen by the eyes of the body, and corporeal when seen by the eyes of the spirit—or both or neither? Bow, arrow, goal and ego, all melt into one another, so that I can no longer separate them. And even the need to separate has gone. For as soon as I take the bow and shoot, everything becomes so clear and straightforward and so ridiculously simple."
>
> "Now at last," the Master broke in, "the bowstring has cut right through you." (Herrigel, 1964 [1953]: 88)

In working up a role, the unmediated self of the actor, the mask (*persona)* that is to be acted, and the text that is to be spoken within the flow of action form a triad. The tendency in most Western theatre today is to begin with the confrontation of actor and text and to work towards the persona—a term which in common usage has come to mean character as well as mask. In many of the theatrical forms I shall be examining, this process begins, instead, with the confrontation of actor and mask (always, to be sure, within the context of a more or less well defined set of social and artistic expectations). The text and *mise-en-scène*—the specific patterns of words and actions that emerge—will be shaped by this encounter and will often be improvized within the boundaries established by aesthetic form and social occasion. The ordering of the triad is different, but the essential process of finding a meeting ground for self and other remains the same; so does the need to negotiate playfully (and rigorously) the demands of experience, character, and text.

Some disclaimers are in order. The following chapters are in no sense a survey of masked traditions of the world, of Asia, or even of the localities that are addressed. Rather, I have chosen to concentrate on a few forms of masked performance, and, in most cases, the work of a very few exemplary performers in specific performances. The narrowed focus, while not consistent, is deliberate. Cultures don't create performances. Individuals living in complex and contested cultural circumstances do. The hope is that by drawing closer to an understanding as to how these particular performances proceed, and what is at stake within the various contexts that give rise to and sustain them, we may also come to a clearer understanding about theatre itself as an artistic and social phenomenon.

Using (mostly) theatre and rituals from Papua New Guinea as examples, the following chapter will have more to say about the range, modalities, and psychological underpinnings of masked play—and about the particular allure of masks in the playing. Papua New Guinea seems an attractive place to begin, since its (sometimes surface) otherness is so apparent, making what is shared—and not shared—between New Guinean and Western traditions of performance take on added interest. Papua New Guinea was also, chronologically, the first stop on a physical and intellectual journey that these chapters must in some ways replicate.

Chapter 2 will focus on trance performances in Orissa, India and in Bali, Indonesia that use masks in complex strategies to contain disruptive, chthonic forces that are seen as threatening to the health of the community. The Orissan *Prahlada Nataka* and Balinese *Calon Arang* will receive particular attention in these studies. These forms of ritual/theatre—and the play with identity and consciousness that they involve—will be looked at in relationship to the artistic and religious traditions and understandings that inform them. The chapter will conclude with a consideration of the historical and cultural links between eastern India and Bali, considered in the light of current controversies about interculturalism.

In chapter 3, Balinese *topeng pajegan* will be taken up and a performance by the late topeng master I Nyoman Kakul described and analyzed. I will be concerned with the complex temporal play between past and present that characterizes both the action and the language of Kakul's topeng pajegan, and the use of competing performance conventions and modalities to create some of this complexity. This description will be followed by a translated transcript of Kakul's performance—a performance improvised around the quasi-historical tale of the hero Jelantik's expedition to nearby Blambangan in approximately 1550 AD.

Kakul's performance provides not only an example of the theatrical possibilities of masked play within Balinese contexts, but also a focus for discussing the similarities and differences between certain Asian traditions on the one hand and practices and theoretical constructs typical of Western modern and postmodern theatre on the other. This task is taken up in chapter 5, with the aid of a "taxonomical model" adapted from the work of Richard Schechner.

In chapter 6 the life and work of a former Rajasthani court jester, who now uses his skills at mimicry and disguise to entertain passersby in the streets of Mewar, provides a focus for further observations on the frequently mischievous play between self and other that is central to theatrical practice. Hajari Bhand's street performances also provide an opportunity to examine the interplay between what Victor Turner has termed social and aesthetic dramas, and to explore some of the metaphorical extensions of the mask in performance.

Work and play with Asian performance principles—particularly with principles derived from topeng—have often been important in my own performing and directing over the past twenty years. The interview that constitutes chapter 7 will take up, in more personal terms, attempts to use the lessons of topeng and other non-Western forms of theatre within the contexts of Western performance. James Schevill conducted this interview with me in 1982. I have resisted the temptation to convert the results into essay form, because the interview format allows for a more informal and personal voice—another mask, if you will—and allows me to address my own work as a director and performer in a less inhibited way. I have added some further thoughts, though, in a conclusion that addresses the phenomenon of interculturalism and the role of the mask in contemporary theatre.

Finally, a list of questions that might be asked of various performance traditions—with or without masks, Western or Eastern—is offered as an aid and goad to further field research. These questions, and others inherent in these studies, revolve around the complex of relationships that bind together audience, performers, and that which is performed. Throughout, the mask serves as one touchstone in these inquiries, and play as another.

Some mechanical notes are also in order. Writing, I hope, for a diverse readership, I have chosen not to use diacritical markings for transliterated terms. It's a decision I have mixed feelings about, but the hope is that this will put less in the way of the reader not used to the discourses surrounding these cultures. The reader will also note that when certain terms shift from Indian to Indonesian settings, the transliterated orthography often shifts as well, reflecting changes in pronunciation and writing. Thus the Indic Shakti (divine power personified as female) becomes Balinese *sakti* (mystical power held by a person), Kshatriya as a caste designation becomes *Satria,* and the god Vishnu becomes Wisnu. This is probably just as well, since the meaning of these terms, and even the cultural weight ascribed to gods and heroes, often shifts with the geographical relocation. Following what seems a growing consensus, I have kept nouns in Austronesian languages the same in their singular and plural forms (like the English work "sheep"). Non-English terms (there are inevitably many) are italicized and, usually, explained (or at least, I hope, understandable by context) when they are first used in each chapter. They can be tracked, of course, through the index.

This book has grown out of a series of articles dealing with related concerns written over a fifteen-year period. One of the limitations of a study written over a number of years is that material inevitably becomes dated. Already, changes have occurred that have profoundly affected the practice of masked performance in Papua New Guinea, India, and Bali (as well as scholarship and performance in the West). In Papua New Guinea, for example, my visit came the year before independence transformed a colonial confederation into a separate nation-state, placing great stress on local traditions. In Bali, Kakul's performance not only came in the last years of his extraordinary career, but in the year before electricity (and, with it, television) was brought to his village and to most of the island. One of the *Prahlada Nataka* troupes of Orissa I witnessed has toured England and North America since my first visit. I have not been able to revisit all the sites discussed in the past few years, and, though some recent changes will be noted, in general I have left the performances described as witnessed—within the contexts that obtained when they were observed and documented. I have not hesitated, though, to include emerging critical viewpoints that have affected my ever changing sense of what these performances are about and what they have to offer. The performances documented are, in any case, not so much typical examples of the traditions studied as they are exemplary of the theatrical and performative possibilities within these traditions. Kakul and Hajari Bhand were not typical performers, any more than Olivier was a typical Shakespearean actor or John Coltrane a typical jazz musician: as masters of their art, they exemplify the possibilities of specific traditions even as they act (pun accepted) to transform those traditions in response to a rapidly changing world. Indeed, the ways in which performance in general and masked performance in particular play in the creases of constantly shifting temporal frames will be one of the recurring concerns of this work.

James Clifford notes that ethnographers are more and more like the Cree hunter called to come to Montreal to testify about a complex hydroelectric scheme. The hunter had been asked to tell about his way of life. When asked to swear that what he was about to say was "the truth, the whole truth, and nothing but the truth," he demurred. "I'm not sure I can tell the truth [. . .] I can only tell what I know" (Clifford 1986: 8). In this context, the problem is that what I know, or think I know, about these performances, about their history, and about their significance keeps changing in relation to further research, further thinking, and further reading. Thus many of the chapters based on older articles have significantly changed as new perspectives have found their way into the analytical weave, forcing a reconsideration of old issues and the taking up of new ones. I have also taken the opportunity to correct errors as I (too often) found them and to make some stylistic changes when I could no longer stomach my previous words. Such is the transitory (and performative) nature of information in the age of the computer. The obligation to leave signposts showing where and with whom I have traveled (intellectually as well as physically) and pointing to the testimonies of other travelers (some of whom have seen the territory in similar ways, and some of whom have not) has militated for the inclusion of numerous citations. I hope these will prove more helpful than burdensome.

Figure 1. Iatmul Mai Mask. Mindimbit, Sepik River, Papua New Guinea.

Chapter 1
Playing and Masking
Observations on Masked Performance in Papua New Guinea and Beyond

Victor Turner points out in his studies of African Ndembu rituals and in his later, more theoretical, writings that ceremonial performances do not occur at random, but at times of crisis and renewal (1967: 94–111, 1969: 94–96, 1986: 24–27). Drawing from Van Gennep's work on rites of passage (1960 [1909]) and on Bateson's observations on the framing of play (1972b [1955]: 177–93), Turner notes that performance activities tend to cluster around "liminal" occasions—times when continuity and change, past and future are held in an uneasy balance, on a threshold, "betwixt and between" the old and the new. Janus-like, performance activities play in the gaps in continuity created or acknowledged by these occasions.

> They are performed in privileged spaces and times, set off from the periods and spaces reserved for work, food, and sleep. You can call these [occasions] "sacred" if you like, provided that you recognize that they are the scenes for play and experimentation, as much as of solemnity and rules. [. . .] Both the performances and their settings may be likened to loops in a linear progression, when the social flow bends back on itself, [. . .] puts everything so to speak in the subjective mood as well as the reflexive voice. (V. Turner 1986: 25)

Weddings, funerals, anniversaries, exorcisms, and preparations for a hunt or battle all constitute examples of liminal occasions that embrace and sustain performance, along with initiation rites, carnivals, and, in Papua New Guinea, "pay-back" ceremonies held to redress grievances between communities, the dedication of spirit houses and health facilities, and high school graduations. Elaborate "sing-sings" are often held to mark such occasions in New Guinea and its neighboring islands, and frequently these sing-sings feature the display and wearing of extraordinary masks.[1]

D. W. Winnicott (1989 [1971]: 1–25, 107–10), a British psychoanalyst interested in the play activities of children, conducted research that may help to explain some of the human dynamics at work in the creation of the masked performances that traditionally cluster around these liminal occasions. Winnicott observes that the earliest manifestations of play in infants and the first use of "illusion" by small children almost invariably occur in response to the temporary absence of an attending adult. He notes that such an absence interrupts continuity in the child's developing sense of the world and thus creates a "potential space" for play: a gap in continuity that needs to be filled.

Winnicott points out that the first game a child learns to play is ordinarily a variant of "peek-a-boo," and that the playing of this game often occasions the child's first laughter. The initial pattern of this rudimentary game is as constant as it is familiar: the attending adult is present and visible, momentarily disappears from view, and then reappears. The momentary disappearance creates anxiety and excitement; the reappearance short circuits this anxiety and releases the built-up energy in the form of laughter. An interesting activity takes place as the child discovers that this pattern of activity can be repeated and "played"—as it becomes a game. The child begins to anticipate the re-emergence of the adult's face, and pleasurable anticipation replaces anxiety—so long as the adult reappears within an acceptable period of time. As the excited child begins to play the game, that child will frequently seek to take on the role of the adult initiator, hiding his or her face, then revealing it to the adult, who often assumes the child's attitude of surprise and relief. Expressions can be changed, the length of time varied. As anyone who has ever played this game with an infant well knows, it can evoke a seemingly insatiable desire to perform and repeat the various possibilities of hiding and revealing the face's presence.

Eventually, Winnicott observes, the child learns to employ "illusion" in order to sustain pleasure through longer periods of discontinuity—longer absences on the part of the attending adult. The child invests specific objects with animate qualities—a favorite stuffed animal, perhaps, or a blanket with its own repeatable name—and plays with these objects, talking to them, inventing scenarios for them, filling in the "potential space" left by the adult's absence. Thus the child's capacity for imaginative creation and play are called into being at times when a developing sense of continuity is threatened; but what begins in apprehension and anxiety is transformed into a pleasurable and highly charged activity, eagerly sought after, involving the presence, animation, and "participation" of chosen objects.

Winnicott calls the objects invested with animate qualities used to prolong this play time "transitional." They are "transitional" in that they help to bridge, or effect transits, across gaps in continuity—gaps between the world as it is known to be from past experience (including the presence of the adult) and the world as it is momentarily perceived (without the adult's presence). Winnicott goes on to label the activities bridging these gaps as "transitional events." He suggests that the capacity for human creativity is engendered in these first successful attempts to transform anxiety-laden breaks in continuity into pleasurable periods of play. His observations end in marveling at the capacity of human beings to transform patterns generated in order to stave off anxiety into modes of activity used to induce pleasure; he argues that the ability to employ "illusion" in this manner is a necessary strategy for the maintenance of sanity.

Turner's many studies of liminal events can be seen as extending Winnicott's observations into the realm of adult behavior. Winnicott's use of the term "transitional" is congruent with Turner's use of "liminal." Both describe events called into being by the experience of gaps in continuity that afford "potential space" for play. The similarity of Winnicott's findings to Turner's provides a significant indication that the connections between child's play and the "playing" of adult performances indeed run deep.

In the observations that follow, I have found it helpful to treat Torajan effigy figures, the life-sized puppets used in Batak funerary rites, and New Guinean masks as "transitional objects," and the performances that involve these powerful artistic objects as "transitional events." In so doing, the intent is not to single out New Guinean (or Torajan or Batak or Ndembu) behavior as being peculiarly "child-like," but, rather, to point out how patterns underlying often elegantly structured and socially effective adult performances can derive their form and appeal from what seem to be universal childhood strategies for survival and growth. Ultimately, the hope is to cast a light, however faint, on the genesis and ontology of performance as a human phenomenon.

Effigies and Ancestors

To the west of New Guinea, high in the mountains of the Indonesian island of Sulawesi, balconies have been carved into the sheer cliffs that rise above rice fields of the Torajan people. In these stone balconies are set row upon row of life-sized wooden effigy figures, or *tau-tau.* Male and female, these "person-like things" (to roughly translate "tau-tau") stand or sit at the wooden balcony rails, as though they were there to keep watch over the everyday actions below their collective gaze (fig. 2). Torajan tau-tau, and the ceremonies associated with them, provide excellent examples of the use of "transitional objects" and "transitional events" by adult societies.

Some time after a person of high social standing dies in Tanatoraja (the term commonly used to designate the mountainous inland territory occupied by Torajans), a huge feast and funeral is held, complete with ritualized keening, songs, dances, water buffalo fights, pig and buffalo sacrifices, an elaborate exchange of food and gifts, and, in the funeral for a queen that I witnessed at the village of Kete in 1975, a brief Baptist ceremony. In the Kete ceremonies, most of these events were overlapped, so that a dense texture of sound, color, and movement was created—claiming a new space

Figure 2. Tau-tau figures set in a cliffside to honor the dead. Tanatoraja, Sulawesi.

Figure 3. The tau-tau of a queen joins representations of other members of her family. Kete Village, Tanatoraja, 1975.

here and floating a new sound there—all amidst the general hub-bub. At the end of all of these events, a red cylindrical coffin containing the body of the queen was carried up a treacherous ladder and set into a narrow, deep niche dug high into the cliffsides that dominate the rugged Torajan landscape. A wooden door was set in place; the remains would be undisturbed and allowed to decay, along with a miniature model of one of the ship-like homes traditionally inhabited by the Torajans. In one of the larger, balcony-like niches described above, a seated tau-tau in the image of the late queen that had been prominently displayed throughout the elaborate ceremonies of the past several days was installed next to similar effigy figures of the deceased's ancestors and relatives (fig. 3).[2]

The tau-tau figure is considered to contain and preserve something of the spiritual essence of the honored dead and may be taken down, paid homage to with offerings, and even given new clothes in the years to come. The use of such representative objects as containers for spiritual force

Figure 4. A carved wooden water buffalo head guards a Torajan home. Kete Village.

and power among the Torajans is also evident in the ritual killing of a water buffalo and the placing of a life-sized wooden image of the buffalo's head as a protective device on the front of Torajan homes and granaries (fig. 4). The water buffalo is highly regarded by Torajans for its courage and strength and as a carrier of souls after death. The residual power of the sacrificed buffalo is understood to enter into the wooden head and to serve the ongoing interests of the family who have sponsored the sacrifice and the installation of this icon. Similarly, on a communal level, the assembled tau-tau look down protectively from their lofty perches, creating the somewhat eerie impression of an ancestral audience overseeing the village life that continues below—as though the ancestral portrait hall of a great manor had been made three dimensional and brought into public space. By installing and honoring these figures, the Torajans manage to preserve a sense of the past in the present and to span the gaps left in communal identity by the loss of valued individuals.

The "potential space" created by the loss of the queen is acknowledged and filled with sounds and activities—"transitional events"—that both mourn the dead and address the needs of the living. The decorated coffin, the small copy of a Torajan home, and most important of all, the tau-tau figure of the queen constitute "transitional objects" that partially fill the gap created between the past and the present. These objects may also, in the future, provide traces of a life once lived, and of the care that went into marking its end.

The Past in the Present: New Guinean Masks as Transitional Objects

Appearing as hybrids of the animate and inanimate worlds, masks are particularly effective "transitional objects" in performance events that cluster around "liminal" occasions. In the West, the mask has been devalued and is generally regarded as a cosmetic disguise, rarely used on the stage and often deprecated in the metaphors of everyday speech. People are accused of "masking" their intentions or feelings, or of "hiding behind a mask." Actors are praised for their abilities to reveal the feelings of the individual character "behind the social mask." The tendency is to speak of the mask as an impediment to expression, protecting and hiding the individual, corrupting understanding, and disfiguring truth.[3] In Papua New Guinea, though, as in many other areas of the non-Western world, the tendency is to regard the mask as an instrument of revelation, giving form to the ineffable and providing a nexus between the individual and those communally defined forces that shape one's sense of human possibilities. Commonly, this is accomplished by linking the mask to an ancestral presence, thereby bringing the past into the present.

One of the oldest "transitional objects" related to masking is a human skull, overmodeled with clay, discovered in Jericho and dating from before 6,000 BC (Lommel 1972: 217–18; Pernet 1992: 36–38). Most likely, this is an ancestral skull, preserved in a strategy to retain the deceased person's power and to fill the void occasioned by his death. The practice is widespread: in the Americas, such overmodeled and decorated ancestor and trophy skulls were treasured in Aztec and Incan cultures and in the Arctic northwest; they have been fashioned more recently in many locations in Melanesia, and examples can still be found among the Iatmul—a people who make their homes on the banks of the Sepik River in Papua New Guinea and who practiced headhunting into this century.

Sometimes, these overmodeled skulls are used in performance. Gregory Bateson (1958 [1936]: caption to plate XXVII) reports that the "portrait skull" of a dead man "chosen for his good looks" would be set up as a doll's head and "prodigiously ornamented." This *mbwatnggowi* figure would then be used in puppet-like fashion, appearing "as a Jack-in-the-box" over a raised curtain during initiatory rites that promoted the prosperity and fertility of the village. Thus a natural link between the world of the living and the world of the dead was deployed—playfully—as the focal object of future-oriented ceremonies.

Not surprisingly, such objects may also be used in mortuary rites. The history of a custom once prevalent among the Lake Toba Batak of Sumatra provides an example of how, through symbolic substitution, such practices may lead to the fashioning and deployment of masks or, in this case, of puppets, in performances designed to honor the dead. The origins of the *si galegale* puppet—still sometimes used when a prominent man dies without leaving an heir—are given by P. Leo Joosten:

> When in former times a man of note had died without having children, a big doll with movable limbs was made. This doll was made to dance [in order] to set the dead man's soul at rest. The dead man's skull was put on the doll's shoulder[s], the teeth were blackened with soot, the eye-sockets filled with red fruit. The doll was dressed up in traditional clothes with a wig of horse-mane and a hornbill's head on top of the [skull]. Then it was put on a little wagon and taken around the village. Weeping, the doll embraced the dead man's relatives and officially took leave of all. (1992: 61)

Joosten explains that a Batak man who died with no children to carry on his familial line was doomed to an afterlife "among the lesser ghosts and nameless slaves of the netherworld." Such a ghost could be dangerous to the living. By making a puppet featuring the deceased's skull—a puppet that could be controlled by the living by means of concealed wires—a final set of actions could be added to the dead man's life, performed in the betwixt and between time before dawn and the required disposal of his earthly remains that evening. By adding this posthumous chapter to the narrative of a life receding into memory and the shadowy realm of the dead, the living sought to "recall the past, remind the dangerous ghost of his previous state in life, and thus prevail upon him to leave the living in peace" (1992: 61).

In current practice, a wooden head, unpainted, with finely carved features, has replaced the actual skull of the deceased. The puppet thus formed is manipulated, as before, with hidden wires; music reinforcing its movements, the animated doll inclines its head and reaches out its hands in an uncanny way, commiserating with the living *and mourning the dead* (fig. 5). The process of symbolic substitution has allowed for a "better," more useful narrative: the identity of the doll has been shifted to represent the "missing" son, who will mourn his father and thus rescue him from an ignominious after-life.[4]

While not always deploying objects so literally tied by ontology or history to the dead, the bringing of images and actions bearing the traces

Figure 5. A demonstration for tourists of a si galegale puppet, traditionally used to mourn the dead. Samosir Island, Sumatra, 1993.

of the past into the present is central to the aesthetic concerns and performance practices of the Iatmul. In 1974 I observed a rehearsal for a sing-sing that was to mark the opening of a new "spirit house" (*haus tamboran*) in Magendo. The mythological history surrounding a previous haus tamboran, destroyed by missionaries at about the time of World War I, was to be celebrated in song and dance. As the rehearsal progressed, an old man explained past events involving the death of a child, an evil spirit, male-female disputes, and the coming of the child's spirit to live in the haus tamboran and teach the people of Magendo better ways to grow sago palms and to fish. The sense of the past was immediate and physical: an older haus tamboran stood *there*, across the swamp, the reeds the child was found in were *here*, near the rehearsal ground.

In the myth, a child named Wok had wandered into the haus tamboran—the domain of adult males—and had been killed by an evil spirit painted there by his uncle. After trying to disguise the cause of the child's disappearance by hiding his body in the reeds, the uncle is confronted by the child's mother and accepts responsibility for the sad events: his painting had attracted the spirit portrayed and he had lacked the power to control its powers. He then tears down the old spirit house and builds a new one—in which the child's protective spirit comes to dwell. The arguments revolving around the prerogatives and responsibilities of males and females within the society were clearly charged with meaning for the villagers rehearsing and watching; the playing out of this myth could be seen as addressing imbalances of power in sexual politics, as well as celebrating a literal reclaiming of ground from the missionaries' influence. The past was being contextualized in the present, the present in the past. Once more, a new spirit house had been built, referencing and replacing the haus tamboran of the pre-missionary days. The story now being rehearsed shadowed this historical event, offering a hope of renewal, while at the same time containing a warning "in the subjunctive mood" that sexual politics within the society could make a mockery of their efforts.

As the rehearsal progressed in front of the new spirit house, an old woman with a searing voice led the singing, while young dancers, accompanied by pulsating drums, moved in the manner of totemic birds, coming to alert the dead child's mother of her child's death and his location among the reeds. Boundaries separating past from present, male from female, youth from age, and human from animal were thus all being played with and shown to be porous in the story's narrative, rehearsal, and enactment.

> Just as the subjunctive mood of the verb is used to express supposition, desire, hypothesis, or possibility, rather than stating actual facts, so do liminality and the phenomena of liminality dissolve all factual and commonsense systems into their components and "play" with them in ways never found in nature or in custom, at least at the level of direct perception. (V. Turner 1986: 25)

Beyond "the level of direct perception," however, this "playing" was not at all disconnected from the concerns of everyday life—from "nature" and "custom." Despite (or because of) the imaginative range encompassed by its narrative and the elaborate use of music, costume, dance, and storytelling conventions that would frame playing and set it apart as performance, the conflicts of gender, age, and species embodied in the myth's retelling clearly resonated with "social dramas" familiar in the audience's daily lives. All during the rehearsal, a village headman was making arrangements for appropriate food and housing for guests, and tending to other practical matters that would provide the proper context for the performance. The people of Magendo were reclaiming their history while preparing to dedicate a new spirit house for future communal use; by employing the subjunctive "frame" of performative play within the "potential space" created by this event, they could both celebrate the significance of this occasion and reflexively tease its significance.[5]

Another instance of the playing out of events from the past in ceremonial performance occurs regularly in Makehuku, a village in the Highlands of New Guinea. A group of village males dressed in loincloths, their bodies smeared with gray-white mud, their heads completely covered by unglazed clay masks with broadly molded, grotesque features, advance silently. Some have bows in their hands. There is a sense of readiness, perhaps stealth, in their movements as they approach a group of round huts with thatched roofs (fig. 6). These "mudmen" re-enact the successful meeting of a moment of crisis in the collective past of their village. As the story was told to me, once, long ago, a marauding band from a neighboring village came to Makehuku in search of revenge. Alerted, the villagers of Makehuku deserted their homes and hid on the muddy banks of a nearby river. After a long time had passed, the villagers dared at last to return to their homes. They walked cautiously, covered with mud from the river banks. The marauders who remained took the silent, mud-smeared figures who were approaching to be ancestors coming to chastise them for failing in their raid, and they fled.

Although in recent years the mudmen have been performing this event several times a week for tourists, traditionally (I was told) the performance would be given at sing-sing gatherings with other villages at pay-back ceremonies where grievances among villages are adjusted, and where communal identity is of paramount importance. No individual names are given to the masks, nor are the molded features intended to indicate the personalities of individual ancestors. What individual character a mask may have is left to the imagination of the mask's maker. No "enemies" are portrayed. There is no dialogue or dramatic conflict. In lieu of "dramatic illusion," what is important—at least in traditional settings—is the reactivation of a successful moment that defines the villagers of Makehuku as a group. Edmund Carpenter, who has studied the mudmen, is now dubious about

Figure 6. The "Mudmen" at Makehuku. Highlands, Papua New Guinea, 1974.

the historicity of the event supposedly commemorated, and of the "traditional" status of the mudmen's silent procession (Schechner 1988: 76–77). Whether the event described is historically accurate, a mythic construction that has come to be regarded as historical by the villagers, or the rationalization of a simulacrum, however, the structural relation to an imagined or observed past remains the same. So deeply embedded is the pattern that where an historical event does not exist, it must be invented in order to provide the necessary antecedent.[6]

The re-enactment or recalling of a successfully resolved moment of crisis in the ancestral life of a community is, then, a common subject for performance in New Guinea. While not all such performances are masked, masks are frequently deployed; their liminal status between the world as imagined and the world as observed, the animate and inanimate, the quick and the dead, provide a particularly effective way to evoke the past. In studying (non-masked) Australian aboriginal rites, Mircea Eliade (1959: 5–6, 1965 [1958]: 68–72) has termed this process of reactivating the past by means of performance one of "reactualization." According to Eliade, in "reactualizations," "secular time" is stopped, and "primordial mythical times made present."

My own observations in Papua New Guinea are somewhat different. As I understand it, the villagers of Magendo and Makehuku deliberately play with time in an acknowledged interfacing of past and future defined by the occasion of performance. The audience still understands itself to be living in an ongoing present. "Secular time" is "stopped" only in that day-to-day activities and tasks are by and large given over to the viewing and performing of ceremonial enactments. This cessation and redirection of day-to-day procedures creates, in Winnicott's terms, a "potential space" for the reactivation or "reactualization" of events from the communal past, now superimposed upon an ongoing present that may even suggest new meanings to these "transitional events." Such events may be drawn from Eliade's "primordial mythical time," or from an historical one; in one dance I observed at a high school graduation in New Ireland, an incident from World War II was being recalled. What is important is that the stories and images that give testament to the power of the past be manifested, contained, and celebrated in the liminal present.

While such masked performances in Papua New Guinea can be viewed as having the conservative function of maintaining group identity by glorifying the power of the past, they also have a more creative function—extending the sense of the possible through the imaginative attention lavished on the masks and on the activities that bear witness to their animation. Winnicott's citing of the earliest "playing" of childhood as the training ground for the human imagination is apposite here, as is Turner's stress on playful experimentation and "subjunctivity." The word "play" is well chosen for performance, and among those things that theatre can play with best are the ever shifting relationships between past and present, and between mask and actor.

Visitation: The Mask as Spiritual Conduit

Often in New Guinean performances, the mask not only recalls an ancestral presence, but is understood to function as the conduit for a "visiting" spiritual entity, coming from the past into the contemporary world of the spectators. In many shamanistic performances around the world—from Siberia to Sri Lanka in Asia, and, more generally, from the tundra of North American Eskimos to the rain forests of West Africa—masks are used to facilitate the entry of a "spirit helper" into the performer's body (Lommel 1967: 19; Eliade 1964: 93, 165–68, 179; Campbell 1988, 1989). Like the wooden buffalo heads and tau-tau of the Torajan people and the ancestral skulls of the Iatmuls, such masks are regarded as vessels for attracting a spiritual force—one that is here channeled through the mask and into the dancer's body. The *tubuan* dance of the Tolai people of New Britain, traditionally performed at mortuary rites escorting the dead from the world (but observed by me in 1974 at another liminal event: a high school graduation), provides one example of the use of the mask as an instrument of visitation.

On a green and grassy field, about twenty young men beat percussion instruments and chant a repetitious refrain in an ancestral language (cf. fig. 7). Eventually the tubuan figure emerges, responding to the music and the repeated invocations. The figure is an immense, walking, dancing pile of leaves with a six-foot-tall conical head, painted black with a red and white smile, round eyes, and a pom-pom at the pointed top. The first row of the pandanus leaves that comprise the armless body of the tubuan are red, the other fifteen or so are green. The tubuan is performed by a male dancer, but it is thought of as a "female" ancestral figure, a spiritual entity called from the *momboto*—a past time of great but anarchic power (F. Errington 1974: 113–21).[7] To say that the performer represents or acts the part of this spiritual entity is to use a Western gloss for what is happening. For the dancer and for the audience, the understanding is that the tubuan has entered the dancer's body through the medium of the mask in an act of visitation.

After emerging into view, this extraordinary figure bows its head and raises it again, twists and pirouettes toward the musicians, and then sticks its long conical head in the direction of the assembled audience, shaking it vigorously. These movements are greeted with general merriment. After shaking its head at all those seated around its newly claimed territory, the tubuan prances and hops about in the center of the human circle formed by the onlookers, as the audience's laughter increases. Suddenly, the tubuan seems to become aggressive and menacing. It moves toward the musicians, first shaking its pom-pomed head in their faces, then turning and

Figure 7. Musicians play slit log drums and chant invocations to figures from an ancestral past at a New Ireland high school graduation, 1974.

Figure 8. Making a Uramot Baining mendaska mask. New Britain, 1974.

wagging its immense round rear at them. The alternating joviality and aggressiveness characterizing the tubuan's movement give ample play to the dynamic force that the dancer has invited to possess him and provide opportunities for the audience to express a range of reactions to its visiting embodiment.

A tension between elements of playfulness and of danger mark both the event and its traditional context. If the performer/maskmaker fails either to fashion the tubuan mask successfully or to contain its spirit within his body during performance, he can become seriously ill. If he can summon and contain the power of the tubuan successfully, he demonstrates his own power and gains prestige (F. Errington 1974: 224–26). Similarly, the tubuan itself, though from a dangerous time in the people's prehistory, confers its power in a beneficial way upon those who can summon and contain its presence. The tubuan, then, is both a figure for power and a source of power itself.[8]

As Winnicott notes, play with transitional objects is "inherently exciting and precarious," owing to the active interplay between that which is subjective and that which is objectively perceived (1989 [1971]: 52). This characteristic ambiguity and the accompanying tension between elements of playfulness and danger is deliberately heightened in the tubuan performance and is even more evident in performances held in the nearby hills of New Britain by the Uramot Baining, a people who make and wear huge *kavat* and *mendaska* masks of framed bark cloth (figs. 8–9). These masks "represent" leaf and tree spirits from the bush who are associated with the momboto time and who are said to have aided the ancestors of the current Bainings. Traditionally, these masks are worn at harvest time in a sequence of ceremonial dances lasting all day and all night, which, taken together, serve to celebrate the newborn, initiate the youth, aid the sick, and mourn the dead, but variations on these dances are also now held for the completion of significant community projects, such as the erection of a school, health clinic, or Christian church.[9]

The kavats and their companions are called forth by the rhythmic striking of bamboo tubes of various lengths and by singing and chanting about contemporary village events that require the spirits' attention, as well as by the setting of roaring bonfires, blazing eight to ten feet in the air. Being bush spirits, the kavats dislike fire and are drawn to these blazes by their desire to stamp them out. Thus, as the fires die down to a level of two or three feet high, young male dancers—their bodies glazed with a peaty substance, clay, and bush honey, the huge kavat masks on their heads, and a penis covering called a *limid* literally pinned onto their skin—dance into the fire, vigorously stamping on the flaming sticks. The dancers' feet are not treated in any way, yet the performance lasts for hours as the fire is frequently restoked and the orchestra keeps up the repetitive, rhythmical music associated with spiritual world of the kavats. It is understood that

Figure 9. The mendaska mask modeled by its maker.

a dancer who has allowed a kavat spirit to possess him has conferred a blessing on those assembled, and the audience's attitude throughout this dangerous performance is essentially festive. At a performance that I witnessed, a kavat dancer picked up a small child from the ring of spectators and took it through the fire with him. As I gasped, the child's laughing father told me not to worry, that the kavats were mischievous spirits, but that once attracted to the village they could only have a beneficial effect.

As in many performances that depend on trance inducement, the music acts to signal the spirit's presence for audience and dancer alike, thus enabling trance behavior to "attain its full development," and to create a recognizable social context for these extra-ordinary actions (Rouget 1985: 323–26). In Gregory Bateson's terms (1972b [1955]), the music acts as a meta-communicative device, establishing a frame of "this is play; this is different; the usual rules don't apply" for the performance activities nested within the larger occasion. In this case, of course, play has taken on functions of ritual; "this is play" is also, paradoxically perhaps, "this is sacred." As Johan Huizinga noted in his seminal work on play, *Homo Ludens*, this paradoxical pairing of play and ritual is built into the procedures of both phenomena, and "the unity and indivisibility of belief and unbelief, the indissoluble connection between sacred earnest and 'make-believe' or 'fun,' are best understood in the concept of play itself" (1950 [1938]: 65).[10] By including references to present-day concerns in their invocations, those summoning the kavats playfully conflate myth and reality, past and present, and sacred and profane, into a charged field of action that is established in an interface between usually reliable and separable temporal categories.

When a Tolai dancer puts on a tubuan mask and responds to the invocatory drumming and chanting that summons the tubuan spirit to take possession of his body, or when a possessed Baining kavat dancer tramples out raging flames, they are participating in adult activities involving procedures strikingly similar (if more complexly elaborated) to those described by Winnicott in his study of children's first experiments with play and illusion. As in the childhood play strategies, these events bridge gaps in the continuity between past and present and effect transits across the boundaries of experience.[11] For the dancer and his audience, of course, the animate nature of the mask is not illusory, but active and participatory. Experientially, map and territory have become one; within the frame of the dance, the dancer has become what he represents. This is a significant difference from the child's play described by Winnicott, though it is presaged by his comments on the precariousness of the subject/object relationship in play (1989 [1971]: 47, 52). The child's relationship to its transitional objects is itself complex, as Herrigel's Zen master points out: "We would say that (a child) was playing with the things, were it not equally true that the things were playing with the child" (1964 [1953]: 49). Though the exploitation of the ambiguities inherent in "the play frame" vary from instance to instance in the play activities of children, the funeral rites of Torajan and Batak peoples, the elaborate masked rituals of New Guinea, and in numerous theatrical activities of East and West, actions that arise out of anxiety and apprehension are turned into celebrations of the human capacity to renew and enjoy life through the devising and carrying out of "transitional events."

A Sepik Myth: The Discovery of Performance

In Mindimbit, another Iatmul village on the Sepik River, I witnessed a short "play," already alluded to in the introduction. This performance deserves a more ample description, since it not only exemplifies many of the tendencies noted above, but also offers an Iatmul account of the genesis of the performing arts.

On a sunlit field, what appears to be a gaily decorated, walking haystack appears out of an improvised enclosure of pit-pit grass. He is followed by another, similar figure. The bodies are almost entirely covered with reeds attached to bamboo hoops. The incredible, long faces are carved from wood, partially overmodeled with clay, decorated with dozens of cowrie shells, plumed with feathers, and festooned with flowers. These are brothers—Mulai Mai and Yembogai Mai—ancestral figures from the archaic tumbuna time and prominent figures in Iatmul creation myths (see fig. 1 and color plate I). The figures strut and waddle about, bells on their ankles, talking, chanting, grunting, and bleating in voices amplified by bamboo tubes that the dancers carry inside the layers of reeds. The brothers, fresh from battle, are full of pride in their victory, strutting about and congratulating themselves on their strength and prowess. Villagers crowd around, some waving handkerchiefs and joining in the shuffling process. But something seems to be wrong. The victory celebration seems incomplete. From time to time, the shuffling procession mysteriously comes to a dead halt, creating obvious gaps in the performance. The brothers lack the means to give their victory its desired significance or the celebration its wanted scope.

Two more figures emerge from the pit-pit grass enclosure. These are the sisters, Mulinja Mai and Yembogeja Mai. They are played by male dancers, but their parabolic shapes move somewhat mincingly and they talk, chant, grunt, and bleat in slightly higher voices than their brothers'. They seem to wish to join the procession, but the brothers brusquely reject them, reminding them that they had no hand in the fighting. The sisters sit on the log and sulk while the brothers continue the intermittent trumpeting of their own valor. The sisters then rise. They pick up another log, this one hollowed out—a simple slit-log drum (*garamut*)—and they bring this hollowed log into the center of the field. The brothers seem curious and puzzled. They start competing to see who can leap furthest over the log (and in the process, to the delight of the audience, send a would-be ethnographer scrambling for cover). The sisters inform them that they had another game in mind and hand them each two small sticks. The two brothers begin to beat out rhythms on the garamut—tentatively at first, then with greater and greater sureness and joyfulness. The villagers join the dance, and the figures exit amid great laughter and glee.

The Mai (sometimes spelled Mwai) family has discovered rhythm, music, dance, and song, and that discovery has given them a means to preserve their victory and give it enduring significance. The past can now be invoked in the present and a future-oriented sense of continuity is given to the life of the village. The martial exploits of the brothers will henceforth be available as an ongoing source of strength. Indeed, I suspect that my own discomfiture when face to face with the leaping Mulai Mai was good-naturedly perceived as evidence of this strength. With the Mai family's discovery of song, dance, and theatre, past and present can be joined, and "potential spaces" can now be performatively filled by "transitional events" that provide both solace and enjoyment.

Richard Schechner (1988 [1977, 1973]: 98–104) has speculated that the need to mark special events in crisis-oriented hunter and warrior cultures might have as much or more to do with dramatic origins than the marking of agricultural cycles. Though it is probably fruitless to seek a universal source for theatre (it generally seems to emerge from a confluence of sources, including storytelling, shamanic rituals, and mimicry), the Iatmul myth of theatrical origins is consonant with this idea. More significantly, perhaps, the actions of the Mai family suggest that the impulse for celebration and "play" is endemic to the theatrical process, and not a degeneration from a "purer" ritualistic mode. Studies of the classical Greek theatre suggest that it, too, might have grown, in part, out of the celebration in song and dance of the exploits of past heroes, as in the choric odes that Herodotus tells us were performed in honor of Adrastus at Sicyon.[12] Certainly Aeschylus' mythological and historical plays are closer to this model than the later and more individualistic and psychologically centered treatments of myth by Sophocles and Euripides, in which the mask often seems a somewhat arbitrary device decreed by tradition. Ellen Burstyn remarked in a talk at Brown University in 1975 that the history of Western theatre can be seen as the progressive shedding of masks as the civilization moved more and more towards an ethos centered around the individual. That progression gave us Hamlet and Blanche Dubois (as well as *People* magazine and the late night talk show), but it has deprived us of equivalents to the enlivening presence of the bleating Mai family or the fire-stamping kavats, and distanced us from our own medieval theatrical heritage. Recent work by Peter Schumann's Bread and Puppet Theater, Ariadne Mnouchkine's Théâtre du Soleil, and others in the West, however, have indicated a new interest and vitality in the theatrical mask as a means of capturing images that play between our own communal past and present.

Modes of Performance

This recent reawakening of interest in the mask in the West is symptomatic of the broader interest of contemporary theatre practitioners in exploring non-naturalistic theatrical techniques and, more generally, the modalities of performance itself—"The Way(s) of How" as the title of a George Coates piece of the 1970s suggested. New Guinean masked performances—from the mudmen of Makehuku to the entranced kavat dancer of New Britain—challenge Western assumptions about the nature of theatrical experience. Is it accurate to call what these men do "acting"? How many different modes of performing are there? How many different ways to wear a mask or play a part? If lines are to be drawn between these different modes, then where might such lines be drawn? And how firm are they? Such questions are bound to come up in considering such performative traditions.

The deeply rooted relationship between playing and performing may provide a starting point in sorting out various performing modes. In his study of the play behavior of infants, Winnicott (citing Melanie Klein), calls attention to the child's developing sense of what is "me" and what is "not me" as being crucial to play with "illusion" (1989 [1971]: 130–31). One way of differentiating among performance modes would be on the basis of different kinds of play between "me" and "not me" that are involved. As a tool for further discussion, I am suggesting such a continuum of experiential states, or modes of performing, that might be included in the broad spectrum of activities that has been covered by the term "performance"—each distinguished by a different relationship between "me" and "not me." This continuum would begin with the experience of performing within everyday life, continue through the experiences of pretending and character acting, and conclude with the experience of being visited or possessed by a spiritual entity other than one's self while in a performance situation:

```
          performance in   pretending   acting in   visitation
           everyday life                character
"me"---------|---------------|-----------|----------|---------"not me"
```

In the past, it would bother me slightly when colleagues from other departments within the university would assert, in good-natured fellowship, that they, too, were actors, that they, too, performed. As both a teacher and an actor, I knew that my experiential sense of these two activities held them to be quite distinct. Still, as sociologist Erving Goffman (1959) pointed out and as Eric Berne (1972) has emphasized in psychoanalytic literature, there is surely a lot of performing and scripting going on in the presentation of self during everyday life. The teacher lecturing or leading discussion is, after all, a good example. What is performative in this instance is the use of a "self" that is reserved for particular, bracketed, and frequently more public occasions in place of the complex of selves experienced and projected on other, more private occasions. Thus a shy man in his personal dealings with others may become witty and self-assured in the classroom or on the office floor, or a man whose day-to-day conversation may be casual and full of expletives may become studied and meticulous.

This capacity to maintain multiple selves for use with different people or on different occasions is at the heart of the capacity to engage in theatrical play, but it is distinguished from other modes of "performing" by the fact that (in a reasonably well-integrated personality) the bracketed self is only "not me" in the sense that it is "not like me when I am acting in other situations or with other people." The play is between one "me" and another "me." Masks would be inappropriate to this mode, since there is no clearly defined "other," only other ways of behaving, of being "oneself." Storytellers and stand-up comics construct their personas within this mode, and Spalding Gray has theatricalized its ambiguities—portraying himself telling stories about himself in various real-life situations—with startling results.

"Pretending" involves a definite, unsynthesized play between self and other. To pretend to be what one isn't implies a putting-on of the attributes and characteristics of another without integrating those attributes into the self. Often, pretending can be seen as failed acting: "indication" is the technical term for such internally unsupported performing. At other times, however, with different expectations in force, such pretending might be an appropriate mode of playful behavior—establishing another's characteristic manner or response to a situation while telling a story, for example. Brecht, with his analogy of the street scene (1964: 121–28), calls upon such examples of playful pretending as the basis for an alternate aesthetic for acting:

> I usually picked as my example of completely simple, "natural" epic theatre an incident such as can be seen at any street corner: an eyewitness demonstrating to a collection of people how a traffic accident took place. [. . .] The demonstrator acts the behavior of driver or victim or both in such a way that the bystanders are able to form an opinion about the accident. [. . .] The actor must remain a demonstrator; he must not suppress the "*he* did that, *he* said that" element in his performance. He must not go so far as to be wholly transformed into the person demonstrated. (1964: 000)

In the hands of a master storyteller and mimic such as Dario Fo, use of this demonstrative approach can produce compelling theatre without the illusion of character transformation. Fo does not assume the identity of others, he is Dario Fo showing us things *about* those others—for his amusement and for ours.

In a related, inverse approach to performing, those involved may function as iconic representatives of "others" without trying to convincingly assume the voice and bodily movements of those who are nominally portrayed. This approach, like the instances of pretending cited above, is referential. While the demonstrative actor or storyteller shows us characteristic attributes of another's behavior while maintaining his or her own essential identity, the performer engaged as an iconic reference takes on the exterior look of another, but makes little attempt to match this assumed appearance by internally identifying with the other that is referenced. In both cases, a synthesis of self and other is denied. Examples of such iconic representation include American Halloween celebrations, in which children wear masks on trick-or-treat visits (or used to in less paranoid times) and masquerade balls, in which masks were frequently held on a stick as though to emphasize their essential separation from the wearer's face and person. Other examples include carnival and religious processions, pageants and *tableaux vivants*, and the *ramlila* and *raslila* performances of India—in which small boys do not *act* as the divine epic heroes of the *Ramayana* or the *puranas*, yet are nonetheless treated as their representatives on earth (and, indeed, as the gods themselves) by the audience (Schechner 1985: 151–211; Hawley 1981). It is typical of this mode of performance that contextual complexity makes up for the lack of illusion and ambiguity in characterization.

The actors (and often non-actors) in Robert Wilson's early theatre pieces —dressed as Freud, Stalin, Queen Victoria, Einstein, Frederick the Great, or scores of dancing golliwogs—were often called on to function in this mode of iconic representation, and so, essentially, are the "mudmen" of Makehuku. Some of the "mudmen" I talked with in 1974 spoke of becoming bored with the repeated performances for tourists; deprived of the sing-sing context, their iconic representation of the ancestors had lost much of its meaning, and performing had become just another job. It will be interesting to see whether, separated from the traditional contexts that gave the actions social meaning, the events take on a more "dramatic" aspect, characters become more personalized, and the mode of performance accordingly shifts.[13]

Most actors—including those working in the Berliner Ensemble and those portraying the Iatmul Mai family—aim at a transformation of their identities, however temporary and bracketed that transformation may be. Stylistic matters aside, this is the performative mode traditionally associated with drama—masked or unmasked—and also used by performers, such as Lily Tomlin, who display their transformational skills in revue sketches and by actors in certain historical recreations and theme parks. Richard Schechner, playing with Winnicott's terms, has characterized the desired state as "not me/not not me" (1985: 109–115): "Olivier is not Hamlet, but he's also not not Hamlet; and the reverse is also true: Hamlet is not Olivier but he is also not not Olivier" (110). Thus many modern rehearsal techniques such as Stanislavski's "magic if" (1961 [1933]: 43–67), Lee Strasberg's emphasis on "affective-memory" (1987: 110–22), and Michael Chekhov's "imaginary body," "imaginary center," and "psychological gesture" (1953: 63–93, 1991: 58–106) are essentially strategies—starting from different points in the working triad of text, actor, and imagined persona—to short circuit the distinctions between self and other that Winnicott describes as being so "precarious" during play. The result of this short circuiting is an amalgam: the illusion of "character." It is an illusion both "controlled" and experienced by the actor.

The eighteenth-century disagreement between David Garrick and Denis Diderot on the nature of the actor's art elegantly reflected the actor/character's murky ontological status. Garrick, in a letter written in 1769, insisted that the master actor "will always realize the feelings of his character, and be transported beyond himself" and that the greatest moments on the stage occur "when circumstances, and the warmth of the scene, [have] sprung the mine, as it were, as much to [the actor's] own surprise, as that of the audience" (in Cole and Chinoy 1970 [1949]: 136). Diderot countered in *The Paradox of Acting*, written in 1773, by pointing out the evidence of calculated craft and control in Garrick's own performances.

> Garrick will put his head between two folding doors, and in the course of five or six seconds his expression will change successively from wild delight to temperate pleasure, from this to tranquillity, from tranquillity to surprise, from surprise to black astonishment, from that to sorrow, from sorrow to the air of one overwhelmed, from that to fright, from fright to horror, from horror to despair, and thence will go up again to the point from which he started. Can his soul have experienced all these feelings, and played this kind of scale in concert with his face: I don't believe it, nor do you. [. . .] Can one laugh or cry at will? One shall make a show of doing so well or ill as one can, and the completeness of the illusion varies as one is or is not Garrick. (in Cole and Chinoy 1970 [1949]: 168)

Diderot cites further proof of the chicanery involved in creating such "complete illusions": Garrick once confided to him that, if his acting was "astounding," it was "only because [he] constantly exhibited a creature of the imagination that was not [him]self" (Cole and Chinoy 1970 [1949]: 168). But this "proof" only highlights the ambiguous experience of self that the character actor lives with—"not me/not-not me." The "feelings of the character" that Garrick describes himself as realizing, even as he is being "transported beyond himself," are bound up in the creation and acceptance of a malleable persona—a mask (or, to judge from Diderot's account, a series of masks of the same character in different emotional states), reacting to shifting circumstances "in the warmth of the scene."[14]

Diderot's paradox states that, when the actor seems most emotionally involved, the actor is in fact most in control. But Garrick poses a paradox of his own: when he is at the height of his powers and most "in control" as an actor, he experiences his feelings and actions as though they are happening to someone else; he is "beyond himself"—not actively guiding the situation (as Diderot assumes), but, rather, caught up and even "surprised" by the "instantaneous emotions" elicited in the course of carefully planned and rehearsed actions. The writings of psychologist Mihaly Csikszentmihalyi (1975, 1993: 179–206), suggest that the paradoxical state Garrick describes is precisely the state of consciousness that makes play so exciting and desirable to the player. Csikszentmihalyi calls such moments "flow episodes" and characterizes them as unstable but highly pleasurable times when "one is aware of one's actions, but not the awareness itself" (1975: 45). "Action follows action according to an internal logic which seems to need no conscious intervention on our part. [. . .] we experience it as a unified flowing from one moment to the next, in which we feel in control of our actions, and in which there is little distinction between self and environment; between stimulus and response, and between past, present and future" (1975: 43).

In other words, the bridging of categorical gaps that Winnicott ascribes to transitional events is accompanied by a loss of "self-consciousness." As actor and action experientially merge, the "ego" or "self-construct" of psychoanalytic jargon becomes superfluous (1975: 49). Caught up in a "flow episode," ego-directed questions that frequently "flash through an actor's mind," such as " 'Am I doing well?' or 'What am I doing here?' or 'Should I be doing this?' [. . .] simply do not occur" (1975: 45). As Csikszentmihalyi points out, these (often brief) "flow episodes" are enjoyed by rock climbers, musicians, surfers, chess champions, dancers, and many others, as well as actors. What is peculiar to the character actor, though, is the use of a persona to short circuit the "self-construct" and thus—"in the warmth of the scene"—to plunge into the logic of (fictional) circumstances "as if" freshly encountering them in the flow of (usually well-rehearsed) actions. The "flow experience," then, is abetted by the sense of "not me/not-not me." The use of the double negative is appropriate, since, ideally, all prior decisions and questions of identity are now absorbed in the actions: once the persona has been created to focus, shape and direct energy, the ontological questions surrounding "me or not me?" "simply do not occur."

As Garrick points out, these experiences can be contagious, and it becomes difficult for the audience to distinguish between the actor as engaged in the internal logic and resultant actions of the character and the fictional character that is being enacted. Ads for popular movies often play on this notion, stressing the illusion created by this synthesis, and touting, say, Robert DeNiro's or Meryl Streep's or Dustin Hoffman's transformational skills, their ability to *be* the character (most recently and preposterously proclaiming on the front of videotapes for sale that "Tom Hanks Is Forrest Gump"). This play with illusion and identity lends an uncanniness to the actor (forcing burials outside of sacred ground and selling magazines that purport to describe what they are "really like'). As Bateson notes, this uncanniness is potentially inherent in the nature of the frame "this is play"; even in the simplest instances of animal play, there is a range of unsettling ambiguities present:

> [T]he message "this is play" sets a frame of the sort which is likely to precipitate paradox. [. . .] Paradox is doubly present in the signals which are exchanged within the context of play, fantasy, threat, etc. Not only does the playful nip not denote what would be denoted by the bite for which it stands, but, in addition, the bite itself is fictional. Not only do the playing animals not quite mean what they are saying but, also, they are usually communicating about something which does not exist. At the human level, this leads to a vast variety of complications and inversions in the fields of play, fantasy, and art. (1972b [1955]: 182)

The character actor exploits these multiple paradoxes to create a playful set of ontological ambiguities that can be either entertaining or upsetting —sometimes to actors themselves, as well as to their audiences. Coleridge's famous description (written in 1818) of the complicit audience indulging in a "willing suspension of disbelief" is one formulation of the audience's contribution (see Dukore 1974: 588), but I suspect that Stendahl's reaction (written in 1823) is more typical of the audience's experience. He describes a drifting in and out of "delicious instants of complete illusion," sometimes concerned with the flow of fictional events, and at other times concerned with the skill of the performers—or, no doubt, a hundred or more other matters, only some of them cued by the show in progress (Dukore 1974: 681).

So far, the examples used to discuss this mode of performance would seem to preclude the use of actual masks. Surely masks could never duplicate the quicksilver changes of expression Diderot describes Garrick as achieving. Although a skilled mask dancer in the right mask can create nuances of expression by a tilt of the head or even a shift of the body, plasticity of emotional response is inherently limited in mask work. But masks *are* used, and used well, in this mode of performance; what they lack in plasticity, they can sometimes make up in clarity and amplitude.

The *Natyasastra,* a Sanskrit manual of and commentary upon acting, written or compiled sometime between 450 BC and 200 AD and ascribed to the sage Bharata-Muni (1967 [1951]) outlines two approaches to what I have been calling character acting: one is that of *lokadharmi* (the path of nature/the world) and the other is that of *natyadharmi* (the path of art/dance). Where lokadharmi recycles the forms of action found in daily life, natyadharmi deploys what Eugenio Barba (1986: 114–22, 1991: 34–53) has been calling "extra-daily" gestures in order to replicate a world that is not immediately present to the five senses—a world of the past, of the gods, of essentialized states, or even of grotesque and cartoon-like states of being. Where lokadharmi stresses more conversational dialogue and familiar movement, natyadharmi stresses music, dance, poetry, and song in its reconstructions of the world (see also Vatsyayan 1980: 1–14, 178–88; Gupt 1994: 236–47).[15]

It is here, in these more fanciful renderings of the world, not as seen, yet as felt and experienced (Plato's parable of the cave comes to mind along with Winnicott's child with a gap to fill) that masks and mask-like makeup tend to appear. Yet, interestingly, actors working in these genres—*kathakali* actors and *chhau* dancers in India, for example—also commonly state their goal as "to become the character." As Phillip Zarrilli points out, the kathakali performer saying this does not mean that all is left to spontaneous connections of feeling: a mastery of the kinetic traces involved in dancing the various character types or displaying the appropriate *bhavas,* or states of feeling, is involved (1990). Still, most Indian performers I have talked with describe as ideal something very close to Csikszentmihalyi's notion of "flow," in which mastery is bound up in the movement itself, and the movement is connected to the spiritual and emotional state (bhava) of a character, or, frequently, a succession of characters being portrayed.

Masks have something else to offer performers in this mode, besides their concreteness and ability to represent epistemologies other than the everyday. They can be constructed to play further with the confusion of identities—conforming to the face in more or less human contours, but revealing something of the actor's face behind the mask. Much of the actor's skill comes in knowing how to blend the mask with his or her own face, body, and voice in order to create a disturbing and/or pleasing illusion that is both affirmed and denied by the manifest duality of mask and actor. To do this is to take advantage of what Stendahl notes as the natural tendency of the audience member to shift points of view while attending to the ambiguous stage illusion. To do this is also to add a level of complexity, and hence, of fun, for both artists and audience members. This strategy is observable in many masked theatre traditions, some of the best known being Japanese *noh,* Javanese and Balinese *topeng,* and the Italian *commedia dell' arte.*[16]

The potential "complications and inversions" within the play frame of performance are more and more the focus of contemporary theatrical play. While the character actor's mode of performance, based as it is on illusion, has enjoyed a privileged status in the conventions of modern drama that have evolved in the West since the Renaissance and is readily observable in dramatic traditions around the world, Brecht's epic theatre and other self-reflexive forms (including Balinese topeng, the work of such postmodern author/directors as Richard Foreman and Charles Ludlum, and even MTV videos of popular songs) can be seen as playing with this flow—establishing and then breaking the flow of the character, while maintaining a flow of performance. Such theatrical traditions also frequently alternate between narrative and dramatic modes of address and call for switching back and forth among the alternative modes of "acting in character," "pretending," and presentating self as performer. Masks and puppets lend themselves particularly well to this sort of ontological acrobatics, since they may alternately contribute to the illusion of character or be foregrounded as artifice, according to the treatment they are given.

Possession or, as I have preferred to call it, "visitation" (desiring a somewhat less loaded, mystical, and mad-sounding word for this phenomenon, and one closer to the terminology used in the sites I have studied) takes the ambiguities inherent in the play frame and completes the inversion: for the kavat or tubuan dancer and for those believers in the audience, the "illusion" experientially *becomes* "the reality." Indeed, from the point of view of the entranced performer or convinced audience member, "illusion" is no longer an appropriate word. If character acting is ideally marked by "an awareness of one's actions, but not the awareness itself," then visitation involves a loss of "the awareness itself," too. The atmosphere attending such alchemical performances tend to be highly charged, and, depending on the nature of the spiritual entity tapped, may be characterized by laughter, fear, reverence, or some combination of all three.

For the performer, this mode is experienced as a passive state. At least in its pure form, it is alien to my own experience and, with certain exceptions such as "speaking in tongues" in the Pentecostal church, it is outside of the experiential range of most performers in the West. Jerzy Grotowski's stress on a *via negativa* for the actor—an elimination of blocks rather than an accumulation of skills (1969: 17)—indicates a Western interest in the actor as a passive vessel; but the tubuan dancer, the kavat dancer, and performers in some of the traditions discussed in the studies that follow take the possibilities of performing through a via negativa far beyond Grotowski's use of that phrase. If we are to respect the testimony of those involved (see, e.g., Belo 1960; Lewis 1971; Halifax 1979; Kalweit 1992; and the next chapter of this book) then we must deal with this phenomenon not as metaphor or pedagogic aid, but as an experiential reality.

Visitation is characterized by a loss of the sense of "me" and an engulfment of the self by an entity that is considered "not me"—with an attendant loss of conscious control and a scanty memory of what took place while performing. When masks are used to facilitate this transference of identity—as they frequently are—they tend to be large ones that completely obscure the identity of the performer; this tendency holds true in Africa and parts of Asia, as well as in Papua New Guinea. As a mode of performance, visitation is most frequently encouraged in religious and curative rites, and many of the performers are themselves priests or spiritual healers.

Visitation is distinguished from certain forms of madness characterized by extreme dissociation by the ability of the performer or the society to control the entrance into and the coming out of this behavioral state. As Robert Wessing once pointed out to me (1984, personal communication), one could carry the metaphor of visitation farther: if the body is considered—as it often is—a home for the soul, then in visitation the home is loaned to a guest, while in madness the guest takes over the home. In madness, then, play has ended. The continuum proposed reveals itself to be circular; the unmediated "me" of everyday life—the self—is contiguous with, and potentially threatened by, the "false self" that has taken over control of the madman's daily actions.[17]

In talking with men who undergo trance possession, or visitation, while performing with masks in Papua New Guinea, Bali, and India—many of whom have experience as character actors—it is clear that they regard these two modes of performance as discrete. Ritual performers familiar with the process know whether or not they have been acting or in trance, just as accomplished actors have a clear sense as to whether or not they are pretending. In other words, though there may be degrees of accomplishment within each mode of performance, a quantum leap seems to be required to get to the next mode along the "continuum."

The actor's experience, of course, does not always correspond to the audience's perception. Every actor has nights when he or she feels outside the character's logic and actions, and yet the audience applauds his or her simulation. Ritual performers I talked with have cited times when they have feigned trance. This is not always a matter of failure. Indeed, because of the common association of masking with trance, there is a complex interplay between the rival performative modes of character acting and visitation, and several traditional forms involving masks deliberately play with these gray areas of experience and perception.[18]

Traditions may shift from one of these modes to another—usually, though not necessarily, in the direction of secular and aesthetic play. Within certain traditions, the choice of mode may be determined by external circumstances (the time of day, the audience present, the consecration of a mask, the "purity" of the dancer) or it may be left open to be determined in the flow of performance. Moreover, just as the Brechtian model of theatre may call for alternation between demonstrative and mimetic approaches to acting, the modes of character acting and visitation may alternate within a given ritual performance.

The tradition of possession may also be used to color the mimetic experience, allowing the New Guinean Mai performer to claim mischievously that the *masalai* spirit he was playing had enjoyed my bumbling presence. Such coloration of the experience and perception of performers and audience members is not limited to Eastern theatre. In English, we talk of certain actors as having "presence." In Spanish, such actors may be said to "have *angel.*" In Bali, actors who have this charismatic quality are said to be blessed with *taksu,* a spiritual quality or presence that, while not possessing the actor, is felt to accompany and reinforce the actor's words and actions, commanding the audience's attention. Artaud's sense of the actor seeking to join with his "double" or "soul from the other side" (1958 [1938]: 134–35) is akin to this perception, and Artaud himself makes the link between his terminology and the shamanistic traditions that have been an important seedbed for theatre: "To join with the passions by means of their forces, instead of regarding them as pure abstractions, confers a mastery upon the actor which makes him equal to a true healer" (135).

The pervasive use of such terminology gives ample evidence that, even in the West, where the extreme development of the individuated self makes it very difficult to discuss trance or visitation without recourse to vague mysticism or a dilution of experience through rationalization, a vestigial sense of this mode of experiencing and perceiving is strong enough to color our ways of thinking about, talking about, viewing, and making theatre—playing in the creases of our knowledge, teasing the capacities of logic, reveling in paradox, and creating a complex of artistic phenomena that Lévi-Strauss once likened to a national park system for "savage thought" (1966 [1952]: 219).

Notes

1. An earlier draft of the first half of this chapter appeared as "Masking and Playing: Observations on Masked Performance in New Guinea," *World of Music* 3 (1981): 5–25, portions of which have been reused by permission of the editors. Partial funding for my 1974 research in New Guinea and Indonesia was provided by the Department of English of Brown University, under a Bronson Grant. Much of the material presented here under the heading of "Modes of Performance" was originally presented under the title "Possession and Mimesis as Interacting Modes of Masked Performance" at a panel on "Meaning and Problems in Masked Performance" during the Northeast Anthropological Association Convention, Hartford CT, April 1984. This material was later revised for presentation at the South Asian Conference of the University of Wisconsin in March 1985, and at the American Theatre Association Convention in Toronto, Ontario, in August 1985.

2. For more information on the Torajan people and their funeral rites see Volkman (1979) and Nooy-Palm (1988).

3. For example, note this section in Uta Hagen's widely used (and generally excellent) text *Respect for Acting,* in which Hagen describes a "prominent film actress" she was coaching:

> Her previous orientation to acting consisted of finding a mask to hide behind. She believed that the outer dressing of the part—age difference, historic difference, national difference—contained the real essence of acting. For her, acting was only a craft when it was miles away from her, and when it was used to illustrate something totally different from herself. [. . .] She had only one wish: to put on a mask, to disguise herself. (1973: 27)

Though Hagen's metaphor is certainly understandable, she shows little comprehension of the actual procedures or aesthetic principles involvled in masked performance, such as those discussed in chapter 3 in reference to Balinese *topeng*.

4. A similar evolutionary history has been constructed for the intricate and extraordinary *malanggan* masks of New Ireland, also tracing them from the use of overmodeled skulls (Pernet 1992: 84–87), while, in broader strokes, Ernst Kris has traced the origins of the comic caricature through stages of symbolic displacement involving effigy magic as an intermediate step (1952: 189–203). The point I am making is not that this is a necessary evolutionary process—cultures can have masks without a history of decorating skulls—but that it is a logical one, made possible by the mask's ability simultaneously to evoke qualities of the durative and the transitory, of the material and the ineffable. The death masks in Egyptian, Mycenaean, Roman, Chinese, Inuit, and Incan cultures—used as burial objects or as reminders of the dead to be contemplated by the living—may also be seen as "transitional objects" spanning a gap between the worlds of the quick and of the dead and conflating the ephemeral and the enduring. The frequent use of masks in performances that reference and give form to figures from the past follows naturally from this capacity to embrace temporal and ontological ambiguities.

5. A more complete account of this rehearsal is quoted from a letter written by me in 1974 in Schechner (1985: 52–54). Schechner's commentary touches on many of the issues raised in this chapter. The same essay (36–116) explores in detail the play between historical re-creation and artistic elaboration involved in performing—and documenting—the past, and suggests the phrase "restoration of behavior" to cover these and other activities. For more on male-female tensions as they affect musical traditions in New Guinea, see Gourlay (1975).

6. In practice, of course, the differences between history and myth are sometimes difficult to discern. In Moem, another Iatmul village, I was told a story of how the last evil spirit had been driven from the village. The story was told in striking cadences and in specific detail. I was then asked to tell an American story. While I thought of Paul Bunyan and his Blue Ox Babe or, stretching a point, Bre'r Rabbit and the Tar Baby, my host asked for "The Story of How the Americans Went to the Moon." I tried, but his story was much more convincing. It is no doubt true that performance and history act in a loop so that the original event slides towards the subjunctive under the influence of its re-enactments (Schechner 1985: 36–116). Yet, as Schleiman's discovery of Troy through careful attention to the details of the *Iliad* amply demonstrates (see Ceram 1967 [1951]: 26–40), specific knowledge of the historical past often remains complexly embedded in myth.

7. Although Frederick Errington's research was done on the tubuan performances on Karavar Island, much of what he says seems to apply to Tolai practices. C. S. Valentine (1961) suggests that among the Lakalai of New Britain, the tubuan dancer is not considered to be possessed.

8. The containment of dangerous entities within masks is a familiar phenomenon and is the focus of the following chapter. For an early and influential comparable study based on Nigerian traditions, see Horton (1963: 95–99); for a detailed treatment of this aspect of Sri Lankan ritual practice, see Kapferer (1983, 1986). Comparative studies stressing this phenomenon are found in Bourgignon (1966, 1973).

9. Most of my information about the Uramot Baining performances I observed in 1974 was received from Lepan Lea, a young Baining man who has been collecting the folklore of his people. I was also aided by the people at Rabaul Excursions of New Britain. George A. Corbin (1979, 1984) has since provided the most extensive and useful accounts of Baining art and culture, and I have also drawn upon his research.

10. Huizinga deserves to be quoted at greater length as he argues for a profound linkage between ritual and play activities:

> Primitive society performs its sacred rites, its sacrifices, consecrations and mysteries [. . .] in the pure spirit of play. [. . .] The function that is operative in the process of image-making or imagination [. . .] is a poetic function; and we define it best of all by calling it a function of play. [. . .] The sight of the masked figure [. . .] carries us beyond "ordinary life" into a world where something other than daylight reigns; it carries us back to the world of the savage, the child and the poet, which is the world of play. (1950 [1938]: 49, 63–65)

Although Huizinga's vocabulary is now out of date (it is now difficult to use "primitive society" as a meaningful construct, for example), his intuitive connections are supported by the work of Turner and Winnicott.

11. Schieffelin (1976: 217) takes a similar approach in giving a detailed and fascinating account of how another New Guinean ceremony, without masks, fills "a gap in the journey of the dead." In the observations that follow, it should be noted that not all members of an audience, nor, for that matter, of a culture should be expected to have the same epistemological understandings. Individual members of the audience may vary a good bit as to what they believe is "really" happening. As Marjorie Halpin has commented, "Whether people believe that the transformation is real, or whether they only pretend that it is real, is irrelevant [. . .] the new identity itself is an artifact of the larger whole—the ritual frame" (1983: 223).

12. A "euhemric" theory of the dramatic origins, emphasizing an urge to represent historic deeds at the tombs of ancestors, was advanced by Ridgeway (1966 [1910]), but lost ground to the theory of the Cambridge anthropologists that a "spring dromenon" provided a ritual model for Greek tragedy. That argument, though, based on conjectural reconstructions of rituals and the supposition that the tragic festival was inherently bound up in the worship of Dionysus, has become suspect. An account of the Adrastus ceremonies as reported by Herodotus and a critique of the evidence can be found in Pickard-Cambridge (1927: 135–42). More recently, critics such as Else (1965) have stressed the role of storytelling traditions; but Herodotus's account of a dithyramb that honored Adrastus as a local hero remains an intriguing precedent.

13. There is a photograph in Malcolm Kirk's remarkable *Man as Art* (1993 [1981]: 94) that suggests the possibilities of just such a transformation. A dancer from the Chauve area in the Chimbu province in the Highlands appears in a clay mask elaborated with bamboo horns and with fingers accentuated by bamboo tubes. Kirk suggests (1993 [1981]: 140) that the costume and mask are elaborations on the Asaro (Makehuku) mudman tradition; though no information is given about dramatic contexts, there appears to be a movement towards individualization and theatricalization of the borrowed icon. Kirk also notes (in another context) that "in the Eastern Highlands masks are sometimes used in small ceremonial plays or farces that are designed to amuse and instruct" (140).

14. Roach (1993 [1985]: 93–159) treats both Garrick and Diderot at length and is more sympathetic to Diderot's view. For a wealth of statements from contemporary actors regarding the relationship of the emotional life of the actor to that of the character, see Bates (1988: 69–100). Recent scientific evidence suggests that Diderot underestimated the involvement of the actor. Tests involving the altering of breathing patterns and facial musculature to mimic emotional states indicate somatic changes (in heart rates, blood composition, muscle tone, etc.) in trained actors (see Bloch, Orthous, and Santibañez-H. 1987; Ekman, Levinson and Friesen

1983; Schechner 1988: 261–75). The basic emotional states that both teams of researchers have codified, by the way, are in general conformity with the "stable emotions" (*sthayibhavas*) listed by Bharata-Muni: love, mirth, sorrow, anger, energy, terror, disgust, and astonishment (1967 [1951]: 102). Similar categorical grids have frequently provided the starting places for mask-makers to elaborate and essentialize human emotional states.

15. It is Gupt (1994: 19–40) who suggests the very early date of 450 BC for at least some of the *Natyasastra* (usually dated between 200 BC and 200 AD). Gupt's reading of the concepts lokadharmi and natyadharmi stresses that, while the path of lokadharmi is closer to mimetic representation of the "natural" world, both approaches involve a profound transformation of that world through the medium of performance.

16. For the use of masks in noh theatre see Teele (1984) and Keene (1966). Among the many works on commedia dell'arte, see Duchartre (1966 [1929]); Oreglia (1968); and Rudlin (1994). Useful overviews of masks and their usage are presented in Lommel (1972); Bihalji-Merin (1971); and Mack (1994). The masks used on the classical Greek and Hellenic stages present an exception to the remarks about mask size in this mode, since they covered the entire head; for a study of these masks which includes a comparison with those of the commedia and noh, see Wiles (1991).

17. Psychiatrists Luh Ketut Suryani and Gordon D. Jensen (1993) have recently provided a provocative study of the relationships of trance (which they define very broadly) and possession phenomena in Bali to multiple personality and possession disorders as encountered in the West.

18. In chapter 3 I make a case for Balinese topeng being one such form that deliberately encourages a blurring of the line between visitation and character acting. Frank Hoff (1985) notes a similar juggling of ontological identity in Japanese noh and argues that the intentional blurring that results is central to the aesthetics of noh and subsequent Japanese theatrical traditions.

Chapter 2
Dealing with the Demonic
Strategies for Containment in Hindu Iconography and Performance

Just as play frequently flirts with danger, artistic activity in general and theatrical works in particular often dwell on dreadful events and nightmarish presences. From the murder of Agamemnon and the unleashing of the Furies, to Macbeth's bloody deeds and tormenting Witches, to Grand Guignol and the Theatre of Cruelty, the imagination seems to follow a need to push against the boundaries of experience and to wrestle artistically with the visions encountered there, at some threatening edge of our sense of what it means to be alive. The discussion that follows focuses on a set of related artistic and psychological strategies found in Hindu iconography and performance in Orissa, India and Bali, Indonesia. Discussed in the order of their accessibility to Western understanding, all of the traditions described use artistic means to manifest—and partially contain and control—the felt presence of chthonic and, sometimes, demonic forces. Masks figure prominently in these enterprises, and the theatrical performances described exhibit some striking similarities in the ways in which ritual magic is combined with mimetic play while giving form to force. They also indicate a range of options open to theatrical artists working in these Asian settings as they juxtapose various modes of performance for the sake of both entertainment and efficacy.[1]

Visages of Glory

Throughout South and Southeast Asia, carved images of monstrous, disembodied heads frequently dominate the facades and entrance portals of Hindu and Buddhist temples, public buildings, and even private homes (cf. fig. 10). The eyes bulge, the nostrils flare, the teeth are bared, the jaws are open, and the canines are enlarged to form menacing fangs. Hair may curl from the lower jaw and horns sprout from the top of the head, while flames

Figure 10. A Kirtimukha stone relief in the wall of a twelfth-century temple. Uluwatu, Bali.

swirl around the entire countenance. Often, hands reach out directly from behind the ears, with fingers spread wide and fingernails elongated to grotesque proportions in order to enhance their calculated frightfulness. Leaf and floral patterns billow out from these chthonic forms; fecund as well as frightening, they are carved with a sense of playful indulgence in the demonic that links them in spirit to the devils on Romanesque church portals and to the gargoyles of gothic cathedrals. Like the gargoyles, these robustly demonic images function, paradoxically, as protective icons. They are apotropaic: designed to turn potentially destructive power against the forces of evil, by means of artistic play.

In India, these demonic faces used to ward off evil are referred to as Kirtimukhas, or "Visages of Glory" (fig. 11). In Puranic myth, Shiva was approached by the demon Rahu, a leonine messenger from the world-conquering Titan, Jalandhara, and asked to surrender his *shakti*—his physical bride and his spiritual force. In a fury, Shiva sent forth a burst of energy from the "eye of enlightenment" in his forehead and, instantly, this power took shape as a horrendous, lion-headed demon, insatiably hungry and irresistibly strong; Rahu's leonine appearance was mirrored in its countenance, and his ferocious power surpassed. "The apparition's throat roared like thunder; the eyes burnt like fire; the mane, disheveled, spread far and wide into space" (Zimmer, 1972 [1946]: 180). Jalandhara's terrified demon messenger craftily took refuge in the all-protecting benevolence of the almighty Shiva himself. Called upon as protector, Shiva bade his monstrous creation to consume itself, which it voraciously proceeded to do, until only the ravenous head remained. Pleased, Shiva declared, "You will be known, henceforth, as the 'Visage of Glory,' and I ordain that you shall abide forever at my door. Whoever neglects to worship you shall never win my grace" (Zimmer 1972 [1946]: 181–82). The myth accounts for Kirtimukha's place of honor on the entrance gates of Shaivite temples in India and provides some clues as to its significance: the Visage of Glory is emblematic of Shiva's power in its destructive but ultimately containable aspect.

The "worship" of a divine but horrific icon, representing a potentially destructive side to the godhead, is common to systems of Tantrism—an approach to Hindu and Buddhist worship that focuses on the power latent in sexual energy and usually addresses itself to the "female" aspect of the divine, frequently in its more horrific forms (see Avalon 1978 [1918]; Mookerjee and Khanna 1977; Bhattacharyya 1992). As Tantric Shaivism spread and the Visage of Glory became a popular icon in the Indianized states of Southeast Asia, the names and myths associated with its origin varied. In central Java and in Angkor, the Visage became identified as Batara Kala, a voracious demonic presence spawned when a drop of Shiva's semen shot into the ocean and was swallowed by a fish (fig. 12). The name Kala also invokes Time as a ravenous destroyer and has become a generic term for demonic beings in Southeast Asia. In eastern Java the most com-

Figure 11. Kirtimukha carved on the face of the ninth-century Mukhtaswara Temple. Bhubaneswar, Orissa.

Figure 12. Kirtimukha carved over the entrances and portals of a tenth-century temple complex. Prambanan, Java.

Figure 13. Bhoma as Kirtimukha guards the entrance gate to the fifteenth-century Pura Kehen. Bangli, Bali.

mon identification is with Banaspati Raja, a leonine "Lord of the Forest." In Bali, where a variant of Hinduism still holds sway, the Visage has taken on a multiplicity of forms but is most commonly identified with Bhoma, a demonic son born to the earth goddess, Prithivi, fathered by Vishnu while he was in the shape of a rampaging wild boar (fig. 13).[2]

In all its various manifestations, the Visage of Glory is associated with the animal world as well as with the divine. Moreover, the frightful icons are frequently accounted the progeny of divine anger and lust, precisely those "baser" instincts most carefully suppressed in daily human life. The Tantric strategy is inclusive—embracing and giving form to the irrational and the disavowed. Like homeopathic medicine (and inoculation), it seeks to counter the power of that which is poisonous by introducing poison to the system in carefully measured doses. In their affective range, the icons generated by this inclusive strategy run from the whimsical to the awe-inspiring. As Zimmer notes of the Indian Kirtimukha, "Images of this kind allow for a kind of jocular intimacy with the powers of destruction. They represent the 'other side,' the wrathful aspect of the well-known and well-loved divine powers. When properly propitiated, such presences give support to life and ward away demons of disease and death" (1972 [1946]: 183).

During ceremonies that take place in those liminal times when the continuity and health of the community are endangered—and the powers exercised by the "demons of death and disease" become most threatening—these horrific yet divine presences are frequently given more active form. Perhaps the most spectacular use of the Visage of Glory to ward off trouble-causing demons occurs during the treacherous passage of the corpse to the burial ground during a high-caste Balinese cremation (see color plate II). An immense, brilliantly colored Bhoma image, fashioned of wood, split bamboo, paper, and balls of unspun cotton, is affixed to the back of the multi-tiered tower used to transport the corpse on its raucous and whirling way to dissolution. Looming up over the cloth-wrapped body, this monstrous demonic head protects the vulnerable soul trapped within until it can be released by fire, and reassures the community that the proper steps have been taken to counter destructive forces.

Becoming the Icon: Narasimha in Orissa

"Proper propitiation" of divine presences capable of warding off the "demons of death and disease" can also extend to more explicitly theatrical performances, in which fanciful icons for wrathful aspects of the divine are animated and deployed. In the village of Baulagaon, Orissa, a four-foot-high wooden lion mask is venerated in the temple of Vishnu. The mask is reputed to be 160 years old. It has a green face with prominent red nose and forehead, a crimson protruding tongue, a flaming mane, and an elaborate crown. The figure represented is Narasimha, the wrathful "man-lion"

Figure 14. The face of Narasimha functions as Kirtimukha in a Puri-style *pata* painting celebrating Rama and Sita. Bhubaneswar, Orissa.

avatar of Vishnu, who came to earth to destroy the blaspheming demon tyrant, Hiranyakashipu (who was Rahu's uncle, it should be noted, and whose sister—Rahu's mother—was named Hiranyasimhi: Golden Lioness). A similarity to the leonine Kirtimukha is evident, and, indeed, a truncated version of Narasimha—with only head and forearms showing—is now commonly used in Vaishnavite temples and paintings as a substitute for the Shaivite Visage of Glory (fig. 14; Eschmann 1978b: 109–10). Priapic lions are commonly used in India as guardian figures to Shaivite, Vaishnavite, and, especially, Shakti temples; the role of beast-protector seems to have passed naturally to the man-lion incarnation of the godhead itself.

For generations the mask at Baulagaon has been used to help cure illness. Patients are brought to the room where the mask is stored and ceremonies are conducted to awaken its curative powers. At the adjoining temple, the mask is given a daily *puja*—a ceremony of welcome—and on Narasimha's name day it is publicly honored with an especially elaborate puja during which the priest who presently cares for the mask, Arjun Satapathy, frequently becomes entranced and loses consciousness. Arjun Satapathy reports that his grandfather, a Tantric adept, wore the mask in the streets of Baulagaon to protect the village from an epidemic; its ritual function seems to have preceded its use in connection with a dramatic text at Baulagaon (Arjun Satapathy 1983, personal communication). Since at least 1880, though, masks like this one have been used to capture the furious spirit of Narasimha avatara in spectacular theatrical performances of the Orissan *Prahlada Nataka.*

As of 1994, there were at least fifty-five active *Prahlada Nataka* troupes—composed mostly of subsistence farmers—performing in the Ganjam District of Orissa, with a few more in the adjoining Srikakulam District of Andhra Pradesh. While many of these troupes perform only once a year as an act of devotion, others tour throughout the region, performing at town fairs, temple holidays, and privately sponsored ceremonies. Performances can last as many as seven nights, but the common tendency is to condense the text for a single long night's performance lasting anywhere from ten to twenty hours, with two troupes playing simultaneously, pitted against each other in competition (*bedi*). There are several textual variants in Oriya, attributed to various local rulers; but all that I have found essentially derive from a version composed in approximately 1880 that was sponsored by and attributed to Raja Rama Krishna Deva Chottaray of Jalantara. Influenced by Telegu models, the Oriya text drew from several previously existing musical, poetic, theatrical, and ritual conventions to fashion a new synthesis, combining the theatrical strategies of mimetic play and visitation and featuring large and striking masks of Narsimha that allow for a great deal of variation (see, e.g., figs. 15–18).[3]

As noted in the previous chapter, the use of masks as conduits for "visiting" spiritual entities is a widespread phenomenon. Whether taken from

Figure 15–18. Papier mâché Narasimha masks used in *Prahlada Nataka* performances in the Ganjam District of Orissa and in neighboring villages of Andhra Pradesh.

the ancestral past, from the mythic elaboration of divine powers, or from the realm of animals and spirit-helpers, these entities are understood to be drawn through the mask into the body of the performer and are then theatrically contextualized in the contemporary world of the spectators. As with the Baining *kavat*, these animated icons are often used in exorcistic rituals and serve both as representations of power and as the source of power itself. The process involves iconographically manifesting the "other side," acknowledging the manifestation's power, and then harnessing that power within a theatrical domain.

Most Hindu performance forms in India stress elements of theatrical play within a fictive framework, elaborating both the mythological stories themselves and their theatrical means of representation. In these forms—in *kathakali*, *yakshagana*, and Purulia *chho* (or *chhau*) for example—gods frequently appear as characters, but the actualization of a divine presence is vestigial or works metaphorically, through mimesis.[4] There are still some performance forms in India, however, that adhere more closely to the procedures of "visitation" outlined in the preceding chapter (*prasanna*—"arriving"—is the term most frequently used in Ganjam). These forms stress the actualization of the divine presence itself and tend to forgo the mimetic elaboration of a mythological story. One such form is *gambhira*, traditionally performed in the Malda region of West Bengal and representative of a tradition once widespread in eastern India. In this tradition, masks are used to manifest aspects of Shakti—the active "feminine" energy most often represented as Durga or Kali, and whose forms include Narasimhi: half woman, half lioness, the Shakti counterpart to Narasimha (fig. 19). The dance movements used for Narasimhi are frenetic and flailing, and lunges in the direction of the audience are greeted by squeals of fear and delight from children scrambling for cover. A poem in praise of Narasimhi, however, makes clear her protective function, saluting her as "the goddess who humiliates the pride of giants and demons, who gives bliss and happiness, whose nature is immortal and whose halo is refulgent" (Ghosh 1979: 71).[5]

In chapter 1, I noted a tension between elements of playfulness and of danger that often characterizes ritual performances in Papua New Guinea. In Hindu cultures, elements of danger are supplied by the divine origin of the powers invoked, the frequent emphasis upon the wrathful and often bestial "other side" of these divine powers, the mirroring of the demonic that is a part of the Tantric strategy, the artistic skill used in manifesting the frightful aspect of this divine and potentially destructive power, and, where trance is involved, the sense that the wrathful "other side" is really present—that the dangers are not only metaphorical, but actual.

More playful elements are afforded by the "jocular intimacy" with figures for divine energy offered in Puranic myth, the possibilities for fanciful artistic treatment of these figures, and, most important here, the playful-

Figure 19. Narasimhi mask used in a gambhira performance. Aiho, Malda, West Bengal, 1983.

Figure 20. Shri Arjun Satapathy offers puja to a Narasimha mask prior to a *Prahlada Nataka* performance. Baulagaon, Ganjam, Orissa, 1980.

ness inherent in the ambiguous and paradoxical procedures of theatrical contextualization. The transformation of a human actor into a chimera of man, god, and beast may bring delight as well as awe. The capacity to turn dreaded forces inside out and lay claim to them as protective forces through the medium of artistic play can bring an exhilarating sense of the capacity to conquer fear.

The syncretic form of Orissan *Prahlada Nataka* maximizes this tension between threatening and playful elements by allowing for both the actualization of a divine presence by means of trance and the mimetic elaboration of a mythological story. An intriguing result of this juxtaposition of visitation with mimetic play is that both the mask's power and the degree to which that power can be theatrically contained may vary from performance to performance. To understand how this works, it will be necessary to describe a typical *Prahlada Nataka* performance in greater detail and to indicate its shifting modes.

Before the performance begins, while the other actors are putting on their costumes and makeup, the actor/priest who is to wear the mask of Narasimha removes a (frequently red) cloth from the mask and conducts an elaborate puja, welcoming the spirit of the mask as an honored guest in accordance with time-honored procedures (fig. 20). Flower petals are strewn on the mask's headdress, water is blessed and sprinkled over the mask's face, a coconut is offered up to the mask, cooling sandal paste is rubbed on the mask's forehead, and incense is lit and held up for the mask to breathe. Throughout this ritual welcoming, the mask is treated with reverence. Sanskrit *mantras* are spoken and appropriate *mudras* (ritualized hand gestures) are performed to invoke Narasimha's presence and blessings, while the orchestra plays interlocking drum and cymbal patterns. Finally, all the actors and musicians gather around the mask and sing invocations to Vishnu, while the actor/priest tosses flowers towards the mask, lights a camphor flame, and moves it about the mask's face as an act of worship:

Hail to thee, Shri Man-Lion! Hail Shri Hari!
[. . .]
Appearing suddenly in your fourth incarnation,
You saved the troubled gods
And fulfilled the wishes of Prahlada,
Emerging from the pillar and killing the demon Hiranya.[6]

While this ritual is not viewed by the audience, the knowledge that it is being performed both at regular intervals in the temple and immediately before a performance is important to audience and actors alike. The puja signals and enhances belief in the mask's divinity—in its power as a performing object and in its effectiveness as a spiritual conduit. The actors of Baulagaon tell of a nearby village that also had a Narasimha mask used in *Prahlada Nataka* performances. Pujas to the mask lapsed, they say, and the performer who used to wear the mask received a dream in which the spirit of the mask stated that, because he was not being properly worshipped, he would no longer take part in performances. The mask became so heavy that no one could lift it.

Prahlada Nataka performances take place in the road outside a temple or in an open field, with a set of bleacher-like platforms installed at one end for the actors to pose and dance upon. The production style is boldly theatrical, mixing raucous music, vigorous dance, operatic song, melodramatic dialogue, and calculated spectacle. The reverential tone of the dressing room seems to be completely overwhelmed in the broad theatrical display. As in most Asian (and other non-Western) theatre, the performance begins with music. The orchestra consists of two drums *(mrdala)*, four sets of medium-sized cymbals *(gini)*, a harmonium, a small oboe-like instrument *(mukhavina)*, a conch shell used to signal Narasimha's climactic arrival, and, sometimes, two long trumpets to mark other entrances. Throughout the performance, a variety of musical effects are used to create excitement and to support the dramatic action. Entrance flourishes, chanted Sanskrit *slokas*, and folk elements are freely mixed with the ragas and talas of Karnatik classical music. The principal narrator *(gahaka)* and a chorus of "play-back" singers (a term taken from the dubbing practices of popular Hindi film musicals) do not enact or represent characters but, rather, present themselves humbly as devotees of Vishnu, or, sometimes, as surrogates for the author:

> Oh learned pundits, listen with pleasure to the style of this play. Do not find fault if it fails to have the proper grace of poetry, for I am unlettered by nature. Even in dreams, I have kept poor company. Yet I take courage, keeping the deeds of Hari [Vishnu] always before me.

After preliminary greetings to the audience, Ganesha, the elephant-headed son of Shiva and the bringer of auspicious beginnings, is invoked in both Sanskrit and Oriya:

> Pray to thee, oh Lord Ganesh! Dwarf-in-stature, fat-of-body, elephant-headed, big-bellied one! Who is beautiful! Whose neck is garlanded with the sweet smelling flowers sought after by the bees. Whose tusk is broken and whose body is red with the blood of his enemies. We pray to thee, son of the mountains' daughter, remover of obstacles, and fulfiller of wishes! Grant us your blessing!

An actor wearing a red papier-mâché elephant mask comes forward and ascends the bleacher-like set of stepped platforms, sitting on a crude throne set up at the top (fig 21). With a bang on a strategically placed floorboard that has been deliberately left loose, he rises dramatically and proceeds to execute a spectacular whirling and spinning dance, moving diagonally up and down the steps. The dance is made all the more spectacular by the restricted vision offered the actor—usually a child—through the wooden or papier-mâché elephant mask that he wears. After Ganesha gives his blessings for the performance, Saraswati, the goddess of learning, is invoked. Impersonated by a boy in female dress, she also gives her blessings to the performance.

Neither the actor dancing in Ganesha's mask nor the boy impersonating Saraswati are understood to be entranced or possessed by the spirits of those deities. Rather, they "stand for" the deities, honoring them. To

Figure 21. Ganesha gives his blessings.

dance well with Ganesha's mask requires great skill; but the mask itself is treated as a costume, not a spiritual conduit. No pujas welcome this mask's spirit. It is kept in a property trunk, not a temple. With a good dancer, the mode of representation is clearly that of the character actor: he enacts Ganesha in spirit and body. With less skilled performers, iconic representation of the deities may suffice. In either case, the mode of presentation is in contrast to that used when an actor/priest puts on the Narasimha mask and is understood to *become* the man-lion avatara of Vishnu.

The next section of the performance introduces the demon tyrant, Hiranyakashipu. His *Dwari,* or doorman, enters first, in splendid costume and with bright red makeup. He sings his own praises and dances in a vigorous, whirling fashion, his sword sweeping through the air:

Gaudy slippers on his feet,
The braggart doorman comes to court,
A killer-chopper is in his hand.
The audience trembles at his command.
Hear me, you who assemble here,
For I am Hiranyakashipu's man.

Introduced to the audience and his fictive court as the greatest of warriors and "Thorn of the Three Worlds" by his flamboyant sentry, Hiranyakashipu himself now enters (fig. 22). At Baulagaon he entered on a dummy elephant (supported by two men), accompanied by attendants and announced by trumpets and fireworks. His costume is even more splendid than that of his vainglorious herald's, while his makeup, like the Dwari's, is bright red, and set off by a "diamond-studded" mustache and—frequently—by round-rimmed sun glasses. The demon king dismounts. His voice is commanding. His movements as he spins up and down the stepped platform are athletic; he dominates the treacherous space. Everything is calculated to display strength and confidence. Like the sentry, he begins by singing his own praises in the third person:

Hiranyakashipu, Lord of Demons,
With all his ministers comes to court.
Set with precious stones and gems,
His crown outshines ten million suns.

He exults in his power and good fortune. He has been granted a boon from Brahma rendering him impervious to death by the hand of god, man, or animal, in daytime or at night, inside or outside of a house, on the ground or in the air, by any weapon known to man. Seemingly invincible and at the height of his powers, this demon has become a tyrant over the three worlds, and has forbidden the worship of Vishnu.

As the dialogue shifts from the third person form of address characteristic of these entrance songs *(daru)*, other characters are introduced to people the dramatic world. The tone of the dialogue used in dramatic exchanges varies greatly. In Bharata-Muni's terms, the performance shifts back and forth stylistically between the elaborate and elegant conventions of *natyadharmi* theatre and the more plainspoken mimetic play of the *lokadharmi* approach. These shifts are evident in the text as well as in the vari-

Figure 22. Hiranyakashipu in performance.

ous kinds of movement used. Singing to his wife—played by a young man in women's clothing and makeup—Hiranyakashipu uses lushly romantic poetry:

Oh Pandanus-colored Queen, sit here by my side.
Take away love's agony with all your knowing ways.
Come and make me cheerful, bells tinkling at your waist.
Wipe away all sorrow with the sweetness of your kiss.

In contrast to this elegant and erotic sung verse, a corrupt old priest satirizes the astrologer's craft in comic spoken prose:

Listen to the placement of the stellar constellations. The ram is into the goats, the bull is into the cows. The twins are coupled up. The crab is in a hole in the rice

Figure 23. A boy actor playing Prahlada.

paddy. The lion is deep in the forest. The virgin is in the whorehouse. The scales are in a goldsmith's sack. The scorpion is in a pile of manure. The archer is with the Kshatriyas. The goat is in the water tank. The fish is in the water. And the water carrier is in my pay. Since they're all there together, this horoscope is really powerful!

Finally Prahlada's birth is announced and he is presented at court. Played by a pre-adolescent boy, he spins in, dressed in a miniature version of his father's costume, singing the praises of his father's arch enemy (fig. 23). Hiranyakashipu announces that he will educate his son, and instructs Prahlada never again to invoke the name of Vishnu; but his son refuses to obey his command and defiantly reels off Vishnu's various names: Hari, Narayana, Krishna, Keshava, Rama. The list goes on and on, provoking his father's demonic wrath. In the ensuing action, many attempts are made to force Prahlada to give up his worship of Vishnu. Gurus try to catechize him. Strongmen dance about him menacingly and try to bully him with drawn swords. Still Prahlada persists in his devotion. Furious at his son's obstinacy, Hiranyakashipu himself attacks Prahlada with knives, but the blades won't penetrate. Prahlada is offered to the goddess Chandi as human sacrifice, but she turns on the demon servants who hold him captive. He is set on a wheel of fire, but emerges unscathed. He is thrown from a cliff, but is caught by mother earth. He is trampled by a mad elephant, but it is the elephant trainer who perishes. A snake charmer is called in and sets a live cobra around Prahlada's neck, but the child is not harmed by this and continues to sing Vishnu's praises.

As the play goes on through the night, the scenes heat up dramatically in a kind of nightmare version of Orissan family life: the father tries to keep his son on course, the son rebels, the mother is caught in the middle, desperately trying to make peace:

King: Wisdom has left you, foolishness prevails.
You won't heed my words and defy me still.
Prahlada: It is evil of you, defaming Shrihari.
I can never abandon His lotus-red feet,
Threaten me though you will.
Lilavati: Don't torture your father. Accept his advice.
Abandon these prayers to Shrihari.
I am your mother. Please, hear what I say.
Oh son, I beg you, be wise.
Prahlada: Have you no fear, opposing Shrihari?
Consider it carefully! [. . .]
King: Stop all this chatter and fall at my feet!
Or you haven't a hope of staying alive.
[. . .]
Prahlada: Cut off my head and roll it on the ground!
I cannot abandon Hari's name.
Lilavati: If he prays to Hari in his madness,
It does you no mortal harm.
What glory could you earn by killing a child?

It would only bring you shame.
King: I will surely kill him if his mind's on Sowri.
Don't dare contradict my aim.

Intriguingly, there is little hint of this domestic turmoil in the Puranic sources, and its prominence in the theatrical representation of this story provides a striking example of the ways in which theatre and myth incorporate the "raw stuff" of "social dramas" as they sustain and regenerate themselves (cf. V. Turner 1986: 105). In talking to audience members and the families of performers, it was particularly the women who stressed that, along with its other attractions, *Prahlada Nataka* is appealing precisely because "it's a story about a family." They clearly empathized with Lilavati's position as frustrated family peacemaker, caught between an adamant husband and a rebellious son.

Throughout the long evening's passage, narrative and dramatic dialogue are juxtaposed, as the gahaka and play-back singers support dramatic songs, move the story along, or comment on events. Dramatic action frequently yields place to devotional songs celebrating Prahlada's faith and Vishnu's protective power. Sometimes actors enter fully into character, while at other times they demonstrate their character's behavior or even break character to take a glass of water or adjust a costume. The bedi system of competitions, pitting one troupe against another, further complicates this playing with modes. The two competing troupes play out the action more or less simultaneously, within view of each other, adjusting the text and even the sequence of events to keep abreast of each other, and vying for the audience's attention. When this contest format is followed, the action may be halted from time to time by a sponsoring temple committee, and the often illiterate farmers playing Hiranyakashipu or the boys playing Prahlada are challenged to face each other head to head, sing Sanskrit slokas from the text, and expostulate on the meaning of these verses. This complex shifting among modes creates a highly charged, extremely flexible ambiance for theatre, leading up to the climax of both the mythological story and the performed event.

As Hiranyakashipu whirls his son about in a rage, a conch is blown, signaling that the actor/priest who will wear Narasimha's mask has arrived behind a screened enclosure set up in what has so far been the audience's domain; he is now ready to make his entrance. The music becomes frenzied. Prahlada states that Vishnu is "inside, outside, all in all, and everywhere"—even in the pillars of the entryway. The furious demon king advances menacingly with his giant property club and knocks aside the screen functioning as pillar. The actor/priest bursts forward, the huge Narasimha mask in place. Audience members and many of the actors may clasp their hands in reverence. More likely than not, the actor/priest is in a deep and violent trance as he moves towards the blaspheming Hiranyakashipu (fig. 24). The spirit of Narasimha is understood to have entered the actor/priest through the medium of the mask. In trance, he does not *play* Narasimha, he *is* Narasimha—or at least his body has become the container for Narasimha's visiting spiritual force.

As Narasimha, he is not man nor beast nor god, but a divine amalgam of all three. It is dusk within the world of the story and—ideally—dawn in the actual time of performance: neither daytime nor nighttime. The audience knows that in the puranic narrative Hiranyakashipu will be killed on the threshold of his home—literally a limen, betwixt and between inside and outside; it also knows that he will be disemboweled by the god-beast's claws (no weapon known to man) while held across his lap (neither on the ground nor in the air). Brahma's troublesome boon has been circumvented and Hiranyakashipu's demonic rule is about to end.

Narasimha is pulled to a chair by several large men hauling on ropes attached to his body and is held there, facing the actor playing Hiranyakashipu, who keeps a safe physical distance (see color plate III). Although the priest is not a large man, the strength of his possession is such that it takes considerable effort to hold him back. Hiranyakashipu declares that he is about to die, repents his evil deeds in song, and warns his son that good fortune can only proceed from good deeds. Prahlada moves to Narasimha's side, sings to him, and calms him. The mask is gently removed. The actor/priest who has worn the mask is carried away, limp and unconscious, his eyes rolled back. Away from the field of performance, he will slowly be brought back into consciousness by the sprinkling of holy water.

Shri Arjun Satapathy, the actor/priest who wore the Narasimha mask in Baulagaon, explains that an alternative ending is possible. If the actor/priest who is to wear the Narasimha mask does not go into trance, then the story can be completed mimetically. Narasimha would attack Hiranyakashipu, place him on his lap, and mime the disembowelment of the demon tyrant (1983, personal communication). Evil would still be contained, but this time through metaphoric procedures deployed within the realm of theatrical representation. When trance is achieved, however, theatrical representation yields to the actualization of Narasimha's presence. Theatrical play with demonic forces leads to and is superseded by the visitation of Vishnu as Narasimha.

In practice, the ending that manifests trance possession is preferred as more exciting theatre as well as more effective ritual, but the manner of enactment may depend on the strength of the possession. Shri Satapathy explained the following sequence of events and artistic choices. Behind the screen set up as pillar, the mask is brought to him, and there he performs a puja to the mask. If he has been lax in fasting before the performance, or has otherwise been "impure," or if the gods do not will it on a given occasion, he may not go into trance. As the mask is being placed on his head,

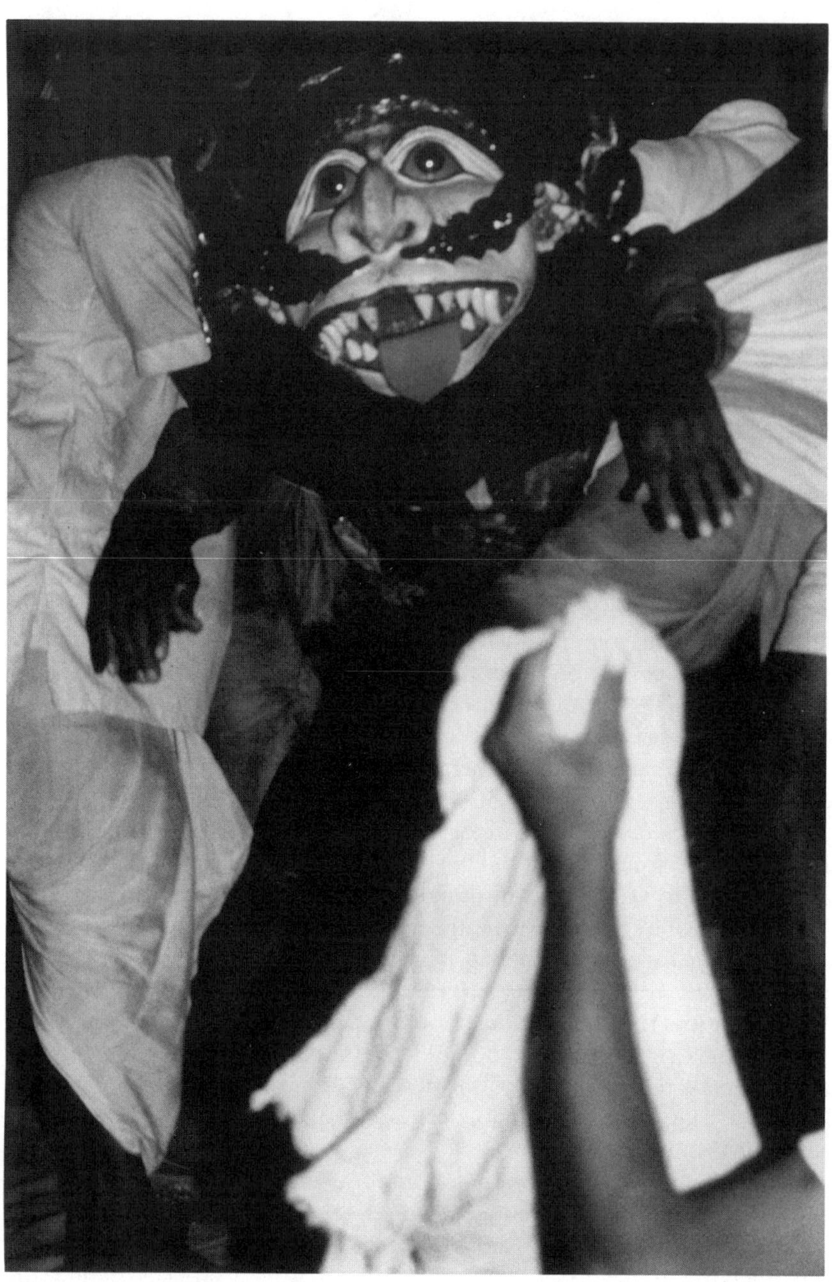

Figure 24. An entranced Narasimha performer being restrained.

he will know at once whether or not the trance is effective by an unnatural weight to the mask, a feeling of heat on his face and a general sense of "wildness" setting in, and he will signal those around him in the screened enclosure. If he is not in trance, then he must represent Narasimha's fury in the mode of the character actor, and the disemboweling of the King will be mimed.

If he is in trance, the bringing forth of Narasimha's spirit is sufficient to provide a symbolic victory over the relatively powerless manifestation of the demonic represented by the actor playing Hiranyakashipu; but Arjun Satapathy will remember little from the time he enters from the screen/pillar to the time that the boy actor playing Prahlada sings to him and calms him:

> When I first put on the mask, my legs tremble, my knees and thighs tremble, too. My body becomes very heavy and my neck and face become like fire. My eyes burn. My whole body takes on a different form that I can't describe. Once the mask is on, I lose the sense of my body. All the other members of the troupe stand by to restrain me. Sometimes, they say, twenty-five people catch hold of me, and still they can't control me. (1983, personal communication)

These alternative procedures for containment of the demonic are said to have been in effect since the turn of the century, when an actor playing Hiranyakashipu was killed by an entranced Narasimha performer during a performance of *Prahlada Nataka*. Containment of the demonic can be a dangerous business.[7]

Descriptive examples of endings observed in various performances may help to clarify the range of choices available to *Prahlada Nataka* performers. In one performance, the Narasimha trance appeared to be relatively mild, perhaps feigned. Narasimha could be handled with ease by those holding him and the actor/priest seemed to have a measure of control over his actions. Hiranyakashipu picked up his oversized property club made of cane and decorated with brightly colored paper and signaled the orchestra to play louder and faster. Another such club was placed in Narasimha's hands. As drums and cymbals played frenetically, a carefully controlled combat was acted out. Hiranyakashipu circled around Narasimha, striking out at him and taunting him. Narasimha—held in check and moved around in a circle by his handlers—lashed out wildly at Hiranyakashipu. After Narasimha had been goaded into a state of frenzy, Hiranyakashipu knelt before him. Narasimha was then dragged over to the bleacher steps that formed the stage and was calmed, and Hiranyakashipu lay down across his lap in a static pose that imitated the iconography of temple statues and Puranic paintings. Holding this tableau completed the story and the performance.

In another performance the trance began mildly, but, as Hiranyakashipu sang his advice to Prahlada, Narasimha became more and more violent and difficult to constrain. The property club had already been placed in Narasimha's hand, but—on a signal from the actor playing Hiranyakashipu—one of the handlers took the club and held it symbolically in front of Narasimha, while Hiranyakashipu knelt before him. Narasimha was then forced back into his chair, his arms pinned back, and Hiranyakashipu lay ever so briefly across his lap to complete the truncated action and end the performance.

During one contest, the trances on both sides were violent, and the masks were removed from both actor/priests so as to continue the performances. On one side, the mask itself was placed on the chair where Narasimha would have sat; on the other, the limp body of the unmasked dancer was addressed as Narasimha. At Baulagaon, the actor playing Hiranyakashipu came before us and excused himself from forming the final tableau, explaining that the trance was too dangerous for him. Narasimha's visitation had supplanted the need for iconographic fulfillment of the story, but he seemed aware of our own Aristotelian expectations of a beginning, middle, and end, played out within mimetic form. He was sorry, but it couldn't be done.

There are other local variations used to emphasize the power of the trance or elaborate the movement toward a dramatic close, but these instances should suffice to indicate an ability to move flexibly among narrative, dramatic, iconographic, and ritualistic modes, depending on the effectiveness and power of the trance as it develops. Despite the preference for trance, in no case did the audience seem disappointed. All the endings were appropriate within the alternate strategies afforded by the flexible traditions of *Prahlada Nataka.*

The Container and the Contained: Rangda and the Barong Ket in Bali

Balinese preoccupation with the demonic is well-documented. As Hooykaas has written:

> A Balinese is constantly harassed by hordes and armies of malevolent beings of the most divergent shape, function, abode, and time of activity—one would nearly say: as many as a playful mind during many hours of leisure can imagine. When the exorcist priest [. . .] has had a good teacher and himself has a good memory, he enumerates tens, dozens, scores of names and locates them everywhere in our immediate neighborhood. [. . .] He has to convoke them, to regale them, and finally to invite them to go home to their respective quarters. (1973: 8; see also H. Geertz 1995; Howe 1984)

Direct propitiation is one way of dealing with the demonic forces lurking within the Balinese cosmos. Thus, garbage-like offerings and blood sacrifices (*caru*), suited to the lowly tastes of such *bhuta kala*, are spread out on the ground at most important functions, and priestly invocations are made (see Eiseman 1989: 226–34).

In keeping with their love of the theatrical, though, the Balinese also deploy a more creative and playful strategy of dealing with these demonic nuisances: animalistic figures, *barong*, are created, consecrated, venerated, danced with, and turned against this inchoate legion of demonic forces. The most popular of these playful and powerful beasts is carved in the image of Banaspati Raja—one of the many names ascribed to the leonine Kirtimukha icons in this area of the world—and is known as the Barong Ket (fig. 25). Like the Kirtimukha icons, the Barong Ket manifests demonic and animalistic qualities in order to defend against lesser manifestations of these powers. Balinese chronicles record this function mythically: Giriputri, an aspect of Shiva's Shakti, appeared to King Jayakusuna of Loripan and helped him to rid his land of sickness by luring the disease-provoking demons into a single great demonic form: the Barong Ket. This Barong would contain the demonic forces safely as long as he was paraded and given offerings at specified times (de Zoete and Spies 1973 [1938]: 94, 294).

As an animated extension of the strategies behind the guardian faces of Shaivite temple gates, the Barong Ket can and does function independently in his confrontations with lesser beings that populate the chthonic world. In the Balinese village of Sideman, for example, "when disease and death increase at a disturbing pace," he is led from his place of honor in the chthonian temple *(pura dalem)* by the temple priest and representatives of the palace and, animated by two young men, paraded around the city to accept the offerings of various families and community groups and to confer his blessings (Ramseyer 1977: 190). More festively, at the Galungan holiday and at other propitious times, clubs of young men parade with the Barong Ket of their wards through town and village streets and beyond. Bandem and deBoer describe the shaggy beast in the exercise of his apotropaic function: "The eight foot frame of his body is shaggy with white palm fibers and a little bell and a mirror hang from the animal's tail. [. . .] His magical beard, made of human hair, waggles as his jaw clacks at crossroads and village corners, chasing the bhuta back into the outer darkness" (1981: 118; see also Mead 1970 [1939]). However serious the Barong Ket's purpose on such occasions, his style is frolicsome. In deploying him, the Balinese take full advantage of the "jocular intimacy" with demonic and divine forces that Zimmer notes as a possibility with Hindu systems of belief and iconography. When deployed theatrically, however, Banaspati Raja is traditionally paired with an "adversary"—a witch-like manifestation of potentially destructive power most commonly known to Westerners and Balinese alike as "Rangda" (fig. 26). This is a far less playful figure, and a far more difficult one to decipher.[8]

My own most memorable encounter with Rangda took place in 1975, when I journeyed to a village on the outskirts of Denpasar to witness a

Figure 25. The Barong Ket playing with the audience at a mapajar performance. Jimbaran, Bali 1991.

Figure 26. Rangda mask being restored by its carver, I Wayan Tedun. Singapadu, Bali, 1975.

performance of *Cupak*—a wonderful tale that deals with themes of human imperfection, sibling rivalry, and the struggle for self-respect. I had read accounts of the story in various older sources, had co-translated an epic version of the tale, and had commissioned a set of masks for a production to tour New England schools. Still, the story is now rarely produced in Bali, and I had never managed to find a production. Luckily for me, the village of Sumerta had hired a visiting troupe. With great anticipation, then, I watched as Cupak, the gluttonous, cowardly, ugly brother, and Grantang, his all-too-perfect "twin," were introduced through the leisurely conventions of Balinese *arja*—a form sometimes referred to as "Balinese opera." I was particularly interested in how the climactic confrontation between the two brothers would be handled in production, since the sources I was using varied greatly on this point. Before that confrontation, however, the heroic Grantang has to save a princess from the lustful clutches of the giant Benaru, while Cupak cowers in a tree.

When the performance reached this point of the tale, "Benaru" emerged: as Rangda. Eyes bulging, fangs bared, tongue extended and "enflamed," dugs flapping, and fingernails reaching out grotesquely while holding a white cloth marked with magic formulae, the frightful masked figure advanced on Grantang (cf. H. Geertz 1995: 54–55). Suddenly, the lion-like form of the Barong Ket rushed past Grantang, replacing him in battle. Manned by two agile dancers, the beast's gilded and mirrored leather coat glinted in the light of the kerosene lamps. His red jaws snapped open and shut; white flowers studded his human beard. The *gamelan* music fastened loudly and insistently on a single note pounded out on brass metallophones, while the accompanying drumbeats rose in crescendo. Rangda's white cloth swept across the Barong's head, and the actor playing the front half of the mythic animal fell to the ground in a seizure, kicking his legs as though in an epileptic fit. Pandemonium seemed to break loose. Men with drawn swords rushed forward to attack the Rangda (cf. fig. 27). When their *keris* failed to penetrate the witch-like figure, they turned the blades against themselves. Protected by trance, their skin could not be torn by the blades of their keris; still, they struggled in what appeared an orgy of self-destructive energy, throwing themselves down on the blades and pushing these blades with all their might against the resistant flesh. Priests circulated in the scene, disarming men, carrying the now still and prone Barong dancer into the adjacent temple, and, eventually, bearing off the exhausted Rangda performer as well. In the confines of the temple, he would be gently brought out of his violent trance possession.

The performance was over. Yet, the climax of the tale had not been reached. Worse, the "wrong side" seemed to have won, and the "princess" had been abandoned by audience and actors alike. Still, no one but me seemed bothered. Clearly, something of great theatrical and human interest had taken place; but what it all signified I couldn't fathom. Dramati-

Figure 27. Rangda's daughter, Rarong, being attacked by "keris dancers" in a performance for tourists. Batubulan, Bali, 1991.

cally, the incidents seemed to make no sense whatever. Symbolically, the seeming victory of the evil witch (who had somehow replaced the lecherous male giant, Benaru, of the source narrative) mocked almost everything I thought I understood about dramatic plots in Bali and the symbolic roles of Barong and Rangda. Wasn't Rangda on the side of "evil"? Didn't the forces of "good" have to overcome the forces of "evil," or at least neutralize them within the theatrical and dramatic action? And wasn't it specifically the Barong's function to protect the entranced dancers and the community from Rangda's power? Was this, then, an ill omen? And didn't anybody else care about the rest of the barely begun story? Audience members assured me, though, that nothing had gone awry and there had been no ill omens: "The Barong and the Rangda needed to dance."

In retrospect, the performance strategies I later observed in the Orissan *Prahlada Nataka* provide some clues. As in the Orissan performance, a story had been cannibalized by a ritual: a mimetic representation had first incorporated and then been supplanted by an act of visitation. In the Balinese instance, though, the mimetic envelopes deployed are strained far more by the chthonic presences invoked. If a non-consecrated Rangda mask had been used—and if the Barong Ket and Rangda had not "needed" to perform—then Grantang could have defeated his adversary, saved the princess, and the story would have proceeded to its climax and conclusion. In such a case, the Rangda mask would have functioned as nothing more nor less than a powerful theatrical image of demonic force, meant to be defeated within an unfolding fictive world. The gender switch would pose no problem for the Balinese audience. The Rangda mask would be used as a *pamurtian*—a demonic form that characters possessing magic powers can transform themselves into at will (not unlike the shape-shifters of science fiction). Rangda makes a good pamurtian, all the more so because of her "feminine" wildness.[9]

But this performance of *Cupak* was staged when appearances of the consecrated Rangda and Barong masks venerated at the chthonic temple of Sumerta were called for by "unclean" *(sebel)* conditions in the village. The *Cupak* performance had been commissioned specifically to provide a context for the appearance of these figures. More often than not, when these sacred masks are grafted onto a play they manifest a strength too explosive for the framework of the fictive world to bear. This is quite acceptable to Balinese audiences. A story may work its way to its own conclusion, or it may yield to ritual procedures needed to contain forces far too powerful to be dealt with by ordinary theatrical means. The resulting pandemonium is deemed both theatrically exciting and ritually effective.

It is in some respects unfortunate that Rangda has become so identified with one of her dramatic roles, that of the widow/witch of Girah featured in performances of *Calon Arang*—a story set in eleventh-century Bali, in which forces of "black magic" and "white magic" do battle (see color plate IV). In the pura dalem, the mask is called Ratu Dalem; she is "Monarch" of the temple and, by extension, of the chthonic realm. In the temple, and at appropriate public ceremonies, she is elevated along with the Barong Ket, and is venerated with pujas strikingly similar to those used for the Narasimha avatara mask in the temples of Orissa (fig. 28). As a pamurtian, Rangda's mask is used theatrically to represent the wrathful aspects of shape-shifting gods as well as demons: of Durga, of Siwa (Shiva), and of Wisnu (Vishnu: fig. 29). As Bandem and deBoer point out, even as widow/witch, Rangda functions in a paradoxically protective way: within the metaphoric world of the *Calon Arang* story, Rangda is the mistress of black magic and the container of all that is monstrous and evil; but within the ritual, she functions as the protector of the community, defusing the power of those who practice black magic and directly challenging human malefactors to match their powers against "hers" (1984: 126–29).

Both the Barong Ket and Rangda are manifestations of the chthonic "other side" of the Hindu cosmos. Both are venerated as protective figures, and deployed to keep different forms of evil at bay through strategies of containment. To set Rangda against the Barong Ket is to provide each a worthy opponent and an opportunity to display its powers. Their ritual and theatrical confrontations should not be interpreted as a pitting of "good" against "evil"; nor is a strong showing of Rangda a bad omen. An essentially weak Rangda might be of value as the pamurtian of a demon-to-be-vanquished in mimetic theatre, but it could be of no protective use to a Balinese village. The powers manifested by Rangda and the Barong Ket are ultimately to be harnessed ritually, within the domain of the temple, and not within the metaphorical world of dramatic representation. Still, their "need to dance" is important as a way of confirming their powers, and of "giving play" to the forces that they contain, and all that those powers may signify.[10]

The seemingly self-destructive frenzy of the keris "dancers" indicates the dangerous and potentially destructive nature of the powers contained by Rangda. Indeed, like the wrathful "other side" of Shiva that she sometimes portrays, Rangda is a projection of everything that the Balinese abhor and try to separate themselves from in their day-to-day lives. In infancy, shows of aggressive anger are systematically discouraged (Bateson and Mead 1942: 148–63). In adolescence, the canine teeth of Balinese are ceremonially filed so as to underscore the separation of the human from the animal world. Conventional wisdom, though, teaches that these efforts are never entirely successful. Humans retain their links to the animal world, and unruly emotions can never be entirely eliminated. The human microcosmos *(buwana alit)* is considered a faithful copy of the divine macrocosmos *(buwana agung)*, and as long as destructive, unruly forces are found within, they must be figured as part of the cosmic world of forces without.

Figure 28. Rangda, Rarong, and the Barong Ket honored together at a temple festival near Pejeng, Bali, 1991.

The sometimes combative, and ultimately complementary, relationship between Rangda and the Barong Ket bears a closer look. There is a strong link to the animal world evident in apotropaic masks around the world, including that of Rangda. In tropical zones (and sometimes well beyond them), that link is most commonly made with the most powerful predators of the jungle: the lion and its close relations. David Napier (1986) details iconographic similarities among these figures that revolve around transformations of the image of the lion, and he constructs a possible history of these leonine apotropaic figures in Greece, North Africa, and South Asia and Southeast Asia, taking note of Kirtimukha, Narasimha, the Barong Ket, and Rangda herself, as well as Humbaba of the ancient Near East, and a host of figures from archaic Greece. To his list might be added a sizable bestiary of fantastic figures that can be linked to the Kirtimukha

Figure 29. A Rangda mask used as a pamurtian for Wisnu in a performance of *Godogan* (the Balinese Frog Prince). Sanur, Bali, 1979.

tradition and its Buddhist variants: the *shi-shi* of Japan, the Snow Lion of Nepal and Tibet, and the lions and dragons of China and Korea (see also Miyao 1987; Park 1987), as well as such far-flung icons as the Jaguar figures of Meso-America and the monstrous, fanged, and pop-eyed *xwexwe* and *swaihwe* masks that show their distended tongues in the Pacific Northwest (Lévi-Strauss 1982).

Most intriguing are Napier's remarks on gorgons and gorgoneion of archaic Greece who appear around the seventh century BC on Syracusan reliefs, as apotropaic figures on Athenian warriors' shields, and as leonine masks in Tyrens. Medusa, of course, is the most famous gorgon, and her mask-like severed and snake-wreathed head could turn those who looked upon her to stone. Some of the gorgons pictured on archaic vases and reliefs are smooth-faced and hag-like, in the manner of Medusa, while others are bearded, with definite leonine features, and still others seem a hybrid of lion and witch, with brows that show definite traces of the ancillary tufts

Figure 30. The entrance to Goa Gajah. Pejeng, Bali.

of hair typical of the lioness. If Napier is right in his admittedly conjectural history, then the model for these icons with glaring eyes, flared nostrils, gnashing fangs, wild hair, and thrust-out tongues came to Greece from India via the Phoenician sea trade (1986: 83–187). It might be remembered in this regard that Durga, in particular, has the lion as her vehicle and constant companion; as noted below, she also shares stories, iconographic details, and ritual functions with the man-lion, Narasimha.

In Bali, perhaps the most striking instance of the transferability of the leonine Kirtimukha image to a witch-like visage is the giant, monstrous face that guards the entrance of the eleventh-century hermitage cave, Goa Gajah at Bedulu (fig. 30). Recognizable as feminine from the style of jewelry in her oversized ears, the witch's head has usurped Kirtimukha's place as protector, and it is Rangda's familiar, bugged-out eyes, flared nostrils, and unruly hair that are featured in the icon, along with an enormous, fanged maw that is extended to form the entryway itself (see Kempers 1991: 117–22). Given the curious interchangeability of lion and witch within this widespread iconographic tradition, it is little wonder that Narasimha can inherit theatrical traditions from the Shakti cult and that the leonine Barong Ket and witch-like Rangda can reside together as co-protectors within the chthonian temples of Balinese villages.

Napier notes that the arresting presence of leonine apotropaic faces can in part be traced to an ambiguity of emotional affect. The ferocious expressions of these lion-like creations do not correspond to any of the recognizable sets of characteristics that have been identified with displays of "primary" human emotions (see Ekman and Friesen 1975): the eyes are too enlarged and the mouth pulled back too far for anger (cf. Bateson and Mead 1942: 175); the nostrils are too flared for fear; the characteristic distended tongue matches neither anger nor fear; and sometimes a trace of mirth seems present. While they do not depict any stable human emotion (a *sthayibhava* in the categories of the *Natyasastra* that modern studies in emotion seem regularly, and for the most part unknowingly, to replicate), Oohashi Tsutomu points out that they do bear a striking resemblance to the "threat display" as identified by ethologists (1987: 136–38). This is the transitory expression made in response to danger—all senses alert, caught between fear and fury—that serves as a warning and may precede a ferocious attack, or, for that matter, a grudging retreat. One striking transposition of this threat display onto the human face is in the Maori warrior's fearsome grimace, made with the eyes bulged out and tongue protruded. Another, less complete version, gives us the image of the staring "evil eye" displayed apotropaically on Mediterranean (and Balinese) ships.

While the mimicry of threat displays—especially those of powerful predators—may well account for some of the widespread appeal these figures have, and the mixed feelings they engender, Napier briefly proposes another possibility. Apotropaic figures characteristically exaggerate *all* the instruments for gaining sensory information: eyes, ears, nostrils, tongue, and fingers are commonly rendered larger than "natural." Not only are all Rangda's sensory organs exaggerated in her oversized face, but her fingers, too, are extended by the use of grotesque nails of buffalo horn. Napier suggests that Rangda's appearance may have a particular resonance with the human brain's monitoring of sensation (1986: 205).

Through signals arising from touch and movement, the rest of the body is continually monitored by the brain, but it is not monitored democratically. Graphic reconstructions of the proportionate representation accorded parts of the body within the somatosensory area of the brain's neocortex yield a "homunculus" with a tiny body and huge face, hands, and tongue (fig. 31, from Teyler 1975: 47; see also Kandel, Schwartz, and Jessell 1991: 370–74, 707, 610–11). A frontal drawing following the proportions

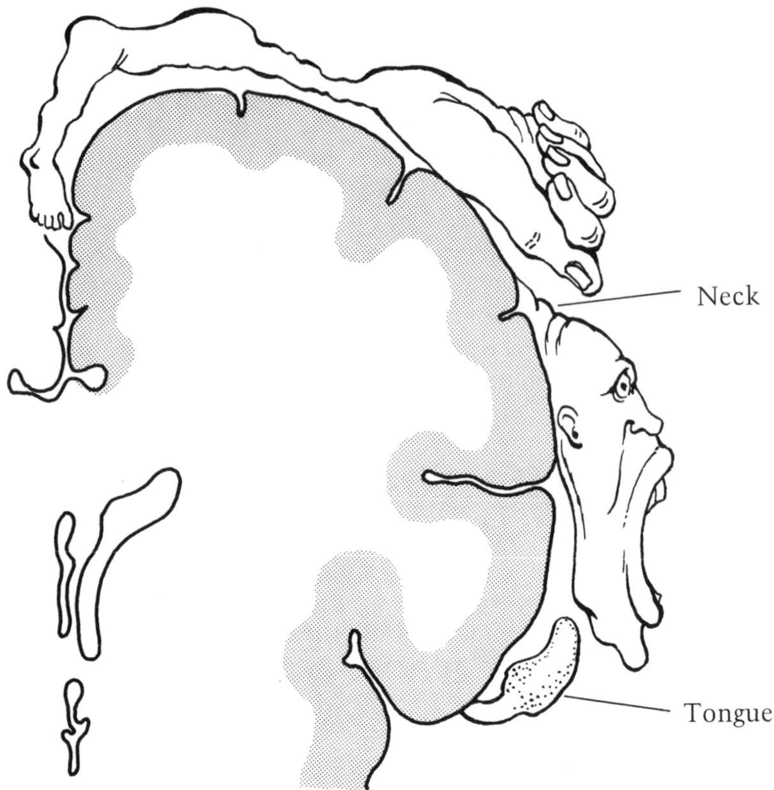

Figure 31. Graphic representation of the proportionate attention given to areas of the body by the human brain's motor cortex; a "homunculus" that mirrors the organization of the primary somatosensory cortex (originally published in Teyler 1975: 47; reproduced here by arrangement with W. H. Freeman Company).

indicated would produce an image shaped very much like the Kirtimukha: all head and hands, with bulging eyes, huge nostrils, and a very prominent tongue. Perhaps significantly, this is essentially what my then four-year-old son Aaron "naively" recorded when he first encountered Rangda in 1974 (fig. 32).

Rangda and her many cousins around the world share these oddly proportioned features. If these demonic and demon-like figures have an "archetypal" appeal (see Snow 1983), then that appeal may lie not so much in the genetic transmission of universal and cultural archetypes (as Jung proposed), but in an intuitive projection of the somatosensory structures themselves, as revealed to us through our constant, hierarchized monitoring of our own bodies as they move and encounter the world beyond the self. Rangda and her many relatives, then, may be first and foremost images

Figure 32. First impressions of Rangda as drawn by Aaron Emigh, age 4. 1975.

of raw sensation (subject, of course, to culturally constructed values and associations). In an inversion of Tantric wisdom, our imaginative sense of the world may be seen as prefigured in what neuroscientist Antonio Damasio (1994: 70, 155–60, 223–44) has called "the body-minded brain."[10]

Whatever the source of their appeal, Balinese and Orissan ways of playing with these potentially destructive forces tend to strain the strategies of playful containment close to the breaking point. Still, the keris "dancers" are protected in their fury and—unless something awful happens (as it sometimes, though rarely, does)—the powers of Rangda are eventually controlled within the temple, the mask of Narasimha is once more wrapped in cloth, and the performers who have worn these frightful masks and temporarily lost their awareness of selfhood resume both their everyday consciousness and their everyday lives. Theatrical and ritual encounters bear a great deal of psychic weight in Balinese and Orissan public life. In Orissa the calling forth of Narasimha provides excellent theatre, an emotionally charged event, a way of reflecting on familial tensions, and immediate evidence of a divine protective presence. In Bali, where—despite recent new technology and a flood of tourists—occasions for performance are still frequently linked to exorcistic needs within the community, to avoid this dangerous path would be to risk disaster on the one hand and the trivialization of both religion and theatre on the other.

Bali and Orissa: The Kalinga Connection

The question inevitably arises whether there are historical as well as aesthetic ties between these Orissan and Balinese performance forms. The simple answer is yes; but the nature and extent of such connections remain subject to considerable speculation which can become heated by hegemonic claims for a Greater India on the one hand and an understandable resistance to such claims on the other (unless, of course, these claims prove useful to Balinese in countering more pressing hegemonic pressures from Java). It is further complicated by the "archetypal" nature of the masks themselves: it is hard to determine where paths of diffusion end and where incidents of independent creation begin.

The Balinese religion, *Agama Hindu Bali*, or *Agama Hindu Dharma*, is an amalgam of Hindu and Buddhist beliefs and practices with indigenous animistic traditions (see Swellengrebel 1960; Eiseman 1989). In studying Balinese religious and cultural traditions, it is often difficult—sometimes impossible—to say where Indic strains end and indigenous ones begin. Still, while it may be impossible to determine precisely how Indic ideas, iconography, and performative traditions may have helped to shape the encounters (generically referred to as *mapajar*) of Rangda and the Barong Ket within Balinese theatre, or what common ancestry—other than the Kirtimukha tradition—these performances might share with *Prahlada Nataka* and its related forms in eastern India, enough is known to venture some guesses. The observations that follow are my attempt to do just this, in the hope that others will be able to come up with more definitive answers. I offer these tentative conclusions in part because I have become intrigued by the thorny issues involved, and in part because I feel that the issues may have a bearing on contemporary concerns about "interculturalism." Those interested in staying on the main path—the subject of masks and their usage and meaning—may wish to regard what follows as a lengthy (and optional) footnote.

The figures of Rangda and the Barong Ket are sometimes identified as prime examples of indigenous traditions that persist in Bali. Thus the narrative track to David Attenborough's documentary film *Miracle of Bali: Night* (1968), attributed to John Coast, asserts that

> The spirits that exercise the most power over the minds of the Balinese are neither remote nor impersonal. They are, on the contrary, creatures that the people know intimately and personally. Nor are they some recently imported deities from India, or anywhere else. But they are gods whose origins lie directly in Bali. [. . .] And the most important and friendly of them all is a magnificent, shaggy creature—the guardian of the village—the Barong. He it is who plays an important role in the most spectacular of temple rituals. The Barong [. . .] does battle with the hideous witch, Rangda, the embodiment of evil.

In contrast, Ramseyer (1977: 190) concludes that "one must in all likelihood look outside of Bali for the cultural-historical roots of both figures." Jane Belo (1949: 32) suggests that "the hideous witch" Rangda probably derives from Durga—Shiva's shakti—and the Barong Ket from the Buddhist iconographic tradition that produced the Snow Lion of Nepal and Tibet and the snapping New Year's dragons and lions of China, Korea, and Japan. As the associations with the Kirtimukha figure traced above indicate, it is likely that the figures of Rangda and the Barong Ket owe a great deal to iconographic influences arriving from outside of Bali, and especially, though not exclusively, from the direction of what is now India.

The Indic influence on Balinese culture was absorbed gradually over several centuries. It arrived both directly and indirectly—from Java and by way of China and other countries to the north and east. The notion that the New Year's lions of China and other East Asian countries where Buddhism had taken hold could have coupled with the thriving Kalas, Bhomas and Banaspati Rajas of the Southeast Asian Kirtimukha tradition to produce the Barongs of eastern Java and Bali is appealing, involving the recombination of divergent strands from a common source. Bali was not the only island in the Indonesian archipelago to provide a welcome home for such progeny: in addition to their close relatives in eastern Java, the Barongs of Bali can claim more distant cousins in the wild boars animated by up to fifteen men that are deployed in ceremonies of renewal and propitiation connected to ancestor worship in Kalimantan (Revel-MacDonald 1988: 79). The possible patterns of dispersion are many, and so are the possible points of origin, with intriguing possibilities for cross-breeding among traditions that have ample common ground, and have enjoyed periodic points of contact over hundreds, even thousands of years.

Since at least the start of the first millennium, Bali seems to have been involved in the sea trade connecting India with the Indonesian archipelago and points east. We know from Valmiki's *Ramayana* (written prior to 200 AD), Kalidasa's plays (probably written around the fourth century AD), and from archeological evidence that sandalwood and garuwood, nutmeg and cloves, bronze bowls, pottery, and gold were all being brought from the Indonesian archipelago to India (Ardika and Bellwood 1991: 230; K.S. Behera 1993: 123). Bali seems to have been an active port of call in this two-way maritime traffic. As a center for the making of the large bronze drums that characterized the latter stages of Vietnam-based Dong-Son culture in the first century AD (the largest of these drums having been made in the Balinese village of Pejeng, with casting molds found elsewhere on Balinese soil), Bali would have needed copper and tin, probably from points further west, as well as trade links to mainland Southeast Asia (Ardika and Bellwood 1991: 227–30; Kempers 1991: 16–31). Recent archeological findings of rouletted ware and inscriptions of Indian origin in Sembiran—an ancient port in northern Bali—match those found in Manikapatna of eastern India and indicate not only that Bali was involved in extensive local trade with Java and other parts of Southeast Asia during this period of time, but that it most likely had significant direct contact with trading vessels from India:

> Bali, during the early centuries AD, was probably located on a major trade route which delivered spices and fragrant woods from the Moluccas and Lesser Sundas to ports in Western Indonesia. These ports, including Sembiran, were presumably visited by both Indian and Indonesian traders, the latter perhaps sailing to India in their own vessels as well. (Ardika and Bellwood 1991: 230)

By 670 AD, Chinese travelers on their way to the monastery at Nalanda in northeastern India report a culture with definite Buddhist elements as well established on Bali (Ramseyer 1977: 37). In general, the cultural influences from India seem to have intensified in the archipelago at about this time, and the temple and monastery architecture of what is now Orissa had a substantial influence on the great monuments of ninth and tenth-century central Java (Coomaraswamy 1985 [1927]: 157). Also by the late ninth and tenth centuries AD, Sanskrit epigraphs and statuary bearing an eastern Indian influence were being produced in Bali in increasing numbers (Stutterheim 1935; Lansing 1983: 24–31). Markers of eastern Indian blood types (but not of southern or western Indian blood types) have been discovered in the endogamous Bali Aga (Old Balinese) village of Tenganan—probably established in the tenth century—and in a Buddhist priest's family in Karangasam (Breguet et al. 1982: 60, 311–15; Chockkalingam et al. 1982). Archeological and serological findings, then, seem to indicate at least intermittent contact with travelers from India throughout the first millennium AD, with a marked increase in cultural influence from the seventh century AD onward, culminating in the absorption of settlers coming directly or indirectly from eastern India, some of whom assumed priestly roles.

While there are indications that traders and settlers from up and down the eastern coast of the Indian subcontinent—from present-day Tamil

Nadu all the way to Bengal and Assam (as well as voyagers sailing around Cape Cormorin from ports as far away as Gujarat)—all had contact with the cultures of the Indonesian archipelago and mainland Southeast Asia, the evidence suggests a particularly strong connection between Bali and the very region where the Orissan *Prahlada Nataka* was developed and where it still flourishes. Historically, the name most often associated with this region is neither Orissa nor Andhra Pradesh: it is Kalinga.

The name "Kalinga" creates some confusion, since it has been used to designate tracts of land along the eastern coast of the subcontinent that have sometimes been much larger, and at other times considerably smaller, than modern-day Orissa. In Ashoka's reign (third century BC), in Kharavela's (first century BC), and once again during Chodaganga's (twelfth century AD), "Kalinga" was used to designate the vast expanse of land connecting the river deltas of the Godavari and the Ganges. Even in Ashoka's time, though, there was a division of northern and southern units of Kalinga for administrative purposes, each with centers of power sometimes associated with the name "Kalinganagaram" (Rajguru 1968: 35–36). The northern "core area" was centered in the Mahanadi River basin near modern-day Bhubaneswar of central Orissa. Under Ashoka and Kharavela, the principal political center of what was referred to as "Kalinganagara" was in this region (A. K. Das 1991: 3), and this seems to be the "Calingae" whose wealth and power was lauded by Pliny in the first century AD (Orissan Institute of Maritime and Southeast Asian Studies [1993]: 2).

Buddhist *Jataka* stories of the fourth and third centuries BC, however, already mention a kingdom of Kalinganagaram centered in what is now the coastal boarder region of Orissa and Andhra Pradesh. The capital of this kingdom, Dantapura, was a maritime center distinguished by a sacred relic said to be Buddha's tooth. Though political borders were in a constant state of flux, throughout most of the first millennium AD and beyond, from the rise of the Guptas in the early fourth century AD until the reconquering of the north by Chodaganga in the twelfth, it was this more southern "core area," spanning the deltas of the Rishikulya and Vamsadhara Rivers and now roughly comprising the northern-most district of Andhra Pradesh (Srikakulam) and the southernmost district of Orissa (Ganjam), that was most often referred to as "Kalinga" (Sahu, Misra, and Sahu 1979: 19–22; Orissan Institute of Maritime and Southeast Asian Studies [1993]: 2): this area is virtually co-extensive with the territory involved in the development of *Prahlada Nataka* and its Telegu predecessors.

While both the northern and southern Kalingas seem to have been active trading centers of considerable antiquity, Ptolemy, writing in the second century AD, states that the principal point of departure (*apheterion*) for ships bound for Southeast Asia was immediately to the south of a town named Paloura. "It was from here," says Ptolemy, that "ships ceased to follow the littoral and entered the high seas," working their way up the coast before making the treacherous passage across the Bay of Bengal in order to reach the rich islands to the east (K. S. Behera 1993: 124). This port (possibly at or near the site of the former Dantapura) is generally thought to have stood near the contemporary village of Palura on the shore of Chilika Lake in Northern Ganjam. The area around Palura seems to have remained actively engaged over many centuries. Following Ptolemy, the *Periplus Exo Thelasses* (compiled 250–500 AD) again mentions "Paloura" as being near the point of departure for ships headed east, while archeological evidence points to nearby Manikapatna, at the mouth of Chilika Lake, as a notable port in Kalinga, also active for several centuries (K.S. Behera 1993: 125).

What emerges from the archaeological and inscriptional evidence at hand is the impression of a well organized and well sustained trading network that connected the Indian subcontinent with Rome to the west and Southeast Asia and China to the east throughout the first millennium AD, with ports of the old southern center of Kalinga playing a central role in the east-bound traffic. This pattern, sustained over several centuries, would account for the South Indian rouletted ware, Sri Lankan coins, Chinese porcelain, and Kharoshthi inscriptions from northwestern India all found at Manikapatna on Chilika Lake, and the fact that these archeological remains substantially match those found on Bali at Sembiran (Behera 1993: 128). It also supports Kalidasa's fourth-century salute to the ruler of Kalinga as "Foremost Lord of the Ocean" (Orissan Institute of Maritime and Southeast Asian Studies [1993]: 5). If I read the evidence correctly, this central role of Kalinga in the sea trade with Southeast Asia was to have a significant impact on the later development of Balinese culture.

Accounts by Chinese pilgrims traveling to and from India from the fifth to seventh centuries AD confirm that ships bound for Southeast Asia in search of gold, bronze, spices, and fragrant sandalwood continued to work their way up the subcontinent's coast to the ports of Kalinga before crossing the Bay of Bengal on the seasonal winds of the northeast monsoon. The period from the seventh to the ninth centuries was a particularly turbulent one on the eastern coast of India, marked by the conflict between Shaivite and Buddhist regimes and the frequent breakup and realignment of political entities. The area constituting present-day Ganjam seems to have remained active as a maritime center and for most of the seventh century constituted a separate border state, Kongoda, with its spiritual center in the Mahendragiri mountains. Perched precariously between a Buddhist kingdom to the north and a Shaivite stronghold to its immediate south—both with aggressive leaders—the area was sometimes merged with the one, sometimes incorporated into the other, and received cultural influences that were Buddhist and Shaivite, Oriyan and Telegu (Rajguru 1989: 35, 54–68).

It has been conjectured that substantial migrations may have taken place during this time of flux and turmoil. This is supported by indications (though they are disputed) that members of the Sailendra dynasty that established rule in Sumatra and central Java over this period of time were recent arrivals to the archipelago, bringing the Devanagri script with them, as well as new ideas in art and architecture, and by tantalizing lore in Java that "20,000 families were sent to Java by the Prince of Kling [Kalinga]. These people prospered and multiplied" (K. S. Behera 1993: 125; S. C. Behera 1982: 190–97; Majumdar 1972: 227). Whatever the basis for this legend, contact continued and intensified over the next few centuries. In the tenth century AD, inscriptions indicate a custom house still in existence on the shores of Chilika Lake, while inscriptions in eastern Java from the ninth to eleventh centuries continue to give the traders of Kalinga pride of place in listing the home bases of the many foreign merchants (K. S. Behera 1993: 130). Whatever the origins of the Sailendras, so pervasive was the presence of the merchants from Kalinga that "Keling" became a generic name for people of Indian origin in the records of Southeast Asia (K. S. Behera 1993: 124; Coomaraswamy 1927: 157). Indeed, an origin story of the village of Tenganan—the same Bali Aga village where traces of eastern Indian blood have been found (and which formerly had a very active *Calon Arang* tradition)—has it that founding ancestors of that village were a man and woman named Kaling and Keling (K. S. Behera 1993: 130).

In 882 AD *topeng* players (masked dancers) and shadow puppeteers are mentioned in the first Balinese inscription that has been found, listed among those exempt from certain taxes (Lansing 1983a: 30–31). Though it is not known what kinds of masks were worn by these "topeng players," Balinese scholars (Bandem and Rembang 1976: 3, 11) are inclined to believe that animal masks and masks used to worship ancestors came first (quite possibly long before this inscription) and Napier (1986: 193) proposes that the use of demon-like masks to project and control ambiguous aspects of the Brahmanical god-head may have played a vital role in reaching an accommodation with threatening aspects of these new gods, as well as in advertising the powers of a new priesthood (cf. Wallis 1979: 45). It is an interesting conjecture—one worth returning to later.

At the beginning of the second millennium AD, while the sea trade with India was still active, a Balinese Hindu prince named Airlangga ruled (from 1011–1049 AD) over both his native island and eastern Java. This period provides the setting for the *Calon Arang* story—the most frequent narrative context for Rangda's appearances. The sea trade with eastern India waned shortly after Airlangga's rule. Then, after a period of relative isolation, from the mid-fourteenth to the sixteenth centuries waves of more fully "Indianized" immigrants arrived from the Hindu courts of Majapahit in eastern Java as Java itself gradually came under the sway of Islam, culminating in 1615 with Majapahit's fall. By tacit agreement, Bali—now controlled by the exiled elite from Majapahit—became a Hindu enclave within a predominantly Muslim world. During this transitional period, there was little contact with India but frequent contact—both friendly and hostile—between the Balinese and eastern Javanese courts—these contacts giving rise to many of the stories used in Balinese topeng performances (including the performance by I Nyoman Kakul documented and discussed in chapters 4 through 6).

Cut off from India and more or less isolated from the later developments of Indian Hinduism—most notably from the growing emphasis on *bhakti,* or personal devotion, and the related elevation of Krishna to the status of a personal savior—Balinese culture preserved traces of conservative Hindu traditions on the one hand while, on the other, these traditions, never purely Indic, were allowed to develop freely within Balinese contexts. The Indic idea of reincarnation, for example, was adapted to suggest the likelihood of reincarnation into the same patrilineal line of descent. As Napier notes, Balinese culture and religion is not so much "Hindu" as it is an ongoing "interpretation of Hinduism" within shifting Balinese contexts (1986: 188–93)—a process metaphorically akin to the accommodation of a face to a mask.

During the period of most intense contact between Eastern India and Southeast Asia (approximately the seventh through the eleventh centuries AD), the Shaivite and Buddhist strains of religion that vied for dominance both had a strong admixture of Tantrism, involving the female aspect of the godhead as the embodiment and source of energy and power. As Boon points out (1990: 163), there is no evidence for an organized practice of Tantric sexual rituals or the elaboration of the philosophical underpinnings of such practices in Bali, but the influence of Tantrism is dispersed across a wide range of ritual practices and beliefs in Bali (cf. Barth: 261–62). Belo's evidence for the links between Rangda and Durga focuses on the treatment of Shakti in her various aspects and of ways to access power for good or evil through her—aspects of Tantrism that clearly reached Bali. In the *Calon Arang* story that often provides a dramatic frame for Rangda's appearances, Calon Arang herself, the widow/witch of Girah, is the disciple (and some say the reincarnation) of Durga. Intriguingly, the entire story of the widow-witch shadows and parallels the history of Airlangga's mother, Mahendradatta—a Javanese princess (daughter of the powerful Makutavangshavadhana) who married the Balinese prince, Udayana, and who seems to have been a worshipper of Durga herself.

As her history is told, after her illustrious father's death Mahendradatta is exiled to a forest by Udayana because she practices witchcraft. Incensed at Airlangga for encouraging his father to remarry, and then left with an unmarriageable daughter after she becomes a widow (the literal meaning of "rangda"), she carries on a war of black magic against her son's kingdom. To gain power for herself, her daughter, and her pupils in the black arts, she goes to the cemetery, digs out corpses, eats the members, drinks the blood, and decks herself in entrails in what amounts to a grotesque parody of extreme Tantric practices.[11] Calon Arang's identity clearly merges with Mahendradatta's as she empowers her students (including her daughter, Rarong) in the black arts, and wages war on Bali's children. At the end of Calon Arang's story, the widow/witch's book of black magic is captured by a ruse and turned against her till she is defeated—first in her demonic form and then in her human one—by Mpu Bharada, Airlangga's spiritual representative (Covarrubias 1974 [1937]: 328–30; Eiseman 1989: 316; Belo 1949: 27–30). Her defeat is rarely performed, though. As noted above, in performance a further inversion takes place: Rangda's own power as Queen of the Witches will be used to thwart the local practitioners of black magic, challenging them to try their powers (their *sakti*) against hers (Bandem and deBoer 1982: 139).

The complex of Rangda/Durga/Mahendradatta is born out by statuary as well as textual evidence. Belo points out that in the Balinese village of Kubutambahan a statue in the attitude of Durga killing the buffalo-demon Mahisasura looks very much like the present-day Rangda—sharp fanged, enflamed, with an elongated tongue and drooping breasts (1949: 27–28, plate XIId). Belo also displays the photo of an earlier statue, dating from the eleventh century, that can still be seen in the Balinese village of Kutri (27–28, plate XIIa: see fig. 33); it is said to commemorate Mahendradatta—also in the form of Durga slaying the buffalo-demon. Icons of this subject are extremely popular to this day in northeastern India (see fig. 34); in Orissa such icons date back to at least the seventh or eighth century AD (see H. C. Das 1992; Fischer, Mahapatra, and Pathy 1989: 83). The narrative and its accompanying icon clearly reached Bali, but the subject is quite rare in Balinese iconography and performance. Indeed, though chthonic temples are extremely plentiful in Bali, there are very few icons specifically honoring Durga. Rangda even seems to have taken on some of Mahisasura's attributes: like the buffalo-demon in the original tale, in the full narrative of *Calon Arang* she must be killed first in the demonic and then in human form.

Is the ambivalent attitude toward Rangda evident in Balinese practice bound up with an ambivalence toward the Indic Shakti cult and its association with a powerful antagonist in east Java? It may be well to remember here the reverence with which the buffalo is treated in Tanatoraja, and that Balinese royalty are frequently cremated in buffalo-shaped containers. Was there an attempt at Kutri (where Mahendradatta is said to have died) to convert the scourge of Airlangga's kingdom into a protectress through the strategies of artistic inversion and containment commonly used in the Kirtimukha tradition? These historical considerations might account for some of the ambivalence evident in the Balinese treatment of Rangda.

Figure 33. Eleventh-century stone relief at Kutri, Bali, said to commemorate Mahendradatta as Durga.

Figure 34. Early twentieth-century temple painting of Durga killing Mahisasura in his human form. Jayapur, Koraput, Orissa, 1983 (now painted over).

As evidence of that ambivalence, note Eiseman's summary of his interviews with keris "dancers":

> All mention that they see flames coming from the face of Rangda—rays like the sun. They don't see them when her back is turned—only when she is facing them. And her face and cloth are on fire. And they are both scared and angry at her and want to kill her. Ordinarily, on those occasions when Rangda appears at other ceremonies they harbor no ill will towards her. They readily and freely recognize Rangda's importance in the village, and understand her power and magic. But, when the feeling of possession comes on at a Mapajar, they cannot control themselves and rush at her. (1986: 382)

Though I have never seen self-stabbing in India, it is not unusual for worshippers of Shakti to go into trance in order to display and celebrate the goddess's protective powers. During the time of the spring *samkranti* in mid-April (the same day designated as New Year [*nyepi*] in the Balinese solar calendar), chosen devotees stand on swords, walk on fires, roll on thorns, and swing from hooks piercing their backs. I know of no instance, though, when these activities could possibly be interpreted or felt to be directed *against* the goddess. It is Kali, Narasimha, and the demons that they counter who are enraged, not their devotees. There seems little doubt that the figure of Rangda is closely associated with Tantric beliefs and practices related to the Durga/Kali/Shakti figure of the Hindu Tantric tradition, and that her essential protective function has been preserved; but new elements, variations, and inversions of the tradition have emerged that stress the danger of the powers narrowly contained within her mask. The question remains, though, how Rangda found her way into the Balinese theatre—and why the theatrical appearances of Rangda bear such a striking relationship to those of Narasimha in Orissa.

In tracing the theatrical precedents for Narasimha's entrance in *Prahlada Nataka*, and the related *bhagavata mela*, *terukkuttu*, and *kuchipudi* forms of Tamil Nadu and Andhra Pradesh, Ulrike Emigh and I were led time and again back to pre-existing theatrical forms used to celebrate the power of Shakti figures in eastern India.[12] Ceremonial processions featuring variants of these masks and involving trance are still observable in eastern and southern India. In the Koraput district of Orissa, a form of mask theatre known as *desia nata* has been performed for at least four hundred years and has clearly contributed to the stage conventions of the *Prahlada Nataka*. During the Mahiravana episode of the desia nata version of the *Ramayana*, Ravana's son tries to takes refuge in Shakti but is rejected by her; Durga (in the form of Kali in the performance I witnessed) goes into a violent trance and is restrained in a manner strikingly similar to that used to contain Narasimha's wrath in *Prahlada Nataka*.

Desia nata is in turn related to a still older form of ritual drama. In many locations throughout Orissa, performances of *danda nata* traditionally begin with a trance dancer in a mask of Kali—her tongue grotesquely extended—while other masks are still occasionally used in remote areas to dramatize tales of devotion to Shiva and Shakti in which the terrifying Shakti figure becomes the paradoxical protector (Dash n.d.; see fig. 35). Textual evidence suggests that this tradition dates from a time when a resurgent Shaivism was wresting control from Buddhism in Orissa, probably around the eighth or ninth century—at the height of the sea trade with Java and Bali (Dash 1983, personal communication). The Shakti dances of *gambhira* (Ghosh 1979) may well be older still (see fig. 36); they display a variety of horrific forms that theatrical play with the Shakti figure can take—including the leonine Narasimhi—and indicate the theatrical fecundity of these traditions as well as a willingness to play with sectarian boundaries. In Bhaliagara, near the Andhra Pradesh border, and in a small village just a few kilometers from the old palace of Jalantara, where *Prahlada Nataka* was composed and first performed, the custom still exists for a dancer to become entranced as Kali, processing through the streets and sometimes becoming enraged; there, as elsewhere in Ganjam, Shakti masks are honored in temples (see fig. 37).

Precedents exist for the transfer of Shaivite and Shakti practices to the worship of the Vaishnavite deity Narasimha (von Steitencron 1978: 29–30). Indeed, the Narasimha story itself may derive from the similar encounter of Kali with the charmed Darika—still played out as part of the repertory of *chho* troupes in West Bengal and in the *mudiettu* of Kerala. In the final scene (which comes at dawn of a mudiettu performance, just as it does, ideally, in the *Prahlada Nataka* and, for that matter, in *Calon Arang)*, Kali is depicted as ripping open the demon's abdomen and adorning herself with a garland of the bloody entrails (Zarrilli 1984: 43–44).[13] Eschmann notes that Narasimha worship is related to Shaktism in its use of Tantric elements and, in another context, states that "the story of Prahlada and his unfailing devotion to Vishnu has not only become a heart piece of Vaishnava theology but is an important link between Vishnuism and Shivaism. Narasimha is the furious *(ugra)* aspect of Vishnu *par excellence* and therewith also that aspect of Vishnu with the highest affinity to Shiva" (1978: 102, 104). This affinity is especially close to Shiva's Shakti in its furious aspects.

It should be noted here that the *Prahlada Nataka* has its own somewhat ambiguous treatment of Shakti figures. These are not unprecedented in Orissan Vaishnavite literature. Fabri (1974: 205–6) includes a fascinating translation by C. H. Tawney of the *Story of Phalabuti* from the popular eleventh-century *Ocean of Streams of Stories* (*Katha-sarit-sagara*). The story purports to tell of the initiation of a witch.

Kalaratri was of repulsive appearance. Her eyebrows met, she had dull eyes, a depressed flat nose, large cheeks, widely parted lips, projecting teeth, a long neck,

Figure 35. A now rare mask of the Birdcatcher of danda nata, who is saved by his devotion to Shakti. Ganjuguda, Phulbani, Orissa, 1983.

Figure 36. Kali mask used in a gambhira performance. Aiho, West Bengal, 1983.

Figure 37. Shakti mask honored in the Takurani temple. Behrampur, Ganjam, Orissa.

pendulous breasts, a large belly, and broad expanded feet. She appeared as if the creator had made her as a specimen in his skill in producing ugliness. When I fell at her feet, after bathing and worshipping Ganesha, she made me take off my clothes and perform, standing in a circle, a horrible ceremony in honor of Shiva in his terrific form, and after she had sprinkled me with water she gave me various spells known to her, and human flesh to eat that had been offered in sacrifice to the gods; so, after I had eaten man's flesh and had received the various spells, I immediately flew up, naked as I was, into the heaven with my friends, and after I had amused myself, I descended from the heaven by command of my teacher, and I, the princess, went to my own apartments.

As a Vaishnavite drama, *Prahlada Nataka,* like the *Ramayana* long before it, not only co-opts the narratives and possessions of Kali, it also subordinates the goddess in her various aspects to the all-inclusive Vishnu to further glorify his name. In one of the attempts on his life Prahlada endures, he is offered as a human sacrifice to Chandi (another of Shakti's furious aspects). In yet another, he is pitched off a cliff and rescued by Budevi (Mother Earth). In both instances, the goddesses subordinate themselves to Vishnu and act as his devotee's protectors. In a third attempt on Prahlada's life, he is made to face a creature summoned by black magic:

An ugly shaped Kruttika appeared from the sacrificial altar. It had huge sharp teeth, a long flowing tongue, long hands spread wide, pendulous breasts, hard nails that flashed like lightening, unkempt hair, and was shouting frightening cries at the top of its very loud voice. The fifteen fires in its mouth still blazing, it ran at terrific speed right towards Prahlada, intent on attacking the supreme jewel of the Lord's devotees.

Kruttika, too, is moved by Prahlada's devotion to Vishnu and comically turns upon the hapless Brahmans who summoned her into being. The description of her bears a striking resemblance to the Balinese Rangda (a resemblance confirmed by maskmaker Laxmi Dhanu Mahapatra of Ganjam when shown her picture in 1994). Could Rangda's horrific appearance be derived in part from that of a Kruttika? Is this yet another possible link between the Tantric traditions of India and horrific figure of Rangda? The point here is that the Shakti tradition that reached Bali was neither uniform nor uncontested; it left plenty of room for new interpretations.

An art historian might trace aspects of Rangda's appearance and behavior to individual manifestations of Shakti in her many horrific forms and in her Buddhist counterparts. The pendulous breasts and grin could derive from Chamunda, the long tongue and entrails from Kali, the tusks from the boar-like Varahi, the white face from Mahadevi, the role of child killer from the Buddhist Hariti (who was also converted into a protectress of children and is prominent in the iconography of eleventh-century Bali), while Lakahi of Nepal is reputed to have a similar white cloth that she uses as a weapon.[14] There other traces as well of the Shakti tradition. Tests of the protective power of Shakti while in a state of trance and the staged resurrection of a man who has feigned death as a corpse are part of the ritual panoply that accompany gambhira, danda nata, and Seraikella *chhau* dances—all forms that stem from a common tradition of Shakti worship in India, while variations on these activities accompany Rangda's theatrical appearances when they are ritually centered (Bandem and deBoer 1985: 138–42). The weight of evidence clearly suggests that, even though the Orissan *Prahlada Nataka* was not written until approximately 1880 and the *Calon Arang* drama as currently performed in Bali may be as recent as 1890 (Bandem and deBoer 1982: 132), both the Balinese theatrical forms deploying Rangda and the Orissan *Prahlada Nataka* developed independently from a common tradition involving trance-inducing Shakti masks—each making its own variations and inversions within and upon that complex tradition.

On the night of the full moon of the month of Kartika, people of Orissa float small boats with candles on the Mahanadi and Rishikulya rivers, commemorating the fleets that once sailed east from the ancient ports of Dantapura, Paloura, Pithunda, and Chelitalo. Though the origin of the name is debated, this ceremony is called *Bali Jatra.* On the island of Bali, it is common for small children to float paper boats with candles in them in the river. Phalgunadi (1984) calls attention to this ceremonial link and also notes a range of gastronomic, linguistic, and cultural affinities between present-day Bali and Orissa. To his list might be added the prevalent use of black-and-white-checked cloth, the occurrence of double and single *ikat* tie and die weaving (sometimes with quite similar patterns, as in the wedding patterns of Tenganan and Sambalpur), a similar treatment of space and turbulence in popular paintings based on the Hindu epics, the holding of objects between the feet while carving, the existence of the only shadow puppet tradition in India using small, opaque puppets similar to those originally used in Bali and in Java (Pani n.d.), the somewhat unusual technique of making slits below the eyes of masks instead of in the center of the pupils, the habit of holding handkerchiefs in the right hand (in the manner of Rangda) while dancing (evident in desia nata, *Prahlada Nataka,* and numerous Telegu forms), the existence of an ancient hermitage cave framed by the yawning maw of a tiger that could have provided inspiration for Goa Gajah (see Sahu 1984: 205–8), and, perhaps significantly, a relatively caste-free approach to the performing arts in Orissan villages as well as in Bali. More specific indications include the startling similarity between the layout of the Bali Aga village of Tenganan to villages in Ganjam (with houses abutting each other in long parallel rows and central buildings such as granaries, schools, and rehearsal rooms set in the midst of these row houses), the comparable power and sanctity accorded the mountains of Gunung Agung and Mahendragiri, and the inclusion of the small and frequently dried up Mahendratanaya River of the Mahendra valley among the sacred rivers of India enumerated in Balinese prayers (K. S. Behera 1993: 129). While many of these connections and affinities may be otherwise explained or attributed to chance, together they argue for considerable cultural influences on Bali from the direction of Kalinga including, very specifically, that part of Kalinga which has been the seedbed of *Prahlada Nataka.*

A little over a decade ago, J. Steven Lansing reviewed the evidence for transmission of Indic values to Bali in (1983a: 15–49; 1983b). Though skeptical of the evidence for direct contact (much of which has appeared since his article), Lansing stresses the role of theatre in inculcating Indic values and familiarizing people with Hindu myths and their characters. Citing the several inscriptions from 882 AD onward that indicate groups of performing artists, including topeng dancers and shadow puppeteers, made their way through Balinese villages with court and temple sponsorship (1983a: 30–31), he suggests that "Performances were perhaps the most significant instruments of 'Indianization,' for it was through them [. . .] that Mount Meru came to be transplanted to village shrines, and an Indic world-view based on written texts came to be shared by ordinary villagers, few of whom presumably read Sanskrit" (1983b: 420). Lansing is writing of Balinese performances by Balinese artists that were inspired by Indian myths, but the shared ritual elements and structural similarities of *Prahlada Nataka* and other eastern Indian forms to the Barong and Rangda confrontations suggest that more direct theatrical borrowings may also have taken place. It seems likely that forms of Shakti trance dancing such as appear in danda nata were brought to Java and to Bali during the last centuries of the first millennium AD, and that these ritual and theatrical forms had a major impact on Balinese theatrical and cultural history. Both the *Calon Arang* and *Prahlada Nataka* traditions seem to have developed from the same hybrid seed—grafted onto a resurgent Vaishnavite faith in Orissa and transplanted into receptive new soil in Bali.

Even this is not the whole story, though. A longer and still more complex history seems to be involved. In discussing how India may have influenced Southeast Asia, the tendency is too often to oversimplify "India" itself and to negate the thousands of years of interaction already existing between South and Southeast Asia. In this oversimplified history, India becomes the alien carrier of a rationalized metaphysic, Southeast Asia the land of irrational animism; both of these representations are at the very best dangerous half-truths, however, developed in support of claims to a Greater India that were once useful to Indian nationalists in countering the presumptions of English colonists. It is necessary to look more closely at the ethnic and cultural mix that formed Kalinga.

The foothills of the Mahendragiri range in Orissa—the same mountains that gave Mahendradatta her name and that find their way into Balinese prayers—are dominated by Austro-Asian and Dravidian tribal populations. In this area, there are tall, man-sized puppet masks that slip over the entire body and look very much like the *barong landung* masks used exorcisti-

Figure 38. Large processional mask (prabhat) used to honor Shakti. Chikiti, Ganjam, Orissa, 1983.

cally in Bali (see Slattum 1992: 101–3), and like certain Shakti masks used in the more low-lying areas of Ganjam (fig. 38). These puppet-like masks (*prabhats*) are built, it might be added, on the same principle as the piles of leaves fixed to hoops used by mask dancers in New Guinea and in the pre-Hindu enclave of Trunyan in Bali (Bandem and deBoer 1985: 3–12). Also in these Orissan hills, in the village of Borokadanda, there frolics yet another version of the Barong: a two-man tiger that cavorts at weddings and feast days and is presided over by a huge mask of Narasimha (fig. 39). The similarity of the puppet-masks of Borokadanda to the New Guinean and "pre-Hindu" Balinese examples suggests there may be a prehistory to this story; there is no reason to assume that the influences all flowed in one direction, or that they took hold all at one time.

The Indian mother goddess with a vengeful and a benign side is generally conceded to be non-Aryan in origin. She may be first evident in the (probably) Dravidian and Munda cultures which predated Harappa. These cultures were overwhelmed by the Aryan invasion, but not without leaving their imprint on the invaders.

> That many of the gods in the domestic and community shrines are of grotesque and alarming aspect reveals the immensity of the challenge that untamed and, to large extent, untamable nature, in all its sub-tropical violence, posed to the people who settled there. [. . .] The first image with which the inhabitants of India pictured nature was that of the great mother—prodigiously fecund and at the same time destructive. The grotesque terra-cotta figurines unearthed from pre-Harappan and Harappan settlements do not differ greatly from the violent images still favored by most rural Indian communities today. [. . .] In the wake of natural, and perhaps human, catastrophes old, outworn images and symbols have been revalorized, such as the figure of the black goddess Kali. (Lannoy 1971: 18)

Some cultural historians lay particular emphasis on the development of the mother-goddess figure among the Dravidian peoples of South India (see Kinsley 1975: 96–97). It has yet to be determined what, if any, direct links existed between the Dravidian cultures of India and the Australoid peoples who crossed land bridges into Indonesia, Melanesia, and Australia some forty to fifty thousand years ago, leaving their traces in the current population of Bali (Breguet 1982: 59–60, 315). Less vague, though, are the links between the Austro-Asiatic peoples of tribal India and the populations of Southeast Asia (see Zide 1968). Racially and linguistically, the Munda speakers of eastern Indian are close kin to the Mons and Khmers of mainland Southeast Asia and somewhat more distant cousins to the Austronesian-speaking populations of the Indonesian archipelago and the further Pacific. These Austronesian speakers seem to have come to Bali about 5000 BC, bringing an economy based on wet rice cultivation, and intermingled with previous populations (Breguet 1982: 53). The Austro-Asiatic peoples who reached India seem to have similarly brought with them a wet rice culture, along with linguistic and cultural contributions

Figure 39. Tiger-like prabhats and giant kings and queens frolic during the festival of Holi. Borokadanda, Ganjam, Orissa, 1983.

(Solheim 1975). Kalinga itself, it is worth noting, is considered a name of Austro-Asiatic origin (Orissan Institute of Maritime and Southeast Asian Studies [1993]: 2), and the Shailodbhava Kings of Kongoda, who kept their spiritual home in the Mahendragiri range and may have profoundly influenced the history already traced, seem themselves to have been of Austro-Asiatic origin (S. C. Behera 1982: 39–50).

Indic visitors were not, of course, the only ones to find Bali, nor were they the first neighbors bringing new cultural luggage. The island formed part of the Dong-Son culture that spread (probably) from southern China and took hold throughout Southeast Asia and Melanesia from around 500 BC to 100 AD, featuring bronze drums inscribed with figures that may indicate already well developed dance traditions (see Cravath 1986; Newton 1988). The gong and metallophone music used in Balinese productions (including *Calon Arang)* seems to owe far more to the growth of this culture than to any Indic elements; and, as already noted, the largest Dong-Son drum of all is in the village of Pejeng in Bali; it features mask-like faces with staring round eyes (not unlike icons still used in the Maprik region of the Sepik River basin). Variants on the lost-wax process of bronze casting practiced in the Dong-Son culture are also prevalent among the Austro-Asiatic peoples of India; what early contacts and influences from Southeast Asia might this betoken? I do not mean to suggest that cultural influences are restricted to ethnic migratory patterns. There were ample opportunities for a continuing exchange of ideas and practices as well as people. As I. W. Mabbet notes, "Indians visiting South East Asia were not alien invaders, but familiar neighbors, visiting with new luggage" (1977: 9–10). Between 1000 BC and 1000 AD, sea-faring traders based in the Indonesian archipelago were also active, moving from the Bay of Bengal to the South China Sea. Not enough is yet known of how these adventurous traders might have affected Indian (or Chinese) beliefs and customs, but there is no reason to believe that cultural influences, any more than peoples and goods, consistently flowed in any one direction.

K. B. Das and L. K. Mahapatra, an Orissan folklorist and anthropologist respectively, note that "it is always difficult for [Indian] ethnologists to find out which are purely tribal customs, traditions, and myths and which are not. More often than not, they come across a syncretistic amalgam, or even integrated synthesis of elements drawn from tribal cultures, scriptural instructions of the Aryan tradition, and from the systematized forms of the Dravidian traditions. In the nature of cultural development of any region or of any people at any time in its history, such cultural inflow and outflow in many directions is the rule rather than the exception" (1979: 5). Staal has noted that in the interplay between Aryan and Dravidian cultures within India known as Sanskritization, "almost all giving (was) based on prior taking" (Staal 1963: 274). Eschmann (1978a, 1978b) suggests that Narasimha—the god of the pillar—carried with him strong associations with the goddesses in pillar form worshipped in the Khond communities of western Orissa, and was Hinduized as Khambeshvari. Surely the Austro-Asiatic peoples of eastern India have had their roles to play in this process, and there is every reason to believe that cultural borrowings between South and Southeast Asia paralleled this complexity.

What I am suggesting is that performative traditions, as well as linguistic and agricultural ones, may well have flowed south and west before returning towards the east; and that the Tantric traditions that took root in Bali may already have been nurtured in common ground. While independent invention is always a possibility, it is difficult to regard the dancing Shakti figures and not think of the "feminine" *tubuan* coming from the wild *momboto* time in an act of visitation during mortuary rites of New Britain; on the gables of the men's spirit houses in Iatmul villages, distant female cousins of the Kirtimukha and the guardian witch of Bali's Goa Gajah can be found—tongues distended, horrific countenances in place (fig. 40).

We probably will not be able to fill in the blanks more precisely until further archeological work is done to define the nature of the trade contacts between South and Southeast Asia, a reassessment is made of the contributions of the Austro-Asiatic and Dravidian populations to "classical" Indian culture in general, and more is known about the early cultural and historical links connecting the Indonesian archipelago to India, southern China, mainland Southeast Asia and Melanesia. This much, though, seems clear: the current *Calon Arang*, like so many performative traditions, emerged after many passes from many directions, traces of which were kept and altered in a continuing process of accommodation, invention, and interpretation. It seems likely that both the Balinese *Calon Arang* and the Orissan *Prahlada Nataka* fundamentally grew out of related ritual and theatrical traditions connected to Shakti worship, and that these traditions were themselves made possible by thousands of years of a partially shared prehistory. Whether there was a further cross-pollination after the sixteenth century, borne, in part, by Western merchant ships, is unclear. What *is* clear is that the identities of Rangda and the Barong have been adjusted over the centuries to specific Balinese circumstances and have evolved as "laminates" of Balinese cultural history—retaining essential links to the Shakti and Kirtimukha traditions of Indian performance and iconography, while adding distinctive Balinese attributes, as these powerful masks are pressed into new roles with new meanings in the shifting contexts that define Balinese life and performance (cf. Belo 1949: 18–20).

As new intercultural contacts are made and internal changes take place, further changes are taking place, too, and at an accelerated pace. The twentieth century has already seen a number of these. If Bandem and deBoer are correct in dating the current version of *Calon Arang* from about 1890, then some interesting historical questions emerge. F. A. Lefrink, a Dutch

Figure 40. Gable mask guarding a spirit house (haus tamboran). Angoram, Sepik River.

scholar, observed a "keris dance"—in the context of a rice ritual and unconnected to any narrative—in 1896. He describes "as many as a hundred half-naked figures rushing furiously back and forward, repeatedly making motions of stabbing *themselves and others*" (quoted in Lansing 1983a: 64, emphasis added). How was it that self-stabbing became the dominant form of entranced action accompanying the *Calon Arang*? What was its particular appeal as a new theatrical element? It is difficult not to see some associations between this ritualized (and protected) self-stabbing, cued by feelings of rage when facing the powerful mask of Durga/Mahendradatta/Rangda, and the mass public suicides with similar swords that greeted the Dutch "conquest" of Southern Bali in 1906 and 1908:

> As the Dutch soldiers approached the palace (at Badung) the main gates opened and a silent procession emerged—the entire court, led by the raja, dressed in white cremation gowns with flowers in their hair and wearing their krises and jewelry. At a signal from the raja, the high priest plunged a sacred kris into his breast. The Dutch opened fire as the Balinese turned their swords upon themselves. According to eyewitnesses, court ladies disdainfully hurled their jewels at the soldiers, while Dutch artillery fired at the people and the palace behind. (Lansing 1983a: 48)

This mass suicide (*puputan*) was seemingly both prefigured (one is tempted to say rehearsed) and reflexively replayed in the then new theatrical form syncretically taking shape—with the crucial difference that the Dutch demons (as they are portrayed in the theatre and sometimes in statuary at temple gates) were not containable within the contexts of the temple system. Masks evoking one time of historical turmoil seem to have been used to reference and inform actions in another. Social drama and aesthetic play were reflexively bound up in a life and death dialogue about the state of the world and what could be salvaged from it.

Similarly, soon after the bloody killings that followed the failed communist coup of 1965 and left from 50,000 to 100,000 people dead in Bali alone, the *Calon Arang* troupe of Penarukan, a village near Krambitan, decided to train their keris blades against each other rather than against themselves. The result is shown in startling detail (though with its historical significance obscured with Jungian rhetoric) in Harvey Bellin's 1975 film, *Bali: Mask of Rangda*: entranced men run full tilt at each other, swords drawn, straining in vain to make their blades penetrate their neighbors' flesh. Besides becoming popular in Krambitan, this variation was also taken up around 1970 by a trance club outside of Denpasar in a village said to contain an unmarked mass grave of many killed in 1966. To judge from Lefrink's report, this option was always there, but had not made theatrical sense until the bloody reprisals that pitted neighbor against neighbor and family member against family member changed the forms of action that must have seemed most significant for the reflexive "play" of theatre and ritual.

And what does all of this have to say about interculturalism? Simply that, though the pace may be quicker now and the solvents more powerful (cf. F. Turner 1991: 267–72), it is not an entirely new phenomenon; that it has been threatening in the past as well as in the present, and sometimes for good reasons; that there are no pure cultures out there and the "anthropological present" within which we often reify "culture" is a fiction; that, even so, "cultures" have a way of adapting and changing what they choose to receive or have foisted on them; that we have some common biological ground to work on, though it is not a smooth one; that when cultures do manage to produce a synthesis that works—one that takes hold and fits the needs, aspirations, and fears of the people most directly involved—it is a lot like finding a meeting ground with a good mask; and that masks themselves have played vital roles in helping this process along.

One more change during this century must be mentioned. For over four decades now, in daily tourist performances commonly performed with non-consecrated masks, the Rangda and the Barong Ket have been used as pamurtian figures in a story spun off from an incident in the *Mahabharata* (see Bandem and deBoer 1981: 147–48). In skillfully directed productions, meticulously timed for commercial purposes, the "self-stabbing" is imitated by the isometric straining of arm muscles, and the forces manifested by Rangda and the Barong Ket are predictably controlled within the realm of mimetic play. Under Western influence, visitation has yielded place to illusion as the preferred mode for these performances. There are many who hold this relatively tame performance, with no trance, no threat of injury, no black magic, and no graveyard watches, to be far more dangerous for the artists involved (see Picard 1990).

Mimetic play with visitation is not limited to tourist productions, however, nor is this mode of performance alien to Balinese traditional practice. It is also important in topeng—a form of mask theatre in Bali that now takes its story matter from quasi-historical chronicles and which, in its most traditional form, features prominently the demonic-looking mask of a priest arriving from the direction of India (*"bharat"* denoting both "west" and "India" in Indonesian). That priest's name, appropriately, is Brahmana Keling, and in his person are played out yet again the strategies of containment common to Balinese and Orissan masked theatre.[15]

Notes

1. An earlier version of this chapter appeared under the same title in *Asian Theatre Journal* 1, 1 (Spring 1984), pp. 21–39. With the permission of the publishers, I have amended this article and have added quotations from the *Prahlada Nataka* and the final section on Bali and Orissa.

Partial funding for research in Bali was provided by the English Department of Brown University under a Bronson Grant in 1974–75. Funding for exploratory research in eastern India with William O. Beeman and Amy Catlin was provided by the Smithsonian Institution in 1980. Further research on *Prahlada Nataka* and related theatrical and ritual forms in eastern India was conducted with Ulrike Emigh on a grant from the Indo-U.S. Subcommission during 1982–83 and in 1993 under a grant from the American Institute of Indian Studies, with further support from the Government of Orissa. Initial work connecting theatrical theory and practice with readings in neuroscience has been funded by the office of the Dean of the College, Brown University. I was assisted in my research in India by Rob LaBelle, Mark Plesant, Jeffrey Eugenides, and K. S. Dora, as well as by Ulrike Emigh. Material used in the last part of this essay, on "the Kalinga Connection," was developed through presentations at the University of Hawaii in 1985, at the University Northern Illinois in 1986, and for the Orissan Institute of Maritime and Southeast Asian Studies in Bhubaneswar and the Indira Gandhi National Center for the Arts in New Delhi during 1994. Carol Babiracki, Robert Wessing, L. K Mahapatra, and K. S. Behera all provided valuable bibliographic advice for this section.

2. I have drawn from a number of sources in tracing this history. The debt to Zimmer's work on the Kirtimukha icon (1972 [1946]) is already noted. For the identification of the Kirtimukha with Batara Kala and Banaspati Raja, see Holt (1967: 107) and Ramseyer (1977: 68). For the story of Batara Kala, see Forge (1978: 30). An alternative version is given in Covarrubias (1974 [1937]: 291). For the story of Bhoma (also referred to as Boma), see de Zoete and Spies (1973 [1938]: 293, 327). Bosch (1960) treats the spread of this image into Southeast Asia and, since the original version of this essay appeared, Napier (1986: 193–205) has studied the phenomenon, along with parallel developments in archaic Greece.

Curiously, Rahu himself later loses his head to Vishnu's discus while attempting to drink the nectar of immortality. His head—the only part reached by the miraculous nectar—is said to dwell eternally in the heavens (like a malevolent and voracious Cheshire Cat) and to cause lunar eclipses. His visage sometimes replaces Kirtimukha's on Vaishnavite iconography, since it bears witness to Vishnu's power and vigilance as the world's preserver. As will become apparent, such inversions and co-optations are typical in the strategies addressed here.

3. There are several related forms of theatre in the Telegu language that predate the authoring of *Prahlada Nataka.* The story of Narasimha forms a part of the kuchipudi repertoire of Andhra Pradesh and is the heartpiece of the bhagavata mela performances near Tanjuvor. For information on bhagavata mela, see Jones (1963) and Richmond (1971). One striking difference between these forms and *Prahlada Nataka* is in the composition of the troupes: kuchipudi and bhagavata mela performances are only danced by Brahmans, while most of the members of a *Prahlada Nataka* troupe are drawn from lower caste farmers. The precise relationship of the Oriya text to Telegu precedents in the area is not yet clear. Most believe that the Oriya text of *Prahlada Nataka* was a new syncretic creation drawing on Orissan folk traditions as well as "classical" Telegu models, and not merely a translation; but this issue is much debated among the performers and there is one troupe in an extremely remote village just over a river from Ganjam in Andhra Pradesh that performs a version in Telegu (though their text may be a translation from the Oriya). The principal author of the Oriya text was probably Goura Hari Paricha, a noted poet of the nineteenth century employed by the court at Jalantara, though other suggestions have also been made (see Panda 1973; Pani 1983; Mahapatra 1986; Patnaik 1992). I hope to resolve some of these issues before publishing the text in English translation. The story of the play's transmission from court to village is a fascinating one, revolving around a remarkable family of per-

formers from a Oriyan speaking fisherman caste in Ichhapur, Andhra Pradesh—the Durga Das cousin-brothers—but that story, also, will also have to wait.

4. By mimesis, translatable as representation or imitation, I am referring to a procedure, not a style. Use of the word need not be limited to "realistic" modes of representation. For clarification as to the representative nature of divine figures in kathakali, see Zarrilli (1977: 48–56). Gupt (1993: 93–102) points out similarities and subtle distinctions between Aristotle's use of "*mimesis*" and Bharata-Muni's of "*anukarana*"; the Sanskrit analogue lays still greater stress on the transformational properties of artistic representation.

5. For further information on gambhira, see Ghosh's article (1979: 53–77). Besides Prof. Ghosh, I am indebted to Asutosh Bhattacharya, Durgadas Mukhapadhyay, and the performers of Aiho for information about this form—one that has been recently undergoing transitions that are de-emphasizing the aspect of visitation and integrating more story elements into the presentations. Konishi (1981) provides a useful summary of mask forms in South Asia in general and eastern India in particular.

6. This song and all other quotations from the text of *Prahlada Nataka* are translated by Dhiren Dash and myself from a text edited by Bhagaban Panda (1973). A full translation is in progress, with additional help from Jiwan Pani. The performance described is typical of many seen, but corresponds most closely to the one viewed in Baulagaon in 1981. The Baulagaon group has recently ended a period of inactivity. Their mask is a particularly old and beautiful one and the performance I witnessed there, being my first, is particularly strong in my memory.

For assistance while researching *Prahlada Nataka* and related forms of theatre in Orissa, I am indebted to Raghunath and Sanjukta Panigrahi, Gopinath Panigrahi, P. C. Misra, L. K. Mahapatra, K. B. Das, S. N. Rajguru, D. N. Patnaik, Nayan Chand Patnaik, D. N. Pathy, Bankini Satapathy, and, especially, Dhiren Dash, K. S. Dora, Biswa Bihari Khadanga, Simanchalam Patra, Arjun Satapathy, and Raghunath Satapathy. In 1994, over 150 principal performers, gurus, and managers gathered in Chhatrapur under the auspices of the Central Sangeet Natak Akademi and the Ganjam Secretariat to assess the state of their art and try and set a course for its preservation and continuance. It was a remarkable event, and I learned a great deal from those in attendance.

7. The strategy can backfire. C. Geertz (1973: 115) cites examples of Rangda performers in Bali becoming permanently deranged, and I, too, have heard of such cases. The mask is said to "turn" on the performer, a reversal of the apotropaic strategy. On a broader social level, the playwright V. J. Tendulkar has pointed out how the rituals of Shakti worship were appropriated and used by Naxalite terrorists in Bengal in the 1960s (cited in Naipal 1979: 92).

8. There is already a considerable literature on Rangda and the Barong Ket. Much of this is both informative and provocative, but it is bewildering *in toto*; and where the literature seems most clear, it is often contradicted by Balinese practice. The studies by Bateson and Mead (1942), Belo (1949), Covarrubias (1974 [1937]), Foster (1979), C. Geertz (1973), Holt (1967), Lansing (1974), Snow (1983), and Napier (1986) all offer valuable insights, each from a different perspective, and each with its limitations. The most comprehensive source of information about the theatrical appearances of these figures is still de Zoete and Spies (1973 [1938]). Bandem and deBoer's study (1984: 118–47) for the first time offers valuable historical information about these figures and stresses Rangda's role as protectress. Also of particular interest are Eiseman's richly detailed studies of the Barong and Rangda mapajar in his village (1986: 344–86, partially contained in 1989: 146–54, 293–321)

and Hildred Geertz's thoughtful and informative text for the exhibition catalogue, *Images of Power*, featuring many drawings of Rangda made in the 1930s (1995).

At least four films depict confrontations between Rangda and the Barong Ket: Bateson and Mead's *Trance and Dance in Bali*, Harvey Bellin's *Bali: Mask of Rangda* (Hartley Productions), David Attenborough's *Miracle of Bali: Night* (a Xerox/BBC film), and *Barong*, an Indonesian Film marketed by Film Forms International. Psychological interpretations are imposed on the material in the first two instances—drawn, in the first case, from a Freudian base that may not apply and, in the second, from Jungian assumptions that have little to do with the symbology of events as articulated by the Balinese. The Indonesian film is of the commercial performances offered daily for tourists. All three films of traditional performances have idiosyncratic elements embedded in the action; but, as shown above, a certain amount of variability is deliberately built into the procedures, and regional variations abound. Significantly, in all three films of traditional performances, things do not go "as planned" and Rangda proves more powerful than the Barong.

Among Balinese performers, I am particularly indebted to I Made Bandem, I Nyoman Kakul, I Nyoman Sumandhi, I Wayan Suweca, I Wayan Dibia, I Nyoman Wenten, I Nyoman Catra, and I Gusti Windia for their insights into these matters.

9. The sexual identity of the Rangda figure is complex. Her flapping dugs certainly identify her as a female, and I have been told that masks have menstrual periods calculated for them and cannot perform during these times. Still, the mask can be used as a pamurtian for male deities and it is always danced by a male performer, using a grotesque, almost parodic version of "masculine" dance movement. The result may be thought of as the grotesque inversion of the androgynous theatricalizations of refined male heroes in Balinese and Javanese theatre, played by strong women or by extremely graceful men. Mary LeCron Foster (1979) discusses this sexual ambivalence in psychoanalytic terms. These issues are also dealt with in far greater detail in a recent article on "Gender-Bending in Bali" by myself and Jamer Hunt (1992).

10. I hope to address in greater depth some of the ways research on the workings of the brain might inform the study of performance (and perhaps vice versa) once I can better trust my purchase on the information coming out of the fields of neural and cognitive science. The diagram of a humunculus presented here (fig. 31), in Napier (1986: 205), and in Teyler (1971: 47) is an over-simplification, of course, but one that I think points in an interesting direction. It is based on a drawing by Penfield and Rasmussen (1950) designed to represent the proportionate dedication of neurons to various body parts in the area in the neo-cortex that monitors and mediates motion. The homunculus derived is more vivid than the one constructed for the adjacent somatosensory cortex itself (though very similar to it in its proportions) and it is therefore often used in its place (cf. Kandel et al. 1991: 707). This substitution accounts for the lack of representation for genitalia. According to Kandel and Jessell, the brain actually has ten different somatotopic representations of the body, each with discrete sets of neurons involved in monitoring different modalities of sensory information: movement, pressure, temperature, pain (Kandel et al. 1991: 367–83). The image shown here specifically represents the right hemisphere of the brain which controls the left half of the body—the same hemisphere that is most strongly associated with affective response, metaphoric thought, and artistic activity (though, in this case, it is my understanding that an image of the left hemisphere would yield similar results). The somatosensory cortex sends the information received out to the posterior parietal cortex, where integration with other sensory information takes place and forms a more complete "overall picture of the body" (Kandel et al. 1991: 383). It should not be surprising, then, once the impor-

tance of the sensory information gleaned through other sense organs is factored in, that the eyes, ears, and nose would be represented as much larger in apotropaic masks than in a humunculus representing the somatosensory area (or the motor area) alone. Sensory information is also integrated with associational areas of the cortex dealing with categorical constructions and with memories that are linked to emotional cues and value judgments, but that is another story, one only beginning to emerge with any clarity, and one that should eventually have much to tell us about the construction of emotional experience and of meaning through theatrical events. For those interested in pursuing this thread, Damasio's book (1995) provides one useful starting point, and Edelman's recent work (1992) another.

While there seem to be certain archetypal (or at least extremely widespread) attributes shared by demonic and apotropaic masks worldwide, the values—positive and negative—attached to these images vary greatly from one culture to another. One interesting hypothesis to follow would be that these differences have a great deal to do with the role of the body within the larger ethical constructions of the culture (contested though these may be): hence, the lowly and usually less ambiguous position of the devil mask in Christian traditions (see Napier 1986: 15).

11. A sensational account of the practices parodied is given in Colaabavala (1976: 56–72). The association of Rangda with graveyards is a strong one. In Jimbaran, I witnessed the start of a cycle of mapajar performances in 1994. It began with the placement of the masks of Rangda and her two companions over skulls dug up for the occasion. The ritual performers are said to be summoned from their sleep by the call of the mask. They dress in the appropriate costumes, come to the graveyard in the dark hours of early morning, place the masks on their heads, and discourse at length in Old Javanese (cf. Eiseman 1989: 311–312). It is a remarkable event to witness, and one that, again, indicates the strong associations the mask has with the past and with death.

This popular history of Airlangga and Mahendradatta is challenged by more recent readings of the evidence that suggest that Airlangga ruled in East Java, while his brother ruled in Bali, and that their mother, far from waging war as a widow, predeceased Udayana by a number of years (Kempers 1991: 39–40). Still, this is the popular version of the history as recounted in at least one version of *Calon Arang*.

12. Richard Frasca (1990: 133–66) has similarly found far-reaching connections between the popular terukkuttu tradition in Tamil Nadu—a tradition that embraces the Narasimha story as well as others involving possession—and rituals celebrating goddess figures. Our research indicates that the iconography for Narasimha masks up and down the eastern coast of India invariably follows the iconography associated with Shakti figures. In northern Andhra Pradesh, the masks look very much like Shakti masks themselves. In Tamil Nadu, they are clearly influenced by the heads of Yali (Kali's carrier in this region), as carved on southern temples.

13. It is not certain which way the borrowings of story patterns between Narasimha and Kali flowed originally. Stories of both appear first in the Mahabharata (200 BC–200 AD) and are elaborated throughout the Puranic period; Narasimha seems to have been popular in Orissa in the fourth and fifth centuries AD (Eschmann 1973b: 112). During the centuries under consideration here, however, Kali had become more important in eastern India, with Narasimha coming back into prominence with the rise of Chodaganga and Vaishnavism in the twelfth century AD, often as a figure that could bridge Shaivite, Vaishnavite, and Shakti practices. Thus, von Steitencron points out Narasimha's role as an important transitional figure in establishing the major Vaishnava temple of Jagannath in Puri on grounds once dedicated to the worship of Shakti (1978: 26–30). For a history of the Narasimha story, see Soifer (1991); for Kali's history, see Kinsley (1975).

14. Most of these variants of the Shakti figure in India are described in Aryan (1980: 32–33). For the story of Hariti as known in Bali, see Ramseyer (1977: 49). Covarrubias (1974 [1937]: 355) points out the parallels with Lakahi.

15. Brahmana Keling's story is told in Dunn (1983). A topeng pajegan performance of this story as performed by I Nyoman Catra (1989) has been translated by Fredrik deBoer and I Nyoman Sumandhi (unpublished manuscript).

Chapter 3
Playing with the Past
Visitation and Illusion in the Mask Theatre of Bali

Not all masks portray otherworldly beings. Masks may also serve to essentialize the character traits of human agents in history, legend, and contemporary society. Most of the masks used on the Greek classical and Hellenistic stages, for example, portrayed not *the* other, but *an*other—a forsaken wife, a once-proud ruler from the legendary past, a recently conquered enemy from Persia, a slave bearing terrible news, or even a comic caricature of Socrates or Cleon. Gods, too, were represented on the Greek stage, but when they were they took on a decidedly human aspect. Similarly, the face-like masks of the Japanese *noh* theatre were created to depict human agents with stories that bind them to the past, or gods and demons in essentially human form. The half-masks of the *commedia dell 'arte* of Renaissance Italy had a more prosaic field of reference; they were based upon the human faces one could see in the contemporary streets of Venice. The actor's own face was reshaped for comic effect, and in that reshaping into a comic type, eccentricities and excesses of character were revealed through a mischievous remodeling of brows, cheeks, and noses and the addition of flowing mustachios or angry carbuncles.

Topeng is a popular form of theatre in Bali that also uses masks—both full masks and half-masks—in order to re-present the human face; topeng *pajegan* is an old and particularly demanding version of that form in which one man portrays all the characters—male and female, noble and ignoble, tragic and comic, past and present, human, demonic and divine. In topeng, as in Greek tragedy and Japanese noh, even the chthonic and godly characters appear in essentially human form, and the topeng pajegan performer's many masks—his many personae—reveal a wide range of attitudes toward human life. The movement between past and present, tragic and comic, and human and divine frames of reference is complex as the lone performer puts on these masks, turn and turn about, in order to dance, tell

Figure 41. I Nyoman Kakul at his home. Batuan, Gianyar, Bali, 1975.

stories, make jokes, and perform vital rituals; this movement between and among frames is accomplished in part through a subtle referencing and manipulation of the rival aesthetic procedures of visitation and possession on the one hand (the most common Balinese term is *rauh*, a "coming")—and mimetic representation and illusion on the other—modes of performance that have been outlined in the previous chapters. What follows is a detailed account of one such performance of topeng pajegan, acted by I Nyoman Kakul (fig. 41) in the village of Tusan, Bali, on February 6, 1975.[1]

On the day I first met Kakul, he checked a calendar, found it to be a particularly propitious hour to begin study, gave me my first lesson, and invited me to live in his family compound for the next several months while I studied masked dance. In the months that followed, as I watched Kakul teach and perform, daily had him wrench my resistant body into something approximating the proper shapes for Balinese dance, and met with other performers and mask-makers on the island, I came to understand topeng as a form of theatre that mediated between the rituals of ancestral visitation I had recently seen in New Guinea and the theatre of character and illusion that I had studied and practiced in the West. I also grew to have a great respect and liking for the form of topeng, and for the men and women who sustain it.

Kakul had a stroke soon after I left Bali. Paralyzed and unable to talk for several years, he died in 1982, at the age of seventy-eight. I hope that, along with its other purposes, this account will serve as a testament to his artistry.

Performance and Occasion: The Clustering of Events

Topeng is usually performed as part of the festivities accompanying a wedding, a cremation, a tooth-filing ceremony, or an *odalan*—an occasion held every 210 days in each temple, when the gods and ancestors come down to their appropriate shrines in the temple to be honored.[2] It is the Balinese custom to mark these liminal times of transition and renewal with layer on layer of music, theatre, and ceremony, filling up the "potential spaces" until they are *ramai*—a Sanskrit-derived term that means both busy and beautiful (see Becker 1979: 230). For some events, the performers will be drawn from the villages themselves. For others, a specialist will be hired from outside the village. In February 1975, at Tusan, Kakul was hired to perform topeng pajegan as a part of the ceremonies leading up to the cremation of a *Brahmana* (Brahman) priest. Kakul himself was a *Sudra*, one who is *jaba*—outside the castes of privileged status—but his fame as a performer added luster to the activities planned.[3]

As usual, Kakul traveled to his work by public conveyance, his baskets of topeng masks and costumes competing for space with the chickens and goods that other passengers were bringing to market. As the bus approached Tusan, the road wound around a bend in the river Unda. On one side were green hills and a huge, gnarled banyan tree that marked the entrance to the village. On the other side, across the river, a vista of terraced rice fields stretched out toward the sea. A parade of villagers, dressed in brilliant reds and greens and yellows, with white cloths tied around their heads, came flooding out onto the road from the village. The cremation itself would not be held for three days, but already much of the village life was given over to the activities surrounding this event; the sense of holiday contrasted sharply with the mundane world of the bus and its passengers. Many of the villagers were carrying brightly colored gilded umbrellas. Others were striking small gongs of different sizes to create a joyful interplay of pitches and rhythms. Rice cake offerings of pink and yellow and white were piled high on silver trays perched on the heads of several of the women. As the bus stopped, Kakul opened his eyes and reached for a basket of masks.

By the time the baskets of masks and costumes had been carried to a central courtyard, the procession was returning. The rice offerings were set down. Kakul was greeted as visitor, guest, and hired expert. The manner of greeting was determined by caste and conditioned by his renown as an entertainer. A group of priests sat in a pavilion—laughing, trading stories, chewing betel nut. They greeted Kakul with enthusiasm and he returned their greetings, maintaining the extreme attitude of respectfulness that befits a Sudra in the company of Brahmana priests. This behavior was in marked contrast to the demeanor he exhibited a short time later, apart from the priests, at a huge feast of turtle meat and hotly spiced rice. Here, Kakul was animated and filled with expressive energy—an extraordinary storyteller set down among friends (see figs. 42–44).

Before the feast had finished, perhaps a hundred village men poured into the center of the village in answer to the sound of beaten wooden gongs, or *kulkul* , and took up a huge structure of thick, crossed bamboo trunks that supported an enormous, larger-than-life image of a white cow, decked with gilded embellishments. This figure would become the burning sarcophagus of the deceased Brahmana in the cremation to come. A strident and boisterous gong ensemble formed and the cow was borne aloft by the villagers. The entire structure was spun about in the main square and then carried at a breakneck pace down the dirt road, accompanied by gongs and a cacophony of shouts and laughter (fig. 45).

This clustering of activities—"ramai" in the extreme—is typical of the occasions when topeng is performed. Processions, feasting, beating of gongs, shouts, and laughter are deliberately overlapped, creating an event of great density; and while these particular events were appropriate for a cremation, a similar overlapping of events would mark a wedding, a tooth filing, or an odalan.

Figure 42–44. Kakul tells an anecdote at the feast before his performance. Tusan, Klungkung, Bali, 1975.

Figure 45. The cremation sarcophagus is paraded prior to Kakul's performance at Tusan.

A Balinese Actor Prepares

As the villagers returned up the road, sweating under the burden of the white wooden cow, Kakul moved to a relatively isolated area and began preparations for his performance. An offering had been prepared for his use. Standing over the offering, he spoke formulaic *mantras* in Javanized Sanskrit, invoking earth, air, heavenly ether, and the nine manifestations of the Hindu godhead to bless his actions as performer. *"Om awighanam astu,"* he began, "Let there be no hindrance." He did not make any effort to hide this ritual of preparation; neither did he make any effort to display it (see fig. 46). While the mantras concentrated Kakul's energies on the performance to come, the use of Sanskrit placed him in touch with the traditional path of access to a divine world. In employing the language of the Brahmana priests, Kakul stepped out of the vernacular and, in so doing, stepped outside the caste-based linguistic conventions that would define him as a Sudra in the social structuring of Balinese life. By using the language of the priests and of the distant past, he began to assume the position of a mediator between history and contemporary realities—a role in which the day-to-day social obligations and caste-based rules of etiquette can and must be suspended.

Following the speaking of these mantras, Kakul headed for the performance area. A curtain had been set up in a large courtyard, and a temporary structure of woven mats was set behind the curtain, Kakul changed into his topeng costume with help from an assistant. This is an elaborate procedure. The topeng performer wears one costume for all the characters that he portrays; only the masks and headdresses change. Composed of many layers, the costume is hot, uncomfortable, and spectacular. Over white pants and a flowing white cloth that falls between the legs, a brilliant assortment of bands, cloaks, and tabards are arrayed. The green, red, blue, purple, and black expanses of material are all embellished with gold ornamentation, while fringe drips from the tabards and glittering sequins dot leggings, wristlets, and collars. At last, a ceremonial sword (*keris*), is wrenched into position, its handle poised over the dancer's right shoulder, and its sheathed blade forcing the whole costume to billow out to the left (see color plate V).[4]

This costume is very unlike the ordinary dress of the Balinese. Although topeng stories are drawn from chronicles detailing ancient wars, and the dance vocabulary has its roots in the martial arts of the Indonesian archipelago, the relationship of the costume to the court or military dress of the fourteenth and fifteenth centuries is obscure. The costume is designed to evoke and exalt that period, not duplicate it. It belongs to the marginal performance time between the past and the future.

His costume in place, Kakul then turned to the unopened basket of masks and spoke the following words:

Figure 46. Kakul says his mantras while preparing to perform.

Om, honored grandfather,
Om, honored grandmother,
Please wake up in order to dance.

He brushed his hand across the basket three times, then opened it and arrayed the masks in the order they would be used. After the performance, on closing the basket, he would speak to the masks once more, give them an offering, again call them "honored grandfather" and "honored grandmother," and bid them return to their "heavenly homes." Using a flower, Kakul sprinkled "holy water" onto the masks and onto his own face. He then held a burning stick of sandalwood incense up to the nostrils of the masks, breathed in the incense himself, and spoke further mantras in Javanized Sanskrit, asking divine blessing for his performance. The flower is emblematic of Siwa (Shiva), the water of Wisnu (Vishnu), and the burning incense of Brahma. All in all, the ceremony, including the holding up of incense for the masks to "breathe," can be seen as a simplified version of an Indian *puja,* such as given the Narasimha mask by the actor/priest of Baulagaon.

As the Rangda and Barong performances indicate, there is a long and still-vital tradition of trancing and spirit visitation evident in Balinese theatre and life. In deep trance (*kerauhan*—"entered"), untutored spirit mediums are said to speak in ancestral languages and transformed voices, prescribing ways to propitiate neglected spiritual entities (Bateson 1970 [1937]; Connor, Asch, and Asch 1986). Pre-adolescent girls in trance, *sanghyang dedari,* are similarly "smoked" with incense and perform dances they have never rehearsed, in unison, their eyes closed (O'Neill 1978). In the small village of Trunyan, a "pre-Hindu" enclave in Bali, a set of masks may be found bearing a distinct similarity to ancestral masks of New Guinea, complete with costumes made of dried banana leaves (Bandem and de-Boer 1981: 3–16). The origins of both the sanghyang dedari dances and the ceremonies in which these *berutuk* masks and costumes are used probably predate the influence of Indian and Javanese courts on Balinese life and theatre. Drawing from both Indic and more ancient sources, however, the Balinese Hindu religion (*Agama Bali Hindu*) has, since its inception. embraced this tradition of visitation.[5]

At the odalan ceremonies that most often provide the occasion for topeng performances (see fig. 47), gods and ancestral spirits are called down to visit their shrines and activate the temple by the *Kidung Wargasari* (the Song of Spiritual Essence):

This fragrant sandalwood incense
Is offered to invite you,
Ancestral spirits,
And hasten your journey to earth,
Coming from Majapahit.

Figure 47. Prayers are offered at a Balinese odalan. Mas, Gianyar, Bali, 1975.

Everything is ready for you
To leave your holy mountain
With all your heavenly followers.

You journey here from heaven,
Flying through the sky,
Mounted on your powerful carriers,
Accompanied by your great retinue.
Clothed in your fiery raiments,
You enjoy your journey greatly,
Passing each other, weaving in and out,
As you fly through the sky.

Lord Siwa is coming,
Together with the ancestral host.
They come down from heaven,
Delighting in their journey and coursing through the sky,
Dressed all in brilliant colors
That please the heart.
The followers arrive first,
Making themselves known.

The signs of Lord Siwa's
Arrival are at hand.
The earth trembles.
Thunder resounds in the air.
The sky is filled with clouds
And rain pelts the earth.
Wind rages over all the world,
Felling trees as it blows.[6]

Lured by the same sandalwood incense used to "smoke" trance dancers and mediums and to prepare the topeng pajegan dancer and his masks, the ancestral spirits are depicted as leaving their "holy mountain," Gunung Agung—a volcano that dominates the Balinese horizon from many points on the island, including Kakul's home village of Batuan. This sacred mountain provides a fixed point for the Balinese sense of direction, as well as a home for both the Hindu deities and the ancestral host from Majapahit—a feudal Hindu empire of east Java from the twelfth to the sixteenth centuries to which most Balinese trace their ancestry and whose chronicles are very important in the topeng repertory. The topeng performer generally faces Gunung Agung in performance, including the honored ancestors and deities in his performance; and it is there that the topeng masks may be thought to return to as their "heavenly home." The brilliant-colored "fiery raiments" of the ancestral host, along with their sportiveness and love of display, remind one of nothing else in Bali so much as the costumed topeng performer. Indeed, the Balinese word for an actor's "presence" is *taksu*—the same word used for ancestral spirits visiting family shrines (see Dunn 1983: 122–34; Young 1980: 93–103).

Topeng draws from the tradition of visitation—but in topeng the tradition is used to buttress and underpin mimetic representation. The topeng dancer does not show any evidence of performing in trance. The taksu that holds an audience enthralled is often accounted a divine gift, but the dancer seeks inspiration, not possession. Still, his approach to characterization through the mask is informed and supported by the tradition of visitation.

Occasionally, when I would bring a new mask home, Kakul would take hold of it with his right hand, supporting it on his palm from behind so that it was fully visible to him. He would turn it first one way, then another, and make it look up and down. He would play with the movement, adjusting the speed and the sharpness of definition, until he was satisfied that he had found how the mask moved best; how it wanted to move. Only then would he put the mask on his face and begin to move his body, bringing the mask to life, making an amalgam of mask and self that, for lack of a better word, can be called character. Always, his words would be about the demands of the mask. When he liked a mask, he would say, "This one lives." When he didn't like a mask, he would disparage it as having no life in it. This method of seeking out the will of the mask is typical of topeng performers I have watched at work (cf. frontispiece).

Unlike the sanghyang dedari dancer, the topeng performer first learns to dance by rote, the body being pushed and pulled into proper shapes by the guru (cf. fig. 48). Bit by bit, by imitation and by the direct manipulation of limbs, the performer assimilates the dance vocabulary needed to portray a range of masked characters. The masks themselves are not used at all at this stage of the training, and the dance vocabulary, along with sample choreographies, are learned by type: a refined king, a strong warrior, an enfeebled old courtier. This rigorous training in the stylistic demands of topeng character types provides an objective framework for the interpretation of specific masks. Those masks themselves make their own, very specific demands, and work with a new mask begins with a respect for a mask's separate "life" as an objective other.[7]

It would be a mistake to think of the process of character formation as impersonal. To my surprise, when I was studying with Kakul, he would repeatedly criticize my facial expressions as I grimaced while awkwardly trying to make my feet, arms, and body work together in excruciatingly unfamiliar ways. The mask was not a disguise, he stressed. If the face of the actor behind the mask did not register the character of the figure dancing, the body would move wrongly, and the mask would be denied its life. The dancer might be technically proficient, but he would fail to properly animate the mask. He would be derisively called a "carpenter"—one who just pushes wood around (Jenkins 1978: 48). Ana Daniel, another student of Kakul's, notes that, while Kakul stressed diligence in practice and the cultivation of a state of "total receptivity," he also emphasized an intensely personal commitment to the inchoate character: "You must feel the life,

Figure 48. Kakul teaching his granddaughter to dance, 1975.

the flow from your heart, from your soul. [. . .] All expression dwells within you. It must come from inside and pass through you" (1981: 100, 117).

After I left Bali, W. S. Rendra, the Javanese poet, playwright, director, and political activist told me how his grandfather prepared to perform with a new mask. The procedures he described exemplify this dual attention to self and other. When Rendra's grandfather acquired a new mask, he, like Kakul, would take it in his hand and turn it this way and that, trying to sense the spirit suggested by the mask: its life. He then placed the mask on his bed, by his head. As he slept, he purposefully interjected the imagined spirit of the mask into his dreams, and in these controlled dreams invited the spirit of the mask to witness the most important events of his personal history. Working backwards in time, he finally dreamed his own birth. In that dream, the embodied spirit of the mask took the "brother" placenta (cf. Lansing 1974) in his hands. After this dream, the dancer was considered able to let the spirit of the mask enter his body and, through his body, the life of the mask was able to find expression, animating and making specific the dance movements previously learned by rote and type. A meeting ground for self and other had been found. The dancer was not possessed, but his behavior was transformed (1975, personal communication). While I have never heard these precise procedures described or seen them practiced in Bali, Ron Jenkins reports the following interview with an unidentified dancer in Bali: "My father used to spend many days in meditation with his masks. He kept them in a special place in the house and sometimes slept with them next to his pillow. Today it is sad the young dancers have little time for this. They put their masks in a box and use the box to sit on. This is not the way to find Taksu" (1978: 48). This suggests that techniques similar to the one Rendra described may have been used in Bali.

Introductory Dances: The Shaking of the Curtain and the Entrance of the Ancestor

As Kakul arranges his masks in the order they will be used, the *gamelan* orchestra begins to play. Brightly, quickly, gaily, wooden hammers fall on the bronze keys of the metallophones with perfect and seemingly effortless precision, forming intricate interlocking patterns that are embellished by the striking of several small bronze pots and the playing of sweet-voiced flutes, marked by the regular sounding of a large and a medium-sized gong, and urged on by the rapid play of drums. Attracted by the music, the audience has begun to arrange itself in a large oval in the courtyard. The orchestra is at one of the small ends of this oval; the decorated curtain that hides Kakul's preparations is at the other. At either side of the curtain, gilded ceremonial umbrellas have been stuck into the ground. There is no other "scenery," no further isolation of the dancing space from the space outlined by the audience.

Children gather first, sitting cross-legged or stretching out on the ground, their faces bright and expectant. The performance had been "scheduled" to begin at four o'clock. It is now seven o'clock and kerosene pressure lamps are being stoked and hung overhead to provide illumination as the daylight dwindles. No one seems to mind. Things happen as they are ready on ceremonial occasions, or when the time is propitious. Clock time is regarded as a relatively unimportant convention on these occasions and has little to do with when things begin or end. Gradually, adults begin to fill in behind the children, forming several more or less attentive "rows" of people sitting cross-legged, squatting, and standing, while others look casually on from a distance. Casual banter blends with the music.

Behind the curtain, arrayed in his colorful and gilded assortment of tabards and cloaks, his keris handle poised over his right shoulder and his costume billowing out behind him, Kakul makes a final check of the masks to be used—an extraordinary assortment of kings, beasts, heroes, rogues, and buffoons (cf. fig. 49). He takes the smiling, red mask of a proud *patih* (a principal minister of the court), I Gusti Ngurah Lepang, in his hand, regards it for a second, then sets it in place. A partial wig is slipped on so that the black hair falls to Kakul's shoulders, and an elaborately carved and gilded leather headdress, studded with flowers and sticks of burning

Figure 49. Masks of I Ketut Kantor, Kakul's son, laid out for a performance. 1993.

incense, is placed over what remains of Kakul's own gray hair. Leaves are fixed along the sides of the mask, blurring the dividing lines between mask and face.

Kakul sets himself in position for his entrance. A guttural sound emerges from his throat. One hand gives a quick shake to the curtain, while the other makes last-minute adjustments. Signaled by the lead drummer, the gamelan starts to play the eight-beat, cyclical melody of *baris gilak*, traditionally associated with the dancing of warriors. Kakul shakes the curtain harder. A rush of sound from a set of overlapped small cymbals attends its movement. Again, the curtain shakes, more violently this time; again, the shaking of the curtain is accompanied by a rush of percussive sound, bringing to mind the auspicious shaking of the world that accompanies the coming of the ancestral host in invocatory songs used in temple ceremonies.

Kakul parts the curtain in the middle and, as the red-faced patih, enters the space defined by the expectant audience (fig. 50). His head makes small, sharp, and sudden movements. His legs are bent, the feet set wide apart and firmly planted on the earth in a position derived from martial arts. The fingers move quickly in multiples of the musical pulse, as though they are antennae testing the air of an unfamiliar world. The warrior alertly scans the new space, his hands elegantly moving up to the gilded lacework helmet as he glances about him. Ominously, perhaps suspiciously, with a sense of great strength and consummate control, he moves forward. The walk is extremely "unnatural." The body seems coiled and tense. The feet pivot out on each step, maintaining balance and readiness. The hands sculpt the air in graceful, smooth lines. Suddenly the patih focuses his attention on a ceremonial umbrella. With a quick cross-step, he moves toward the umbrella and rises up on one foot, remaining poised in the air as the orchestra dramatically halts for two beats. Kakul seems immense. The music resumes and Kakul lifts his gilded cloak in a display of grandeur and pride. He walks more quickly now, claiming the oval as his own, dominating the space, his rapidly moving fingers still testing the air. Or is he reacting to the presence of the audience?

Kakul has never danced with this orchestra before. Still, the cymbals and drums seem to extend the movement of his body into sound, creating an experience of synaesthesia in which sound and movement are one. A small, flashing movement of a knee or elbow signals Kakul's intentions to the lead drummer, and the drummer signals the rest of the orchestra in turn by a rhythmic code. As Kakul suddenly pivots around and stops in a pose of arrested motion, the full gamelan once more stops with him. Eventually, the space claimed, the display completed, the proud patih disappears through the split curtain and it closes behind him.[8]

Behind the curtain, Kakul removes the mask and headdress of the patih and takes up another mask. This mask is tinged an odd greenish-blue and

Figure 50. Kakul as Patih Lepang, the first character to enter through the curtain.

features plump cheeks and a mischievous grin. It has a distinctly comic cast and belongs to Pasung Grisgris (fig. 51), a patih who once, in fourteenth-century Bali, in an inspired, desperate, and ultimately unfortunate moment, grafted a pig's head onto his king's body. The new mask in place and another headdress set above it, Kakul draws up a chair to the curtain, takes

Figure 51. Kakul as Pasung Grisgris, the second, more comic figure in his introductory dances.

the folds that form the opening in his hand, and gives them a shake. Again, the cymbals and drums accompany this motion with a rush of sound. The gamelan is playing another variation of baris gilak, the warrior's tune. After teasing the audience by playing with the curtain, Kakul throws it open and reveals the mischievous patih perched on top of the chair.

The gestures he makes now are quite different in effect from those of the proud red-faced patih who has just exited. Rather than dominating the space with the alertness of a threatened warrior, he plays with the dynamics of the performance situation, openly toying with the drummer, daring him to follow his rapid gestures, teasing the musicians and the audience, and occasionally even punctuating the gamelan's music with a salacious gesture copied from the behavior of European tourists: right elbow bent, closed fist abruptly raised, free hand slapping the biceps of the right arm. The dance follows the same basic choreographic pattern; but the tone is lighter, more playful, with a touch of parody. The audience responds to the shenanigans of Pasung Grisgris with howls of delighted laughter. His antic display completed, Pasung Grisgris, too, returns to the unseen world behind the curtain that opens, lets him through, and swallows him up again.

The gamelan changes melodies. This time the sound is gentler, not so insistent, manic, or forceful; there is an almost seamless thirty-two-beat cycle marked by the gong strokes. Kakul takes up the mask of an old man and regards it for a moment. This is the only one of his masks that he himself has carved. He fixes the mask on his face and sets a flowing mane of white hair upon his head. The character is I Gusti Dauh Bale Agung (fig. 52), aged minister of the royal court of Gelgel in sixteenth-century Bali. To the audience, though, he is simply the *tua*: the old one. The curtain shaking is again repeated, as it will be for each new character. This time, though, the shaking is less vigorous and Kakul parts the curtain to reveal himself as an old man sitting on a chair, surveying a new space, taking in the audience, hearing the music, adjusting his costume, and gathering energy for his dance. First one hand, then the other begins tentatively to move to the gentle music. Gradually, energy and confidence seem to return to the aged courtier, and he takes a standing position. After further adjustments, the sight of the ceremonial umbrellas seem to awaken a sense of pride in battles waged long ago and lodged in an old warrior's memory of his past.

The old man begins to dance, slowly at first, then faster and faster. The music keeps pace and grows louder as the aged dancer grows more and more energetic, finally overextending himself, carried away in his proud enthusiasm. A series of rapid turns leaves him off-balance and he stumbles toward the audience, barely managing to stop himself from falling into its midst. The audience roars with laughter. Slowly, the ancient courtier collects himself, breathing slowly. He reaches out to shake the hand of a small child who is looking up at him with an enraptured smile. He seems about to resume his dancing, but instead reaches suddenly up to his flowing mane

Figure 52. Kakul as I Gusti Dauh Bale Agung, the old man (tua) that ends the sequence of introductory dances.

of hair and grabs hold of an imaginary louse. He looks at it and the audience laughs. He pinches the imaginary pest and tosses it in the direction of the delighted audience. Twice more, he hears the music playing and starts to resume his dance. Each time, he reaches instead for lice—once on his leg, another time on the back of his neck. Finally, he shakes off these distractions and begins to dance. He is more careful this time and there are no more stunning turns, but he manages to recapture a sense of human dignity and authority before exiting through the curtain. The obligatory set of introductory dances, or *pengelembar*, is over. No words have been spoken, and none of the characters portrayed will reappear. But a world has been introduced, and a range of human response demonstrated. Perhaps a third of the performance time has elapsed.

Accompanied by an elaborate interplay of movement and sound, the pengelembar characters enter through the curtain into a neutral space created from unadorned Balinese earth and demarcated by a ring of spectators. As Kakul enters as the proud patih, I Gusti Ngurah Lepang, his brilliant costume, his mastery of a special vocabulary of movement, and his concentrated energy set him apart. The audience regards him as extraordinary, but the hypersensitive, abrupt, and prideful display of the patih may indicate that the world of the audience is as challenging to him as his world is to them. A distance is established between a character emerging from a world dominated by the ways of the past, and the audience living and watching in the present. The actor moves as a character from the world of the past into the world of the present in a sort of foray across boundaries of time and association.

The pattern is that of a rite of visitation, but the playing out of this pattern has been theatricalized. The audience knows that behind the curtain lies Kakul's basket of masks and changing table. Kakul himself is not a man entranced or possessed; he is a performer in triumphant control of his actions, choosing to portray first one character, then another, adjusting his costume, signaling to an unfamiliar orchestra his intentions as a dancer, determining the dynamics of the performance.

The first dance references the aesthetics of ancestral visitation to establish a division between the world of the past and the present. The next dance plays with that sense of division. Pasung Grisgris's teasing and playing with the orchestra and audience is as direct and immediate as it is mischievous. As the boundaries between worlds are violated, laughter occurs. The third character presented in the pengelembar, I Gusti Dauh Bale Agung, the tua, is far more "human" than either of his predecessors. He makes further excursions across the boundaries separating the storied world of the past and the mundane world of the present. When the old man reaches out and touches a child in the audience, he is engaging in a form of contact that would be unthinkable for either the proud patih or his antic opposite.

Figure 53. Ida Bagus Alit performs in a tua mask he has made. Sangeh, Bali, 1993.

While Kakul's specific choice of masks is made from a range of options, the order of appearance of these characters is not arbitrary. While the number of pengelembar characters varies from performance to performance, and the inclusion and choice of middle characters (topeng *arya,* comic noblemen) is up to the discretion of the dancer, a strong and proud patih (patih *keras*) almost invariably comes first, and a somewhat eccentric old man (the tua) almost invariably enters last (fig. 53; see Bandem and deBoer 1981: 54–55).[9] By playing with the theatrical possibilities inherent in the representation of visitation, a framework for performance is established that will allow for a playing back and forth between the world as it is imagined to have been, and the world as it is usually experienced to be.

Storytelling: The Languages of Topeng

Topeng is not only a dance theatre, it is also a storytelling theatre, rich in verbal interplay. The introductory dances stake out the means of playing back and forth between the distant past and the immediate present through modulation of the degree of artifice used, through control of the directness of contact with the audience, and, most importantly, through the use of humor. This play between the past and the present, the distant and the immediate, the grand and the mundane, is at the heart of topeng.

The stories of topeng are drawn from the *babad dalem*: the chronicles of the kings. These chronicles are not contained in one central and authoritative collection. They are the work of numerous court poets and genealogists, Brahmana employed to glorify the ancestral heritage of their various *Satria* (Kshatriya in Sanskrit and Indian usage) lords—drawing from inscriptions on copper plates (*persasti*) and from oral tradition. Beginning in the sixteenth century and continuing into the early years of the twentieth, these court scribes wrote out their semi-historical chronicles on sheets of dried and boiled palm leaves, known as *lontar*. The quasi-historical works that were produced by this process report the coming of the Majapahit expeditionary force to Bali in the fourteenth century and relate incidents centered around the often warring Hindu princedoms that were established in Bali during the years that followed Majapahit's decline and fall around 1520 AD. The story used by Kakul in Tusan relates to an invasion of Blambangan, Java, by an expeditionary force sent in the mid-sixteenth century by Dalem Baturenggong, who ruled the Balinese kingdom of Gelgel, now located in the province of Klungkung.[10]

Kakul's immediate source is contained in a small notebook of stories he has collected, drawn from the lontar, that he often refers to while choosing and preparing a performance. As with many of the babad stories, variants exist, stressing the roles of different historical figures. Kakul thus has a wide range of interpretations available to him and he can shape the stories in any one of a number of ways. He does not quote from the babad. Instead, he creates various storytelling personae and through them improvises on the babad's story-line.

The first such storyteller to enter is the Penasar Kelihan (fig. 54). His entrance, accompanied by the usual shaking of the curtain and flourishes of cymbals and drums, reveals him to be proud, flamboyant, and commanding. He has the hearty laugh of an enthusiast and dances in an exaggeratedly macho fashion that pushes the dance to the edge of parody. The mask of the Penasar Kelihan covers the face only as far as the upper lip, leaving the jaw free to move. Kakul's mask (a somewhat unusual one) has huge, wide eyes that bug out of the purple mask and impart a look of perpetual apoplexy.

After performing for approximately half an hour, Kakul now speaks for

Figure 54. Kakul as Penasar Kelihan.

the first time. The words that he utters are half sung, half chanted in Middle Javanese, a literary language used by poets in Bali from the seventeenth to the nineteenth centuries in composing *kidung*—romantic poetry to be sung in groups or used in the courtly *gambuh* drama that depicts the life of Majapahit. (see Bandem and deBoer 1981: 28–48, Vickers 1986). The particular words used begin the *Kidung Tantri*, a Javanese equivalent of the *Tale of a Thousand and One Nights*: "A story is told of the King of Patali, rich, proud, and full of dignity." The use of the ancestral language is more important than the content of the words used here. Most audience members would simply identify the language and style of singing as *ucapan* gambuh, speech of the courtly gambuh theatre. The audience would also be cognizant of the theatrical association of this mode of speech with the Majapahit Empire (Wallis 1979: 45, 58).

After playing with the gamelan, with the audience, and with his character's joy in seizing control of the playing space—combining the topeng dance vocabulary already defined as belonging to the world of the past with exclamations and hearty laughter that place him in a most immediate present—the Penasar Kelihan stops short and speaks in yet another ancestral language, Old Javanese, or Kawi (see Zoetmulder 1974; Zurbuchen 1987). The mode of delivery is guttural, authoritative, chanted. The themes and characters associated with this mode of delivery originate in the Indian epic tradition, notably in the *Ramayana* and the *Mahabharata*. From 900 to 1500 AD these epics were translated and reworked in the Hindu courts of Java, becoming Javanized in the process. Kawi began to appear as the language of Balinese courts as early as 994, and passages from the Javanized epics still serve as sources of ancestral wisdom (Wallis 1979: 82–83). Like the chanting Tolai musicians invoking the *tubuan* in a forgotten language, or the rural performers of *Prahlada Nataka* invoking Ganesha in Sanskrit, Kakul begins by "speaking the past" (cf. Becker, 1979: 211–16).

The first words that the entire audience can comprehend are immediate and personal: the Penasar Kelihan is happy to be here, strutting, dancing, and telling tales. He is especially happy, he says, because he has just become a bachelor again—inviting the audience to laugh at the age-old joke with his own infectious laughter. Once again, the mode of address is more important than the information given. The use of colloquial Balinese recontextualizes the present in the "potential space" thus far dominated by the languages of the past. The encouragement to laughter grants the audience permission to participate playfully, if vicariously, in the leaps from past to present and back again, licensed by the occasion of performance.

This is a mode of play that a Balinese audience is particularly well prepared for by skills in communication necessary for their daily lives. I have referred to the Penasar Kelihan as speaking "colloquial Balinese." In fact, the nature of "Balinese" is far more complex than this would indicate.

Miguel Covarrubias, in his pioneering *Island of Bali*, describes day-to-day language practices as follows:

> When two strange Balinese meet, as for instance on the road, they call each other *djero*, a safe, polite way of addressing someone whose title is unknown. Since there are no outward signs of caste, [. . .] strangers talk in the middle language, a compromise between daily speech and the polite tongue. Should, however, one be of low caste and the other a nobleman, it would be wrong for them to continue talking in this manner, and one of the two, probably the high-caste man, will ask the other: "*Antuk linggih?*"—"Where is your place (caste)?" which is answered by the other man's stating his caste. Then, the usual system is adopted; the low man speaks in the high tongue and the aristocrat answers in the common language [. . .] two distinct, unrelated languages with separate roots, different words, and extremely dissimilar character. It was always incongruous to hear an educated nobleman talking the harsh, guttural tongue, while an ordinary peasant had to address him in the refined high Balinese. (1974 [1937]: 50–51; cf. Eiseman 1990: 130–46)

Even with the tendency in Bali today to use the status-marking modes of language less—usually preferring the school-taught and far more egalitarian Indonesian language for the purposes of business and scholarship (cf. Barth 1993: 233)—it is an insult in south Bali to be termed "*sing nawang basa*," one who doesn't know the language (Wallis 1979: 43). The Balinese are very sensitive to relationships among context, speech, and action. The theatre plays with this consciousness, both reinforcing the sense that different words and actions properly belong to different contexts and delighting in the leaps from context to context provided by an expert performer.

As the Penasar Kelihan, Kakul abruptly shifts to the respectful vocabulary and mode of address appropriate to high Balinese in order to address humbly his as yet unseen lord and king, Dalem Baturenggong, and to pay homage to the Hindu deities and consecrated ancestors. For the first time, he places himself as a character within a world of illusion—one with interconnected social relationships and the capacity to sustain a "plot." At first, this world of illusion is referred to as "here in ancient Bali." It is then particularized as being "here in Gelgel," invoking the nearby ancient capital. The Penasar Kelihan identifies himself as a servant to Dalem Baturenggong, thereby specifying the time of the story as being approximately 1550.

This world of illusion, though, is abruptly shattered almost as soon as it is established. After a vigorous bit of dancing and a mischievous *kekawin* refrain from the *Ramayana* describing the young monkey Angeda rising high on his tail in order to insult the demon king, Rawana, Kakul momentarily drops the story and even the character of the Penasar Kelihan altogether and speaks of a "here" that is definitely Tusan at the present moment of performance. His use of the "crude" low Balinese is made even more immediate by the deployment of the local Klungkung dialect as he chides the Satria-led gamelan for rushing during the dance and makes fun of himself as a mangy "old dog." The contrast between the behavior of the new persona and the humble pleadings of the Penasar Kelihan as he tries to avoid his king's curses could not be greater.

So far, the audience only knows the historical time and locale of the story to be told; yet, Kakul has deployed Middle Javanese, Old Javanese, and high, low, and medium Balinese, and has given to each its own sense of decorum, its own mode of being. Before the performance is over, he will also deploy Modern Indonesian and Archipelago Sanskrit. What A. L. Becker notes about Javanese *wayang kulit* is true also of Balinese topeng:

> [There is] an extraordinary fact about the language of wayang, a fact of great importance in understanding what is happening at any given moment. A wayang includes within it, in each performance, the entire history of the literary language. [. . .] I do not mean here what might be said of English, that it reflects its history in vocabulary, syntax, and phonological variation. That is also true of modern Javanese. The difference is that in the shadow play, the language of each of these different eras is separate in function from the others. [. . .] One could even say that the content of the wayang is the languages of the past and present, a means of contextualizing the past in the present and the present in the past, hence preserving the expanded text that is the culture. (1979: 232)

Topeng's "content" can similarly be seen as the presentation and contextualizing of the languages of the past and present.

These various linguistic worlds having been established one by one, and the process of contextual leaps set in motion, Kakul, as the Penasar Kelihan, begins to concentrate on the story itself, providing expository information, freely dropping into crude dialect for immediacy and humor, soaring into recitations from the *Mahabharata* in Kawi to invoke an ancient warrior's ethos, and singing sections from the *Kidung Malat* in Middle Javanese to invoke images of courtly grace and elegance. As Kakul leaps from frame to frame, he assumes three essential roles while still wearing the mask of the Penasar Kelihan: he is servant in an illusionary world of ancient Gelgel, the proud reciter of epic poetry, and the mangy "old dog" of a performer. Alternating these roles, Kakul manipulates the flexible vehicle chosen from the babad stories recorded in his notebook. As Penasar Kelihan, he quotes kings and ministers as the story unfolds, ever sensitive to their bearing and manner as language shifts appropriately in the caste-conscious world of ancient Gelgel.

Another Storyteller: Common Sense and Extraordinary Happenings

For all the textual and contextual leaps, the world of "ancient Bali" invoked by the Penasar Kelihan is coherent in its formulation and rigorous in its demands. The singing of the kidung selections in Middle Javanese evokes an image of elegance and courtly grace consciously derived from the Courts of Majajpahit: as the king is about to enter, "the air is transformed. It is all gentleness and prettiness." The recitations in Kawi of lines from the Javanese *Mahabharata* and *Ramayana* give a sense of divine purpose to the power and elegance of the Court. In this world, every man has his place in a hierarchical chain. The king humbles himself before the gods and holds his dignity among men as inviolate. Warriors pledge their lives to their kings and command the service of their men. Thus the Penasar Kelihan, low on the chain but not at the bottom, humbles himself before his king and commands his lackeys without ceremony to "Pack up! Get ready for a fight!" "A small ring is a bracelet for the finger," sings the Penasar Kelihan. The implication is that, by extension of this principle, the king is a god on earth, the Penasar a king to his servants.[11] The sense of form repeating form as the scale increases and diminishes is given its most elaborate expression by Jelantik, the eventual hero of the story, when he likens the "macrocosmos" *(buwana agung)* of the spiritual world to the "microcosmos" *(buwana alit)* of the physical world and states that "the microcosmos finds expression in the body of every man."

The world of ancient Bali as presented by the Penasar Kelihan is one that needs vigilant defense. He recites from the *Mahabharata* that "since time immemorial, the warrior's path has been one of action." In this story, the order of the world is in jeopardy because of the disfigurement of an image of the king. While such shocks to the world's ordering demand redress and give rise to drama, they also open the way to humor. The Penasar Kelihan himself, though, cannot fully exploit the humor latent in the instability of such a world. With his love of epic verse, his exaggerated dance posture, and his hearty enthusiast's laugh, he is quintessentially an advocate and advertiser for the ethos and splendor of "ancient Bali." But the Penasar does not tell this story alone: he alternates storytelling functions with the Penasar Cenikan, or younger storyteller (fig. 55).

In topeng *panca,* the company form of topeng, these characters work in pairs and are understood to be "brothers."[12] They are invariably in the service of the kings, heroes, and adversaries whose deeds the chronicles relate. They are also, most importantly, mediating characters between the heroic world of the past and the mundane world of the present. Coming from the past into the world of the present, these characters may talk about anything from esoteric Hindu mythology to birth control programs or tourists falling off motorcycles while they provide exposition for the "plot." More often than not, their talk is humorous, and their characters are designed to maximize the use of humor as they assume their roles as mediators.

As with any good comedy team, the "brothers" have contrasting styles. The Penasar Kelihan is the straight man, full of self-importance and bound to the world of the past by word and gesture. The Penasar Cenikan, on the other hand, has the freedom from constraints of a comic innocent. He walks upright, arms by his sides, in a casual manner that violates all the

Figure 55. Kakul as Penasar Cenikan.

carefully established decorum of the legendary world. His speech is almost always in contemporary Balinese. When he does sing a kidung selection or quote kekawin poetry, the result is often parody. In his light, nasal voice, he often makes fun of the pretentiousness of his older sibling. Like his brother, he wears a half-mask; but his is of a far more "natural" appearance. The performer's own mischievous eyes show through the empty eye sockets. Kakul gives him a common and unprententious name: I Ketut Rai. His very lack of pretension gives him a license to speak his mind. The word "penasar" is fashioned from *dasar*, the basis or foundation. As I Gusti Windia, a great comic performer of the new generation explains it, "Between the morning of youth and the nighttime of old age, there are the everyday activities of life. This is shown by the penasar clown going through the business of the day. He is the foundation of what people do in their lives" (quoted by Jenkins 1994: 26).

In Kakul's topeng there is a marked difference in tone as the Penasar Cenikan takes over the storytelling. As in the introductory dances, the movement is toward the human and the contemporary. Speaking almost entirely in Balinese after a self-deprecating passage from the *Kidung Malat*, the Penasar Cenikan does not mock the heroic values espoused by the Penasar Kelihan—he speaks as an outsider to the heroic world that supports those values. His speech is full of expletives revealing an attitude of wonderment toward the events he must relate: *"Pih!" "Beh!" "Aduh!"* The idea of becoming a great warrior himself amuses and pleases him, but the assumption of the role of "Ketut Rai the Invincible" is not convincing, and it is with a sense of surprise at his own words that he recounts his noble reply to his lord's suggestion that he stay at home with his wife rather than go off to war—a report that draws the audience's laughter as well.

And yet, this simple man of common sense must report the most extraordinary happening of the story: the appearance of Jelantik's accursed father in the form of a giant leech who can be restored only by his son's death on the field of battle. The Penasar Cenikan does not pretend to understand the workings of such curses as they fall upon those who disturb the fixed order of the world. He can only relate what he saw and heard, improbable though it might be. He tells the audience that the leech was hairy. He compares it in size and shape to familiar objects of the day-to-day world: a roofing mat, a betel nut canister. He interjects mundane details concerning a fishing pole and bait. He is an unlikely chronicler of extraordinary events.

Rather than disguise the distance between the fantastic world of the ancestral heroes and the mundane world of ordinary people, his wondering presence emphasizes that gap; and, as he plays across that gap, the telling of the story becomes more recognizably human. With his addition as witness, the past contains something more of the present and the audience's own response to such fantastic happenings finds expression. By alternating the Penasar Cenikan's wonderment in the face of the extraordinary events

Figure 56. Another performer as Penasar Cenikan in a company performance at Batuan, Bali. 1993.

he has witnessed and must describe with the Penasar Kelihan's boldly assertive reactivation of the languages and attitudes of the ancestral past, audience members are afforded contrasting ways of approaching stories that define their history as a people.

This fluidity of movement between past and present is aided by the fact that Balinese (like other Austronesian languages, including Javanese of whatever epoch and modern Indonesian) does not employ tense in order to mark temporality: there is no conjugation of verbs. Other time markers abound: I go the river today, I go to the river yesterday (perhaps in the early morning), I go to the river the day after tomorrow. Linguistically, though, the act is the same: I (or a remarkable number of other pronouns depending on who is talking to whom, and who is being included or excluded in the conversation) always *go* to the river, regardless of when the going takes place. This enforced use of the narrative present acts as a powerful solvent on temporal barriers that might otherwise impede the frequently comic oscillation between time markers; and the consequent ambiguities when other temporal marker are dropped make anachronisms far less awkward (though potentially no less playful) than those used in tense-marked narratives.[13]

The Dancing of the Principals

During Kakul's performance, each of the principal characters within the story is accorded a dance. Framed by the alternating voices of the two penasars, king, hero, and antagonist all make their separate appearances. The king is first, and the manner of his invocation is significant. As Dalem Baturenggong, King of Gelgel, is called into the playing space by the Penasar Kelihan, the rate of change from language to language accelerates: Kawi, Middle Javanese, and Balinese succeed each other in rapid succession as if all times are dramatically merging into one in order to accommodate the king's entrance. An interplay is established between expectations appropriate to the rival esthetic modes of dramatic illusion and ancestral visitation. The king's entrance is embedded in an unfolding story and is partially anticipated in the terms of dramatic illusion. He is bidden to come forth among his ministers and his people, asked to enter the "hall of justice" in "ancient Bali." He is quoted as preparing his loyal followers for his entrance, establishing protocol among imagined ministers gathering in an illusionary world. The king is arriving on business. Yet the Penasar Kelihan also sings of his imminent entrance through the curtain in terms of performance and display. He tells the audience that the king will come forth "dancing beautifully." The use of ancestral languages, the deployment of music, the shaking of the curtain, the lack of illusionary scenery, the inclusion of the ancestors and gods in the audience, and the promised emphasis on display, all combine to relate the king's entrance to the traditions of ancestral visitation already theatricalized in the introductory dances.

A similar shuttling back and forth between these rival esthetic modes is evident in the other two appearances of principal characters embedded within the telling of the story. As the Penasar Cenikan calls upon his master Jelantik, he urges him to "come forth" and "reveal" himself, employing terms of visitation, performance, and display. The hero's imminent appearance is also talked of as "going forth," as a departure to Blambangan—the next stop along the line in a developing dramatic "plot." The audience is asked to regard Jelantik's entrance and dance both as an act of revelation, a coming forth from the ancestral world into their own, and as an event within the dramatic line of action, a going forth to another illusionary locale.

Later, when the King of Blambangan, the antagonist of the refined Dalem Baturenggong, shakes the curtain (thereby cueing another frenzied rush of percussive sound), he cries out in Kawi: "Behold, here I come, the King of Blambangan," and warns the audience that preparation is necessary to witness his powerful countenance. The curtain is yanked open and the king thrusts his animalistic hands forward, looking through the opened curtain into the performance oval, demanding to know whom it is he is facing. Is he talking to the warriors from Gelgel who have invaded his territory? Or is he speaking to the audience he sees revealed to him on the other side of the curtain, demanding information from them in a language which is no longer theirs? The ambiguity is deliberate. By shifting back and forth between the modes of illusion and visitation, the performer can playfully toy with the vantage points of the audience. The display format of the introductory dances is now loosely embedded within a developing line of action or "plot," and the result is a theatrical form rich in its ability to awaken wonder while it mediates between the world as the audience ordinarily experiences it and the world as the audience can imagine it to be.

In appearance and movement, the three principal characters of the central story are deliberately fashioned as contrasting figures. Their dances do not advance the story itself. Rather, their entrances are presented as acts of revelation highlighted within the narrative structure. Dalem Baturenggong appears in a white mask with almond-shaped eyes and a fine black mustache (see color plate VI). His headdress is covered with flowers. The gestures the Dalem uses are flowing, graceful, and delicate, imparting a sense of inner strength and great pride. Jelantik's mask is of a more earthy, natural color. The eyes are wider, the smile larger (fig. 57). The stance accompanying the mask is wider, the movements sharper. The debt to the martial arts is clear. As Jelantik, Kakul presents a figure of great dignity and strength, alert to everything about him, but without the hypertension the red-faced patih exhibited in the pengelembar. As Sri Dalem Blambangan, King of Blambangan and "villain" of the evening (fig. 58), Kakul wears a red demon's mask with bulging eyes, large boar's tusks, and a protruding tongue over which there is an opening to allow for speech. Covering his hands are white gloves equipped with six-inch fingernails made of water buffalo horn and tufted with animal fur. He is revealed perched on the back of a chair, legs wide apart, hands thrust aggressively forward and to the side, with fingers spread apart and trembling.

These masks and the postures and movements associated with them do

Figure 57. Kakul as Patih Jelantik.

Figure 58. Kakul as Dalem Blambangan at another topeng pajegan performance (Photo, Rucina Ballinger).

not derive from descriptions in the historical chronicles, but, rather, from performance tradition and typology. In Balinese terminology, the king is *halus*, his minister *keras*, and the demon king *kasar*. The mask used for Dalem Baturenggong could also be used for any other refined king; and the mask used for the Sri Dalem Blambangan can also be used for the god Mahadewa in his terrible aspect. The point is not to present these figures "as they were," but as they ought to be imagined. The story is a scaffolding used to show essentialized images of human capabilities and epistemologies—of different ways of knowing and of being in the world.[14]

Bondres: Joking and Reflexivity

The dramatic line of action comes to an end with the report of Patih Jelantik's death on the field of battle. With that event, a successful synthesis of the thematic lines enmeshed within the dramatic "plot" is achieved. Jelantik's father is freed from his curse and the honor of Gelgel is preserved in a single heroic action. Yet the performance continues. Indeed, the Penasar Cenikan's report of the resolution of the dramatic themes seems perfunctory, and the audience's interest intensifies and quickens rather than dissipates with the entrance of the next character. It is time for *bondres*—a parade of clowns offering jokes that seem ever so loosely connected to the dramatic action. For the Balinese audience, this is a happily anticipated part of any topeng performance. In Kakul's performance, the jokes bear a direct relationship to the themes and actions of the dramatic "plot": the jokes work reflexively, turning the audience's attention back upon those themes.

The Penasar Kelihan touts the ethos of "ancient Bali." The three dancing principals of the dramatic plot embody that ethos. The Penasar Cenikan stands in awe of it. King, hero, villain, and servants all function in their given orbits within this ethos. The next three characters to appear offer alternative modes of behavior that cannot be assimilated within the structure of values shared by the warriors, courtiers, and kings of "ancient Bali." There seems to be no place for them within this tale of noble deeds, yet come they do (as they always will). As I Gusti Windia explains, "The bondres are the interferences of our lives. [. . .] The bondres clowns are always interrupting the king's plans the way that distractions in our lives interrupt the things we want to do" (quoted in Jenkins 1995: 26). Through these bondres characters, Kakul is able to position himself outside the realm of punctilious behavior and the tragic praxis of heroic self-sacrifice. The truths of this realm are revealed to be (not false but) partial.

The first in this succession of clowns, jokesters, and outsiders is named Si Mata Mata (fig. 59). His very name—loosely translatable as One-Who-Looks-Out-For-Himself—is an affront to the noble values of Jelantik, who sacrifices his life for the restitution of his country's honor and the salvation

Figure 59. Kakul as Si Mata Mata.

of his cursed father's soul. Si Mata Mata's first "word" is a sneeze, immediately violating all the elaborate linguistic protocol thus far used to narrate the babad episode of Jelantik's mission to Blambangan. He then proceeds to string together nonsense syllables that resolve themselves in inanities and obscenities, assuring the audience that, even if they don't catch the words, they won't miss the meaning. The "meaning" is to be found precisely in the assault on the elaborate linguistic structure Kakul has himself created, composed of layers of language drawn from the distant and honored past, as well as the "high" and "low" levels of speech used in the status-conscious present. Si Mata Mata performs acts of linguistic vandalism and the audience roars with laughter.

The range of the assault broadens as Si Mata Mata proceeds to sing an "Indonesian national anthem," repeating the phrase "defend the country" over and over again in modern Indonesian. Each time the phrase is uttered in singsong fashion, the audience laughs. The joke here seems to be concerned with the awkward fit of the values extolled in Jelantik's story to the ambiguous loyalties the Balinese feel toward the contemporary nation-state of Indonesia. Kakul forces this comparison by insisting that he, Si Mata Mata, began the fighting on the beaches of Blambangan by singing this Indonesian refrain. The claim is preposterous, of course, and the audience's laughter reveals that they are in on the joke, knowing Si Mata Mata to be a braggart and a liar. I believe that the joke goes deeper, though, and that the audience's laughter may also reveal an awareness that the "truths" associated with the chronicles of the feudal past can lose their certainty when applied to the realities of the present.

Jumping from his transparently vainglorious claim to be the true hero of the dramatic events at Blambangan, Si Mata Mata next acknowledges the laughter that he has generated and points out one laughing member of the audience as "his girlfriend." The mask of Si Mata Mata makes this joke doubly funny. The mask appears to represent something between a pig and a man and the lower jaw is hinged so that when the character talks, it opens to reveal a set of wonderfully hideous crooked teeth. The aspect of this mask is as far from the heroic countenance of Jelantik as it could possibly be; and to think of this mask as the object of romantic attachment is to engage in delicious nonsense. Wearing this mask, Kakul does not simply portray a piggy man; he presents a laughable monument to human swinishness.

In this anti-heroic mask, Kakul proceeds to dance *baris*—the warrior's dance related historically, musically, and choreographically to the heroic dance of Jelantik. The performance is an hysterically funny parody. The audience delights both in Kakul's making fun of his own mastery of dance, and in the violation of the dignity and grace he brought to Jelantik's appearance in the performance oval. The effect is not, finally, to make fun of Jelantik, nor to negate the importance of his presence; rather, it is to amplify the scope of the world represented in performance so that it can contain both the feudal hero and his contemporary antithesis.

The next character to emerge, Desak Made Rai (fig. 60), further expands the scope of this world. Until her entrance, the play has been all male. The first vernacular words spoken by the Penasar Kelihan express his happiness at becoming a bachelor once again. The Penasar Cenikan takes Jelantik's suggestion that he might wish to stay with his wife rather than march off to war to be preposterous nonsense and draws the audience's laughter as he mentions the "sacrifice" of leaving home. Jelantik's heroic dance, accompanied by an all-male orchestra, is derived in part from the male skills of martial arts, and a blustering macho pride pervades the movement and speech of the Penasar Kelihan. Into this world, Desak Made Rai enters: flirting, teasing, cajoling the orchestra, and accusing a Brahmana in the audience of trying to pinch her.

Kakul's female impersonation is funny, to be sure, but the jokes here do not all poke fun at womanly ways; the masculine world that Desak Made Rai intrudes on is made fun of as well. When Kakul, as Desak Made Rai, performs dances intended for women, they are not parodied. In other dance forms in Bali, the ideal male heroes—Rama, for example, or Arjuna—are often performed by women. The understanding seems to be that in the ideal person male strength is combined with feminine grace. The world of traditional topeng is essentially masculine in its conventions and concerns, but the entrance of Made Rai partially redresses an imbalance even as it sets in motion a new line of jokes.

The appearance of the final bondres character creates an even more startling intrusion into the world of warriors, kings, and courtiers. Pulling his brightly colored and gilded cape up over his head and shoulders so as to reveal the stained white lining, Kakul emerges as Cucul, a shivering, whining peasant, far too caught up in his own domestic problems to feel himself a part of history (fig. 61). As a Sudra, an outsider, Cucul's concerns are not those of the kings, warriors, courtiers, and merchants who comprise the *triwangsa,* or upper three castes. His deeds and concerns will not be chronicled. Jelantik's noble self-sacrifice and the defeat of Sri Dalem Blambangan mean far less to him than the fact that his wife has just left him.

There is a circularity about the dialogue of the story. The first line of vernacular dialogue forms a joke about a man's happiness at being rid of his wife. The last line of vernacular dialogue is spoken by a man who is desolate because his wife has left him. The very first lines of the play tell in an almost forgotten language of "a king, rich, proud, [. . .] full of dignity" and "truly magnificent" (a king, by the way, who was in the habit of killing off his brides). The last lines of the play are spoken in plain speech by a poor man who wishes his wife would come back home. Having created a

Figure 60. Kakul as Desak Made Rai (Photo, Rucina Ballinger).

Figure 61. Kakul as Culcul.

Figure 62. The statue of an historical king recreated in the image of a Balinese dancer.

world dominated by kings and warriors, Kakul, the Sudra performer, ends the story with the image of a common man, at once comic and pathetic, caught outside the glorious world of noble heroes and demonic villains.

Once again, in a far more elaborate manner, the movement has been toward the human and the contemporary. Within each section of the performance, the same pattern is discernible. In the introductory dances, the arrogant red-faced patih yields to the lovable old man. The Penasar Kelihan yields his role as narrator to the far more prosaic Penasar Cenikan. The high-flown sung and chanted languages of the ancestral past yield to Balinese vernacular speech. The heroes and villains of the chronicles yield the playing space to the clowns of the bondres. The fantastic and eccentric Si Mata Mata yields to the all too familiar Cucul. This pattern is cyclical. Fantastic and extraordinary figures keep appearing from the remote past; but, time and again, these figures are supplanted by other figures far closer to human life as experienced in the present. It is not that the noble and demonic personages of the chronicled past are obliterated: on the contrary, topeng performances serve to keep these characters alive (see fig. 62). The performances also serve to contain these figures, though; and this playful process of reciprocal revitalization and containment is finally what topeng is all about. In the process, it celebrates the vitality of the present, as well as the grandeur of the past.

Topeng and Caste

Clifford Geertz notes that Balinese ceremonials provide "public dramatization of the ruling obsessions of Balinese culture: social inequality and status pride" (1973: 335). Certainly caste roles are important in the drama enacted by Kakul: Jelantik is aware of himself as an exemplary Satria warrior; and the kings and servants who provide the occasion and support for his actions within the dramatic world of illusion all see themselves as acting within a matrix of values and possibilities that are largely caste-determined. In Kakul's performance at Tusan though, much of the humor of the bondres section seems to play against this caste-consciousness, and in each section of the performance there is movement away from the rigors of caste-conscious behavior toward more encompassing images of humanity.

Caste, though sometimes an important determinant of behavior in Balinese life, does not determine whether or not a man may be a performer, nor what roles he may perform. Kakul, though a Sudra, is particularly well known for his depiction of refined kings, as well as for his bondres characters. There are Brahmana performers in Bali who are particularly well known as Penasars. In topeng panca and related full-company forms, it is not unheard of for a Brahmana or Satria performer to be playing a cringing servant to an overbearing prime minister played by a Sudra. After the  performance, the language conventions will be reversed and the protocol appropriate to the caste distinctions outside the theatrical roles will be reinstated. This dispersal of roles across caste lines can be played with, as when Kakul teases the Brahmana for "trying to pinch" Desak Made Rai, and, most notably, when he steps out of the role of the Penasar Kelihan to joke about himself as an "old dog" without much hair left and chastises the leader of the gamelan (who happened to be a Satria in Tusan), for playing faster than he wished.

It would be far too pat to call topeng pajegan a "ritual of status reversal" (Turner 1969: 166–203); but it is necessary to point out that, while topeng performances do dramatize situations based on "social inequality and status pride," the range of attitudes portrayed in handling these dramatic themes is complex. The most startling instance of this complexity comes in Kakul's last appearance in the playing space.

Sidha Karya: The Performer as Priest

The performance is not over. Although there will be no more mention of Jelantik and his mission, and no more jokes reflexively playing back upon his heroic actions or their contexts, Kakul will enter through the curtain and into the playing space one last time. He wears a white mask of hideous aspect, with a gaping mouth and protruding teeth—not unlike the Kirtimukha variants in Balinese temples. On his head is an unkempt wig made of horse's hair. The character is Sidha Karya (fig. 63), and his appearance is necessary in every topeng pajegan performance.

Sidha Karya is also a character from the babad, recorded as having lived during the reign of Dalem Baturenggong. But his story is independent of Jelantik's and he would appear whether or not the topeng story was "set" in Dalem Baturenggong's reign. As he himself states, his appearance is required if the event is to be "successful"; indeed, his name identifies him as the one the completes and makes successful *(sidha)* the sacred work *(karya)* of the ceremony. The story of how he got that name is worth relating here, even though there is only a single oblique reference to that story in the performance "text."

After the Hindu migrations from Majapahit, the god Mahadewa came to be associated with the "mother temple" of Besakih, high on the slopes of Gunung Agung. During the reign of Dalem Baturenggong, Dewa Mahadewa summoned a priest known as Brahmana Keling, usually identified as living in Java (but in a place called Keling), to come to Besakih. Dalem Baturenggong was preparing for a great ceremony to be held at Besakih at that time and, as preparations were being made, Brahmana Keling arrived. He told the sentries to deliver to Dalem Baturenggong the message that his brother, Brahmana Keling, wished to be received. On hearing this message, Dalem Baturenggong was puzzled and angry. He denied having any such brother, and refused to meet the wandering priest. Summarily dismissed,

Figure 63. Kakul as Sidha Karya.

Brahmana Keling warned that Dewa Mahadewa would be displeased at the king's actions. Soon after the priest's departure, a swarm of locusts descended from the sky and a horde of hungry rats devoured the rice in the fields. Famine swept the land and many died in a terrible epidemic. Without the rice, offerings could not be made and the great ceremony had to be postponed. Realizing his error, Dalem Baturenggong summoned Brahmana Keling and publicly received him as his "brother." Soon the locusts and the rats vanished. The spread of disease was stayed and rice fields once more turned green. The great ceremony at Besakih was held one year after it had been originally scheduled; and this time, Brahmana Keling officiated as high priest. Dewa Mahadewa was pleased. Brahmana Keling became known as Sidha Karya in memory of the successful event and was appointed the high priest of a temple in Denpasar, the current capital city of Bali.[15]

The story of Sidha Karya is formed around the uneasy sharing of priestly and secular power between the Brahmana and Satria castes in Hindu Bali. As noted in the previous chapter, the name of Brahmana Keling hearkens back to the ancient Kalinga empire of India, and probably places the roots of this story in the early encounters between Hindu priests and the feudal lords of Sumatra and Java, as much as in Bali. Much of the appeal of the story, though, is in its by now familiar patterning: a mysterious, threatening, and potentially destructive force is turned into a force for well-being by a process of recognition and inclusion.

In the babad story, Brahmana Keling, the potential destroyer of Bali, becomes Sidha Karya, the principal intermediator with the gods, once his divinely arranged place in the scheme of things is discovered and acknowledged. The ceremony that ends a topeng pajegan performance does not refer directly to this story, but the treatment of Sidha Karya is patterned around a knowledge of it. Sidha Karya's aspect is awesome in its ugliness and otherworldliness; yet, he is called forth as the emissary of Dewa Mahadewa, manifestation of the Holy Presence, incorporating all divinity within his person. The performance model is again that of visitation, but this time without the wrappings of dramatic illusion. Kakul, the famous dancer, must have undergone a special ritual to gain permission to wear the mask of Sidha Karya.

As Sidha Karya, Kakul will alternately take on the functional roles of ancestral character, emissary of the gods, embodiment of the godhead itself, and intercessor for the assembled audience. In short, he is a mediating figure, adjusting his role within the ritualized proceedings so as to "successfully" deliver the offerings of man to the gods and the blessings of gods to men. The languages used now are Sanskrit and Kawi—the first the medium of communication used by the priests when addressing the Hindu deities, and the second the language associated with the ancestors of Majapahit who brought those deities with them to Bali, and who are still understood to accompany the gods on their occasional visitations "into this world" and "upon this earth."

It is common in Bali for performance genres regarded as "secular" to be given as offerings on religious occasions: stories are enacted to please and amuse the divine as well as the secular audience. It is also common in Bali for acts of offering to be ritually performed with an emphasis on style and grace: the presentation of food offerings is often danced to the accompaniment of music. Topeng pajegan, also called topeng *wali* (ritual topeng), combines these two traditions. Ritual and theatrical frames cannibalize each other. During the performance, seated in a separate raised stall, a real-life priest has been preparing an offering to be used by Sidha Karya: softly speaking mantras, performing appropriate *mudras*, and occasionally ringing a small bell (fig. 64). The ritual framing of the theatrical event quietly sustained in the background is now thrust into the foreground. Ritual patterns of visitation are embraced and subsumed by theatrical presentation, and a theatrical world of illusion is in turn embraced and subsumed by ritual ceremony. The pervasive traditions of visitation pave the way for the introduction of a dramatic world, and this world is then supplanted by the enactment of a visitation.

Throughout, a playful tension is maintained between these two aesthetic traditions. As proud patih and feeble courtier, graceful king and ferocious demon, Kakul alternates including and excluding the audience. As the Penasar Kelihan, he leaps from the role of character to the role of performer and back again. As Sidha Karya, a jumping of frames occurs as Kakul alternates between being a priestly mediator and portraying an embodiment of the godhead. In the overall shape of the performance, a transformation takes place: in the introductory and "dramatic" sections, the performance is to be regarded as an offering; in the Sidha Karya section, an offering is performed. Kakul's private ritual of preparation asking for the gods' blessings leads to the performance of a public ritual in which these blessings are conferred on the community.

Kakul can only take on the role of priestly mediator because of his skills as a dancer and storyteller. A priest cannot perform the Sidha Karya ceremony himself and Kakul would not perform it without previously doing the rest of the performance. We are left with a bewildering and intriguing paradox: the village of Tusan, with a large Brahmana population, must bring in an outside performer, a Sudra, in order to complete successfully a ceremony attending the cremation of a high priest. Within the context of performance, Kakul becomes what he plays. For a time, within the mask of Sidha Karya that he is privileged to wear, he functionally *is* the "priest of dharma"—emissary from the gods and intercessor for mankind.

Kakul's last actions as Sidha Karya constitute what may be the most startling event of the whole performance. The "priest of dharma" takes the

Figure 64. A priest prepares the offering during a topeng pajegan performance. Gelgel, Klungkung, Bali, 1975.

I. Ancestral Mai masks dance at Mindimbit, Sepik River, Papua New Guinea, 1974.

11. A Bhoma head guards a corpse on its way to the cremation ground. Gianyar, Bali, 1975.

III. Narasimha is restrained in a *Prahlada Nataka* performance. Kamagunda, Ganjam, Orissa, 1983.

IV. Rangda and her daughter, Rarong, in a *Calon Arang* performance. Batuan, Bali, 1975.

V. Ida Bagus Alit in full costume performing a topeng pajegan. Sangeh, Bali, 1993.

VI. I Nyoman Kakul dances the role of Dalem Baturenggong. Tusan, Klungkung, Bali, 1975.

VII. Hajari Bhand hawks non-existent wares in the guise of a Gaduliya. Chittorgarh, Rajasthan, 1983.

VIII. The opening scene of Bertolt Brecht's *Caucasian Chalk Circle*, Brown University, Providence, RI, 1977 (set designed by John R. Lucas).

coins from Dewa Mahadewa's offering, throws them toward the children who line the inside of the audience oval, and calls to them in modern Indonesian—the language of the schools. The children scramble to pick up the coins and then run screaming as the terrifying and otherworldly Sidha Karya chases after them. Their faces register fear and thrilled excitement. Sidha Karya, who is also known as the *pengejukan*, "One-Who-Takes-People-Up-In-His-Arms" (Spies and de Zoete 1973 [1938]: 184), then grabs hold of one of the children and bears him aloft. He sets the child down next to the offering prepared for Dewa Mahadewa himself and gives the child some of the food, whereupon the excited child returns to the smiling audience. The performer takes one last turn of the playing space and, still in the mask of Sidha Karya, he exits for the last time through the curtain. There is no curtain call. The music stops. The audience slowly disperses.

Returning Home

Behind the curtain, Kakul removes his last mask. He has performed at an extraordinarily high pitch of energy for an hour and a half and is thoroughly exhausted. His face and body pour sweat. I am amazed to rediscover how tiny and vulnerable this man is who has just embodied a whole universe. The masks are blessed again and put away. As quoted by Daniel, Kakul explains the significance of this second blessing—a giving of thanks to the gods:

> The masks (have been) seen as symbols of the ancestors, and it is my sacred duty to receive their magic, to allow it to enter me and animate the masks, one after the other, until I am exhausted. After the performance, I must make the proper offerings to ensure the departure of any evil spirits who have witnessed the performance. And my offering must be great enough to provide for the return of the taksu on the next occasion of the sacred performance. This is of absolute importance, as is the gesture of thanking the gods. The sacred words (mantras) bind us to our ancestors, to their revelations—to their very existence. (1981: 140)

Layer by layer, the costume is removed. There is time for resting, joking with friends, polite exchanges with the Brahmana and Satria patrons, the drinking of a strong, clear, distilled liquor called *arak*, and the eating of another big meal. Two of Kakul's sons and several more performers arrive. There will be another topeng performance later that night, this time a secular performance (without Sidha Karya) involving nine actors, including Kakul. A rain squall moves past, causing a delay, and this performance does not start until well after eleven o'clock, and it lasts until about four o'clock in the morning. The rows of children are often asleep now, lying one upon another and waking to appreciate bits of bondres. In between appearances, the performers catch naps behind the curtain. Despite the hour, the audience remains large and appreciative, sometimes chatting as the story slowly unfolds, other times caught up in the antics and entanglements of the story's characters or arrested by the virtuosity of a dance.

After the last character swirls through the curtain, the actors sit together talking, joking, resting, waiting for dawn and the first mini-truck for Batuan. It comes and all pile in, crowding two deep amidst the baskets of costumes and masks. Some of the performers will go directly to the rice fields, while others are free to go home. In a corner of the jouncing mini-truck, Kakul lies with his head against a basket, his work finished, his face serene in sleep.

Notes

1. Earlier versions of this chapter and the translation that follows appeared under the same titles in *The Drama Review* 23, 2 (T82: 1979). I have reinserted some quotations and observations that were omitted from the original article due to space and format constraints, have corrected a few mistakes, added some connective tissue, taken the opportunity to cite Kakul's words as reported by Ana Daniel, another of his students, and added citations to suggest further readings.

Research on topeng was undertaken in Bali in 1975, 1980, 1991, and 1993. Ida Bagus Alit, Ida Bagus Ambara, Ida Bagus Anom, I Nyoman Catra, I Wayan Dibia, I Ketut Kantor, I Made Regug, I Nyoman Sumandhi, I Wayan Tedun, and I Gusti Windia have all taught me a great deal about the nature and use of Balinese masks in my various trips to Bali. In this country, Rucina Ballinger, Amy Catlin, Fredrik deBoer, Andrew Toth, John Steven Lansing, I Nyoman Sedana and I Nyoman Wenten all made helpful suggestions. I am grateful, also, to Richard Wallis and A. L. Becker for lending me copies of their then unpublished works. Finally, there is a pervasive debt to I Made Bandem, who transcribed and co-translated my tape of Kakul's performance, and to I Wayan Suweca, with whom I worked for three years.

2. There are "weeks" of various lengths for various purposes in Bali, and the 210-day cycle is held to be auspicious and worthy of marking since the one, two, three, five, six, and seven day weeks again line up in the same positions at that interval. 420 days is an even more auspicious cycle since the four day week lines up then, too; but that would be too long to wait to honor the gods or celebrate a holiday. Each of Bali's estimated 20,000 temples (not counting shrines within family complexes) calculates its own odalan cycle, so that—even though many of the temples are small—there is an ample demand for performances on the island, especially when the more personal landmarks celebrated by families are factored in. For more on Balinese calendars and their relation to ceremonial occasions, see Eiseman (1989: 173–92), C. Geertz (1973: 389–404), and Lansing (1983a: 53–57). For accounts of Balinese odalan, see Belo (1966 [1953]), Dibia (1985) and Eiseman (1989: 249–64). For accounts of life-cycle ceremonies for individuals, see Mershon (1971) and Eiseman (1989: 84–126).

3. For more on the caste system in Bali, see H. and C. Geertz (1975) and Eiseman (1989: 25–37).

The aesthetic preference for filling in all "potential spaces" is pervasive in Bali (cf. Bateson 1972c [1967]: 149–52). I once asked a painter in Batuan, I Ketut Kantor, one of Kakul's sons and a fine dancer in his own right, which of three paintings by himself he liked best. He unhesitatingly pointed to one of them. To me, all three were equally fine, and I asked why he preferred that particular one. "It has more painting in it," he quickly replied—the canvas was better filled. The preference is never so evident as at ceremonial occasions, and at these times topeng forms but one part—though a vital one—in a busy and intricate tapestry of events. A Mitsui film, *Catur Marga*, shows some of this layering of events, as does Steven Lansing's film, *Three Worlds of Bali*.

4. For an explanation and diagram of the topeng costume, see Dunn (1983: 52–54). Dunn's dissertation is a good source for more specific details about topeng pajegan. The most standard source about Balinese masks in Indonesian is Bandem and Rembang (1976).

5. In the original published version of this chapter (1979), I underestimated the role of visitation in Indian religion and performance, stressing a "Papuan underlay" to Balinese culture in accounting for the prevalence of trance phenomena. While this is not necessarily completely false, the case is far more complex. See the final section of the previous chapter.

6. Translation by I Wayan Suweca and myself (unpublished).

7. Compare the following remarks by Peter Brook. His international company had gleefully and thoughtlessly started to play with a set of new masks brought from Bali, appalling the Balinese actor who had brought them:

> A mask is two-way traffic all the time; it sends a message in and projects a message out. It operates by the law of echoes: if the echo chamber is perfect, the sound going in and the one going out are reflections; there is a perfect relation between the echo chamber and the sound. But if it isn't, it is like a distorted mirror. Here, when the actors sent back a distorted response, the mask itself took on a distorted face. The minute they started again, with quiet and respect, the masks looked different and the people inside them *felt* different. (1987: 220)

One summer, I had the pleasure of teaching in the same program with Carlo Mazzoni-Clementi. As we compared approaches, it was clear that there was a similar process in wearing the masks of Italian commedia—masks that are also both of a type and very particular in their demands on the individual performer. Dario Fo's comments on wearing commedia masks confirm this observation:

> Adapting oneself to the mask is a result of exercise and attention, of technique but equally of instinct. The feel of a mask of a certain structure on one's face, of a mask that forces one to assume a particular appearance and a definite character, involves the choice of precise models of gesture. The various masks which I wear [. . .] compel me to continually change rhythm, timing, and in some cases vocal tonality. Furthermore, I find myself obliged, by awareness and instinct, to heighten or diminish the value of those creatures and attitudes by a shift in the rhythmic progression—pushing onto the legs deliberately but with suppleness, moving and balancing the limbs, or jerking forward while keeping the legs rigid, after the manner of puppets. (1987: 70)

Topeng masks—and Barong masks, also—are made of the soft and light *punyan pule* wood (*alstonia scholaris*) in Bali. This same tree is known as white cheesewood or milky pine in Australia. For detailed accounts of mask-making in Bali, see Eiseman (1990: 207–19); Dunn (1983: 90–113); and Slattum (1992: 124–27). For accounts of Balinese dance training, see Ballinger (1978); Pitt (1982); and Dunn (1983: 109–13, 141–57). More general notes on Asian theatrical training apply from Schechner (1985: 213–60) and Barba (1986, 1991).

8. Dunn (1983: 192–211) includes detailed descriptions, diagrams, and photographs of basic choreographies for the patih, tua, and dalem as taught by Kakul's son, I Ketut Kantor. For an analysis and transcription of some of the music used for topeng see McPhee (1966) and Tenzer (1991: 57–71).

9. Kakul's great rival from Badung, I Pugra, introduced an alternative to the tua which is still occasionally used by others. This is the topeng *munyer*, an effeminate, preening young man with a huge silly smirk on his face and a fan in his hand. The result is similar, in that the topeng munyer flirts with the audience, making more direct contact, has no pretensions of martial glory, and seems much more a part of the world of the present than of the past. It is an exception that shows the strength purpose of the rule.

10. Overviews of the history of Balinese principalities and their links to Majapahit are given in C. Geertz (1980) and Vickers (1989: 38–76). For synopses of the *babad dalem* see de Zoete and Spies (1973 [1938]: 294–311) and Young (1980: 251–62). Worsley (1972) has translated and written a commentary on the *Babad Buleleng.*

11. There is a striking similarity to the "great chain of being" in early Renaissance thought and literature described by Lovejoy (1960 [1936]) and applied to Shakespeare's plays by Tillyard (1943). Indeed, *A Midsummer Night's Dream,* with its complex play with earthly and cosmological hierarchies, comes very near to the Balinese theatrical imagination, as does Shakespeare's predilection for shadowing his "serious" plots with comic variations.

12. For information on the history and traditional practice of topeng panca, see de Zoete and Spies (1973 [1938]: 178–95); Bandem and deBoer (1981: 95–96); and Young (1980: 77–153). Jenkins (1994: 13–45) gives a fascinating report on recent developments of the form, with extensive quotations by I Nyoman Catra and I Gusti Windia, two of Bali's best comic topeng performers at present.

13. Shelly Errington examines the effect of tenseless narrative on a classical Malay text and stresses the difference between such texts (*hikayat*) and what we usually refer to as "history": "Hikayat and other forms convert the impermanent and transitory events of this world into something which endures, at least as it is spoken. Or rather, they do not so much convert transitory events as perpetuate them, carry them into the present in their telling" (1979: 244). Surely, there is an element of this in the retelling of tales from the past within the contexts of the present that marks topeng—one that is reinforced by the referencing of traditions of ancestral visitation. If I am correct in my reading of Kakul's performance, though, a sense of historical difference also plays an important role in his complex use of language(s)—and this sense of historical difference acts as a source of humor and critical commentary (see chapters 5 and 6).

14. Wallis (1979) treats the use of the "alus," "keras," and "kasar" typology in an *arja* performance. Emigh and Hunt (1992: 204–5) relate this typology to ideas about gender. In dealing with Javanese wayang plots, Becker stresses the coinciding of such divergent "epistemologies" as an organizing principle (1979: 224). Anderson (1965) similarly stresses the use of wayang typologies as a means of categorizing and discussing various approaches to life.

15. See also Slattum (1992: 27) and Dunn (1983: 71–80) for other versions of the story and further myths associated with Sidha Karya's character. A brief topeng pajegan version of this story by I Nyoman Catra (1989) has been translated.

Chapter 4
Jelantik Goes to Blambangan: A Topeng Pajegan Performance

I Nyoman Kakul

As Recorded at Tusan, Klungkung, Bali on February 6, 1975

Translated by I Made Bandem and John Emigh

Language Key

During this performance, I Nyoman Kakul speaks in seven different languages, including the distinct status levels within Balinese (see preceding chapter). To differentiate between the various languages and status levels, lines have been set in different typefaces, as follows:

When Kakul speaks in Sanskrit, his words look like this.
When Kakul speaks in Kawi, his words look like this.
When Kakul speaks in Middle Javanese, his words look like this.
When Kakul speaks in High Balinese, his words look like this.
When Kakul speaks in Median Balinese, his words look like this.
When Kakul speaks in Low Balinese, his words look like this.
When Kakul speaks in modern Indonesian, his words look like this.
Stage directions and other explanatory material are set in ordinary italics.

There are three introductory dances depicting a proud warrior, an antic minister, and an aged courtier. The curtain shakes again and the performer re-enters, wearing a purple half-mask with round, bulging eyes. This is the Penasar Kelihan, the "older" storyteller. His bearing is proud, his voice commanding, his laughter hearty, his gestures and dancing flamboyant. Gamelan *music accompanies the entire performance.*

Penasar Kelihan:

(singing snatches from the Kidung Tantri *in Middle Javanese, an archaic, courtly language associated with the theatrical heritage of the Majapahit Empire of east Java):*

A story is told of the King of Patali, rich, proud, and full of dignity. *(dances proudly)* Truly Magnificent! Proceeding now! Aat!

(dancing, mixed with exclamations and laughter)

Ah! Ha, ha, ha, ha! Arah! Hi, hi, hi! Ha, ha, ha!

(chanting lines from the Mahabharata *in Kawi, or Old Javanese, a language introduced to Bali in the tentth entury and still used in the shadow puppet theatre and in chanting the Javanized Indian epics)*

At dawn, the red sun rises. The rustling of leaves on the mountainside joins the harmonious sounds of the frogs, large and small. (exclaiming and dancing some more) Aat!

I'm so happy! So happy! I never get bored, telling you about my happiness! Like today! Why don't I get bored, talking about my happiness? Ayah! Hi, hi, hi! Heh! Why am I so happy? Because, I just now became a bachelor again! Hi, hi, hi!

Oh my Lord and King, I try to follow you loyally. I beseech you, lay not your curse upon me, for I am going to tell your story now. Singeh! Singeh! Please! Please! I pay homage to the ancestors, to those who are already holy. And to the divine trinity, the Holy Lords Wisnu, Brahma, and Iswara. And I pay homage as well to all those who would make the countryside peaceful and prosperous here in ancient Bali. I ask for your blessings. I beseech you not to lay your curses upon me.

And why? Why do I offer up these prayers? Because, I am about to tell you of my Lord, the King here in Gelgel, Klungkung, the great Dalem Baturenggong.

(chanting from the Ramayana*) Spinning round on his tail, the son of Subah rises higher and higher.*

(Dances, then speaks, affecting the local Klungkung dialect) **Aduh! What a chase those noblemen in the orchestra gave me! Now I'm worn out! Already too tired to give you a show! Mind you, I don't mean to criticize. Not just yet. It's my first time here. My first time dancing with these musicians. Their first time playing with me. And I'm very old-fashioned. Just like an old dog! There's not much fur left on my hide and what there is of it is very short. Beh! Moving on!**

My Lord and Master, Dalem Baturenggong, is the ruler of this kingdom. His mind is troubled now, filled with thoughts of His Royal Highness, His Majesty, the King of Blambangan.

What could have broken up their old friendship? Wah! My King sent a proposal of marriage to the Princess of Blambangan, the King's own daughter, Diah Gusti Ayu Nipang. He sent along a portrait, too. A very fine portrait, bearing an exact likeness of my Lord. So how did things get so screwed up? That portrait got fiddled with. By the jealous Princess Diah Bima Cili of Pasurahan. And now, to judge from that portrait, my Lord is fat! With a big fat nose! And bowlegged and splay-footed, too! And Gusti Ayu Nipang isn't so sure that she wants him anymore. And all this has left my Lord and King in a terrible mood! Oh, mother! So much for peacefulness here in ancient Bali! Ruled over by my Lord and King, like an incarnation of the Holy Lord Wisnu himself!

(reciting from the Mahabharata*) Since time immemorial, the warrior's path has been one of action.*

And now the King gathers his closest advisors about him to choose the right man to lead his forces into Java. Keyai Blangsinga is his closest advisor. And next to him, Penget Yeh. To Blambangan! To Pasurahan! Someone must go! Let it be done! Nah! Wah!

(Still speaking in Median Balinese, the Penasar Kelihan now speaks as Dalem Baturenggong. He does not assume completely new voices or characters for these quotations, but remains a storyteller, quoting personages involved in the story with an animated sense of their characters and presence.)

"Honored counselors, all of you who assemble here, what is to be done? Who could best go to Blambangan?"

(reciting from the Mahabharata*)* The answer comes quickly. ***O God-chosen King, I do not hesitate to venture my life in your service.*** *(laughing)* Oh, ho! Ha, ha, ha, ha, ha!

(as Counselors) ***"Oh Lord and Majesty, we shall tell you the man to send as your champion. His lineage is from the Satria warriors of Kediri. His name is I Gusti Jelantik Made Tengahan. On the field of battle, he is the most stalwart of men. Your Holiness, send forth no one but this man. Long ago, he dedicated his life to your wishes. Let him go forth!"***

(reciting from the Mahabharata*) When a warrior is brave, he is dedicated to action. His innermost thoughts are of the battlefield. When a warrior is resolute, he will always find action on the field of battle. The satria caste will scourge the earth of selfishness and human greed.*

(as Jelantik) ***"You are pre-eminent among kings, my Lord."***

(as King) "Release the bonds that oppress the soul."

(as Jelantik) ***"So be it! Let the task fall to me! I shall defend the macrocosmos and microcosmos, the order of the spiritual world and the order of the physical world. For the microcosmos finds expression in the body of every man. And I shall be your Majesty's true champion."***

Bih! His answer to the King is very brave! He would follow the example laid down in the story of *Gatutkaca Seraya*:

(reciting from the Mahabharata*) Over there, Gatutkaca stands. Speak now as a brave son. Kresna already knows you must face the invincible Karna.*

I, too, will be brave.

Wih! Wih! Wih! Pack up! Pack up, servants! Get ready for a fight! *(singing and dancing)* Ndaaaaaaa! *(laughing)* Aruh! Hi, hi, hi. Eh! *(with*

Klungkung dialect) **I'm winded! Out of breath! Dancing too fast! I was almost stumbling there at the end. Hi, hi, hi. Ha, ha, ha, ha! Aduh!**

I could go on forever, talking about the wisdom and greatness of my Lord and King. Whoever is obedient to the King, whoever is steadfast in his service to the King, that man shall go forth as the King's true champion. Yes! Yes! And now the King himself is on his way.

The Prime Minister and all the honored counselors are ready to greet you in the hall of justice. I beseech you, your Majesty, come forward!

(singing from the Kidung Malat, *used in the* gambuh *theatre)* **His shape is so beautiful. His face is so radiant. Before entering the hall, he glances in the mirror and adjusts his temple dress.** *(departing from the* Kidung Malat *text)* Like he's off to the market in Batavia-a-a. *(laughing)* Oh! He, he, he! Ah! Ha, ha, ha! *(singing from the* Kidung Malat, *while the gamelan begins the introductory music for the Dalem's entrance)* **The air is transformed. It is all gentleness and prettiness.**

(as King) "My loyal servants, Open now your ears and hear me well."

(as Counselors) ***"We await your words, oh Lord."***

(as King) "Approach my person now, loyal followers of mine, and take your proper places behind me."

(singing from the Kidung Malat*)* **A small ring is a bracelet for the finger. (spoken) Thus is the world constructed! Ah!**

And now, my honored Lord, I beseech you to pray to the gods.

After the robes of majesty are in place, my Lord, then pray to the Supreme God, lest you receive his curse. (singing) Beautiful, beautiful! See how beautiful!

Pay homage to the gods, that you be not cursed.

(singing from the Kidung Malat*)* **You will come forth, dancing beautifully.**

(as King) ***"Inggih! I salute the Supreme God!"***

"I would receive your blessings now. And also a blessing upon my people."

"My ministers, my people, you must give me your prayers."

"I would now come forth among you."

(as Counselors) ***"Please, come forth, my Lord."***

Dalem Baturenggong:

(Kakul exits as the Penasar Kelihan. As the gamelan plays the King's theme, Kakul changes his mask and headdress and re-enters with the handsome white mask of Dalem Baturenggong, King of Gelgel. The King dances and then exits. The music alters and Kakul again changes his mask and headgear. He re-enters in the half-mask of the Penasar Cenikan, or younger storyteller, named I Ketut Rai. He is without the pretensions of the first storyteller, his walk is more natural, his gestures less flamboyant, his speech more colloquial.)

Penasar Cenikan

(singing from the Kidung Malat*):* **Dressed up in temple clothes, I go to see my love.**

Once more, Prince Karna's story is told.

Aduh! Ah, ha, ha! Here it comes! Karna's story again! Only our hero now is I Gusti Jelantik. What is he feeling, deep in his heart? To lose the battle would be shameful. He must preserve the honor and happiness of Gelgel.

(singing) ***The King's command must be obeyed.***

Aiee! Beh! Nah! But hold on! *(To the gamelan leader, using his caste title)* Slowly, slowly, Cakorda! Let's not get ahead of ourselves! Me, I'm happy! And without eating a thing! I'm happy just getting ready for this battle. A man like Jelantik can set a good example for the people here in Gelgel.

(singing) ***In the end, there will be happiness.***

And why? I'm just a servant. Only a servant. But since I follow a lord who practices *dharma,* a man of the battlefield, why then, even though I'm only of the *Wesia* caste myself, I can be a warrior, too. Just call me Ketut Rai the Invincible!

I would venture my soul for my country, for Gelgel. Listen now to my words, for I am a follower of the great I Gusti Jelantik Made Tengahan!

Pih! That Jelantik was brave and cool, talking to the King.

Rejoice! For Jelantik Made Tengahan will be the defender of the country!

Ah, ha, ha! The King says, "Honored sir, are you ready to go to Blambangan?" And Jelantik answers.

(as Jelantik) ***"So be it, my Lord! Let me go forth! Do not trouble yourself further!"***

(with Klungkung dialect) I am told by I Gusti Patih Jelantik, "You are my servant. Of course, you should come with me and obey my orders." That's what he tells me! "But if you are afraid of dying, why don't you just sleep with your wife at home?" That's what he says to me!

"How else can I prove my devotion to you? On what occasion, if not now? You needn't speak further. For many years now, I have served you faithfully as your loyal retainer. It would be impossible for me to turn my back upon you now. Your kindnesses to me have been many. How shall I bear them? How can I ever repay you?"

That's really what I said to him! So, follow him I will!

(reciting from the Mahabharata*) The brave man shall be victorious upon the field of battle.*

"If you should emerge victorious from the field of battle, then all the gods and celestial nymphs will pay homage to you. But if you should taste defeat upon the field of battle, then you shall be punished by Sang Hyang Yama Depati on the day of your judgment. Eh? Is that not true? You suggest that I might turn my back upon the call to battle. No! Even though I must leave my wife! Nothing could stop me from venturing forth."

(as Jelantik) "Nah! Nah! If that's the way it is, then let's get going."

"So be it, my Lord."

Eh, he he! "But before we leave," says I Gusti Patih Jelantik, "I would speak with my wife, Ni Gusti Ayu Samwantiga. This is a precious time for us, for she is now bearing our child."

"Yes, my Lord. What will you say to her?"

(as Jelantik) "My love, it is true. I must go now and leave you. The King has ordered me to go to Blambangan to seize victory for him on the field of battle. Why must this be? Listen. Listen, for there is a great deal that I must tell you now. Long ago, my father was Prime Minister here in Gelgel. Knowing this, I have questioned the high priest in front of all the assembled ministers. 'My priest,' I have said, 'If a man should become a person of great power, what are the dangers for him, and what are the joys?' "

(reciting from the Mahabharata*) The answer is not long in coming.*

(as Priest) "My son, Jelantik Made Tengahan, if a man of responsibility and power falls in love with his own father's wife, the fortunes of the entire country will suffer and decline."

(as Jelantik) ***"Inggih! But what is the proper action for me? Speak to me so that I may understand. What should I do now?"***

(as Priest) "Properly, you should tear up your ministerial robes, burn them, and throw the ashes into the ocean. That would be correct."

(exclaiming) Beh! Beh!

(as Priest) "But you are a man much honored in this land and one who carries the word of the King. There are many who depend upon you. You cannot afford to act rashly."

(as Jelantik) ***"I am aware of this and do not wish to set a bad example for my people. My priest, please advise me and I shall follow wherever your words may lead."***

That's what he said! Pih! Aduh! I feel so sorry for him. I don't know how long ago these problems began. But some time ago, a voice came rising up from the Unda River in Batu Kerotok. "Son! My son! Jelantik Made Tengahan!" Beh! "My beloved child! My precious nugget of gold!" A cowherd came ambling by. Beh! Just a young boy. "Please! Go and get my son, I Gusti Jelantik Tengahan." Beh!

(as Cowherd) **"Who's that talking in the river? A demon? A spirit? What is it?**

(exclaiming) Nah!

(as Voice) **"Get going! And repeat what you heard to my son."**

(as Cowherd) "Yes! Yes! But what's happening? I don't understand."

Fortunately, I Gusti Jelantik Made Tengahan was sitting in his courtyard.

(as Jelantik) **"Why do you come rushing into the courtyard like this?"**

(as Cowherd) ***"Noble Sir, I heard a voice coming from the Unda River. A voice calling out your name."***

(as Jelantik) **"What voice? Saying what?"**

(as Cowherd, quoting Voice) "Son! My son! Ngurah Jelantik Made Tengahan! Help! It's your father! If you don't rescue me from my curse, I can never reach *sorga*, never go to heaven."

(as Jelantik) **"Really?!"**

And then I Gusti Jelantik picked up a fishing net and played at catching fish.

(as Jelantik) "I'm not sure about this. The cowherd may not be telling the truth."

So he started for the river. And he brought the fishing net with him.

"My honored lord," I say, ***"I wish to accompany you. I truly do."***

(as Jelantik) **"Beh! You go with me?"**

"Please, my lord. I wish to accompany you."

(as Jelantik) **"All right, let's go then. We'll look for some shrimp. Did you bring any bait?"**

"No, my lord."

(as Jelantik) **"Well, go get some bait!"**

We arrive at the Unda River. Beh! We throw the fishing net out to the south. Nothing!

(as Jelantik) **"Where did the cowherd say that voice was coming from?"**

Still nothing there! We throw the net out to the north. Beh! Nothing there, either. By now we're ready to throw away the net. Seret! Pleh! Then we see something shaped like a beetle-nut canister. But it's as large as a ceremonial umbrella. Beh! It's a leech as big as a roofing mat! Aduh! There's the leech, all curled up. And hairy, too. Beh! Mun, mun, mun! That big!

"What could it be, I Gusti Patih?"

(as Jelantik) **"Quiet! Shush!"**

Aduh! Aduh!

(as Leech) "Son! My son! Ngurah Jelantik Made Tengahan! I am your father. Come. Come closer to me. I committed a terrible sin one day, after coming home from the palace at Gelgel. I arrived at home, I entered the house, and I went to bed. My father's wife was lying there. I slept with her that night. And now, if you do not release me from this curse, my life shall never be complete and I shall stay forever in this hellish state."

(as Jelantik) ***"Father, what can I do to release you from this dreadful curse?"***

(as Leech) "The only way is for you to die in the midst of battle. Only if you die on the battlefield, can I end this horrible water-bound existence as a leech."

(as Jelantik) ***"Yes, father. Please. Be at peace now. Allow me to do this for you. I shall become the defender of the macrocosmos and the microcosmos, of the spiritual order and of the physical order, an order that***

finds expression in my own body. I shall sacrifice my life for my father at the same time that I defend the Kingdom of Gelgel."

Nah! All right! Getting on with the story!

Inggih! Inggih! Gusti Patih Jelantik! Come forth! The time has come for you to reveal yourself! Ndaaaaaa!

(Kakul dances briefly as the Penasar Cenikan and then exits through the curtain. He continues to talk from behind the curtain as he changes his headgear and mask for the entrance of I Gusti Jelantik Made Tengahan. First he sings lines from the Kidung Malat *in Middle Javanese in order to give the orchestra a musical pattern to use for Jelantik's entrance and dance.)*

Beautiful rocky heights! Beautiful rocky heights! So beautiful is the sound of the beaten gong!

(as Jelantik) **"Nah! Nah! Get us ready servants!"**

Inggih! Inggih! Gusti! The time is now at hand for my lord to venture forth!

Now his entrance! Now the entrance of I Gusti Ngurah Jelantik Tengahan! If you were to search for another like him, you could only compare him to the Holy Lord Brahma. No one else! Now his departure is at hand! He will pray to the six mother temples of Bali. No one can stop him from going forth. Eh!

Patih Jelantik:

(The curtain shakes and Kakul enters as I Gusti Ngurah Jelantik Made Tengahan. Wearing a handsome orange-tinted mask that covers his whole face, he dances, then exits through the curtain. After Kakul has changed his mask and headgear, the voice of the Penasar Kelihan is heard from behind the curtain.)

Penasar Kelihan:

Pih! His prayer!

Oh, my lord!

(chanting) With scepter in hand, with the knowledge of Saraswati, he prays to the gods. Holy water from the Ganges completes the ceremony.

(The curtain shakes and the Penasar Kelihan enters, speaking) ***Beh! Almost daybreak!***

Meneh! Feel the difference? Beh! The signal for daybreak comes down from the mother temple of Besakih! Beh!

(In the section that follows, Kakul as Penasar Kelihan will repeatedly sing passages from the Javanese Mahabharata, *then roughly translate those passages into the vernacular.)*

At the foot of the mountain, they awake at dawn.

Aduh! They wake up at dawn.

Like shadow puppets shimmering upon a screen.

That's the feeling. Just like shadow puppets on the screen.

The concatenation of the frogs signals daybreak.

Bih! The rushing, cascading sounds of the big frogs. *(imitating the inter-*

locking sounds of the frogs with a rhythmic chant) Ke kung ke ke kung ke kung. Ke kung ke ke kung ke kung.

Answered now by the small frogs.

And the little frogs answer.

Over there, on the far bank of the river.

From the far bank of the river. Beh! A man no longer thinks of his home. He no longer imagines himself in Gelgel.

The cascading of the water.

Beh! The water rushes by.

He dreams no more of returning home.

He no longer wants to go home.

The banks of the river are beautiful! There will I pay homage to the gods.

He makes his offerings.

(singing) ***The priest's wife awakens with her husband. They attend to his duties, singing*** **Malat** ***and blessing the offerings.***

Malat is sung and the offerings blessed.

Inggih! Inggih, Gusti!

(spoken) Prepare yourself. Now he goes to fight Sri Dalem Blambangan. Irika!

Dalem Blambangan:

(Kakul exits through the curtain as Penasar Kelihan and changes into the mask used for the King of Blambangan. This is a mask of the demonic type, with bulging eyes, enormous pig tusks, a protruding tongue, and a hole above the tongue to speak through. He also puts on fur-tufted white gloves with long, quivering, buffalo horn fingernails attached. He perches himself on the back of a chair and begins to speak and shake the curtain vigorously.)

Irika! Yeh! Oh! Ha, ha! Luweh! Ih, ih, ih! Eh! Luweh! Ehhh! Behold, here I come, King of Blambangan! Prepare yourselves! Beware! Yeh! Kascarya! Uduhhh!

(Kakul yanks the curtain open, revealing himself as King of Blambangan, perched loftily on his throne. He continues to speak, reaching through the curtain opening towards the audience and making his long fingernails tremble.)

Ehh! Eh, eh, eh, eh! Who are you people? What do you want here? Ih, ih, ih, ih! Give me your names! What land are you from? Come, come! Speak! At once! Irika! Speak up! Speak up!

(The torso and arms of Dalem Blambangan move to frenzied music. The curtain is then pulled shut and Kakul changes his mask and headgear and re-enters through the curtain as the Penasar Cenikan.)

Penasar Cenikan:

Beh! Such a short fight! The King of Blambangan is dead. Aduh! Ha, ha! The timing was perfect. My lord caught sight of Dalem Blambangan strolling along the beach. *(with Klungkung dialect)* Ahh! We just rolled right over him. He was helpless! *(dropping dialect)* How could the King of Blambangan be killed so easily? Because, long ago he received the curse of Pedanda Bawurawah, high priest of Majapahit. That's true! And now, the warriors return to Gelgel. But my Holy Lord . . . I mean my noble lord! I got mixed up! Well, anyway, I'm out here all alone, so I can say whatever I want! Ha, ha, ha! Now the warriors return, but my noble lord Jelantik has found death on the field of battle. He must be cremated now. Sampunika! Like that! Nah! Nah!

(as Dalem Baturenggong) "Jelantik is gone, but, since Jelantik's wife is now carrying his child, when that child is born we shall name him I Gusti Jelantik Bogol, Jelantik the Brave. And now, since the honor of the country has been defended, there must be ceremonies and celebrations. Let there be splendid performances in three days' time!"

(Kakul exits through the curtain and changes his mask and headgear. The curtain shakes and he re-enters in a mask with a hinged jaw as Si Mata Mata, half pig and half man, One-Who-Looks-Out-For-Himself.)

Si Mata Mata:

(sneezing) Ahchoo! Ahhhchoo! *(nonsense syllables mixed with median and low Balinese)* Ah! Ka, ka, ka, ka. Ka, ko, ko, ke, ka, ke. Ne, ni, ni, ni, ni. Ih, ih, ih, ih. Ay, ay, ay. Aw, aw, aw, off to the palace! Where is it? Off I go now! Hu, hu, hu, hu, hu. Pi, pi, pi, piss, pistachio! Nice! Where now? Sa, sa, sa, sa, sa. Ra, ra, ra, ra, ra. Hi, hi, hi, hi, hi. Don't worry if you don't catch the words, you won't miss the meaning! Sa, sa, sa, sa.

(singing) Defend the country. Defend the country. Defend the country. Defend the country. Defend the country. Defend the country.

That's an Indonesian national anthem for you!

(singing) Remember the gods. Remember the gods. Remember the gods. Remember the gods.

Now I have something I want to say. I followed my lord Gusti Jelantik to Blambangan. I was right there at the head of the army. Started the fighting myself! I did it like this.

(singing) Defend the country. Defend the country. Defend the country. Defend the country. Indonesia!!

Beh! My girlfriend is laughing over there. That's enough about that! In three days' time, I'll be dancing baris. *(imitating the drum pattern of the* baris *dance)* Ka pang an tuk. Ka pang an tuk. Ka pang an tuk. Ka pang an tuk. Wait! Wait! I want to do the real dance now:

(Si Mata Mata begins to dance a parody of the baris, a warrior's dance related rhythmically and historically to the heroic dance that Jelantik performed earlier.) What's next? Bapang, bapang!

(The gamelan starts to play the bapang *section of the* baris *dance, which is also parodied.)* Aduh! I'm tired! Worn out!

(Kakul exits through the curtain. He changes his mask and headgear and reenters in the half-mask of a woman, Desak Made Rai. The character moves with all the coquetry and sly humor of a middle-aged woman who has known life too well for too long.)

Desak Made Rai:

(singing from the Kidung Malat*)* **I gather flowers and give them to you to make you irresistible.**

(laughing) Ah ha!

My lord, I don't know what to do now. There have already been enough performances to complete the ceremonies. Baris has been performed. And* arja. *And gambuh. Performances for three days in a row! Beh! Oh, those* Brahmana *over there are laughing at me. And that one tried to pinch me! I wonder if he'll do that when we're alone. If he does, I'll be very nice to him! Well, I could dance* sutri *for you. No? What about a* legong *dance? The story of Lasem? Or* jobeg*? Please, orchestra, won't you play one of them for me? No? Oh well! Forgive me. I can't perform sutri for you. Maybe another dance then? Oh, dear!

(Kakul exits through the curtain. He changes his mask and pulls his gold-painted cape up over his head and shoulders so as to show the stained white inner lining. He re-enters in the character of Cucul, a miserable villager who seems to be shivering with the chills.)

Cucul:

Aduh! Such a crowd of people gathered in the palace courtyard. All of them so happy! And here I am, so sad and miserable. I don't have any wife. Don't have any children. My wife has gone and left me. Aduh! Bih! If anyone comes to find me, please call out my name. "Brother! Brother Wayan!" What are you thinking about me? Sometimes I feel so dumb! I used to have a wife. There were times when she wouldn't come home for three days in a row. Even though she promised she would never leave me. Nyoman! Nyoman! Aduh! You're so thoughtless and fickle, Nyoman, leaving me like this. All the happy people crowding around, too! If I don't go to the palace now, what shall I do? You've left me feeling like a shattered stone. Nyoman! Nyoman! Won't you please come back home? Aduh! I'd be so happy, if she would only come back home. Aduh!

(Kakul exits through the curtain. The story is over, but the music changes and Kakul puts on a white mask with a gaping mouth, prominent teeth, and an unkempt wig. He will re-enter as Sidha Karya, a priest during the reign of Dalem Baturenggong, who must end each performance of topeng pajegan by performing ritual ceremonies that confer a blessing upon the village.)

Sidha Karya:

(laughing and exclaiming while shaking the curtain from behind) Eh! Ehhh! Ohhh! Ohh! Singeh! Aat! Ohh! Ohhh! Ih, ih, ih, ih, ih, ih! Ih, ih, ih, ih, ih, ih!

Now the Holy Presence arrives. Now Sidha Karya appears. Coming now, into this world.

(chanting the beginnings of a mantra*)* **Om. Earth, air, and heavenly ether.**

(chanting a passage from the Mahabharata*) In a beauteous place, he encounters the devout king.*

(speaking) Make haste! Now he arrives upon this earth!

(Kakul enters through the curtain as Sidha Karya and chants the following dialogue in the manner of a priest, often addressing Dewa Mahadewa, god of the Besakih temple.) Oh Divine Lord, you come down to earth, accompanied by all of your celestial followers, drawn as they are from the several castes. All gods descend now in your person. The people assembled here dedicate these offerings unto you. Please do not feel slighted that this is only a **suci**, *a simple rice cake offering. It will be followed by a* **daksine** *offering of coconut, eggs, rice, cakes, and old coins. There is also a* **tebasan** *offering, especially prepared for Sidha Karya, with rice, peanuts, and chicken brought from Sidha Karya's own village, from Badung. And there is a tebasan* **durmanggala** *offering, all wrapped in coconut leaves to form the shape of a huge gong. This offering is intended for your enjoyment. And to welcome you here, there is a* **prasjengan** *offering, prepared with the meat of a chicken. Please, accept these offerings as your own. (crying out and dancing) Aat! Aat! Aat!*

(As Sidha Karya continues to dance, he sounds the ten magic syllables used to formulate spells in the practice of both white and black magic in Bali.) Sa, Ba, Ta, A, I, Nang, Mang, Sing, Wang, Ya. (crying out) Aat! Aat! Aat! Make haste! Ih, ih, ih, ih, ih.

(chanting in the manner of a priest) Please accept this offering of food. (He cries out, dances, and then mimics Dewa Mahadewa's eating of the offering.) Aat! Aat! Aat! (chanting in the manner of a priest) The offering is now accepted.

(Still chanting in the manner of a priest, he unwraps the gong-shaped tebasan durmanggala.*) This rice, also, is for you to eat. This money is dedicated to you as well. Two hundred* **kepeng** *in old Chinese coins. A ball of thread for weaving forms a part of the tebasan durmanggala, your special offering. All this has been offered unto you. Please accept this offering. Please accept this offering.*

(He hands the offering to a priest, who sprinkles holy water on it while the performer speaks.) **Om. Om. Holy water now blesses this offering!**

Make haste! Behold the movement of the god! (He dances.) Listen to the murmuring of the priests offering up their prayers. These prayers are meant only for you, Holy Lord. Only you are entitled to receive them. The offering is now complete. There is nothing lacking. There is no one here, man, woman, or hermaphrodite, who is entering upon a life of evil. There is no one here to be cursed with crippling defects in their next reincarnation. It is the privilege of the priest of dharma to purify the people of the effects of evil. If anyone here is greedy or selfish, may he be turned towards goodness. May his vices be taken from him, as impurities are separated from molten metal. Here there is a bounteous feast of food and drink. All persons who assemble here know that I am like the priest Bagawan Viswakarma in the **Ramayana**. *My presence is necessary here that this ceremony may be a success.*

(He lights sticks of incense on offerings handed to him by a priest, then cries out.) Ehh! Make haste! Ihhhh!

(Sidha Karya now talks to the children in the audience in Kawi, but the word he uses for "children" also appears in the vocabulary of High Balinese and would be understandable to them.) Now, all you children! (He laughs and takes the old Chinese

Figure 65. Sidha Karya presents the offering and offers a blessing for “every man, woman, and hermaphrodite” at Tusan.

coins in his hand. Then he continues to speak.) Ah, ha, ha! You! Children! This is the priest of dharma. It is my privilege and duty to catch you, eh children?

(Excited and frightened, the children in the audience titter and squirm. Still in the role of Sidha Karya, Kakul now addresses them in Indonesian, the language of the schools.)

Come here! Come here! Uhhh! Eh, eh, eh!

(He throws the coins out towards the perimeter of the performance oval. The children scramble to pick up the coins and then scream and run as Sidha Karya chases after them. Their expressions indicate a combination of fear and excitement. Sidha Karya catches a child, carries him in his arms around the performance oval, and then releases him and gives him some food from the offering. Without removing the mask of Sidha Karya, Kakul makes a final circle within the oval and exits through the curtain for the last time, as the music ends.)

Chapter 5
The Domains of Topeng

I was Kakul's student at the time I taped his performance, on leave from my position as a director and teacher of Western theatre. In the years that followed, I have performed Balinese and Western texts using *topeng* techniques and have continued to teach and direct for the Western stage (see Snow 1986; Reeder 1979; and chapter 7). What follows is an attempt to look at Kakul's performance once again, from other vantage points these activities have provided. As a performer, director, and teacher of acting and dramatic theory, I am concerned not only with understanding what is involved in Kakul's performance—though that task has difficulties enough—but also with how his practice of topeng relates to and is distinct from modern and postmodern experimentation within Western theatre. Ultimately, I want to know what topeng has to teach me as a Western performer, teacher and scholar, and what I am positioned (and not positioned) to learn. This is an approach to these issues, written in the hope that my concerns are not unique.[1]

To make a dent in the agenda proposed, I shall need to take a somewhat lengthy detour into theatrical theory. In 1973 (just before I started to study with Kakul) Richard Schechner published an article entitled "Drama-Script-Theatre-Performance" in which he tried to isolate the various "domains" of activity involved in generating and sustaining theatrical performance. Schechner suggested a "taxonomical model" to be used as a tool in describing the interactions among "domains" that characterize theatrical forms and, in the process, made some interesting observations about the ways in which theatre artists in the West during the latter part of this century have seemed to delight in exposing "creases" between the "domains" indicated in his model (1988 [1977, 1973]: 68–105). Such structural models have their dangers, of course. They may provide complex ways of saying simple things; worse, the models themselves may become reified, encouraging the reader to treat the map treated as though it were the territory. Still, I have found Schechner's model useful in trying to understand how Balinese topeng works as a theatrical genre and, more particularly, how Kakul's performance at Tusan acquires its force and form. As a model designed to indicate domains of activity involved in all theatrical performances, it may also provide a useful starting place for discussing ways in which topeng performances are both similar to, and significantly different from, avant-garde Western theatre since Brecht and Artaud. Artaud's own well-known enthusiasm for Balinese performance and the recent renewal of interest in Asian theatre in general, and Balinese theatre in particular, add appeal to this task.[2]

Drama-Script-Theatre-Performance

Schechner's model has gone through some refinements in his various revisions, but it still consists fundamentally of a series of concentric spheres, with "drama" depicted as "the smallest, most intense circle" and "performance" as "the broadest, most ill-defined disk." In general terms, a "drama" might take the form of "a written text, score, scenario, instruction, plan, or map" which may be transported "from time to time and place to place" and incorporated within the "script" for a particular presentation. This "script" may then be manifested in "concrete and immediate" terms within the larger sphere of "theatre," and what is shown and enacted there may then be encompassed within the domain of "performance"—"the whole constellation of events, most of them passing unnoticed, that takes place in/among both performers and audience from the time the first spectator enters [. . .] the precinct where the theatre takes place to the time the last spectator leaves" (1988 [1977,1973]: 72).[3]

Schechner summarizes the identities of his domains as they apply to the most familiar Western procedures: "Drama is what the writer writes; the script is the interior map of a particular production; the theatre is the specific set of gestures performed by the performers in any given performance; the performance is the whole event, including audience and performers." He further notes that, outside of these spheres of activity, embracing the circumscribed "domain" of performance, is "the domain of everyday life" (1988: 85).

In applying Schechner's model, some theatrical forms may be understood to define and protect the "boundaries" that demarcate these domains more than others. The integrity of any given "domain" may be reinforced and movement to the next "domain" consequently made more difficult. Thus the "dramatic works" of, say, Shakespeare, Ibsen, or Shepard, may be bound, sold, read, and taught in "dramatic literature" classes with varying degrees of success, almost as though they were novels in dialogue form (supplemented by brief descriptions of settings and actions). Then again, at the next "boundary," a director such as Max Reinhardt might work out an elaborate *mise-en-scène*, complete with inflections and nuances of gesture, prior to even meeting his actors. The theatrical "do-

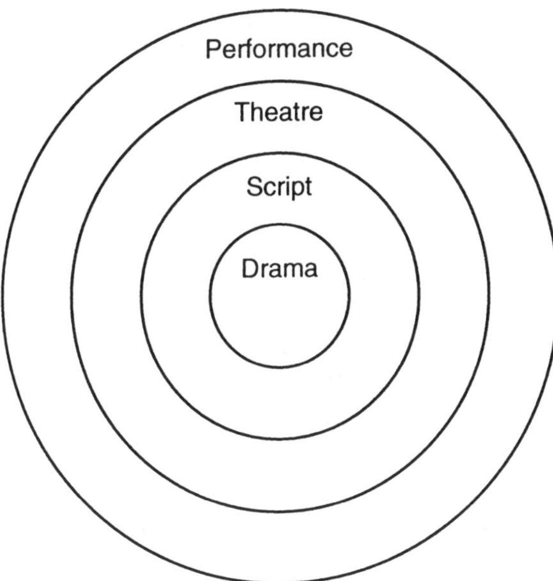

Figure 66. Schematic model of the nested domains of drama, script, theatre, and performance as proposed by Richard Schechner.

main" may be sealed off by "closing" rehearsals to the public while working out the details of theatrical presentation prior to "opening" the work to an audience. The "boundary" between the "domains" of performance and everyday life is also subject to relative degrees of openness or closure. The proscenium arch, the darkened theatre and illuminated stage, the use of elaborate costumes and makeup, or of "extra-daily" movement, are all ways of reinforcing the sense of a separate domain for theatre in order to then communicate across its "boundaries"—of establishing and controlling "aesthetic distance." In common usage, many performance genres are even referred to as "pure entertainment," indicating a supposed disjunction between the events performed and the life that surrounds the performance.

Especially over the past thirty years, there has been a tendency to play with all of these "boundaries," opening them up or exposing them as artificial. The works of such dramatists as Robert Wilson, Richard Foreman, or Lee Breuer have demanded innovative strategies from their editors due to the elaborate interplay between the domains of "script" and "theatre," while the recycling and deconstruction of Arthur Miller's *The Crucible* in The Wooster Group's *LSD* played with the "boundary" between "drama" and "script," creating legal as well as aesthetic dilemmas (Savran 1985). Indeed, the role of the director in interpreting or confronting the dramatic text has probably been the most hotly debated theoretical issue in theatre of recent decades (see, e.g., Grotowski 1969; Hornby 1977; Pavis 1982; Blau 1982; Worthen et al. 1995). These issues are now echoed in questions concerning the reader's or viewer's role being asked by semioticians and critics attracted to hermeneutic circlings: every reader and spectator becomes a director before the circles are exhausted. Ensemble rehearsal procedures, the phenomenon of open rehearsals, the use of environmental stagings by, for example, Schechner, Grotowski, and Harold Prince, and the radical re-examination of the physical and mental relationship of the spectator to the performed action involved in the work of John Cage, Allan Kaprow, and various performance artists all have acted to subvert the integrity of these "boundaries," as do the night club comic's banter with his audience, or Spalding Gray's use of intensely personal experience as recyclable dramatic material.

Schechner's "boundaries," then, are less formidable and static than they may appear. Still, they serve to isolate "areas" for the different sets of procedures used to generate and sustain performances and, perhaps more important, indicate the "potential spaces" in which crucial strategic choices as to what game we are playing may occur and postmodern innovations become possible. Schechner's "domains" are most usefully conceived of as expanding and contracting homes for certain kinds of procedures. Experienced diachronically, their limits are positioned at strategic spots where ambiguities arise; the need for each new circle and category in the model comes from the sense that something else is now happening—that another bundle of procedures is being used.

The model acquires its usefulness as a theoretical tool in helping to point out what is involved in traveling—as performer, as audience member, or as critic—from the home of one set of procedures to the home of another. In this regard, Balinese topeng shares many of the techniques and formal concerns of postmodernism, for it is in the nature of topeng to keep the "boundaries" between the various "domains" of performance relatively open. It is closer to the practice of Brecht, Meyerhold, Foreman, or Monty Python's Flying Circus than to the seamless model of playwriting and production based on the "laws of the necessary and probable" espoused by Aristotle, elaborated by Corneille, reinvented by Ibsen, and systematized for actors by Stanislavsky. Indeed, a fluidity of movement from "domain" to "domain" is quintessential to topeng's strategies and aesthetic life. It is the nature and the consequences of this dynamic movement across the "domains" of performance that I now wish to examine in Kakul's topeng *pajegan* performance at Tusan, tracing the audience's perception of Kakul's performance across the various domains involved.

Before charting a path through the experience of performance, though, it will be useful to apply Schechner's model to the generative process that culminated in Kakul's performance of the story of Jelantik at Blambangan as enacted at Tusan on February 6, 1975. Schechner's use of familiar terms leaves room for ambiguity, and I shall have to make adjustments in the definitions of some of these terms in order to apply his model to topeng. However, as Kenneth Burke noted in explaining the usefulness of his own schematic "pentad": "What we want is not terms that avoid ambiguity, but terms that clearly reveal the strategic spots at which ambiguities necessarily arise [. . .] it is in the areas of ambiguity that transformations take place" (1962 [1945]: xx–xxi). For myself, it is the capacity to better understand and, hopefully, to better effect such "transformations" that is at the heart of this inquiry.

At first glance, Schechner's summary definitions of "drama" and "script" may seem arbitrary to the point of perversity. Drama, after all, refers etymologically to action, and script to that which is written. Why, then, should "what the writer writes" be called the "drama," and "script" be used to designate "the interior map of a particular production"? Schechner's concern in this ordering of familiar and acknowledgedly loaded terms is to place "drama" at the center of the set of procedures that generate and sustain theatrical performance, using "scripting" to refer to the process of elaborating the dramatic nucleus to the point where it might be given theatrical life. This choice is related to (and perhaps determined by) Aristotle's observation that *praxis*—the ordering of the incidents—constitutes the "soul" of a tragedy; it is also consistent with the Indic concept of a dramatic incident providing the "kernel" *(bija)* from which the play must grow (Byrski 1981: 144). "Drama," then, might be redefined as being not so much "what the writer writes" as the sequence of actions, or fable, that is at the core of what he has chosen to write about. In common usage, the terms "drama" and "script" become synonymous in the West (inviting etymological confusion), since we credit the playwright with both conceptualizing the dramatic core and providing the dialogue and stage directions that begin to flesh out that core.

In Schechner's terms, of course, further "scripting" is permissible by the director, and, to a lesser degree, by the actors themselves. In topeng pajegan, however, there is no playwright to provide a script, no director to devise a *mise-en-scène.* There is only the performer, preparing to perform. He begins with the quasi-historical *Babad Dalem* (roughly, "Chronicles of Kings") as handed down to him: one of the stories contained within these "chronicles" must form the dramatic core from which he proceeds. This dramatic core is anterior to "plot" as well as to dialogue—just as, in Greek practice, *mythos* was anterior even to *praxis.* Homer, Aeschylus, Sophocles, and Euripides could and did all reshape the dramatic core of the *Oresteia* (Euripides several times), and so would Sartre, O'Neill, and Suzuki Tadashi many centuries later.[4]

For my purposes, then, "drama" can be roughly equated with the fable or story embedded in one of the *Babad*'s flexible texts, while "script" refers to the patterning of words and actions that will be used to convey and give specific form to this story in the context of a hypothetical performance. "Theatre" continues to describe the "script" as manifest within performance—its "immediate and concrete" expression by the performers. In using this set of definitions (just as in common usage), not all performative actions will be equally "dramatic." Happenings, musical revues, and religious rituals, for example, are all "scripted" and performed, but contain varying amounts of "dramatic" content, and some parts of a theatricalized "script" may be less "dramatic" than others—they deal less directly with an "intense, heated up center" provided by the story matter.

From Drama to Script

On the day before leaving for Tusan, Kakul sat on his porch, a well-worn notebook in his hand. The notebook contained selected babad stories (*caritera*) transcribed from palm leaf manuscripts (*lontar*), along with genealogical charts, useful passages from the *Mahabharata* and *Ramayana,* favorite songs in Middle Javanese from the *gambuh* theatre repertory (in which Kakul also excelled), and *mantras* in Javanized Sanskrit that would be useful for the ritual blessings conferred at the end of the performance (see figs. 67–68). Kakul would peruse the notebook, lean back and close his eyes, glance at the book again, frown, turn a few pages, hum a bit, smile, nod his head, and stare fixedly into space as though lost in an unknown world. Sometimes, he would seem to be napping, and then his hands would begin to move slowly and gracefully, following the rhythms of unheard music. Hours passed in this manner.

Many potential "dramas" were inscribed in Kakul's notebook. He was concentrating on one of these—the story of Jelantik's mission to Blambangan and of his death while saving his King's honor and his father's soul. This story had been fixed as the dramatic core of the performance to be held in Tusan: the village had historical associations with Jelantik's descendants. Indeed, the origins of topeng pajegan in Bali have been traced by Balinese scholars to the celebrating of Jelantik's deeds by one of these descendants (sometimes identified as Tusan by name), using masks brought from Java as booty from this same expedition (Bandem and Rembang 1976).[5] Kakul already knew the story and had performed it before on several occasions. Indeed, he already knew a great deal of the notebook's contents by heart. His concentration was not on learning the story, but rather on the story's transformation from "drama" to "script."

This transformation was taking place through a process that combines procedures of selection and embellishment. In the version of the babad abridged in de Zoete and Spies's *Dance and Drama in Bali* (1973 [1938]: 303), the "kingdoms" of Pasurahan and Blambangan are equally involved in the insult to Dalem Baturenggong, and both are punished. The decisive battle is fought after Jelantik's death by another minister, Patih Ularan, who brings the head of the Dalem of Pasurahan back to his own King. Dalem Baturenggong is so upset by his minister's over-zealous pursuit of his mission that he banishes Ularan and his heirs from Gelgel. The version Kakul performs condenses these actions, eliminating many of the complications and concentrating on Jelantik: his role is made far more decisive and the restoration of his King's honor less equivocal; though Ularan's story is still well known and sometimes performed in Bali, there is no mention of him at all in Kakul's performance.

Some of Kakul's choices may have been determined by his own sources for the caritera, others by aesthetic concerns, and still others by factors peculiar to the occasion for which he was preparing. The themes of filial obligation that are present as a central strand in the story would be particularly appropriate on the occasion of a cremation—the most important (and expensive) obligation a child owes a parent in Bali. Many *Brahmana* priests would be at Tusan, some of whom were well known and greatly respected by Kakul. Apart from its associations with Tusan and with the history of topeng itself, the story of Jelantik's martyrdom would be particularly appropriate for this occasion because of its ethical and metaphysical implications: he would have to make sure to bring these out. At the same time, it would be fun to tease these high priests a bit, and appropriate moments would have to be found for this sort of mischief.

While crystallizing the "drama" of Jelantik's martyrdom, Kakul also embellishes and supplements this dramatic core. This "script-building" is well described by Lévi-Strauss's suggestive term: it is an act of *bricolage* (1966: 16–33). Bits and pieces from many sources are available to Kakul in embellishing the story. Perusing his notebook, he might consider words and sentiments from the Javanized Hindu epics, or songs of praise and grandeur from the Middle Javanese *kidung* literature, to be spoken in their appropriate historical and literary languages.[6] Various topics of current interest and vernacular modes of speech would also be considered, including instantly recognizable and potentially comic speech patterns specific to the Klungkung area where Tusan is located. Familiar bits of comic business would be mentally run through and assigned a place or rejected as inappropriate. Gradually, a tentative "map" for the performance is arrived at, and the sequence of masks to be used is set in mind, along with the appropriate dances.

Kakul does not have to rehearse these theatricalizing elements. He can count on his knowledge of topeng conventions, his kinesthetic training, and the personal precedents he has established in his own practice of topeng to do much of the work of rehearsals. He does not know how skilled the *gamelan* musicians at Tusan will be, nor how extensive their repertory beyond the most customary pieces required for a topeng performance. He will have to be flexible. For now, his preparation consists of deciding how

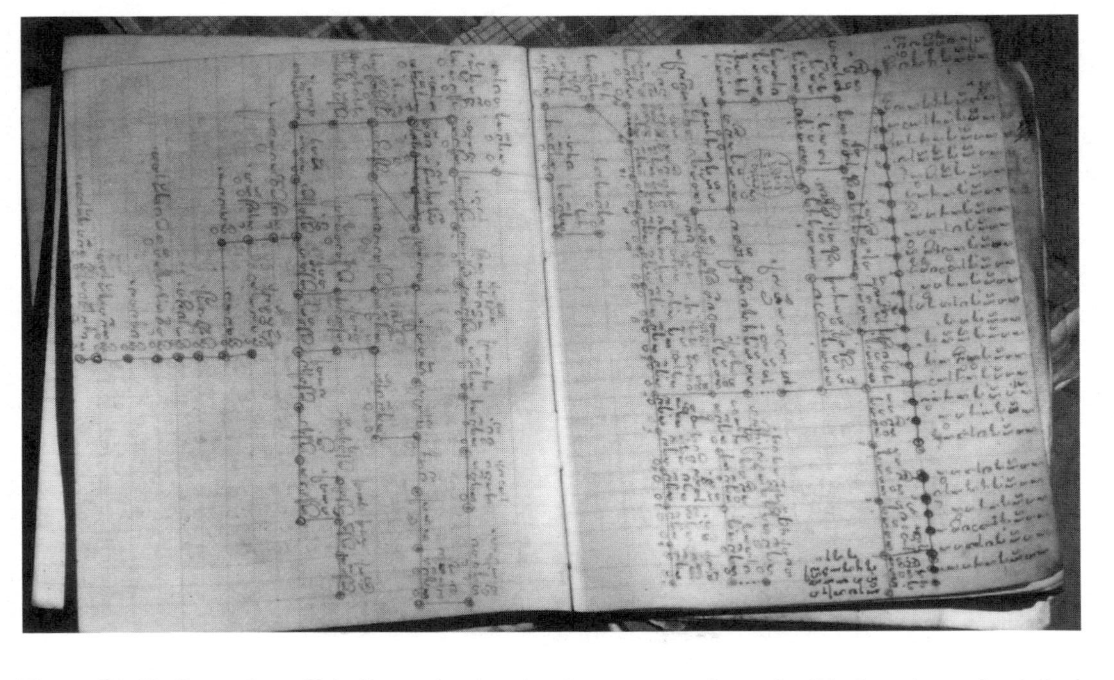

Figure 67–68. Pages from Kakul's notebooks, showing passages from the Hindu epics and a babad genealogy.

the material might be parceled out among his masks, what particular emphases might be given to the story on this occasion, what supplementary material might be appropriate, what special dance movements he might introduce, and what opportunities might be present for jokes and topical comments. The "script" arrived at in this manner is always incomplete.

Roland Barthes's well-known if idiosyncratic distinction between "work" and "Text" are apposite here:

> The work is a fragment of substance, occupying a part of the space of books (in a library for example), the Text is a methodological field. [. . .] The work can be held in the hand, the Text is held in language. [. . .] The Text is experienced only in an activity of production. [. . .] The work closes on a signified. [. . .] The Text, on the contrary, practices the infinite deferment of the signified, is dilatory. [. . .] Like language, it is structured but off-centered, without closure. The Text [. . .] decants the work [. . .] from its consumption and gathers it up as play, activity, production, practice. [. . .] The Text is bound to *jouissance*, that is to a pleasure without separation. [. . .] The Text is that space where no language has a hold over any other, where languages circulate. (1977: 156–64)

Using Barthes's terms, Adrian Vickers points out that the Balinese treatments of the Javanese *Kidung Malat* in the gambuh theatre (which antedates topeng in Bali and informs its practice) are "metatextual": they exist independent of any central, "complete" text and reinvent the story in confrontation with a flexible corpus of written variants that have themselves been influenced by gambuh performances and other performative renderings (1982). Due to its greater reliance on improvisation, the topeng "script" that Kakul creates is still more Text-like and work-resistant. It will remain flexible and never be written down, and Kakul might alter it substantially if the audience reception is right or the weather wrong—adding or subtracting or redistributing material. Still, "scripting" his dramatic material in this manner will allow Kakul to perform with confidence and a clear sense of direction.

From Script to Theatre

The "script" becomes animate in the immediate and concrete "domain" of the "theatre." The suspended ordering of all the considered possibilities and chosen intentions that constitute the "script" must find its life in the movement of muscle and bone, the clanging of wooden hammers against metal bars, the sounding of archaic and contemporary speech, and the display of painted wood and gilded cloth that, for the audience, *is* topeng. A Balinese spectator does not go to see this or that drama performed: the caritera chosen is rarely announced and may not be determined until the arrival of the performers (cf. de Zoete and Spies 1973 [1938]: 37–40). Schechner rightly points out that, while in the West—at least since the Renaissance—the tendency has been to throw emphasis onto the drama and script, in the East the tendency has been to emphasize theatre and performance: Aristotle's despised "spectacle" (1988 [1977, 1973]: 73).

Balinese theatre is a good case in point. Topeng is not lacking in verbal complexity or dramatic content, and the various stories have their separate appeals; but I have never heard Balinese people say that they are off to see a particular story. Rather, they will say that they are going to see a particular form of theatre, or perhaps a well-known performer or group, or even, simply, "the dancing." Topeng is distinguished from many other forms of Balinese dance and theatre by the entire constellation of the masks worn, the instruments, tunings and melodies used, the costumes displayed, the movements executed, and the modes of storytelling deployed. Audience expectations and criteria for excellence are targeted first and last to this theatrical domain.

In chapters 3 and 4, in essay form and through translation, I have already tried to give a sense of the theatrical life of Kakul's performance; such an attempt is doomed to be reductive and illustrates the difference between "script" and "theatre" as "domains" of activity. Leaving aside the thorny problems of translating Balinese into English, the process of moving from performance, to taped recording, to transcription, to translation is a movement away from theatre and back towards script—now reconstituted as a performance text: a sort of pseudo-work.[7] In this process, no matter how many notes and directions are appended, or how many typefaces and photographs are used, the theatrical elements of the production are the first elements to be glossed over or altogether lost.

In performance, it is possible to obscure the process of theatricalization—to attempt to make the theatrical domain transparent, so that the audience perceives activities given shape there as directly representative of happenings in the everyday world.[8] The "fourth wall" of the naturalistic stage is one such theatrical device that works to de-emphasize its own theatrical presence by first isolating the theatrical space and then recreating within that space a vision of the world as experienced outside of the domains of theatre and performance—throwing attention back onto the scripted drama or forward onto social concerns that may be thematically represented. In topeng, however, the "otherness" of the theatrical domain is boldly and flamboyantly declared. The gamelan melodies, the "unnatural" postures and movements of the dance (kinesthetically implanted through an arduous process of direct manipulation), the sounding of archaic language, and the guttural sounds that give this language significance, are all indicative of the theatrical "otherness" of the world as reconstituted in topeng.

In this splendidly realized theatrical domain, the music that Kakul held in his mind while fashioning his "script" is sounded—imperfect, but shimmering and vitally present. The masks are animated. The costumes are adjusted and displayed. The dances acquire specific life as Kakul's bare feet move along the consecrated earth and his hands and costumed body unite with the masks he wears to create a highly theatricalized illusion of characters. Words are now chanted, or sung, or spoken, in a manner appropriate to the linguistic context and the eccentricities of a mask. At times, as in the introductory dances, or *pengelembar*, these theatrical elements dominate, and the "scripting" all but disappears in the display of character and the synaesthesia of music and motion. At other times, as in the narrations of the two Penasars, the scripting becomes the predominant element of the performance, directing attention back onto the dramatic center. Sometimes, as in the moments in which the principal figures of the drama appear, or in the reflexive jokes and parodies offered by Si Mata Mata, scripting and theatricalization exist in a mutual exchange: first one and then the other are held at the center of the audience's attention.

From Theatre to Performance

The theatrical display of topeng is nested within the larger domain of "performance" in such a way as to encourage precisely this sort of inter-play. Contextualized by the occasion which its appearance helps to celebrate—a wedding, an *odalan*, a tooth-filing, a cremation—this theatrical display is both a generator and a recipient of the festive excitement and weight of significance attending the larger occasion.[9]

As the space that will hold the theatrical life is being consecrated, the audience gathers to form a truncated oval, providing an area that is set apart by soft and flexible boundaries. Beyond the human audience is the sacred mountain and the ancestors and gods. The musicians, whose efforts will herald and support the events within this theatrical world, sit among this audience, facing the curtain. As the curtain shakes, and the performer tantalizingly or triumphantly makes his entrance to the sound of cymbals and drums, he is entering a liminal space defined by the presence of the audience—both human and divine. Compare this convention with the use of the curtain common until very recently in Western proscenium theatre. On the proscenium stage, the curtain is raised or drawn to reveal a world apart—often one representing a different historical time or geographical place—and the audience is invited to vicariously identify with the characters portrayed as living in that world. In the Balinese convention, the curtain is at the rear of the playing space. There is nothing to reveal but the architecture and scenery that have always been there—and the actor's changing table, which has been in view during his preparations and can frequently be glimpsed during entrances. No matter where or when the story takes place, the action is thrust into the present moment of performance to realize its theatrical form.

Thus, although the Dutch colonists brought illusionistic scene painting to Indonesia and Balinese artists, internationally acclaimed for their technical skills, have seen such painting used in Java and elsewhere, the only scenery that I have ever seen painted for a Balinese theatrical presentation is a replica of the gateway to a Balinese temple—the "natural" site for a performance. Representations of past times or distant lands would be inappropriate, even though the actions depicted in the dramas putatively take place in India, Majapahit, or ancient Bali. By moving through the curtain and into the liminal space defined by the audience, the actor—usually as character—can directly address the audience in their own time, in their own space, no matter where or when the "drama" is taking place. Such "anachronistic" play abounds in topeng: both as a strategy for humor and as an integral part of its meaning.

There are times during his performance at Tusan when Kakul departs not only from the "script," but also from the process of making the script immediate and concrete through theatrical means. At these moments, sometimes abandoning character, he addresses himself directly to the act of performing. Thus as Penasar Kelihan, the senior storyteller, he chides the *Satria* gamelan leader for setting the wrong tempo:

> What a chase those noblemen in the orchestra gave me! Now I'm worn out! Already too tired to give you a show! Mind you, I don't mean to criticize. Not just yet It's my first time here. My first time dancing with these musicians. Their first time playing with me. And I'm old fashioned. Just like an old dog! [. . .] Beh! Moving on!

Thus, also, as the over-aged coquette, Desak Made Rai, he teases a priest standing nearby. "Oh, those Brahmana over there are laughing at me. And that one tried to pinch me! I wonder if he'll do that when were alone." And thus, he jests about his right to speak as he wishes after mistakenly addressing Jelantik as though he were divine: "But my Holy Lord [. . .] I mean my noble lord! I got mixed up. Well, anyway, I'm out here alone, so I can say whatever I want! Ha, ha, ha!" These are all instances of "metacommentary"—throwing the emphasis onto the act of performing by recognizing the presence of the audience and his fellow performers. An even more significant instance of the potential primacy of the "domain" of performance is the Sidha Karya ritual that ends the performance; but in this instance the play is no longer essentially between the "domains" of theatre and performance (though both of these domains are involved), but between the "domains" of performance and of life itself—in its secular and sacred aspects: "Now the Holy Presence arrives. Now Sidha Karya appears. Coming now, into this world."

Beyond Performance

As Schechner notes, beyond the domain of performance, across an indistinct boundary, is the domain of everyday life—what Victor Turner refers to as *societas*—the activities of which surround, occasion, inform, and in turn may be informed and affected by those events set within "liminal" or "liminoid" circles of performance (1969, 1982, 1989). Further, beyond this domain of everyday life, at least for the Balinese audience, lies the domain of the macrocosmos—the realm of the ancestors, the deities, and of enduring values. One adds these outer realms to Schechner's circles within circles at the risk of calling to mind the childhood joke of listing one's address by giving name, street and number, state, country, the world, the universe. In the child's joke, though, the last two designations are true enough, but superfluous to delivering the mail; and therefore are listed either out of naiveté or silliness. In Balinese performance, these outer domains are operative addresses: characters, audience members, and performers, may be understood to move imaginatively, metaphorically, or actually into or out of these domains.[10] Thus, for the discussion that follows, Schechner's diagram might be redrawn as follows, adding the outer circles and—as he himself has done in his revision of the original essay (1988: 72)—showing his "boundaries" to be less definite, hermetic and formidable than they first appeared (see fig. 69).

Held outdoors, on ground which is only temporarily set apart for theatrical use, the circumstances that surround Balinese performances encourage an active interplay between the domains of performance and everyday life. Audience members come and go on the physical periphery of the performance, joining friends, buying food, flirting, or chatting. In another essay, Schechner has characterized this behavior, typical of traditional theatre throughout much of the world, as "selective inattention" (1988 [1977]: 196–206). The performer, too, may tend to matters of the "real world" while performing: matter-of-factly adjusting a costume piece or chasing away a stray dog. Events and concerns from the "domain" of everyday life allusively play into the content of the "script" and clash with the splendidly set apart world of theatrical conventions. Thus, the Penasar Cenikan, or junior storyteller, interrupts high-flown rhetoric about the demands of *dharma* in order to render a scene in everyday images: "Beh! It's a leech as big as a roofing mat! Aduh! There's the leech all curled up. And hairy, too! Beh! Mun, mun, mun! That big!" Cucul's talk of prosaic concerns—after Jelantik's martyrdom and before Sidha Karya's divine intervention—is even more startling: "Aduh! Such a crowd of people gathered in the palace courtyard. All of them so happy! And here I am, so sad and miserable. [. . .] My wife has gone and left me!" And Si Mata Mata's parody of Indonesian nationalism takes this form of play still further.

The play between the "domain" of performance and the events of everyday life that surround and occasion performance can be complex in topeng, and often results in humor. Ron Jenkins reports acting in a performance held in his teacher's family temple in which his teacher's extramarital affairs were broadly satirized in front of his wife, family, and friends,

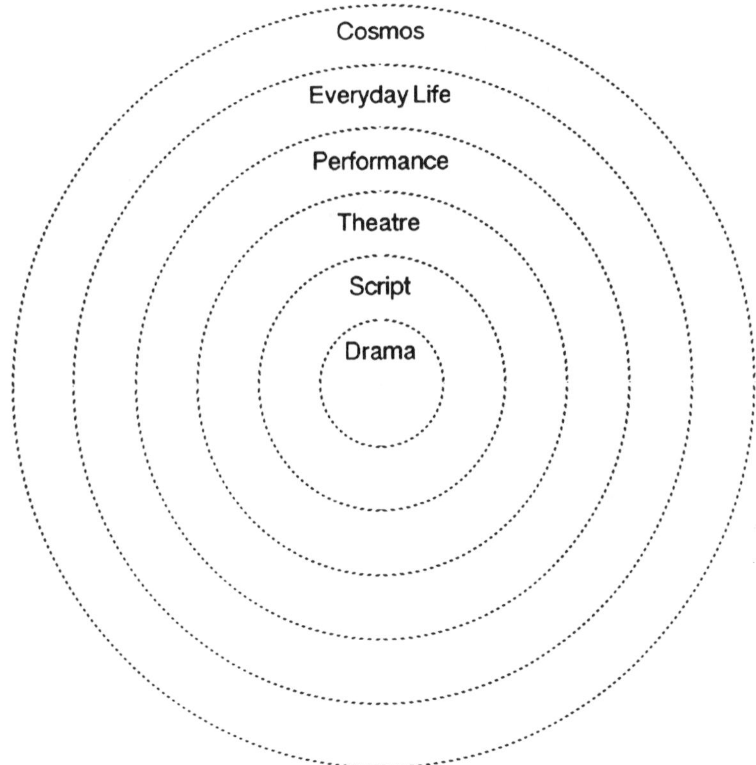

Figure 69. Expanded model of the domains of topeng.

with the teacher himself as the leading performer (1979: 54). Such allusions add spice to a Balinese performance and may serve a therapeutic function. Elizabeth Young makes a case for this humor being socially corrective: by ridiculing inappropriate behavior, the argument goes, proper social behavior is taught and reinforced (1980: 196–239; cf. Goodlad 1971). Young presents the argument well, and I am willing to believe that there are instances of humor in topeng that function along these lines. There is little doubt that Balinese performances can be given a conservative turn. Fredrik deBoer has shown how jokes in Balinese shadow plays *(wayang kulit)* can be used to buttress the traditional social order (1987) and Hildred Geertz has recently recounted a chilling tale of a topeng performance in Kakul's village of Batuan commissioned by princely patrons in league with the Dutch in 1947, during the Indonesian war for independence, in order to incite a crowd to severely beat some Brahmana revolutionaries (1990). Still, the humor involved in, for example, Si Mata Mata's parody of Indonesian nationalism or Cucul's devaluing of history strikes me as having a somewhat different, more mischievous, and perhaps more profound function.

James Boon, in his article, "Folly, Bali, and Anthropology, or Satire Across Cultures" (1984: 160), is similarly distrustful of moral exegesis. Citing Northrop Frye and using the translation and description of Kakul's performance as an example, Boon makes a case for topeng (along with all of anthropological literature) being a species of Menippean satire: "a literary and performative genre based on multiple voices and viewpoints, plural languages, obsessive quotation, pastiche, etymology, blather, and always imbued with a flavor of fragmented parody," where "culture, histories, and languages theatrically, parodically, and apocalyptically converge" (1984: 159). Boon sees this process of setting world against world in an "exegesis resistant" display of folly as fundamentally subversive (1984: 161). In the end, though, the inclusiveness of topeng, indicated by its range of humor as well as its penchant for having peasants and courtiers mingle demonic and celestial beings, may be more important than either its subversive or conservative turns. The performances function to create a vision of the world rendered whole—with all its seemingly mismatched pieces in place. Perhaps the virtual sanctity accorded the topeng pajegan performer by references to his *taksu* and by delegating to him the duty of performing the future-oriented ritual that ends a performance is earned through this capacity.[11]

Kakul's performance as Sidha Karya, "the priest of *dharma*" who intercedes for the villagers in their relations with divine forces and receives the offering on behalf of the gods, is the most striking instance of this playing between the "domain" of performance and life outside of that "domain." The offering he receives has been blessed by a Brahmana priest (*pedanda*) during Kakul's performance, and his acceptance of it and sharing of its coins with screaming and laughing children culminates the playing with boundaries by theatrically joining the "domain" of everyday life with the Balinese macrocosmos of spiritual force and presence. Kakul becomes identified with his role, and, though trance is not directly involved, as noted in chapter four the tradition of visitation that also embraces the ritual use of the Rangda and Barong Ket masks provides a context in which sacred play can occur.

The ritual awakening and the blessings of the masks that precede and follow the topeng pajegan performance, the consecration of the ground, the "dramatic" depiction of heroic ancestors, the inclusion of the gods and ancestors in the audience addressed, the use of languages associated with them, the interpolation of religious maxims and texts into the "script," the public ritual that ends the topeng pajegan performance, and the use of the spiritual term "taksu" to refer to a performer's presence indicate the accessibility of the macrocosmic world of spiritual force and energy to the topeng performer and his audience. Taken all in all, the domains of topeng recreate and celebrate the Balinese cosmos. The aim is not so much to imitate the surfaces of life as experienced—though such imitation has its place in topeng (and that place is in the comic *bondres)*—but, rather, to render and restore a vision of life that is essentially whole, blending experience with cultural knowledge, and what has been seen and reported with all that might well be imagined. As in the strategies of containment outlined in chapter 2, the enterprise is inclusive and encompassing; and the neo-classical unities of place, time, tone, and action can have no place in this more ambitious effort to recreate, celebrate, and contain a vision of life in all its disconsonant and ultimately sacred variety.

The Dynamics of a Topeng Performance

Schechner's model can be applied diachronically to Kakul's performance in an experiential as well as a generative fashion. That is, it can be used to trace the audience's attention as it is focused on the procedures and concerns appropriate to first one and then another of the various "domains" involved in the entire performance process. Tracing this progress, a pattern emerges that may be indicative of a genius peculiar to topeng pajegan as a theatrical from, or, at least, to Kakul's own use of the topeng pajegan tradition.[12] The audience can be seen as carried through the entire performance model, circle by circle, as though moving through its core and emerging through the other side (see fig. 70, p. 188).

As Kakul says his mantras and asks his masks to waken that they might dance, the ground is consecrated with holy water, the gamelan music begins to play, and the audience assembles—joking, socializing, slowly taking up places around the performance oval. The movement is between the "domains" of the macrocosmos and of everyday life on the one hand, and between performance and life outside of performance—both sacred and profane—on the other. The opening dances of the pengelembar harness the music to a theatrical display of virtuosity and brilliance. The play is between theatre and performance, with rudimentary scripting involved in the performer's choice of masks and choreography. The telling of the story, the caritera, begins with the Penasar Kelihan's virtuosic display of an unintelligible language, becomes more complex in its scripting, and eventually closes in on the dramatic center. The oscillations between narration and dance, between the rival modes of visitation and illusion, and between Kakul in his persona as performer and in his role as character, keep all four domains of performative activity in a heated interaction at the temporal center of the performance—with first one and then another of these domains being brought into focus. The appearance of Jelantik himself occurs at the exact center—framed by the appearances of the two Penasars, and (excluding Sidha Karya), with six masks before and another six after. It

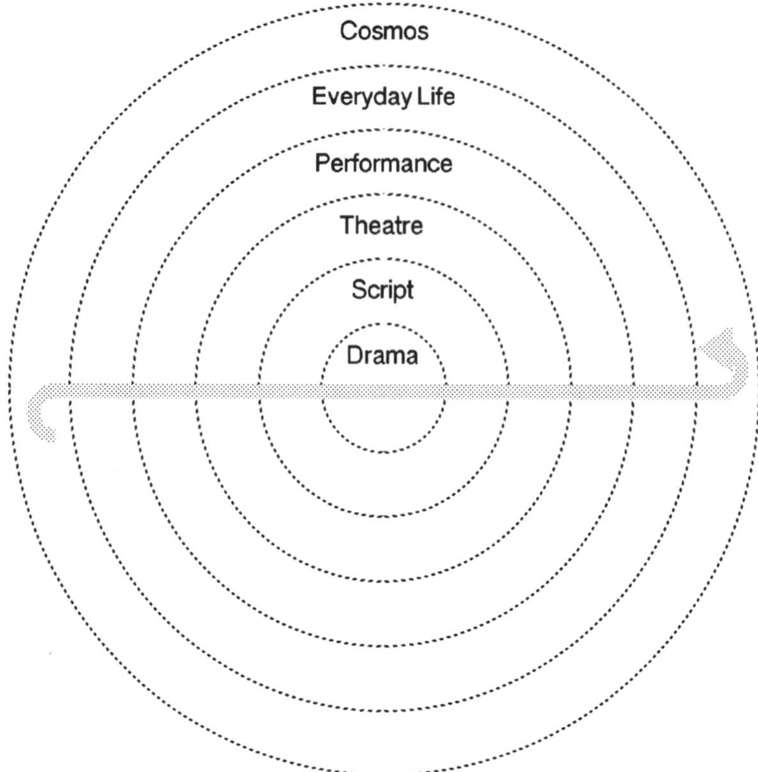

Figure 70. Diagram tracking the audience's attention as it is directed toward various domains during Kakul's performance.

should be noted that, as the drama heats up and the principal characters from the past are summoned to dance, the references to the "domain of performance" become fewer and fewer. With the succession of bondres characters—each with its reflexive view to add and jokes to tell—the emphasis on the dramatic center lessens, with a corresponding increase in attention lavished on the "domains" of theatre and performance. Finally, the Sidha Karya ritual, while it is certainly "scripted" and theatricalized, emphasizes once again an interchange between the "domains" of performance and of the sacred and secular life outside that performance.

The entire event begins with a private ritual that separates the actions of performance from the flow of everyday life (though reminders of that life may be seen within and around the audience's space); it ends with a public ritual that rejoins the concerns of performance with those of that life. Throughout the course of the performance, a priest on a platform removed from the performative focus, but still in view of the audience, prepares the offering for Sidha Karya. Entrances of figures from the past are marked by cymbal clashes and drum rolls as though to emphasize a movement between sacred and secular worlds. The performance may be charted as shown in fig. 71, p. 190.

What the chart cannot show is that—despite the overall movement from private ritual, through secular narrative and comic play, to the emergence of the divine—in each of the major sections of the performance there is a counterveiling movement towards humanization and containment. The startling, hyper-tense, and virtuosic figure of the red-faced Patih yields place to the familiar, somewhat incompetent figure of the old courtier who is free to physically contact the audience. The Penasar Kelihan, with all of his boasting and vainglorious touting of the ancestral ethos, is followed by the Penasar Cenikan, with his far more common-sense view of events. The outrageous Si Mata Mata gives way first to an aging coquette, and then to a simple peasant left outside of the rush of history. Even Sidha Karya moves from a display and celebration of divine power to the sharing of the gods' offering with a small child, and in the process his language moves from archipelago Sanskrit to the Indonesian of the schoolroom before the audience disperses with his blessing and the performing oval once more becomes, unequivocally, a part of "this earth." This movement toward the quotidian and human affirms an essential sanity in the Balinese cosmos, or, at least, of Kakul's inspired play with the confluence of extraordinary and familiar events contained by that cosmos, in all of its variety.

The overall movement from everyday life to artistic activity to ritual and back to the concerns of the quotidian world is familiar in Balinese life. The task of teaching me my first sentence in Indonesian happened to fall to a tailor (and an aficionado of Balinese theatre) who spoke a little English. He decided that the task was important, pondered many options, and then decided to teach me to say: "*Seni ini adala anak dari dunia*" or "Art is the child of nature." The inter-relationships between art and life—in both its secular and sacred aspects—is a recurring theme on the island. A circular progression from nature to art to offering and back again to nature is played out in many variations (see fig. 72, p. 191).

Rice is made into cakes, then colored and stacked high, and decorated and profusely adorned with ornamentation. These works of elaborate artifice are given as offerings to the gods, who enjoy their essence, and are then returned to the people, who enjoy the cakes as food. The performer draws from his observations of the life around him, as well as from familiar historical annals, and, using all of this material, he constructs intricate systems of sound and movement, redeployed through the conventions of his art. This artistic refiguring and inter-twining of the many worlds embraced by the Balinese imagination is then offered to the invited gods and ancestors for their pleasure. It is also (like the gaily decorated offering cakes)

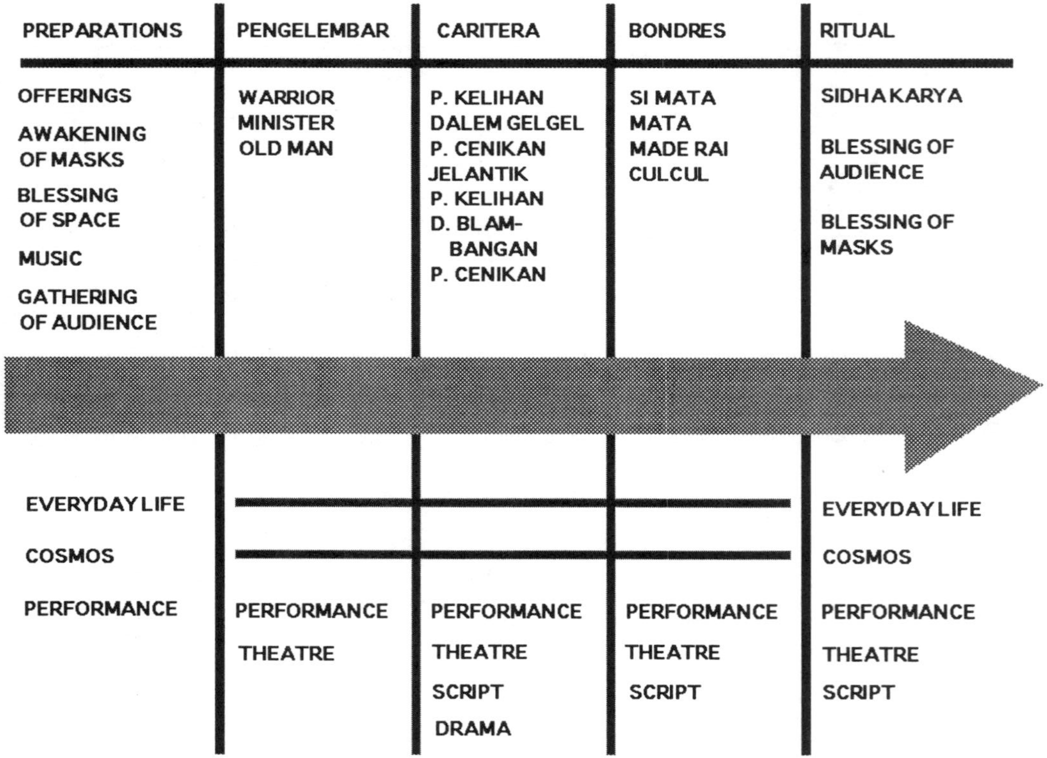

PREPARATIONS	PENGELEMBAR	CARITERA	BONDRES	RITUAL
OFFERINGS AWAKENING OF MASKS BLESSING OF SPACE MUSIC GATHERING OF AUDIENCE	WARRIOR MINISTER OLD MAN	P. KELIHAN DALEM GELGEL P. CENIKAN JELANTIK P. KELIHAN D. BLAM-BANGAN P. CENIKAN	SI MATA MATA MADE RAI CULCUL	SIDHAKARYA BLESSING OF AUDIENCE BLESSING OF MASKS
EVERYDAY LIFE				EVERYDAY LIFE
COSMOS				COSMOS
PERFORMANCE	PERFORMANCE	PERFORMANCE	PERFORMANCE	PERFORMANCE
	THEATRE	THEATRE	THEATRE	THEATRE
		SCRIPT	SCRIPT	SCRIPT
		DRAMA		

Figure 71. Diagram representing Kakul's engagement of domains as his performance moves from private ritual to public ceremony.

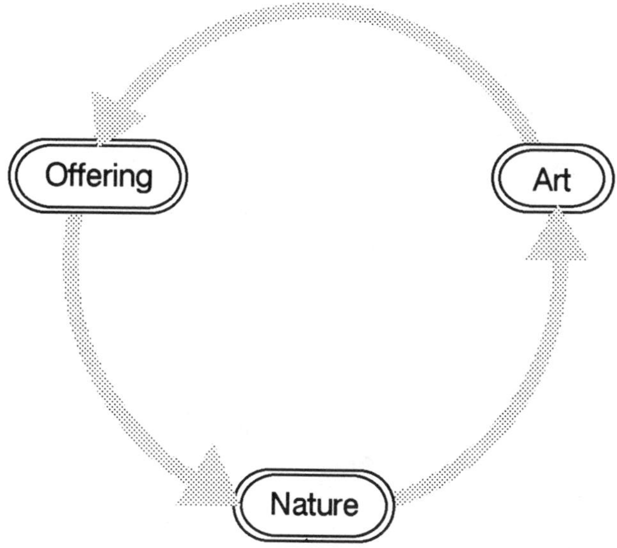

Figure 72. Diagram of the transformative cycle involving nature, art, and offering.

consumed by the earthly audience—an audience equally appreciative of a beautiful movement or a good joke. In the end, the needs and hopes of this audience are the focus of the performer's intercession with those very gods who have shared in the enjoyment of his refashioning of nature as art—as offering, and as delicious entertainment.

An English professor whose unhappy lot it was to instruct me in the beauties of Edmund Spenser's epic poetry once observed that Spenser's verse is not like life, but reading his poetry is a lot like living. Topeng is not "like life," either; but watching a topeng performance is a great deal "like living," and living very well, with all the senses alert, an awakened sense of humor, an appreciation of those who have gone before, and a heightened sense of the consequences and potential of human actions.

Of Limens and Limenoids

In *From Ritual to Theatre* (1982) Victor Turner attempts to point out some of the differences between performances held in pre-industrial cultures and those found in post-industrial settings. Going back to his observation that ritual performances traditionally take place during liminal times—in the margins and thresholds of social experience—he makes a case for post-industrial performance being not truly liminal, but rather (apologizing for the neologism) "liminoid"—resembling without being identical to liminal phenomena. Liminal phenomena are collective and occur at times of renewal or crisis, whereas liminoid works (or plays) mimic attributes of these phenomena, but may be produced at any time by an individual or a group, and are often sold as a commodity. Whereas, in liminal activities, emphasis is characteristically placed on anonymity and *communitas,* in liminoid performances stress is given to the individual innovator—"the unique person who dares and opts to create" (1982: 43). An obligation to follow set forms is characteristic of liminal rites, whereas an emphasis on choice and experimentation is central to liminoid art. The liminoid artist "is privileged to make free with his social heritage in a way impossible to members of cultures in which the liminal is to a large extent the sacrosanct" (52).

Finally, while liminal activities of pre-industrial societies invert and play with the social status quo, they rarely subvert it. "Reversal underlines to the members of a community that chaos is the alternative to cosmos, so they'd better stick to cosmos, i.e., the traditional order of culture, though they can for a brief while have a whale of a good time being chaotic" (1982: 41). Liminoid "entertainments" in industrial societies, on the other hand, are characteristically subversive: "satirizing, lampooning, burlesquing, or subtly putting down the central values of the basic, work-sphere society, or at least of selected sectors of that society" (41).[13]

Noting the differences between Turner's categories in this context should make it clear that the topeng pajegan performed by I Nyoman Kakul at Tusan has attributes of both liminal and liminoid phenomena. The performance—or at least *a* performance—is required by a communal need. The piece begins and ends with more or less prescribed rituals, and many elements within the piece are determined by traditional structures. But Kakul is brought to Tusan as a renowned artist and the script created and performed is his own, for which he receives full credit from an admiring audience. Indeed, now that more information is becoming available about topeng pajegan, and other transcriptions are available, the mastery of Kakul's individual handling of those potentialities within the form becomes more striking. Moreover, the inversions and subversions involved in the scripting are sufficiently complex that two intelligent, informed writers can have opposite opinions about whether the pieces act to subvert or reaffirm societal values. Topeng (Turner might have been amused to observe) exists in a limen between the liminal and the liminoid! And this is precisely its appeal to theatre artists in the West, myself included. It has an immediacy of impact, range of signification, and purposiveness within social mechanisms that are missing in most of the theatre available to us; yet it is not so alien as to be beyond our ken or to lack appeal as a theatrical model.

Topeng, Modern, and Postmodern Theatre

As Schechner points out, the opening up of "creases" between the domains of performance and the playing back and forth across these creases has become common practice in Western contemporary theatre (1988 [1977]: 73). A list of practitioners involved in this tendency would be impressive, with Brecht and Artaud as a somewhat unlikely set of parents and progeny ranging from Richard Foreman to Monty Python's Flying Circus and including Peter Schumann, Jean Genet, Lee Breuer, Robert Wilson, Peter Brook, Peter Weiss, Samuel Beckett, Jerzy Grotowski, Fred Curchack, the Wooster Group, and Schechner himself. The blatant theatricality and reflexivity common to these very different artists has been reinforced and sometimes prompted by the concerns and analytical methods of semiotic and deconstructive studies—particularly those of Roland Barthes and Jacques Derrida. This set of concerns and activities has coincided with a re-emergence of interest in Bali on the part of the theatrical practitioners and theorists. It may be useful to note some striking similarities and essential differences between Balinese topeng as performed by Kakul and recent theatrical theory and practice in the West.

Recorded interest by Western theatre practitioners in Balinese performance begins with the works of Antonin Artaud. It was the capacity of the Balinese performer to project an essentialized vision of life through theatrical means that so attracted Artaud. In his famous essay, "On the Balinese Theatre," he praised the Balinese dancers he had observed in the Dutch Pavilion of the Paris Exposition for their "rigorous" sense of form, their "evocative power," and, most importantly, for their ability to reveal "spiritual states" by means of gesture (1958 [1938]: 192). Artaud's other writings, both before and after his encounter with Balinese performance, indicate a deep affinity with central concerns of Balinese theatrical practice. "The theatre," wrote Artaud, "takes gestures and pushes them as far as they will go. [. . .] It reforges the chain between what is and what is not, between the virtuality of the possible and what already exists in materialized nature" (192).

Plato's parable, in which men see shadows on the walls of a cave and must judge from those shadows what true "forms" outside of their restricted view are distorted and reflected (1944 [1892]), looms behind much of Artaud's writing, and provides the platform from which he appreciates Balinese performance. But Artaud's vision of essential life forms was far darker, more "cruel" than his Athenian predecessor's—far closer, in some ways, to a Tantric adept's worship of Shakti. Beyond his inverted neo-Platonic "forms," Artaud sensed a world of essential "force" that it was the actor's job to embody—always trying to move closer to that embodiment and always doomed to relative failure. "The actor does not make the same gesture twice, but he makes gestures, he moves; and although he brutalizes forms, nevertheless behind them and through their destruction he rejoins that which outlives forms and produces their continuation [. . .] that fragile, fluctuating center which forms never reach" (1958 [1938]: 9). Artaud sought "a pure theatrical language which does without words, a language of signs, gestures, and attitudes having an ideographic value" (192). In Balinese performance, Artaud thought he had found all of this, and an exemplary set of conventionalized gestures which, "in addition to an acute sense of physical beauty [. . .] always have as their final goal the elucidation of a spiritual state or problem" (61).

Working from this neo-Platonic frame of reference, and having available to him only a pastiche of dances and "scenes" from Balinese theatre presented to a predominantly Western audience (Pronko 1967: 24–26), Artaud naturally drew many false conclusions about the specifics of Balinese theatre. In rebellion against the primacy of the playwright in Western theatre as he knew it, and only being able to view samples of Balinese theatre that emphasized dance, he assumed that all theatre in Bali was essentially nonverbal. Looking for "animated hieroglyphs," he overestimated the abstract qualities of Balinese theatre and saw "mysterious signs which correspond to some unknown, fabulous, and obscure reality" (1958 [1938]: 111) where a Balinese audience would see, for example, a warrior looking about him or a king commanding his ministers by means of the familiar conventions of a popular theatre witnessed, *mutatis mutandis,* since childhood. Not having any way of knowing the signals that can pass between dancer and drummer, he believed Balinese theatre to be devoid of improvisation or individual initiative—even more immersed in ritualistic tradition than it is. Not realizing the strengths and paradoxical freedoms that can be the legacy of traditional form, Artaud assumed that theatre in Bali was a director's medium.

In spite of all of these understandable errors in interpreting Balinese performance, Artaud's articulation of the principles of Balinese theatre remains an eloquent testimony to its beauty and inspirational appeal. He was essentially correct in his perception that the Balinese dancer aimed at the "elucidation" of a "spiritual state." The impulse towards archetype and the intensity of signification that Artaud grasped is surely part of the Balinese aesthetic; but it is a part that is counterbalanced by the inclusion of more mundane frames of reference, frequently resulting in humor as these epistemologies clash. It is a shame that Artaud—who loved the Marx Brothers, but whose own theatrical works and projects tended to suffer from an overbearing portentousness—never had the opportunity to observe a topeng performance. The dancing principals do, indeed, seem immense and universally significant in their depiction of essentialized states sanctioned by the Balinese cosmos; but that sense of size and significance is rendered accessible and meaningful to the Balinese by the presence of the immediate, specific, and humorous storytellers and antic clowns who contextualize their appearances. As a tormented alien within his own culture as well as a stranger to Balinese performance, Artaud was doomed to miss the dynamic interplay between the mundane and the metaphysical which characterizes Balinese life in general and Balinese topeng in particular. Yet, it is precisely this interplay in topeng that facilitates in Bali what Artaud was to describe as "the true purpose of theatre: i.e., to create myths, to express life in its immense, universal aspect, and from that life to extract images in which we find pleasure in discovering ourselves" (1958 [1938]: 192).

Artaud's view of Balinese theatre was a Romantic one. Though he admired the cosmic reach of Balinese performance—its seeming access to absolute values, absolutely stated—he felt his audience to be cut off from all that was serious and enduring in human experience. His theatrical inclinations were to shock and startle his audience out of feelings of complacency. Hence, he sought a theatre of "cruelty." He envisioned theatre as an instrument for the radical restructuring of perception and action: "the sky can still fall on our heads and it is the first job of the theatre to teach us that" (1958 [1938]: 79). Artaud exemplifies (though certainly he did not originate) the tendency of the modern avant-garde to take the familiar and to aggressively estrange or "alienate" it in order to force a reconsideration of what, perhaps, has been assumed or unnoticed:

> The identifying signature of avant-garde art, all the way back to Bakunin and the anarchist journal *L'Avant Garde* in 1878, has been an unremitting hostility to contemporary civilization. And its most obvious aspect has been negative: the rejection of social organization and artistic conventions, aesthetic values and materialistic ideals, the bourgeoisie, syntactical structure, and logic. (Innes 1981: 9)

Artaud sought to shatter the metaphysical smugness of positivism and distrusted political mechanisms. For other avant-garde artists, though—particularly those of the political left—the focus of rebellion has been the system of power and prestige enshrined by capitalism. Brecht stated the strategy succinctly: "If we play works dealing with our own time as though they were historical, then perhaps the circumstances under which (the spectator) himself acts will strike him as equally odd; and this is where the critical attitude begins" (1964: 44). In Peter Weiss's *Marat/Sade*—a play influenced by both Artaud and Brecht—the character Marat sums up the avant-garde enterprise in its most positive terms with a statement that director Peter Brook had repeated several times at the end of his production: "The important thing is to pull ourselves up by our own hair, to turn yourself inside out and see the whole world with fresh eyes" (1966: 27).

When employed by a daring performer, the conventions of topeng may also function to encourage a "critical attitude." The significance of the quasi-historical events depicted may be turned about, inverted, and refracted prismatically by the succession of masked characters, each with a different vantage point, a different relationship to "history," and his or her own limited epistemology. This is the sense in which Boon can call topeng "subversive," and this capacity to refocus vision and thought is a substantial indicator of topeng's aesthetic and social vitality (cf. Jenkins 1994: 43–45). To perform their many functions, considerable license is granted to masked performers; but this charge carries its dangers as well: stories are told of performers executed by the Dutch and Japanese for their satiric remarks, and of Balinese performers murdered during the bloody killings of 1966 in retribution for comments made while performing (Young 1980). Despite this subversive potential, though, the strategies of topeng are essentially the inverse of those of the modernist avant-garde. As Boon notes in reference to the initial publication of Kakul's performance, "all the worlds of topeng are made *outside* to each other. [. . .] The tone is less interestedly satiric than disinterestedly parodic" (1984: 164).

There is a great deal at stake in this "disinterested" play. Kakul takes elements of knowledge and experience that are initially "strange" to each other and weaves them into the woof and warp of "normal" experience. Within each unit of the performance text that emerges, the movement is toward the quotidian and human, toward balance, and toward the containment of disparate forces. Each new unit begins with a new challenge to this capacity to balance and contain—be it within the domain of the drama or at the more important interfacing of everyday life with the enduring spiritual forces of the Balinese macrocosmos. In each new unit of action, and within each of the domains as they become appropriate "homes" for aesthetic and social action, the capacity to embrace disparate elements within the expanding circle of performance is triumphantly demonstrated. In topeng, as well as in the ritual performance described in chapter 2, the Balinese seem to delight in a kind of spiritual athleticism: the more dangerous the force and the more otherworldly the form, the more satisfying, therefore, the momentary containment, and the more exhilarating the performance. This attitude is significantly different from the impetus for social revolution or for psychological (or metaphysical) revelation that is characteristically a part of the enterprise of modernism, in which the work of art is posited as romantically antagonistic to life as it is usually lived and perceived in the "real" world.

Richard Wallis has traced a Balinese *arja* performance through its oscillations between the abstract and the familiar—the "traditional" and the "rationalized" in Clifford Geertz's religious and social terms (Wallis 1979; Geertz 1973: 170–89). Many of the same strategies evident in Kakul's solo performance may be recognized in his description of an arja performance of a *Mahabharata* story involving several actors, singers, and dancers:

Text-based feudal vignettes alternate with the details of ordinary, contemporary existence to produce a kind of telescoping effect. In one scene, epic characters may sing in literary languages and posture in highly stylized monumental poses, while at the same time their surrounding attendants busily create down-to-earth Balinese experiences among themselves. The audience can look from one group of characters to the other, adjusting the lens through which it views the respective time and geographic frames. (Wallis 1979: 42)

Wallis stresses the capacity of traditional Balinese theatrical forms to incorporate, play with, and effectively neutralize threatening aspects of modernization through this theatrical juggling of traditional and emergent world-views.[14] Wallis suggests that, just as family planning projects, schemes for national development, a war of suspect morality, and the tastes of tourists may be fastened upon as the subject of a joke or a lecture by a fourteenth-century king's irreverent attendant, the arrival of Portuguese and Dutch traders a few hundred years ago, and, long before that, the coming of priests, traders, and ideas from South Asia may have similarly provided fodder for Balinese performances—cross-referencing and re-contextualizing the old and the new. Such performances help Balinese audiences to clarify and manage their frequently conflicting and constantly shifting spheres of social and religious action—each with its own demands and (sometimes literally) its own language. The theatrical strategy is similar to religious Tantrism in its inclusiveness, and, like the ritual use of Rangda and the Barong Ket that is associated with Tantric traditions, this strategy aims at the containment and inclusion of threatening elements; witness the final appearance of Sidha Karya in a topeng pajegan performance.

By playing with emergent world-views in the context of traditional forms, the strategy allows for change as well as conservation. Kathy Foley has discussed the conservative potential of this process as exemplified in the *wayang cepak* puppet theatre of Cirebon, Java: "As the historical past pulls backward toward the mythical, so the *dalang* (puppeteer) composes his story to pull his audience members back into the vortex of history so the present can become a reflection of the past" (1986: 43). While this capacity to manifest, contain, and celebrate a storied past in a liminal present is certainly not unique to Bali, the prominence of this conservative strain within Balinese theatre and rhetoric has led some observers to postulate that the Balinese conceive of themselves as living in a "steady state" (Bateson 1972a [1949]: 384–402; C. Geertz 1973: 334, 391). Yet, as Foley's own work with the clowns of Sudanese rod puppet theatre (1984) implies, the relationship of Indonesian traditional performance to the historical and mythical events at the dramatic core can be far more complex. Far from demonstrating a "steady state," Kakul's topeng pajegan performance expends much of its energy measuring and remeasuring the distance between the past and present, looked at from different vantage points. If I read it correctly, his performance redeploys and inverts conservative strategies evident, for example, in New Guinean rituals and in traditional performances elsewhere in Indonesia and in Bali itself. His topeng affirms the appeal and validity of contesting world-views drawn from the past and the present, while demonstrating the performer's exemplary capacity to negotiate among them by means of his inspired play.

The utopia suggested by Kakul's performance is one of a complex set of balanced oppositions rather than the denial of new impulses or the supplanting of an old order by a newer one (or the showing up of all orders to be false) that is typically advocated by modernist works. Of course, this utopian attempt at maintaining balance can fail—just as revolutions may break down or create hierarchies more debilitating than those displaced. Such a failure happened, tragically, in 1965–66, when perhaps 50,000 to 100,000 people in Bali were killed following an unsuccessful revolutionary coup from the left (an event foreshadowed in the minds of many Balinese by an unprecedented infestation of rats and the devastating eruption of Bali's sacred volcano, Gunung Agung, after an attempt to hurry the ritual calendar for political ends). Competing modernist and traditional visions of utopia became irreconcilable, and both were doomed to failure.[15]

The metaphoric concern with balance is paralleled and exemplified by the prominent role given the act of balancing within topeng dance itself. Time and again in those dances that celebrate the enduring presence of the past in the context of the present, a performer will swirl full around, abruptly come to a stop with one knee raised, and then hold this balanced posture for two beats (or ten, or eighteen). The gamelan players stop the melody momentarily as the dancer comes into this arrested pose, contributing to the sense of synaesthesia, and accentuating the dancer's balancing feat. It is common in Balinese discourse to express a dislike for being *paling*—of losing one's balance, or becoming dizzy, or losing track of direction. It is also common to express fear of experiencing *lek*—or, as Clifford Geertz interprets the term, acquiring "stage fright" within social gatherings (1973: 401–3). The sudden turns and balances of the accomplished topeng performer (like the movements into and out of trance of the accomplished Rangda performer) may be seen as virtuosic displays of superiority over forces that act to knock one off balance, create a bewildering loss of direction or make one dizzy: paling. The performer's virtuosic mastery of masks that essentialize a vast array of social roles, and his spirited play with the linguistic conventions appropriate to these roles, similarly evoke a triumph over the forces that act to make one out of kilter in social situations: lek. In the microcosm of dance, as in the macrocosms of entire performances and the larger macrocosms that surround performances, the aim is balance and containment.

Balinese topeng, then, is radically different in its essential aims and strategies from the avant-garde movements of modernism. In its non-linear, de-centered approach to narrative and dramatic structure, however, it at least appears to have more in common with postmodern theory and practice in Western theatre. I have already noted the similarity of Kakul's inchoate "script" to Roland Barthes's postmodern concept of "Text." Barthes also penned a rallying cry for postmodernism: "Let difference surreptitiously replace conflict" (1975: 15). The conflict between Patih Jelantik and Dalem Blambangan is not of paramount importance to Kakul's performance (though it provides a logical sequence for the masks and its conclusion must be told, however briefly). What *is* of paramount importance is the richness of play as the various masks enter into the contexts created by this conflict and/or demanded by the conventions of topeng. It is precisely the "difference" of the various masks and the various moments of performance that matters. David Harvey notes that the "postmodern condition" is characterized by a view of the world in which "different realities may co-exist, collide, and interpenetrate" (1989: 41). What is so particularly appealing about topeng, and what seems so strikingly postmodern about it, is the dynamic movement into and out of the theatrical world reconstituted in each performance, and the playing back and forth between past and present, ancestral language and Balinese vernacular, visitation and illusion, character and performer, high caste and low caste, female and male, epiphany and parody, the metaphysical and the social, the fantastic and the mundane.

Elinor Fuchs has summarized the impact of postmodern aesthetics on theatre in the West: "A radical relativizing has occurred that permits theatre artists and their audiences to regard all reality as a bottomless series of illusions in which a central point of view—whether of character, actor, or author—has proved to be the chief illusion. In this 'dizzying regress' the stage is emptied of what we used to think of as reality" (1983). Many postmodernist works take, as their "central premise," "that the shifting illusions of performance constitute the only reality, and that 'character' and the human nature it depicts are mere constellations of performance attitudes" (Fuchs 1983). Harvey describes the effect of this postmodern view: "Cultural life is then viewed as a series of texts intersecting with other texts, producing more texts [. . .] This intertextual weaving has a life of its own" (1989: 49). As Boon points out, Balinese culture itself has something of this feel:

> Like a thousand "Popish" parodies, Balinese institutions, rituals, dramatic arts, and scribal traditions allude to each other in a perpetual reflexivity [. . .] . Everywhere in Balinese ideals and practice we must look beyond any allegorical Machinery to the dialectical field [. . .] from which it emerges. [. . .] Moreover, in its institutions and performances, Balinese culture [. . .] produces the means of exposing all of its allegorical Machineries, not as disguises (for there is nothing True underneath) but as masks. Indeed, everything is masks all the way down, and their symbolics never run out. (1986: 244, 258)[16]

One of the problems of postmodern theory has been a paucity of positive historical examples of deliberately "de-centered" works. The Derridean deconstruction of works supposedly formed around a center of "reassuring certitude, which is itself beyond the reach of play" (1978: 284), has proved useful in exposing the often illusory status of the center itself; but modern works that deliberately mirror a de-centered world tend to do so with the sense of loss and nostalgia evident in the famous opening lines of Yeats's "Second Coming," written in 1921:

Turning and turning in the widening gyre
The falcon cannot hear the falconer;
Things fall apart; the centre cannot hold;
Mere anarchy is loosed upon the world . [. . .] (1956: 184–85)

Even Lacan, who revealed the subjective "I" to be a constructed persona based on the love of a reflected image, found this theory to be problematical in psychiatric practice. It left no whole intact to contain the deconstructed parts. Psychiatrist J.D. Reynaud discusses the fragmentation of "personal functions" in modern (or postmodern society): "The industrialized society is a society of multiple memberships and belongings and, consequently, one in which personal functions differentiate themselves. Each individual occupies various positions, belonging to different hierarchies or different contexts, and playing as many roles. [. . .] [I]n other words, the unity of the persona becomes a problem" (1983: 213–24, unpublished trans. by Mark Siegel). When Derrida calls for positive examples of a de-centered world he must read Artaud's call for "a kind of organized anarchy" out of context (neglecting Artaud's inverted neo-platonism) or lapse into Nietzchean rhetoric, calling for "the affirmation of a world of signs without fault, without truth, and without origin which is offered to an active interpretation" (1978: 292).

This dilemma is not unique to the West. Over a decade ago, Claude Lévi-Strauss summarized the findings of a seminar on identity: "In spite of their distance in space and their profoundly heterogeneous cultural contents, none of the societies constituting a fortuitous sample seem to take for granted a substantial identity: they break it up into a multitude of elements for which, though in different terms for each culture, the synthesis is a problem" (1983 [1977]: 10–11, unpublished trans. by Mark Siegel). Forging a path and an identity among competing functions, hierarchies, and contexts—finding a synthesis—can be a problem for the Balinese, as well; it certainly is for Jelantik, for Cucul, and for the Penasar Cenikan among the masks in Kakul's performance.

Still, the Balinese seem to view the issue in less tragic terms. Putu Wijaya, a Balinese himself and a noted Indonesian novelist and playwright, has, in discussing his own characters, described their need to be "acrobats of the every day" in order to survive (quoted in Zarrilli 1987: 155). Kakul's topeng performance provides a modest example of a de-centered text existing acrobatically, joyously, playfully, and boisterously within a larger cultural field that itself delights in the reciprocal counterbalancing of its many "machineries." Unlike Derrida's envisioned "world of signs," though, the masks (and texts) of topeng, are not "without fault, truth, or origin." They essentialize faults and truths (some of these truths in direct opposition to each other, and some of these faults divinely empowered). They allude to a multiplicity of "origins" through the rituals and rhetoric of visitation, through a layering of historical references, and through the use of highly conventional traditional codes. The multiplicity of the "origins" deployed and alluded to in the gestural and spoken language of a topeng performance may itself be a de-centering device, yet the frequent allusions to a "macrocosmic" world dominated by divinities and ancestors protects topeng from the infinite regress into the self that marks so many postmodern works and which has led some critics to dismiss the entire movement as refried solipsism (cf. Shattuck 1985).

In Kakul's performance, he asserts that both the macrocosmos (*buwana agung*) and the microcosmos (*buwana alit*) made in its image "find expression in the body of every man." Thus, the hero Jelantik proclaims (twice) "I shall become the defender of the macrocosmos and the microcosmos, the spiritual order and the physical order, an order that finds expression in my own body." Within the dramatic domain, Jelantik successfully defends the order of his quasi-historical world from the demonic King of Blambangan; but his ordered world is more successfully challenged by the existence of Si Mata Mata and other masks that bear witness to alternate epistemologies and force a widening of perspectives on both macrocosmos and microcosmos. In performance, all these views of macrocosmos and microcosmos must find their "expression" in the topeng dancer himself. The end result of all of the ritual preparations, kinesthetic training, familiarization with masks and types, virtuosic displays of dance, soundings of archaic and vernacular languages, reflexive play among characters, meta-commentary about the performance, jokes with the audience, and offerings for the village's health and happiness that make up a topeng pajegan performance is an exemplary human act. The dancer shows himself able to embody a range of attributes representative of the entire knowable world and to negotiate its possibilities with strength, grace, and humor.

The techniques that the topeng performer uses to represent his various characters—to wear his various masks—are essentially those of the character actor and, as such, are not unique to Balinese acting. Long before Lacan or Kohut questioned the integrity of the constructed self, the actor's uncanny play with identity was seen in the West as a profoundly disturbing indication of the instability of character—an ontologically subversive activity (see Worthen 1984: 20–21)—as well as a testament to human creativity. As Bruce Wilshire has pointed out in *Role Playing and Identity: The Limits of Theatre as Metaphor*, the actor "thematizes" the struggle to find a self, "project[ing] his mimetic skill and susceptibility into possible modes of being human conjured up through his kinesthetic imagination" (1982: 232–34). Freud described the process of this "conjuring" of possible selves in a letter written in 1931 to an actress bewildered by her inability to keep a safe psychological distance between "her own person" and the "sleazy characters" she represented on stage: "[It is] not that the actor's own person is eliminated (in acting) but, rather, that elements of it—for instance, undeveloped dispositions and suppressed wishes—are used for the representations of intended characters and these are allowed exposure" (quoted in Shattuck 1985: 147). Sam Shepard, discussing his methods as a playwright, in effect amends and amplifies Freud's statement: "It isn't a question of having to write about ourselves, but of contacting in ourselves the elements—forces and tendencies—that are characters. The voices of a lot of external-world characters are inside you" (quoted in Shewey 1985: 122).

The Balinese actor both uses and transcends this amplitude of "the actor's own person" in order to give "representations of intended characters" their life in the theatrical moment. Working within the flexible limits of tradition, hoping for inspiration from his *taksu,* the performer must still tap within himself the "undeveloped dispositions" that will allow him to embody the potential life of each mask. In wearing his many masks, turn and turn about, the topeng pajegan performer becomes a living lexicon of a typology of characters that represent the range of epistemologies within Balinese society and its encompassing cosmos; the effect is to celebrate the variety, difference, and wholeness of a complex and ultimately sacred world as it finds expression within his own person. The artist's integrity resides in the fullness and clarity of his "exposure" of these different "dispositions," these "possible modes of being"—humorous and heroic, demonic and godlike, fantastic and mundane. His virtue is in his living proof that these differing potentialities exist within each individual human being—that a man, or a woman, is not only "created in the image of god," but contains within him or herself all that is divine. In doing this, he embodies the Sanskrit maxim, *Tat Twarm Asi*: Thou art That."[17]

For most postmodern artists and theorists, "That" is suspect. Without this larger sphere of reference, the isolated artist, not the cosmos, becomes the informing paradigm, and the reflexive techniques shared with Balinese topeng lead instead to narcissistic fascination with a dubious self. This is not without potential interest, either as a model of human behavior or as an activity which we might observe, and with which we may empathize; as Beckett has reminded us, "It's human: a lobster couldn't do it" (see Kenner 1961: 16); but it does create a far different affective field for the domains of performance. Caught between mourning a great breaking apart and fooling around with all the leftover pieces, the play of postmodern theatre often turns agonized, conflicted, infected with the (modernist) self-torture of Artaud's noble but ineffectual "victims burnt at the stake." Worse, it (sometimes, too often) becomes frivolous: play without significance or joy.

Notes

1. This chapter has been developed from a lecture given as part of the University of Hawaii's Center for Southeast Asian Studies Distinguished Scholar Series in January 1985. An earlier draft of "The Domains of Topeng" appears in *Art and Politics in Southeast Asia: Six Perspectives,* Southeast Asia Paper 32 (Honolulu: University of Hawaii Center for Southeast Asia Studies, 1989) and has been reworked here with permission of the Center. I am grateful to the University of Hawaii for asking me to speak, and, especially, to Robert van Neil, Flo Lamoureux, Roger Long, John and Lauren Marks, James Brandon, Judy Van Zile, Truong Buu Lam, Elizabeth Wichmann and David Harnish for their hospitality. Many people have contributed to the thinking in this version of my remarks; besides the debts noted in these pages, I would like to especially thank I Nyoman Wenten, I Wayan Dibia, Putu Wijaya, Kathy Foley, Mark Siegel, Mick Diener, and Steven Lewis for their comments, and Ulrike Emigh for her editorial suggestions.

2. The history of interactions between Asian and Western theatre traditions is summarized in the entry "Asian Influences on Western Theatre" by Emigh and Brandon in the forthcoming new edition of *The Cambridge Guide to Theatre* (1995). This entry contextualizes Artaud's interest in Bali in relation to the more widespread fascination with Asian practices (or reports of Asian practices) as examplary alternatives to what many modernist directors and playwrights saw as the deadend of naturalism. A survey of more recent adaptations of Asian theatre techniques in the West is also found in this entry, and in Brandon (1989).

3. Schechner himself takes this approach in giving a history of his own production of *The Tooth of Crime,* beginning with an account of the interactions between himself and playwright Sam Shepard (1988 [1977, 1973]: 73–84). As noted below, in his most recent revision (1988) Schechner has redrawn his circles with far less sense of regularity and clear definition of territory.

4. Claude Lévi-Strauss has commented at length on the multiplicity, malleability, and ambiguity of mythological "meaning":

> There is no real end to methodological analysis, no hidden unity to be grasped once the breaking down process has been completed. Themes can be split up *ad infinitum.* Just when you think you have disentangled and separated them, you realize they are knitting together again in response to the operation of unexpected affinities. [. . .] The unity of the myth is [. . .] a phenomenon of the imagination. (1969: 5–6)

See chapter 4, footnote 10, for further readings on the *babad dalem.*

5. The masks themselves, evidently captured as booty when the palace at Blambangan in East Java was sacked, are now kept in the Jelantik family temple in Blahbatuh—the *Pura Penataran Topeng.* Fifteen in number, they are now regarded as too sacred to photograph, but what may be an old photo of some of these masks is displayed in Vickers (1989: pl. 12). The masks are very similar to present-day topeng masks. "Topeng players" are known to have been performing in Bali since at least the end of the ninth century (see chapter 2), but it is not at all clear how close earlier masks may have been to these captured models, since "topeng"—literally meaning something to cover (*tup*) the face—can be used as a generic word for masks, as well as a more specific one for the masks used in topeng dance/drama. While Bandem and Rembang credit an ancestor named I Gusti Tusan Jelantik with first wearing the masks in performance, Bandem and deBoer (1981: 52–53) state that the first use of the masks in a performance, and the first recorded topeng

pajegan performance, was by Patih I Gusti Pering Jelantik (another of Jelantik's descendants) sometime between 1665 and 1686, during the reign of Baturenggong's grandson, Dalem Dimade. The important point for me here is the specific link to the ancestral past. For years at Gelgel, and later at Klunkung, the masks were used at the odalan (held every 210 days) of the temple linked to the royal family. Though no longer used in performance, such is the power accorded these masks that it said one of the first things that General Suharto did when he ascended to the presidency was to ask that the mask of Gajah Mada of Majapahit from the Blahbatuh collection be transferred to Jakarta as an emblem and source of power and symbol of unity.

6. See also the discussion of the languages used in topeng in chapter 4. For more comprehensive considerations of the various literary and spoken languages used in Balinese performance, see Wallis (1980) and Zurbuchen (1987).

7. The term "pseudo-work" is intended to be consistent with Barthes's distinctions between work and Text. Of course, the "Texts" that Barthes has in mind are themselves written, and the transcribed and translated words of Kakul's performance remain "Text-like"; but publishing this "performance text" at least threatens to convert it into something that might be treated as a "work"—separating it from its "field," holding it apart from its "production," and robbing it of much of its "jouissance."

8. As Susanne Langer (1953: 59–60) pointed out, in a far more sophisticated use of this term, artistic representation can also be made "transparent" after having been set apart, "uncoupl[ed] from practical life," made "subject to deliberate torsion, modification, and composition for the sake of expressiveness," and then made the instrument for insight into "the reality being expressed"—an insight that locks suddenly into place, allowing us to see through the created form to feel a sense of life beyond and behind the artistry. In this sense, topeng very much aims at transparency, with the important exception that the topeng cermonies (like Greek festival theatre), though bracketed and fully indulging in the possibilities of subjunctive play, remain very much "coupled to practical life." It may be worth noting that the pattern she suggests (minus the high art, formalist bias) is reminiscent of the one van Gennep described for rites of passage, one based on discrete stages featuring separation, margin, and return and reaggregation (see chapter 1).

9. See chapter 4, note 2 for further readings on odalans and life-cycle events that sustain topeng and other performance genres in Bali their traditional contexts.

10. This is not peculiar to Balinese or Asian theatre, of course. The use of a cosmological domain in constituting a dramatic and theatrical world has also been noted in Greek and Elizabethan practice (Kitto 1960 [1956], 231–45; Tillyard 1943). Though the Balinese sense of the immediacy of these domains may be greater, the play with them as normative reference points to human actions is no less complex or, sometimes, fraught with paradox and ambiguity.

11. The example given by Hildred Geertz of a topeng performance used to incite violent anger in a crowd offers a significant challenge to this view. Geertz offers her example as an anomaly; it is anomalous precisely because the world is not rendered whole and the audience's angry intervention is solicited instead of the performance moving towards the conferring of a blessing upon all assembled villagers. The more typical movement toward a sense of wholeness by an incorporation of the comic is not unique to Balinese theatre, of course. Shakespeare's subplots (and the presence of Falstaff) fulfilled the same function, and so did Greek *satyr* plays appended to tragic trilogies and Japanese *kyogen* comedies interspersed among *noh* dramas.

12. Elizabeth Young (1982) has transcribed and translated another topeng pajegan, *The Tale of Erlangga*, as performed by an unnamed artist in Sukawati. The script she offers is far more exegetical, and the anonymous artist uses the conven-

tions of topeng pajegan structure in a far less complex and imaginative way than Kakul. Too often, in studying non-Western performance forms, we act as though the culture generates the script, and overlook the contributions of individual genius. The culture may provide the banks of the river; the individual artist is accountable for the force and flow of the current.

13. Turner was to have second thoughts on this issue as he became more and more intrigued by the ways that "cultural performances" and "social dramas" mutually shape each other and turned his attention to carnivalesque traditions in Brazil, coming to the conclusion that. the "anti-structural" nature of the carnivalesque at least has the potential to provide models for change in the "plural reflexivity" that characterizes the symbiotic relation of life and art (1986: 123–38). The next chapter bears on related issues as it follows a trickster and anti-structural agent in India.

14. In the twenty years since Kakul performed and Wallis witnessed the arja performance he describes, modernization schemes, cultural tourism, and all the dangers that might be expected to accompany them have descended on Bali with a vengeance. The men who wear the masks of topeng and the women who, unmasked, increasingly play central comic and heroic roles in the performances now being fashioned—performances that most often blend the traditions of topeng with those of arja to create a relatively new synthetic form called *prembon*—have taken up the challenges posed by Westernization with robust humor and a sharp critical eye. As Ron Jenkins reports, shrill bursts of broken English have now been added to the players' linguistic repertoire, "evil spirits are dressed in imported galoshes, legendary heroes are introduced to government family planning, and fifteenth-century battles are interrupted by tourists looking for souveneirs." I Nyoman Catra, a topeng performer who sometimes arrives through the curtain as a bondres tourist with a prominent sunburnt nose, snapping photos, shaking hands, and demanding the prices of gamelan instruments and dancers' headgear, states the challenge this way: "Our culture needs a filter to modify the influence of Westernization. [. . .] The clowns help us filter out the excesses of progress so that we can change and evolve without losing the traditions that make Bali unique" (Jenkins 1994: 18–19). I Gusti Windia's most popular mask is the malapropism-prone would-be modern village woman, Ratu Gegek. She has been called "a comic incarnation of cultural vertigo," and skewers Balinese males as well as the West with her loopy logic. Windia slyly suggests that "when people leave the temple they will remember the ideas inside the jokes and think about them at home. It is their homework" (Jenkins 1994: 26–27). The strategy of containment continues, and with very high stakes. "Balinese clowns personify the relsilience of their culture's instincts to survive" (Jenkins 1994: 45).

It has recently become popular to hire out just bondres players for large parties and public gatherings, forgoing the elaborate interplay of past and present, halus and keras, that gives topeng its formal richness; still, Catra, Windia, I Ketut Kantor, maskmakers Ida Bagus Anom and Ida Bagus Alit and others of the younger generation have defied dire predictions of its demise and still perform topeng pajegan at temple holidays and family life-cycle ceremonies.

15. The effects of the killings of 1966 on Balinese performance (and the role of performance in those events) have not been adequately studied. For information on the killings and their immediate context see Cribb (1991 [1990]: 241–260) and Vickers (1989: 163–173). It is striking that the essays by Clifford Geertz that did most to perpetuate the notion of Balinese culture existing in a "steady state," sustained by a non-linear, cyclical concept of time exemplified and inculcated by performances (1973: 327–44, 360–411), were researched at the historical moment when the tensions leading up to these tragic events were reaching a breaking point; they were being readied for publication (they originally came out in 1966 and 1967)

even as these killings were taking place. If there are cautionary lessons here, one must be that cultures—insofar as they exist at all outside of the hermeneutic activities of the anthropologist—are not static entities, but, rather, sites where values contest: there are no steady states.

16. Boon's metaphor is reminiscent of (and probably based upon) an account given by Clifford Geertz of an explanation of the Hindu cosmology: "There is an Indian story [. . .] about an Englishman who, having been told that the world rested on a platform which rested on the back of an elephant which rested in turn on the back of a turtle, asked [. . .] what did the turtle rest on? Another turtle. And that turtle? 'Ah Sahib, after that it is turtles all the way down'" (1973: 28–29).

17. The Hindu maxim *Tat Twam Asi*, "Thou Art That," expressing the oneness of microcosm and macrocosm, is first found in the *Chadogya Upanishad*, written by Uddalaka in approximately 600 BC (see Cairns 1992: 29–30; Eiseman 1989: 12–14).

Chapter 6
A Joker in the Deck: Hajari Bhand of Rajasthan

Written with Ulrike Emigh

Hajari Bhand of Chittorgarh (fig. 73) is renowned throughout the Mewar region of southern Rajasthan as a *bahurupiya*—a wandering mimic and comic. Although he only rarely wears masks in his work, his mischievous play with social and psychological identity is another form of masking and provides a fitting complement to the mask-play of *topeng*—another entry point to some of the central issues these traditions share. For two months in 1982–83, Hajari Bhand graciously gave up semi-retirement so that we could document his work and took to the road again—visiting some of the 460 towns and villages that have comprised his circuit and performing twenty-five different roles—including some routines with his son, Janakilal Bhand. In the months that followed, we visited his home to share raw footage from the film we were making and to interview him concerning his life as a bahurupiya and—prior to Independence—as a jester, praise singer, and wit in the Mewar courts.

Using Hajari Bhand's life and work as an example, this chapter is an inquiry into the art and function of the now vanishing bahurupiyas and Bhands of Rajasthan. In *The Fool and His Scepter: A Study in Clowns and Jesters and Their Audience*, William Willeford notes that, "Fools have generally lacked the kind of fully established personal and social identities that can be made the subjects of biography and history" (1969: xix). In some ways, Hajari Bhand's life has followed a scenario of trials and choices that we might think of as typical of the unchronicled jesters who worked at court and on the road in medieval Europe; thus, besides documenting the work of a remarkable performer in a fading tradition, an account of his life and art may also provide an imperfect window to an irrecoverable Western past.

The term "bahurupiya" derives from the Sanskrit *bahu* (many) and *rupa* (form). Hajari Bhand claims to have portrayed several hundred characters over the past forty-five years—creating and recreating a vast assortment of

Figure 73. Hajari Bhand at his home. Chittorgarh, Rajasthan, India, 1983.

Figure 74. Hajari Bhand making up to play the Pagal.

Rajputs and holy men, professional men and tribals, gods and goddesses, tradesmen and rogues, beggars and fools. As one who assumes many forms and playfully takes on different identities, he is aided by the fact that, in Rajasthan, a great deal about a person's occupation, social standing, expected behavior, and speech patterns can still be predicted by the clothing worn. Great emphasis is placed on a bahurupiya's skill at costuming and makeup (see fig. 74). A bahurupiya's disguise is known as a *vesh*—from the Sanskrit *vesa,* for clothing or dress—and the art of presenting himself in makeup and costume is referred to as "doing a vesh." The usually comic pattern of behavior that accompanies the wearing of a vesh is known as a *sang* or *swang.* Derived from the Sanskrit *svanga,* "having graceful action" (Dash 1979: 14), this term now signifies a comic routine. One may refer almost interchangeably to a bahurupiya's vesh or his sang, with a slight shift of emphasis from his appearance to his actions.

Using the streets, courtyards, and marketplaces of Mewar as venues for his veshes and sangs, Hajari Bhand imitates, exaggerates, and sometimes violates stereotypical expectations for comic and dramatic effect. He drops old roles, adds new ones, and frequently changes his patter as the times, his changing interests, and those of his audience require. His art is fashioned from a detailed knowledge of the dress and behavior patterns appropriate to the castes, character types, and figures from mythology that have traditionally comprised the Rajasthani world; and his playful portrayals reflect and help to shape the Rajasthani public's sense of its own identity in its most human terms.

Bhands and Bahurupiyas

The history of the Bhands in India is sketchily known at best. The Sanskrit *bhana* denotes a comic monodrama in which the actor plays many parts (Raghavan 1981: 40–41), while *bhanda* is a Sanskrit term for a jester (Russell and Lal 1975 [1915] 1: 349). Historical connections with the pot-bellied, irreverent *vidusakas* of Sanskrit drama, as well as with the witty parasites mentioned in Vatsyayana's *Kamasutra,* may well be valid (Welsford 1948: 63–64); but ancestors of the present-day Bhands are said to have entered India from Persia with the Muslim courts, and are especially associated with Timur-leng (Tamburlaine), who invaded India in 1398 (Russell and Lal 1975 [1915] 1: 349). As a result of these historical movements, there is still a substantial concentration of Bhands in Kashmir, where a form of farcical drama, *bhand pather,* is performed on Islamic saints' days and other festive occasions; many of the Bhands presently in north India seem to have come down from Kashmir at a later date (Russell and Lal 1975 [1915] 1: 349; Motilal Kemmu 1980, personal communication). Like the Kashmiri Bhands, most Bhands in north India are Muslim. Thus Crooke (1974 [1896] 1: 259) cited figures for Uttar Pradesh, Punjab, and Haryana showing over 14,000 Muslim Bhands living in these areas, but only fourteen Hindu Bhands. In Rajasthan, however, because of strong resistance to the spread of Islam, a separate Hindu caste arose, including Hajari Bhand's ancestors, who served the courts of Mewar as jesters.

The existence of Bhands in the region seems to be of considerable antiquity. G. N. Sharma (1968: 149) quotes the *Samyaktva* of Taruna Prabha Suri, written in 1354, as already mentioning "bhands and troupes of professionals of both sexes performing buffoonery and farce, accompanied by music, dance, and dialogue." The *A'in-i Akbari* of Abu'l Fazl 'Allami makes note of Bhands playing percussion instruments, and "singing and mimicking men and animals" in sixteenth-century India (1978 [1894] 3: 272). In a 1983 conversation, Professor Sharma expressed his belief that Bhands played a vital role in developing the dramatic aspect of the *bhavai* theatre in Gujarat, as well as much of the popular theatre of Rajasthan.

Up until recently, Bhands have corresponded closely both in their function and in their activities to the professional buffoons and "artificial fools" of medieval Europe. The *Ethnographic Atlas of Rajasthan* states that, "known for their ready wit and humor, their art of story telling, jokery and buffoonery, the Bhands provide entertainment and fun to the people of festivals and feasts with the aid of their exciting fables and satires" (Mathur 1969: 60–61). A traditional Hindi proverb has it that a Bhand is "as essential at an entertainment as a tiger in a forest" (Crooke 1974 [1896] 1: 258). Within the Rajput courts, Bhands entertained in the evening hours in military encampments or on hunting expeditions, singing out praises for a good shot or jibing at a missed one. Similarly, they accompanied Rajas into battle—sometimes dressed as a Rajput ancestor—praising brave deeds or making jokes at the expense of both sides. Tulsinath Dabhai of the palace at Udaipur puts the case simply: "Their main function was to make the Raja laugh" (1983, personal communication).

Rawat Kesari Singh, a patron of Hajari Bhand since the days before Independence, stresses that "financially (Bhands) were completely dependent on Rajputs. They were given food, grains, and clothes, and at the marriages and deaths of their family members all the expenses were paid by the Rajas and Jagidars." To earn this support, the Bhand provided his royal patron with amusement, flattering praise, and at times witty and stinging criticism. "It was," says Singh, "a very necessary part of court life" (1983, personal communication).

Like medieval jesters, the Bhands were privileged men; but such privileges have limits and, like their European counterparts, they were in constant danger of losing their livelihood by failing to amuse or overstepping the boundaries of royal humor. K. S. Ada of the Bhartiya Lok Kala Mandal in Udaipur tells a story that illustrates the skills required for survival (1982, personal communication). A Bhand in Jaipur had fallen out of favor with his Raja and been told never to show his face to the ruler again. After he had departed in shame, a great procession was scheduled out of Jaipur. The Bhand coated his buttocks with wheat powder, stationed himself on a hill at the front of the crowd, and bent over, exposing his rear as his monarch paraded by. When asked to explain this extraordinary behavior, the Bhand said that he felt an overwhelming desire to present himself and pay proper homage to his King, but, alas, since he was forbidden to show his face, what else could he do? He was immediately restored to favor.

The practice of performing as a bahurupiya is now associated with Bhands; but formerly members of various castes, including Brahmans, practiced this art, in villages as well as at the courts. The *A'in-i Akbari* lists the "Bahurupi" as separate from the Bhands and notes that in their daytime mimicry, "youths disguise themselves as old men so successfully that they impose on the most acute observers" ('Allami 1978 [1894] 3: 272). The term denotes a professional activity rather than a caste and not all Bhands have been gifted at this particular set of skills: "It is an art, and a gift. Not all can do it," says Hajari Bhand (1983, personal communication).

Central to the art of the bahurupiya is the ability to create convincing impersonations of identifiable types. Impersonations of deities at Hindu temple festivals may have led to performances involving the comic mimicry of social types among such castes as the Rawals by the end of the fourteenth century (Bhanawat 1979: 26–27). Bhands may have adopted these skills to increase their repertory as jesters. These origins are argued for by the fact that in Orissa, where the Muslim courts had far less influence, the term "bahurupiya" is applied exclusively to those impersonating Hindu deities (Dash 1979: 15 and 1983, personal communication); and both Hindu and Muslim Bhands who act as bahurupiyas in Rajasthan now sometimes represent Hindu deities. The combination of mimicry with court jests is a natural one, with or without evolution from divine impersonation. The fourteenth-century Italian buffoon, Gonello, for instance, is said to have "carried various disguises about with him" and to have depended upon his gifts for mimicry and impersonation for the success of many of his jests (Welsford 1948: 14). Whatever their religion, their caste, or the origins of their art, bahurupiyas from Gujarat to Bengal have traditionally prided themselves on the accuracy of their impersonations of men and women from all walks of life and on their ability to deceive even those who know them well. Thus this report from the Punjab Census Report of 1881 (paragraph 529): "One of their favorite devices is to ask for money, and when it is refused to ask that it may be given if the Bahurupia succeeds in deceiving the person who refused it. Several days later, the Bahurupia will again visit the house in the disguise of a peddler, a milkman, or what not, sell his goods without being detected, throw off his disguise and claim the stipulated reward" (Denzil Charles Ibbetson as quoted in Russell and Lal 1975 [1915] 1: 344).

Enid Welsford summarizes the conditions that made the professions of court jester and wandering buffoon possible in medieval and Renaissance Europe as follows:

> It was the existence of the small cultivated court, the sharp distinction but close connection between all classes of society and the comparative rareness of books which made buffoonery so lucrative and popular a profession. The jest books of the 16th century depict variegated but compact little societies, where king, burgher, priest and peasant are perpetually jostling one another, and the buffoon slips in and out licking up something from them all." (1948: 22)

This description applies as well to the princely states of Rajasthan before 1947. With Independence, the social and political system that had sustained the Bhands as court jesters was significantly altered, and the capacity of the courts to offer patronage drastically weakened. For a time, Bhands skilled in the art of the bahurupiya could earn their living through public performances, but the popularity of films and now of television have undercut the support available from the general populace.

Bahurupiyas are becoming scarce, but they have not yet vanished. Babulal Bhand of Gauri in Rajasthan's Swayambhadpur District travels with two younger members of his family throughout the Hindi-speaking region of north India, following "his own sweet will" and earning 5,000 to 10,000 rupees a year. Babulal claims that 2,000 to 4,000 people—most of them Bhands or Naqqals—still earn a substantial part of their income as bahurupiyas (1982, personal communication).[2] Of the over 4,000 Bhands in Rajasthan listed in the 1961 census, R. S. Ashiya of the Bhartiya Lok Kala Mandal estimates that fifty or sixty families still make a substantial part of their income through their traditional skills (1983: 14). Bhands have taken up agriculture, government services, and many other walks of life in order to survive. As members of a scheduled caste, younger Bhands receive educational aid, and Kesari Singh notes a tendency among the educated youth to despise the traditional work of their caste: "They regard it as a shameful profession and feel they should give it up" (1982, personal communication). This attitude is reinforced by those who regard Bhands and bahurupiyas as beggars.

In response to the tendency among townspeople to regard the Bhands as mendicants, Hajari Bhand speaks with dignity, pride, and unconcealed anger:

> I am the Bhand of Rajas and Maharanas. We have been Bhands for a long time. All my forefathers were Bhands. [. . .] I have an allotted area of 460 villages, and I am respected in all these 460 villages. Everyone greets me with respect and I greet them with respect also. I am not a beggar. I am a Bhand. I live in Chittor. [. . .] Now, after the death of the Maharana, I have created my own patrons, and I am recognized and respected by all of these people.[3]

A Bhand's Life

Hajari Bhand was born in March 1922. He does not know the exact date. His father, Kaluji, was forty-six years old when Hajari was born, and Hajari's elder brother, Mohan, was seventeen years his senior. His father performed four or five roles, which he taught Hajari, and his brother taught him more; but he has been largely self-taught, and unlike other bahurupiyas he has never studied under a guru. Both Kaluji and Mohanji were better known as experts at *bhandai*: praising the patron by reciting verses in his honor, or else, if the occasion called for it, criticizing, exposing, or ridiculing him in verse. Kaluji was also head (*patel*) of the Bhand community in the Chittorgarh area and his responsibilities included keeping discipline within the community and organizing ritual functions. As Hajari recalls, "Wherever he went, whatever he did, every sort of work, two or four hundred people would gather. He would hold council and they heeded his word. He would treat everyone with respect."

Hajari's grandfather was Moraji Bhand, who originally lived with his brother Jhoraji in Bhandakakhera—on lands ceded to the Bhands after one of their number had posed as a holy man and tricked Maharana Sajan Singh of Udaipur himself into becoming a disciple (Bhanawat 1974: 15). Family legend has it that Jhoraji became a particular favorite of Maharana Svarup Singh when he appeared dressed as a golden lion at a *shikar*, or hunting expedition, held by the ruler. Seeing the "lion," Svarup Singh shot at Jhora Bhand, who was wearing iron plates on his chest for protection. As Hajari Bhand tells the story, "The Maharana fired and the lion stood up on two legs. As soon as he was hit, he fell to the ground. After five minutes he stood up again. Then he declared 'I am Jhora Bhand!' The Raja cried out, 'He is killed! How did he get here as a lion?'" Jhora Bhand was smeared with animal blood. He had a glass bullet in his hand and showed it to the hunt master. Finally, he removed his disguise and revealed himself, saying, "I fooled you, and now I am your Bhand." He was given over 200 *bighas* of land (about 120 acres) near Mandal, in Bhilwara District.

This event took place in the mid-nineteenth century, beginning a long association of Hajari Bhand's family with the royal courts of Mewar. During the rule of Maharana Fateh Singh, Moraji brought his family to Chittorgarh, while Jhoraji's family moved to nearby Bassi, where the local *zamindars* gave them more fertile land. Every year during the Navaratri festivities preceding Dasahara, members of Kaluji Bhand's family, along with other Bhands, would appear at the *darbar* of the Maharana of Mewar at Udaipur—a custom Hajari continued until recently. During the rest of the year, ten families of Bhands would alternate attendance at the Maharana's court, but the Bhands of Chittorgarh were regarded as particular favorites of the Maharana (Bhanawat 1974: 15–16). Silver coins were placed on lances and given to the Bhands as payment for a good joke or comic routine. During the Navaratri visits, Hajari would receive up to 1,000 rupees in addition to costumes, food, emergency funds to meet specific needs, and, occasionally, more land. At other times, the Maharana would visit their area and the Chittorgarh Bhands would come to entertain. They also worked under the patronage of the local Rajputs of the Bassi and Chittorgarh areas, gave occasional public performances, and were engaged by temples to play gods in religious processions.

In 1936, at the age of fourteen, Hajari was married to the daughter of a Bhand from Indore. He started living with her when he was fifteen, in the house where he still lives. At about this time, Hajari began to perform as a bahurupiya—first in supporting roles and then for a year under the patronage of the Thakur (roughly translatable as "lord") of Bhatyankakhera. Each day he would go to the Thakur's house to eat, and while there he also started to learn the art of bone-setting from the Thakur—a skill he still practices in addition to his work as a bahurupiya.

When he was seventeen, Hajari Bhand came to the court of Maharana Bhupal Singh at Udaipur. While he was at the court, a famous bahurupiya from Jaipur, Ramchandra, arrived. Ramchandra was not a Bhand, but a Brahman who went from court to court practicing the art of the bahurupiya. His paraphernalia and costumes filled an entire railway baggage car. At Udaipur, Hajari saw him win great favor and two hands full of silver rupees by pretending to be a crocodile in the palace lake, frightening and delighting the Maharana. This is how Hajari tells the story:

> The bahurupiya Ramchandra dressed up as a crocodile and plunged into the lake. Someone cried: Oh, where has this beast come from? Bring a gun, someone! By the time they brought the gun the crocodile had dived back into the lake, letting only its snout stick out. As soon as the people handed the gun to the Maharana, the crocodile said: "I am the bahurupiya Ramchandra from Jaipur"!

The officer in charge of entertainment praised Ramchandra's bravery, derided the Bhands of Chittorgarh as having little talent or imagination, and challenged them to appear in a novel disguise or return to Chittorgarh in shame.

Owing to his already evident skills in mimicry, young Hajari was chosen to represent his family. "The next day, I disguised myself as a demon (*raksasa*) first of all. I went among the crowd and many men and women were really frightened. Next, I dressed as a pregnant Pinjari (a woman who cards unspun cotton). I went before the Raja and said, 'Oh, what has happened to me? You, Bhupal Singhji, you have deprived me of my honor!' " As Bhupal Singh tried to conceal his laughter with a handkerchief, Hajari pointed to the Maharana, who had been crippled by polio as a youth, and addressed the crowd: "That one, sitting there, even though he can't walk a step, he still got me pregnant!" Bhupal Singh seems to have been delighted at this flattering abuse. "So Bhupal Singhji gave me 125 rupees and said, 'You did a sang which made us convulse with laughter. Now don't do this any longer.' The Maharana was choked with laughter and he told them, 'Give them 125 rupees and give them good food and treat them well.' "

Young Hajari was not through, however. He disguised himself next as a Gaduliya, an itinerant maker and vendor of iron wares whose caste claims descent from Rajput blacksmiths and swordsmiths of ancient Chittor (see color plate VII)—a claim that the Kshatriya castes deny and resent. His account of his work in this disguise further illustrates how a Bhand exercised his privilege and flirted with disfavor in order to gain greater favor. After many obscene puns about furnishing the assembled lords with iron tools, Hajari shouted out, "I am a Gaduliya. I am one of your ancestors." As Hajari Bhand continues the story:

I said I was a Rajput and shouted all the time. Some two, three people tried to stop my mouth, but the Maharana was very pleased. They said, "Don't shout! We'll give you whatever you demand." The next day the Maharana gave me a reward of 250 rupees. He said the Bhands of Chittorgarh may freely come to the court.

Hajari had successfully gauged his patron's sense of humor and his daring had won him favor. Before the stay was over, he had also performed as a washerwoman, an Afghani aphrodisiac salesman, a shepherd, and a dancing girl. Ramchandra, defeated in competition by the young Bhand, offered Hajari's father 300 rupees a month if he would turn the boy over to him. Kaluji Bhand refused this offer and Bhupal Singh gave Hajari 600 more rupees in appreciation of his skill and heaped gifts of clothing upon him. "Then he told me to come to the palace dressed in those things. I went dressed in them and he said, 'Now you look like a Rajput.' Then I said, '*Khama dhani*—excuse me, Your Highness,' and went back home." Hajari remained a great favorite with Bhupal Singh, and over the years until his death in 1955, Bhupal Singh rewarded and encouraged Hajari's talents by giving him money, a ceremonial sword, and costumes valued at over 20,000 rupees.

Hajari still visits some of his former patrons, such as the Thakur of Orli, Kalyan Singh, and Rawat Kesari Singh, now the elected mayor of Bassi. They express great affection for him and invite him to perform at family weddings and other gatherings. As recently as 1971, Hajari dressed his large family as a group of Bhil tribals and entertained the present Maharana Pramukh of Udaipur, Bhagat Singh. The grateful descendant of the Maharanas rewarded Hajari with 400 rupees. Still, Bhagat Singh does not share the passion of his ancestors for the Bhands' jokes, disguises, and comic turns, and in any case, he does not command his ancestors' treasury (G. N. Sharma 1983, personal communication).

With the dwindling of Rajput patronage after Independence, Hajari Bhand has had to rely more on village audiences, and especially the merchant castes for support. Despite the spectacular success at Bhupal Singh's court, the Bhands of Chittorgarh had anticipated this problem, and by the time Hajari Bhand was twenty years old, he, his brother Mohan, and a neighbor, Champalal Bhand, had begun to go into the villages to perform publicly. Eventually, their travels included villages in the Udaipur, Kapesan, Bhilwara, and Chittorgarh areas, and ranged as far as Banswara, 120 kilometers away, creating a circuit of 460 villages. These villages were shared among six families of Bhands working out of Chittorgarh, while another 250 villages were allotted to a group of Bhands from Devli. Sometimes, villages would be alternated from year to year between cooperating families, and family members would be assigned to play their veshes at specific villages. In the event that a bahurupiya performed his veshes in a place assigned to another, he would have to pay a share of his earnings to the person whose territory he had infringed upon. This practice seems to be less in force now, as fewer Bhands are working in the villages. In any case, Hajari did not need to seek permission to enter the villages we visited, since his high status within the community exempted him from these restrictions.

As Hajari grew older, sometimes one or two children from his growing family would accompany him for veshes involving more than one character. At other times, he would perform with his brother Mohan. Most of the time, however, he traveled alone, leaving bundles of costumes at relatives' houses scattered throughout the district. When arriving at a new place, he found accommodation at a caste member's home, a *dharamsala* (public guest house), or sometimes with the local nobility. In a small village, Hajari Bhand usually performed two veshes a day, one in the morning and one in the afternoon. In large towns, a single vesh might take all day. His stay in a village would ordinarily last one or two weeks. As he performed from shop to shop and door to door, he accepted payment offered by onlookers, and also kept a ledger recording the names of shopowners and householders he entertained. At the end of his stay, he usually appeared in the disguise of a moneylender, a Bania, and collected from those he had entertained, marking the amounts of payment in his record book. Those entertained are expected to give something, be it money, rice, wheat, corn, or other payment in kind according to the season. He estimates that the income from touring half the year amounted to 3,000 to 4,000 rupees.

During his travels, Hajari kept expanding his repertory, picking up ideas from other wandering mimics and inventing new roles based on people he observed in the courts, towns, and villages. "Where I could, I learned, and where I couldn't learn, I taught." Often, he built up characters by observing real-life models over extended periods of time. He tells of attaching himself to a Muslim Fakir for two weeks in order to study his ways. The lengths he might go to in order to master a new role, as well as his adventurous spirit, are shown in his acquisition of the costume of a Behru Jogi, a mendicant Hindu holy man. After approaching a Behru Jogi about obtaining the costume, he was told that he must wear it for one hour a day for twelve years without accepting money before he could earn the right to use it in his work. "Twelve long years, I wore the costume every morning for one hour. While I was acting the role, people would give me flowers and money, but I didn't accept anything from them. If a flower was given, I gave it to the dogs, and if money was given, I distributed it to children." After this long apprenticeship, Hajari Bhand not only acquired the right to use the costume as a bahurupiya, but also "the spiritual powers (*siddhi*) of a Behru Jogi." Hajari once put on the costume to face down a local practitioner of black magic who had threatened a relative of his, drawing a protective circle around the intended victim. He believes that the powers accruing from his disciplined apprenticeship with this costume have helped him gain respect and relative prosperity. "In its name, I am earning my living and working as a bahurupiya."

Hajari Bhand's life has not been spent entirely on the road or at royal courts. He is a leader of the Bhand community in Chittorgarh, has married twice, and has fathered thirteen children—the youngest having been born in 1981. Hajari's first wife died when he was twenty-four. He was remarried to a daughter of Ambalalji Bhand of Jaipur, a Bhand noted for his poetic skills. Of his two children by his first wife and eleven by his second, nine sons and one daughter were still alive in 1983. To support this large family and supplement his earnings as a bahurupiya, Hajari Bhand supervises cultivation of the family lands (now ten bighas). He also earns additional income from assisting with makeup at school plays and "fancy-dress" competitions. Most importantly—and quite apart from his work as a bahurupiya—he also practices as a bone-setter, and his house is frequently visited by people who have broken, sprained, or dislocated a limb. After being introduced to this skill by the Thakur of Bhatyankakhera, he developed it while achieving distinction as an amateur wrestler. He does not accept cash payments for his services, but grateful patients and their parents have given him goats, cows, and building materials through the years. He also performs frequently in the streets of Chittorgarh. Here, Hajari Bhand does not need to keep a record book. Well known by the local merchants, he collects his fees twice a year, at the holidays of Divali and Holi.

Festival occasions are important workdays for bahurupiyas. Bhands may be hired by temples to represent gods and goddesses, or they may portray such figures on their own accord. As a younger man, Hajari used to appear on Divali as the goddess Lakshmi, though in 1983 he considered himself too old to successfully perform this vesh, and during our stay he substituted portrayals of Hanuman and Shiva. On the Muslim holiday of Id, Hajari dresses as a Muslim Fakir (fig. 75), gently satirizes these holy beggars, and collects at least 500 rupees from the amused celebrants. Both Muslim and Hindu Bhands often perform this vesh on Id, and there seems to be no sacrilege or resentment felt by the Muslim community regarding Hajari's comic portrayal, nor on the part of the Hindu community when Muslim Bhands portray Hindu deities.

In addition to performing from shop to shop in towns and villages, Bhands appear as invited or uninvited guests at the weddings of the wealthy merchant castes—these castes having taken over (to an extent) the patronage of the Bhands. While Babulal Bhand most frequently appears at such an occasion as a Bania, making jokes about the merchant caste's historical involvement with the practice of usury and on the new couple's coming economic plights, Hajari usually goes dressed as a policeman (fig. 76). He starts from his home already disguised as an officer, often commandeering bus rides along the way. "Sometimes a policeman shakes hands with me.

Figure 75. Hajari Bhand putting on the costume of a Muslim Fakir.

Figure 76. Hajari Bhand as a Police Inspector.

Sometimes even a police inspector shakes hands. 'Where have you come from?' he says, 'Where have you been transferred from?' 'I've been transferred from Durgapur.' " In this manner, he makes his way to the wedding festivities, sometimes revealing the joke and sometimes not. "Then I address the people of the wedding party. I frighten and threaten people. 'Hey mister! What do you think you're doing?' 'Oh no, Sir. I'm not doing anything.' 'Remove this bus from here! Ho, where is the license for this vehicle?' 'We don't have all of the necessary papers.' " At times, Hajari Bhand will encounter a real policeman at the wedding. "I tell him, 'The number on your belt is upside down.' He corrects the belt and salutes me." At large receptions, he may invoke a public law designed to reduce wasteful expenditures on wedding feasts and order the reception disbanded. "I call the bridegroom's father and ask him: 'How many persons have you assembled here?' '150 persons, Sir.' 'Why did you assemble 150 persons? The government's law does not allow that. The law allows only fifty-one persons to assemble for a feast. Why have you done this?' 'Oh Sir, we'll never do it again.' " As protests mount, angry words are exchanged, and bribes offered, he reveals his disguise and collects liberal fees from the relieved relatives.

Hajari recognizes that fewer and fewer Bhands are now able to sustain themselves by the traditional skills of their caste, and he has exerted no pressure on his children to take up his work. Although many of these children are still quite young, so far only one of Hajari's nine living sons, Janakilal (the second son by his first wife) has taken up the work of the bahurupiya, and his activities are limited to festival days. In Bhilwara, where he works in a flour mill to make ends meet, Janakilal Bhand usually performs for twenty days during the Divali season, six days during Holi, and occasionally travels to the weddings of well-to-do merchants and bankers of the Maheshwari and Oswali Bania castes.

Although he sometimes regrets the drying up of royal patronage, Hajari enjoys working the village crowds. He is regarded with great affection, and mentioning his name evokes smiles, anecdotes, and words of appreciation for his skills as a comic artist and his standing in the larger community. Hajari says that when he was a young man he was offered a contract for performing in the then fledgling film industry of Bombay. Taking his father's advice, he turned down the offer. He has no regrets.

The Art of Bhandai

The ability to give both flattering praise and stinging abuse was central to a Bhand's skills. Both the praise and the abuse are referred to by the generic term, *bhandai.* Bhandais praising a patron might be given as a salutation or as an expression of gratitude. The formula for these bhandais involves naming valued ancestors, praising the patron's worth, and proffering blessings on the patron and his family. These encomiums are often lavish in hyperbolic praise. This is a bhandai Hajari Bhand composed and recited in our presence to one of his traditional patrons, Kalyan Singh, Thakur of Orli:

> Oh Sir, you are the Protector of the Earth, like Chhatrapati Shivaji! The whole earth becomes free and their bonds are broken the moment they look at you! You are like Mahadev in appearance and all baseness flees at a single glance from you! You are more liberal in charity and braver in warfare than any other! You can transform a worthless shell into a jewel worth hundreds of thousands of rupees, such is your worth-enhancing power! This village of Orli where you Rathors rule is like heaven on earth. May God keep you happy forever!
>
> The whole world knows that you are like an incarnation of God. Your name is

known everywhere in the universe. [. . .] May your illustrious Rathor family shine like the sun! Hajari Bhand will go on singing your virtues forever.

Your household estates are like those of a Lord of the Earth. Your heart is large and generous. Oh Kalyan Singh, you are peerless on this earth. Many people come to you with prayers for help in distress and thousands stand in attendance for you. You are Lord of the Earth, Ocean of Mercy, and Giver of Food to us all![4]

While these paeans of flattering praise could be extreme, the abuse of a Bhand who had been offended was to be feared. A Hindi proverb singles out "the rage of a widow, a Bhand, and a bull" as being awesome to behold (Crooke 1974 [1896] 1: 258). Sometimes, this anger could take the form of withering curses aimed at an offending patron. Hajari gave this example:

Oh patron, may you have a long life. But may you be blind in both of your eyes. May you travel forth to foreign lands and be set upon there by thieves and robbers. May all your 32 teeth get broken, just as you near your door. May you be sent to jail and rot there for life after life. May the ominous swallowwort and acacia trees grow outside of your home. Oh my lord, may I never again seek even a grain of corn or a bundle of grass from you!

In these appeals to magic powers for vengeance on an ungrateful patron, the Bhands stand as living examples of a satiric tradition that stretches beyond the wandering bards of Ireland (who were credited with rhyming rats and, sometimes, kings to death), all the way to Archilochus, whose poetic invective was said to have driven King Lycambes to his death (Elliott 1960: 3–48). It is interesting to note that, while most of the Bhands' professional activities are clearly secular, Hajari Bhand—in learning the skills of bone setting and in earning the right to the Behru Jogi's spiritual powers—has independently taken upon himself some of the functions and qualities of the shaman or wizard. Paradoxically, still another link with the traditional procedures of sacred magic may be seen in the use of blatant obscenity in the imagery of this bhandai that Hajari once used to upbraid a Thakur for his lack of generosity:

Thakur *sahib, rajputi* [the courage and benevolence of the Rajputs] is no more. It has gone far beyond the seas. All virtuous Rajputs have been cooked to death in a whore's fart. Poor rajputi moves about, crying, "Where should I go now? Everywhere I wander, I see nothing but prostitutes' legs spread wide!"

The use of graphically obscene imagery is made all the more shocking and effective by its juxtaposition with rajputi—a chivalric code of values that traditionally operates as an unwritten standard of ethics for the Rajput castes. In further upbraiding and insulting the ungenerous Thakur, Hajari Bhand continues to make use of this normative frame of values:

You are a Rajput. I came to your door to ask for your patronage, but you didn't even offer me water. You are the resident Thakur. A fortunate man worth two, three, or four *lakhs* [hundreds of thousands of rupees], and still you don't invite me for a little food. What sort of Thakur are you? You and your kind are not Thakurs, but the thieves and swindlers of the world. And if the Thakurani had given birth to a real Thakur, he would have looked quite different from you!

More frequently, abuse in a critical bhandai was clothed in wit. Kesari Singh says that Court Ministers would sometimes try to withhold payment to a Bhand that had been promised by a Raja, but they did this at the risk of being made a laughing stock in front of the Court (1982, personal communication). The following bhandai in Hajari Bhand's repertory is an example of the kind of abuse such a minister would risk:

Your father is a great slave. Your son is nothing but a slave. And your uncle is a slave to paupers. Your brother is a slave to beggars. Your maternal uncle is a slave to men with monkey shows. Your elder brother wears the sky for his clothes. Your brother-in-law is a slave to fools. Your son-in-law is a slave to *jogis*. This is the kind of family you come from, and you have only increased their baseness. And now I have lost my own honor as a Bhand by requesting money from the likes of you!

In the rough and tumble of Court life, the Bhand's skills at abusive rhetoric could be turned to sport. Sometimes a Bhand would be threatened with the loss of all he had earned if he could not make the Raja laugh, and Hajari Bhand remembers his brother finally winning such a dare by cleverly and outrageously abusing the Raja himself. Motilal Kemmu, who has worked for many years with the Bhands of Kashmir, tells of a mean-spirited Raja who was blind in one eye from battle and threatened a Bhand with death if he could not make him laugh. After going through his entire comic repertory, the desperate Bhand went up to the King and whispered in his ear: "Why don't you laugh, you blind bastard?" The King roared in appreciation of this mention of a taboo subject and handsomely rewarded the fortunate Bhand (1981, personal communication).

As Hajari Bhand's use of the ethical framework of rajputi in addressing the ungenerous Thakur suggests, the bhandai could extend beyond sport or leverage for payment in its significance. Kesari Singh notes that the acerbic remarks of the Bhand were often warranted, and that a wise Raja would listen carefully for words of warning and wisdom in the privileged man's jibes. "Some very courageous Bhands used to point out to the Rajas where they were mistaken and what their wrong actions were. Clever or wise Rajas would never get angry at them, but would reward their service. Some unwise Rajas, at times they would get angry and turn them out of their kingdom. Such things also happened." It is startling for those familiar with Renaissance drama to discover such close cousins to Calderón's *graciosos* and Shakespeare's wise fools still alive in this century.

Hajari Bhand now recites bhandais for generous patrons among the merchant castes in the same manner as he did for his royal providers, sometimes even retaining titles appropriate for Rajputs. Thus the generous payment of cash and a turban by a merchant at Divali was greeted as follows:

Oh Bhandari Raja, you are merciful to the poor and a most lucky King of Kings. Oh great and fortunate Raja, you have brought renown to your family and land. You are like a supreme ruler of the world and your heart is as kind as that of King Hamir. Oh Bhandari Raja, you are incomparable on this earth and there are no limits to your charity. So many persons stand before you, putting forth their requests, begging for alms and help. Thousands of people stand ready to execute your orders. May the goddess Lakshmi and the god Satyanarayan keep you happy and prosperous. Oh World-Renowned-One, may you bathe in milk and prosper in children, as a fortunate King of Kings.[5]

Sometimes the concerns of the merchants form an odd mix with the formulaic compliments and good wishes traditionally extended to royal patrons.

You also are a fortunate King of Kings. May you also swim in milk and prosper in progeny. May the goddess Lakshmi keep your coffers and stores perennially filled to the full. May you make a net saving of 35 lakhs [3,500,000] rupees in the coming year! Oh Master of the World, Bestower of Food and Sustainer of the Poor, I, your Bhand, have come to the door of your palace!

If the merchant class has inherited the flattering praise offered to generous royalty, however, they have also become vulnerable to the sarcasm and humiliation that can be caused by a Bhand who feels himself slighted. By "raising the bhandai" against a wealthy merchant who has refused payment, embarrassment can be heaped upon him and his entire family. Hajari told a story which exemplifies this power of the Bhands to enforce their means of livelihood:

In our Chittor, ______ [an influential merchant] once stopped our being invited to weddings. Four or five of us made a decision. We all gathered and formed a procession. We made Onkarji Bhand ride a donkey, while my brother disguised himself as a witch. We went to the market-place. All the members of the merchant community gathered there, and they asked us: "What are you doing?" "I am ______'s mother, I am a witch!" We were using a shoe as a fan, and Onkarji Bhand was wearing a shoe instead of a bridegroom's crown. Like that, we passed through the market.

In these costumes, they arrived in front of the wealthy merchant's house and began to hurl curses against him, adding the following ill wishes to the recycled curses already cited:

Lord of the Earth, may you never get food or wife, and may your cattle starve for want of fodder! You are killing us, the poor and needy people. May you never enjoy well-being in life! And now this one of us has become a witch in order to take your wife from you and so that you may never enjoy life again. As I have said this, so may it be!

The merchant stayed at home for five days, ashamed at being publicly abused. The women begged him to pay off the Bhands, and finally his caste relations gave the Bhands their fees and assured them that they would always be welcome at Maheshwari weddings.

At times, bhandais can be pointedly satiric, exposing the skeletons in family closets. One Bania who refused to allow payment to Hajari Bhand and his family at a wedding was reputed to have slept with his son's wife and fathered a child. Adapting the vesh that had won him such favor with Maharana Bhupal Singh, Hajari dressed as a pregnant peasant woman and came up to the man in public, accusing him of being the father of the child "she" was carrying, and making not so veiled references to the money-lender's extra-commercial exploits. Although this practice is now rare and the Bhands' power has declined with the weakening of the feudal order, Komal Kothari, director of the Rupayan Sansthan Institute, says that in extreme instances Bhands can still make it difficult to marry off daughters of families known to have incurred their wrath and scorn, for fear of the scurrilous abuse that might be offered by the uninvited guests at such weddings (1981, personal communication).

On the Road: The Artistry of a Bahurupiya

In discussing the criteria for a good vesh, Hajari Bhand stresses care in costuming and makeup, accuracy in the choice of details, and the clear presentation of a character type recognizable to the audience. To meet these goals, first his looking glass, and then his wife and family are consulted before presenting a role publicly. His costumes and properties—his huge coconut-shell begging bowl, for example—are frequently purchased from people he has studied, and his mastery of dialects and accents is particularly impressive—ranging from the rough vernacular of a Pathan street vendor to the polished speech of a Hindi speaking doctor. Mohan Singh Shaktawat and Tulsinath Dabhai of the Udaipur Palace testify that his characterizations were so accurate that he would often go unrecognized at the palace until he revealed his true identity. He enjoys testing the verisimilitude of his portrayals by circulating among those he imitates without being detected, and once he infiltrated a group of Gaduliyas sent to Chittor Fort for an audience with Prime Minister Jawaharlal Nehru. He was selected as one of the spokesmen for the group before revealing himself as a bahurupiya.

Even in his public veshes, where it would be difficult and eventually self-defeating to disguise his identity for long, Hajari often goes out of his way

Figure 77. Hajari Bhand as a Bania, collecting his fees from the merchants of Chittorgarh.

to play to members of the caste or social group he is mimicking. Thus his iron vendor will call out to female smiths of the Gaduliya caste with the peculiar falling inflections typical of Gaduliya intonation, and his garrulous Banjara will seek out members of other castes involved with cattle droving:

Good morning, brother, where are you from? Kanore? How far's Kanore from here? Are these young bullocks yours or not? Brother, we'll meet again if we manage to stay alive. What's the certainty of this life? Any minute, your breath might stop coming out. What's the going rate for salt around here?[6]

More complex is his portrayal of a wealthy Marwari moneylender and wholesaler, commonly referred to as a Bania, while collecting for his services as a Bhand from the Maheshwari merchants (fig. 77).

Hello shopkeeper, which village do you come from? What? You're a Babil? I'm a Porwal. I live in Jaipur. All your accounts with me have to be cleared. Your grandfather took goods on credit and hasn't paid me yet. What's the matter with you? Laughing won't work. You'll have to pay me anyway. Tell me, where should I throw these account books? In a well or in a trough? You tell me where. Remember when you asked me for credit? Oh no, you ask the price of chillies later. First settle your accounts!

Hajari goes from store to store—wool-vested, a red account book under his arm, the sign of Vishnu on his forehead, and a fine patterned turban wrapped immaculately around his head—threatening to charge 4 percent monthly interest on imaginary accounts, complaining about the dwindling of honor among the merchants of Chittorgarh as shown by their lack of zeal in paying their Divali "debts," and citing sometimes exaggerated information on the wealth and earnings of specific merchants being dunned for payment:

You are very rich, too, running those cinema houses. Your son-in-law owns a cinema at Kapasan. Your father has been honored by Maharana Bhupal Singh himself and you are very well off yourself. No wealthy man can ever compare with you!

The accuracy of his impersonation of the Maheshwari moneylender makes this public dunning potentially tense, but usually good humor prevails. Sometimes in his banter, Hajari Bhand will make sport of a familiar merchant, inventing comical failings:

What should I do? Make up for past losses with future profits? We have always been kind, even though we have lakhs of rupees. And Sethji, you too are very well off in every respect, except in education. The only thing causing us losses and trouble now is your illiteracy!

Shop by shop, he incites laughter, pockets small amounts of money for his past services, and stops his patter only to salute generous patrons of long standing with bhandais of flattering praise, or perhaps to share a cup of tea.

The specificity of Rajasthani dress and speech patterns, together with the public nature of much of Rajasthani life, helps Hajari to create easily recognizable character types. Working in the hurly-burly of Rajasthani streets and marketplaces, he must first attract attention: "make a scene." Itinerant vendors hawking their wares are particularly suitable for large crowds, since they also must attract and hold the attention of the milling public. Hajari builds comically on the extroverted behavior natural to these vendors. In these publicly performed sangs, laughter is even more important than accuracy. "60 percent comedy, 40 percent accuracy" was a formula Hajari once offered us—with a huge grin that belied its mathematical precision. The garrulous old Banjara mixes the street cries of the salt seller with his humorous homilies, and the Gaduliya alternates between hawking non-existent bits of ironware and making sexual puns about iron tools or offering to fix up a shopkeeper's worn-out bottom with a good copper nail.

The first vesh that Hajari performs in a new town or village is usually that of a Pathan selling asafoetida (*hing*)—a bitter powder used in cooking and in medicine which is believed to kill germs, cure toothaches, and restore sexual vigor. Wearing white leggings (*salvars*) and a bright orange turban wrapped in the Pathan manner, Hajari accosts people in a broad Afghani accent and uses the stereotype of the Pathan as a rough, proud, and bawdy individual in order to aggressively move out into the public, assess their mood and humor, and announce his presence as a performer:

> The strength of horses, the quickness of peacocks, the power of a bull can all be yours! I've got hing! Pathani hing, Pishori hing, Peshawari hing! Four rupees a *tola*! Excellent hing! Try it once and you'll never forget it! A taste of this hing and a man becomes young and virile again! You'll ring those chimes at night like a glorious bell! Yes, my man, this hing comes straight from Peshawar! Take some and you'll be ready to go the whole night long! Take it at night and you can ring those chimes in the day! Would you take it from a Pathan? Strong like a horse, quick like a peacock, powerful like a bull! This'll make you so hot that you won't even want to leave your bed! Genuine hing! Just one tola and you'll keep it up all night! Stiff and steady all through the night like a Pathan! Four rupees a tola! Look, yours is longer already!

The hing vendor's salacious patter, repeated with variations and with more and more asides to audience members, creates a highly charged field of energy and short circuits all sense of propriety. It thereby opens up future possibilities for a playful "putting on" of the conglomerate of attitudes and attributes that constitute Rajasthani culture and creates an aura of expectation and appreciation for the sangs that are to follow.

Like vendors, religious mendicants must also call attention to themselves in public. Imitating these holy beggars gives the bahurupiya the opportunity to play with the ways in which sacred and secular values interface each other in Rajasthani life. Although Hajari Bhand takes the powers of his Behru Jogi's vesh seriously, the figure cut is that of a jovial mendicant moving through seas of grinning and shouting children like some well-fed and wondrously beneficent pied piper, shouting out praises to Shiva like a divine fool: "Bom, bom, bom! Bhole Nath! Jai Shankara! Hail to Lord Shiva!" His Muslim Fakir is similarly jovial; but his good nature and touch of divine joyfulness and grace is accompanied by an appreciation for cash contributions, thus creating good-humored satire. Hajari moves about accosting the crowd wearing a black *dhoti* and *kurta*, a black Muslim hat, a huge black mustache, beads around his neck and earrings in his ears, and carrying an animal skin to sleep on, a set of tongs (*chimta*) to use as a noisemaker and for defense, and his all-purpose coconut-shell begging bowl:

> Good health to you and your children, too! I'll take alms only if you wish to give alms. Money jangles and returns to the giver! I need my fare to get to Ajmer! He who gives alms buys good health for his family! Oh, Ali! Oh, Haider! Partridges and pigeons, beware the cannon! He who renounces money is granted salvation! Oh, Ali! Oh, Haider! Bless all of you and your children, too! Send me a *paisa* (coin) and a handkerchief edged with gold! I'll take alms only if you want to give alms! Partridges and cows, never ride a wild horse! Give unasked in the name of God! I need my fare to get to Ajmer! He who remembers God prospers and he who forgets God finds ruin! Oh, Ali, send me alms! And make these foreigners here my disciples. I won't go without alms![7]

Less ambivalent in its satiric play with religiosity is Hajari Bhand's depiction of a wealthy Khakiji Sadhu. Amidst invocations to Rama and Narasimha, this prosperous holy man announces that he has come with 350 other *sadhus* from Ayodhya on their way to Rameshwar. "Get ready," he warns "there are hungry and thirsty sadhus in your village here. Devotees of God must be well looked after by the people." And so, he adds, must their 350 cows. "And we've got a few elephants with us, too!"[8]

This strain of social satire, directed against the hypocrisy, greed, and overbearing pride of the wealthy and powerful, is also found playing beneath the mimicking of the Bania, the police officer, a doctor who suggests removal of vital organs and sexual abstinence (fig. 78), and a sanctimonious Congress Party politician. Though satire rarely dominates, it surfaces often, as, for example, when the Gaduliya mentions that people call his caste vagrants and beggars because they sleep in wagons, whereas "the real beggars are the bureaucrats who live in their new houses built with the money of the poor."

Hajari Bhand not only portrays and sometimes satirizes holy men, he represents the deities themselves. Thus, within a tradition that may relate back to the origins of mimetic performance in India, he represents Hanuman, Kali, Shiva (and, when he was younger, the goddess Lakshmi) in non-comic veshes frequently given on religious holidays. For Hanuman (fig. 79), he uses a papier-mâché Ramlila mask, along with a great deal of red dye, a "tail" improvised from materials about the house, and a picture of Rama and Sita cut from a calendar at his home and glued to his chest. He leaps and shouts "Shri Ram!" as he moves through the Divali market, animating the vision of Hanuman generated by calendars, comic books, and popular religious films.[9] His Shiva (fig. 80) glides through the market in a jovial, ecstatic state, blessing goods and people, accepting alms, and

Figure 78. Hajari Bhand as a Doctor.

dancing joyfully outside of the Shiva lingam and shrine in downtown Chittorgarh. This affinity of the fool with the divine manifests itself around the world. The privilege of the fool to rail and satirize is surely related to these touches of divine grace.

The ecstatic quality associated with divinities has its darker, demonic side, as well. Several middle-aged men told us of childhood nightmares occasioned by seeing a bahurupiya as Kali or as a raksasa. Divine inspiration also finds its disturbing and sometimes cruelly comic counterpoint within the bahurupiya's repertory in the portrayal of secular madness. The madman (*pagal*), who calls attention to himself through his own eccentric looks and behavior, is a familiar figure in India (see fig. 74). Hajari portrays a variety of such characters, adding touches of poignancy and comic zest to his professional fool's enactment of the natural fool's behavior. Thus one such fool sits in the middle of the street with blood pouring from his head, pounding rocks together, breaking into manic laughter, and repeatedly shouting out doggerel verse:

Figure 79. Hajari Bhand in the mask of Hanuman at Diwali.

Figure 80. Hajari Bhand as Shiva.

Come children, come! Come on out to play!
I've found a white pebble, made of Pushkar clay!

Another portrayal of madness occurs in a two-person sang based on the Persian story of Leila and Majnun. Majnun (fig 81), a poor young man, falls in love with Leila, a princess. Though love may care little for such distinctions, societies do, and the lovers are not allowed to marry. Majnun goes mad and spends his life crying out for his lost love, haunted by her memory, searching for her everywhere. In the performance, the specter of Leila is played by a young performer, often a son or apprentice of the bahurupiya, and Majnun carries the dialogue. With Janakilal playing Leila, Hajari cried out for her up and down the street, reached for her in the crowd, tore his clothes into shreds, beat his breast with rocks so hard he couldn't perform for two days after, and "mistakenly" embraced bicycles commandeered from shops and children pulled from the audience—combining melodramatic passion with a Quixote-like single-mindedness:

I cry Leila, Leila in the wilderness. Leila haunts my mind, day and night! Where should I look for my Leila? Leila! Oh, Leila! I am ruined for Leila, gone mad for her, drunk with the thought of her! Leila!

Real private affairs often spill out into public space in Rajasthan, and since Hajari Bhand's home is next to the old police station in Chittorgarh he has witnessed many such events. He takes advantage of this in a number of veshes—particularly those involving women. The role of the pregnant Pinjari played before Bhupal Singh and used to expose a philandering merchant is also adapted as a street routine—humorously blaming dignified merchants as the father, calling out for public assistance in collecting support payments, and threatening to give birth in the street. Kesari Singh expresses particular admiration for both the veracity and the comic skill of Hajari's portrayal of a Kanjari woman seeking money from the crowd, claiming police brutality, and flirting outrageously with those who will stop to listen. From a caste traditionally notorious as prostitutes, thieves, and repeated criminal offenders (O. P. Joshi 1982, personal communication), Hajari's Kanjari (fig. 82) is a non-stop talker—pleading, cajoling, protesting innocence, and playing on the audience's sympathy with a glint of humor in her eyes. The laughter generated comes from delight in the play with sexual identity, exploitation of the stereotypical behavior associated with a traditional outlaw caste, satirical allusions to police brutality, and by-play with individual audience members:

We're innocent, sir, but the officer has broken every bone in my husband's body. We don't steal, sir, we're just camping in the neighborhood. We get by begging scraps of food. We keep little puppies and calves, sir, we don't steal. And then the officer comes wearing his shorts and takes away my husband. The sergeant has

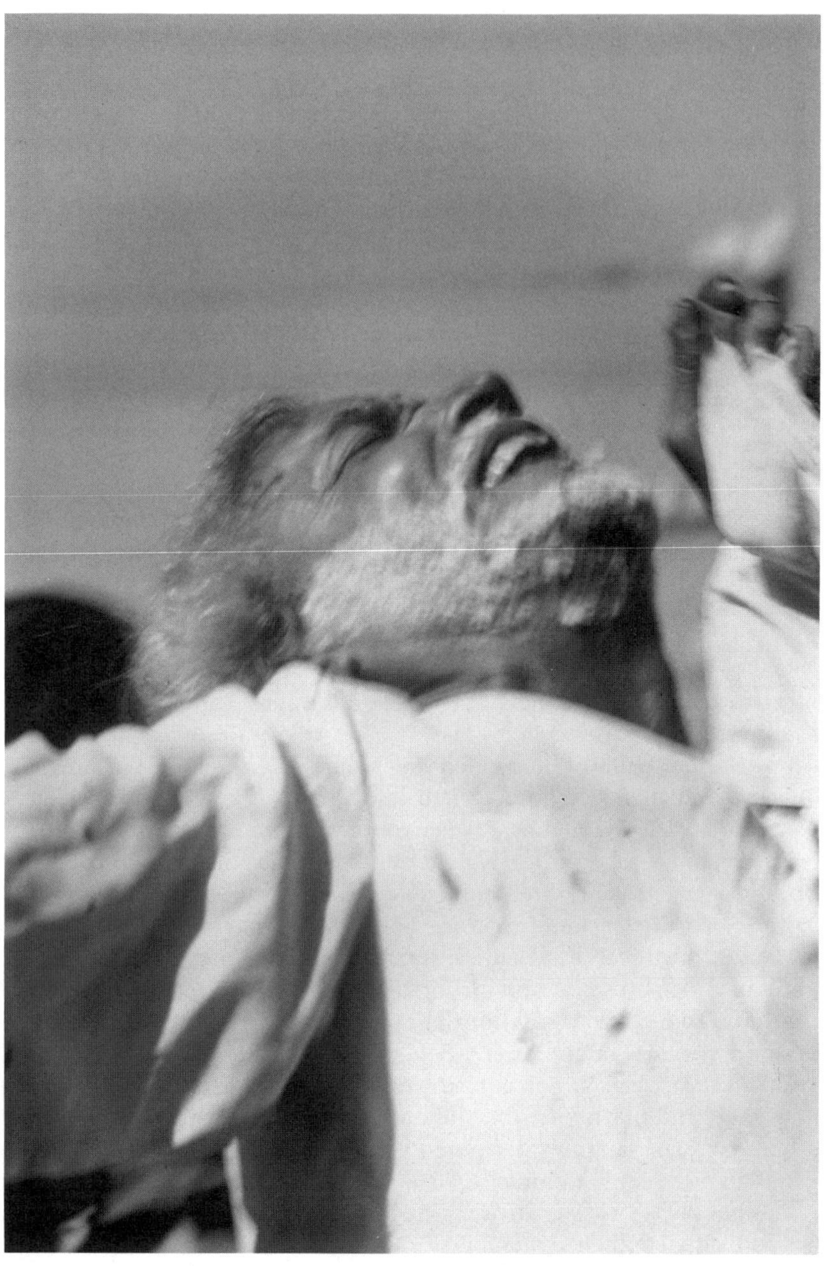

Figure 81. Hajari Bhand as Majnun, the hero of a Persian romance.

Figure 82. Hajari Bhand as an aging Kanjari thief and prostitute.

broken every bone in my husband's body, sir. My daughter, my mother-in-law, her daughter, they're all weeping bitterly, one tear after the other, sir. Come to our camp and we'll feed you some eggs. Sir, if you put up bail for my husband, I'll let you sleep with my daughter.

The technique of bringing private affairs into the public arena is combined with the extroverted bawdiness of the Gaduliya and his "wife" in a sang performed by Hajari and his son, Janakilal, in which private squabbles overwhelm the vendors' professional concerns:

Gaduliya: Bring your scrap iron to me! Buy that ladle you need! Give me your broken scrap iron!
Wife: Oh mother, would you buy a ladle?
Gaduliya: Why do you always shout and create a disturbance?
Wife: Strange! If I sell my wares or do nothing at all, you still say I shout!
Gaduliya: Oh, let me burn your mouth! Look at that, Sethji, just because the country is ruled by a lady, this woman is shouting! I've told her clearly that, being a woman, she shouldn't shout, but she shouts anyway, can't keep her face straight or her mouth shut! [10]
Wife: Lovely language you're using in front of everyone in the middle of the market!
Gaduliya: How dare you interrupt when I'm speaking.?
Wife: You don't want me to sell any goods?
Gaduliya: Sell goods! Goods are sold by men, not women!
Wife: Oh, if a woman shouldn't shout to sell goods, maybe she should stuff a pestle in her mouth!
Gaduliya: What's that about a pestle?! Still shouting! I'll brand you yet! Have you seen my tool?
Wife: Watch out for your tool, it's blunt!
Gaduliya: You want me to sharpen my tool? Have you felt it lately? If you go to another man, I'll get another wife. Shopkeeper, the rains have failed, we're out of fodder, the children need food. How can I feed them when all she thinks of is clothing and jewelry?
Wife: Are you going to buy me a skirt or not?
Gaduliya: See how she shouts!

Perhaps most startling and complex of all the sangs bringing private matters into public spaces is that of the Nakhti (fig. 83)—a woman whose nose tip has been cut off by her husband in a jealous rage—a practice of punishing unfaithful wives once fairly common and still occasionally heard of in villages according to R. C. Pancholi, a Chittorgarh jurist (1982, personal communication). With the cut nose created by tying a piece of cardboard soaked in red dye over his real nose, and a liberal use of stage blood, Hajari enters the streets shouting for help:

Oh sir, my nose has been lopped off! When I was nursing my child, he came and said that I slept with other men! Damn my husband! What'll become of my children now? Where should I go? How could I be an adulteress when I'm the mother of three children?!

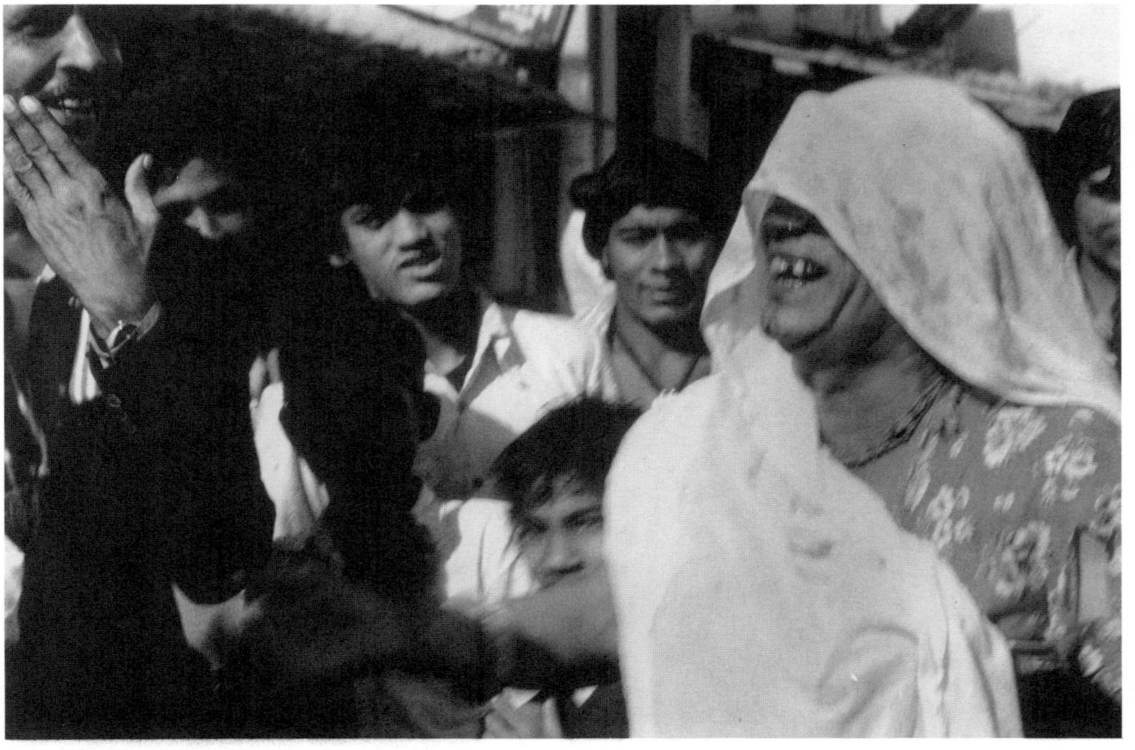

Figure 83. Hajari Bhand as a Nakhti, a woman who has had her nose cut off for adultery.

The audience's astonishment and shock is gradually turned to uneasy comedy as Hajari names one after the other of the onlookers as among the "few" exceptions that she had shared her favors with, praising the discretion of some, disparaging the sexual services of others, and finally stating that the husband's claim that she had slept with every man in the village was preposterous, given the smallness of their home. In the process, both the husband's vicious action, the wife's hypocrisy and prodigality, and the audience's own gullibility and discomfiture become targets for satiric attention and laughter.

These examples show certain artistic principles at work in the construction of the bahurupiya's sangs. Since he is a street performer and must play to a constantly changing audience, the repetition of key phrases abound in the playing—far more so, in fact, than in the limited examples given. Thus street cries, bits of doggerel, and repeated lamentations are used to specify the character and situation for new onlookers as well as to sustain dialogue and character for those who follow the performance from street to street and shop to shop. These key strips of dialogue provide a base for the sang and are then departed from as Hajari improvises within the circumstances offered by the audience's reactions. Many of these improvised bits of repartee with the audience have already been tested in other performances, while a few may be evoked by the particularities of the moment.

Entire performances are built up by recycling old material within new contexts. Thus, the vesh of the pregnant Pinjari, originally created for Bhupal Singh's amusement, can be used to humiliate an antagonistic merchant or to provide public entertainment. Elements worked out for one-man veshes can be built upon in expanded sangs involving two or more bahurupiyas. Janakilal, for example, teamed with his father to perform as a protesting Kanjara being led to the police station by Hajari's stern Police Officer:

Kanjara: I fall at your feet, sir! We walk the straight and narrow path, sir! We don't steal! We are your Kanjaras, completely innocent!

Policeman: Shut up, motherfucker! Keep moving! If you talk too much, I'll whack you with this stick!

Kanjara: Oh, sir! Please don't drag us into the station! What have we stolen? We only steal little things. Have we stolen gold so you're taking us to the police station?

Policeman: Move it! Walk!

Kanjara: Oh, sir! We don't steal. Ask him! We won't steal anymore, sir! We're innocent. Except for a few little necessary thefts. Oh, sir, we didn't steal the goats.

Policeman: How many goats did you steal? Who did you sell them to?

Kanjara: We sold them to Mama, the butcher. But he just died yesterday. What can we do?

Policeman: How many goats? Tell the truth!

Kanjara: Oh, Sir, I only took three goats. And still people say we steal gold!

	Oh, sir, we don't even eat mutton! We are your Kanjaras, getting by begging cold stale food!
Policeman:	It better not happen again! Sit here on the ground, motherfucker! And shut up!
Kanjara:	Oh, sir, I repent, I put my hands in my mouth. What do we steal, sir? By your throat I swear, sir!
Policeman:	You dare swear by my throat?
Kanjara:	I'll never swear by your throat again, sir. We're your Kanjaras, camping in your area, living on food we beg, sir. By your throat I swear, sir. We only steal very small things or gold. Except for gold and small things, we never steal at all!

Though "situation" becomes far more important than "plot," and characters have little chance to "develop" as the street audience comes and goes, it is important to note that—at least in Hajari and Janakilal Bhand's treatments—there is a dramatic progression involved in these sangs. The initial dialogue establishes the situation and character—usually familiar to the audience. Often there is an initial "taking in" of the audience. Thus the Doctor and Police Officer convince many at first by their seeming authenticity, and we have seen the sang of the Nakhti send people calling for help. Gradually, the joke is revealed by greater and greater audacity in the portrayal of character and manipulation of dialogue—as in the Pathan's harangue or in the fight between the Gaduliya and his wife—or through comic by-play with the audience. Thus the Doctor moves from suggesting pills to telling the "patient" that he should only have sex once a year. The performative play involved in the sang of the Nakhti is revealed by her more and more outrageous allusions to supposed secret affairs with audience members. Janakilal's Kanjara goes from protesting complete innocence to pleading with the arresting Officer that "except for gold and small things, we never steal at all."

The overall sense of spontaneous and enlivening play may be more important to a bahurupiya's performance than any of the specific techniques and effects that have been pointed out. To celebrate the end of our work together, and to mark the end of a period of mourning following the death of his elder brother Mohan, Hajari Bhand dressed up his sons and recreated the vesh of the Bhils—a tribal people known for their bravery, loyalty, and zestful appetite for life. With Hajari carrying his two-year-old son and impersonating a Bhil matriarch while spinning in feverish circles with a broad grin on his face, the infectious joy was picked up by the citizens of Chittorgarh as Hajari and his family sang this song:

The King is coming,
Beat the gongs and drum!
The Bhils are dancing,
The Bhands are dancing, too!

To an unusual degree, Hajari Bhand strives for originality while devising his sangs—even when his veshes are shared by other bahurupiyas. He takes pride in the fact that he has developed his own repertory and in his efforts to keep his material fresh. During our travels, we had the opportunity to observe the creation of a new character. While Hajari was performing the vesh of the Nakhti, a real life pagal began to interact with Hajari, saying he would beat up the woman's husband and inviting her to move in with him. Hajari afterwards reflected that the pagal's intervention had been welcome at first, since it gave him something new to respond to in his improvised play. As the pagal began to follow us around, however, demanding money, throwing stones, and taking attention away from the performance, Hajari found his presence annoying. Later that night, we asked him if he could make up a character based on the pagal. Hajari immediately showed us how he would do this, beginning by rearranging his clothes and then assuming a stance that was a slight exaggeration of the pagal's. He then started to repeat a few key actions and phrases of the pagal that had rankled him: imitating the demands for money and swinging his arms in a wide arc as if throwing a stone. As we laughed, he began to elaborate, keeping the words and actions first chosen as touchstones in his widening portrayal. A character that was both an accurate reflection and a comic comment on the pagal began to take on life, as though he was being recreated in the distorting glass of a fun-house mirror.

If the mirror that the bahurupiya holds up to nature is a distorting one, often sustaining stereotypes and poking fun at man's pretensions to dignity, the bahurupiya's playful census of Rajasthani types also provides a dynamic method of airing tensions within the culture. Beyond this, in its cumulative effect, the artistry of the bahurupiya challenges the fixed nature of the very categories that it uses for its field of play. Plato, who distrusted mimetic skills, refers in the *Republic* to wandering "pantomimic gentlemen, who are so clever that they can imitate anything" and suggests sending storytellers with such skills promptly away as disruptive influences, "sweet and holy and wonderful beings" though they may be (1944 [1892]: 155). Plato feared that the mimic would further distort life—already imperfectly comprehended—for the sake of a good laugh or a dramatic effect, and that the net result of his fooling with identities would be chaos. The anarchic juggling of identities by the bahurupiya as "pantomimic gentleman" is particularly striking against a social background traditionally dominated by principles of *karma* and dharma—principles that dictate the obligations and duties, as well as social rank, dress, and occupations of caste members. Plato is at least potentially correct in pointing out the anarchic impetus latent in the mimic's art; but then, perhaps an heretical touch of anarchy has more to do with a comprehensive and humane picture of the world than he would readily admit (at least until his turnabout in *Phaedrus,* which recognizes the need for a streak of madness in art, and in love). The bahurupiya's adroitness at shifting identities while maintaining his comic (and moral) perspective may strike us as particularly commendable in a world that often calls for dizzying shifts of roles that make the unitary sense of self harder and harder to sustain.

Feudal societies in general have tried to answer the call of anarchy by sponsoring pockets of disorder within the system itself. The fool chained to the throne of the king served as a reminder of common frailty, but the chain must have also have functioned as a means of keeping this human symbol for disorder fixed within the compass of the court. The natural fools and dwarfs that so fascinated the European medieval and Renaissance courts as lessons in humility and images of a disorder that cried out for containment seem to have been less popular (though not entirely missing to judge by the vidusaka's distorted shape) in the courts of India. In Hindu caste society, the bahurupiya's ability to take on many identities is similarly appealing and threatening. It can be no accident that of all the Bhands, the Hindu Bhands of Rajasthan seem to have taken particular delight in tapping this tradition to add to their repertory as jesters. If the rigidities of dress and behavior in caste society facilitate the bahurupiya's work, these same rigidities give added meaning to his ability to function.

The bahurupiya's heretical play with the principles of karma and dharma points to a deeper stratum of Hindu philosophy—one expressly articulated in Kakul's performance—that asserts that each human being contains, in microcosmic form, the powers and potentialities of the macrocosmos. As a joker in the deck, a "wild card" in an otherwise carefully labeled pack, the bahurupiya serves as a reminder that, even in the most rigid societies, identities are not fixed. The wheel of karma takes many turns and a prince in one cycle may find himself a pauper in another as the *lila*—or play—of life continues. Small wonder, then, that the rich and powerful would strive to contain and control this disruptive presence through patronage, and that the Bhand's sycophantic flattery is sought after, while his curses are feared. The Bhand as bahurupiya serves not only as an entertaining reflection and distortion of a Rajasthani "human comedy," but as a reminder and immediate demonstration of the mutability of the human soul and the liveliness of the human spirit.

This is, of course, neither a new nor a peculiarly Indian (or Asian) enterprise. At the end of the Middle Ages in Europe, Erasmus followed a similar line of thought while meditating on the fool and writing his *Praise of Folly* (1941 [1511]: 37):

> Now what else is the whole life of mortals but a sort of comedy, in which the various actors, disguised by various costumes and masks, walk on and play each one his part, until the manager waves them off the stage? Moreover, this manager frequently bids the same actor go back in a different costume, so that he who has but lately played the king in scarlet now acts the flunky in patched clothes.

We do not know, of course, how much of this analysis would ring true to Hajari Bhand, who in his day-to-day behavior is as polite and modest as he is outrageous in his professional roles. It is appropriate to end this study with his own joking protest about our work with him:

I wander about. I meet everybody. I get along with everyone. By making people happy, I earn some money. I eat and I drink. I have no problems. Then you people come along and hire me to do all this work and ask me all these questions about this and that. Now, I've got problems!

Notes

1. This essay originally appeared, with minor differences, in the *The Drama Review* 30, 1 (Spring 1986: T109). Another version of this chapter, with diacritical markings, is included as "A Joker in the Deck: The Many Faces of a Rajasthani Bahurupiya," in *The Idea of Rajasthan: Explorations in Regional Identity*, Vol. II: *Art As Communication*, ed. Karine Schomer, Joan L. Erdman, Deryck Lodrick, and Lloyd I. Rudolph (Riverdale, MD: Riverdale Publications; Delhi: Manohar Publications). It is reused by permission of the editors.

Research for this essay was funded by the Smithsonian Institution in 1981 (for investigations jointly undertaken with Amy R. Catlin and William O. Beeman), and by the Indo-U.S. Subcommission in 1982–83. This funding was administered by the American Institute of Indian Studies, whose help is gratefully acknowledged. In addition to the individuals cited in the text, and many others who must go unrecognized, we are indebted to the people of Bassi, Bhilwara, Chittorgarh, Gangapur, Renwal, Pushkar, Kacheriawas, Jaipur, and Udaipur, where we filmed and conducted research: the bahurupiya's work and our own would be impossible without their good will and sense of humor.

A forty-minute videotape, *Hajari Bhand of Rajasthan: Jester Without Court* (NTSC color standard) is available for rental or purchase through Documentary Educational Resources, 101 Morse St., Watertown, MA, USA. VHS copies of this video tape may be viewed in India at the Archive and Research Center for Ethnomusicology of AIIS in New Delhi and at the Rupayan Sansthan Institute, Borunda, Rajasthan.

2. Naqqals are frequently equated with Bhands (Russell and Lal 1975 [1915] 1: 349). In usage, though, *naqqal* seems to be a more generic term for itinerant actors; it derives from the Urdu term for imitation or copy, and is more frequently heard in Uttar Pradesh.

3. The Patron referred to is Bhupal Singh, Maharana of Udaipur from 1931 to 1950, who died in 1955. His successor in the now honorary office of Maharana Pramuk, Bhagat Singh, shares neither his predecessor's enthusiasm for these traditions, nor his means of rewarding them.

Quotations from Hajari Bhand come from taped interviews and conversations held from November 1982 to March 1983. Translation assistance was provided at various times by Komal Kothari, who first introduced Hajari Bhand to us, Rawat Kesari Singh, O. P. Joshi, Ranchor Singh Ashiya, Dinesh Chandra Bhanawat, Shadashiv Shrotriya, Amritjit Singh, and Kanilal M. Bhandari, whose good faith and assistance were invaluable. Further translation advice was provided by Robert Hueckstedt. Karine Schomer and Joan Erdman offered helpful suggestions for writing and editing.

4. Some of the references made by Hajari Bhand in this bhandai may require ex-

plication. "Thakur" roughly corresponds to "lord"; it is traditionally used both as a respectful term of address for Rajput noblemen and as a designation for prominent local landowners and overlords. Chhatrapati Shivaji is one of the many appellations for Shiva—that aspect of the godhead associated with destruction and renewal. Mahadev is yet another name for Shiva, stressing his preeminence among the gods. The Rathors constitute one of the dominant Rajput clans. Rathors have ruled in various localities within Rajasthan since at least the tenth century AD, but are particularly associated with Jodhpur; since the time of Akbar, they have been celebrated especially for their prowess in battle.

5. Divali, or the Festival of Lights, is a festive holiday held in autumn when both ancestral spirits and the goddess of wealth are honored; hence, it is a particularly appropriate time for Bhands to collect for their services and to offer bhandais that praise a family's lineage and wealth. The Bhandaris are a subdivision of the Oswali Bania caste of merchants and bankers. King Hamir (Maharana Hamir Singh) ruled in Udaipur from 1300 to 1363 and was known for both his vigorous defense of Mewar and his generous patronage of the arts. Lakshmi is commonly referred to as the "goddess of fortune" and is understandably important in the religion of the Bania merchants—particularly at the time of Divali. Satyanarayan refers to Vishnu, Lakshmi's consort and one of the principal manifestations of the Hindu godhead; he is especially associated with the preservation of a divinely determined order on earth and in the heavens. Though some Banias are Jains, most consider themselves to be Vaishnavites.

6. The sections of Hajari Bhand's sangs and bhandais quoted in this article have been reworked from Dinesh Chandra Bhanawat's literal translations made from our field recordings.

7. Id-ul-Fitr is a festive Islamic holiday that marks the breaking of the Ramadan fast. The term Fakir comes from the Arabic *fakr*, poverty; Id would be a particularly propitious day for these mendicants to seek alms. Ajmer is a pilgrimage site for Muslims, since it houses the Chisti Dargah, shrine to the thirteenth-century Sufi saint, Mu-in al-Din Sanjari, whose memory is honored by many Hindus as well. 'Ali (b. Abi Talib) was the Prophet Mohammed's son-in-law and heir, the fourth Caliph of Islam (656–660 AD); he is revered by Shi'ites, who hold that the legitimate succession of the Caliphate was through 'Ali and his martyred son, Hosein. 'Ali is also widely held to be a founder of Fakir orders. Haider is another name for him.

8. Khakiji Sadhus are itinerant Vaishnavite holy men who travel in groups; they can be quite prosperous. For Narasimha's story see chapter 2. Rameswaram is a celebrated place of pilgrimage in Tamil Nadu, where Rama is said to have set up one of the twelve great *lingas* (phallic monuments) to honor Shiva.

9. Ramlila performances are held in September-October to celebrate Rama's victory over the demon Ravana, as chronicled in the *Ramayana* and its more recent retellings, especially Tulsidas's *Ramcharitmanas*. While the largest of these ceremonies takes place over thirty to thirty-one days in Ramnagar (outside of Varanasi), smaller celebrations are held throughout North India. Rama (an *avatar* of Vishnu) is aided in his struggle by an army of monkeys under the leadership of the loyal Hanuman; this legendary monkey-general has assumed an important place in the Hindu pantheon. Masks for Hanuman may be made of wood, hammered copper, or, like the one used by Hajari Bhand, of papier-mâché.

10. In 1982 Indira Gandhi was the prime minister of India. "Sethji" is an honorific used when addressing merchants.

Chapter 7
A Capacity for Wonder

Interview conducted by James Schevill

This chapter consists mainly of an interview that poet and playwright James Schevill conducted with me in 1981. Schevill was my colleague and friend throughout the two decades we shared at Brown University, and I directed some of his plays at Brown and at La Mama ETC in New York City. He was interested in updating *BreakOut*! (1973)—a book he had edited on contemporary theatre—and interviewed me for that purpose. Other projects came up, the revision was deferred, and the interview has never been published until now. I have retained its projected title.

I have trouble writing about my own performance work (not unusual, I think) and felt I had come as close to getting my sense of things right in his interview as I was able. The interview touches on many of the themes taken up, turn and turn about, in the preceding chapters, but from the vantage point of what is curiously and aptly called "a practicing performer." This is a somewhat different vantage point—a different self, a different mask—than I have had access to in the preceding chapters. Bernard Shaw once said (as an excuse for writing a second preface) that an old man had no right to change willfully the words of a young one—even if the old man and the young one bore the same name. While I can't yet claim Shaw's longevity, I have decided against unduly fiddling with words that once seemed right, and I have instead added a few footnotes that give further information as seems appropriate. There has, of course, been a significant discussion of the issues involved in interculturalism since this interview was given, and I shall address some of these issues as they relate to the paradigm of the mask in a separate conclusion.

Schevill: Is the energy of experimental theatre shattered today, as Richard Schechner says in recent issues of the *Performing Arts Journal*? (expanded in Schechner 1982).

Emigh: I don't know if the energy is shattered. The sense of direction is certainly not so clear as it once was. By the late 'sixties "experimental theatre" had become a sort of genre with its own conventions: ensemble development and enactment of pieces guided by strong directors, a de-emphasis of the proscenium barrier, the frequent use of improvisation, the breaking open of narrative expectations. "Theatre from Ibsen to Grotowski" could be neatly packaged and sold in the universities. I peddled it myself. In 1971, when we got together what turned out to be the first national festival of "new" theatre, somebody, one of the other organizers, joked that he wasn't sure whether we were celebrating the experimental theatre or helping to bury it.[1] It was an exciting festival—partly because it was the first time that many of the groups had seen each other's work. But one phase of experimentation was over. Certainly that kind of work is less dominant now, and in some ways less exciting when it does appear.

Schevill: How do you think the political climate has affected experimental theatre?

Emigh: Well, it's been depressing. For all of us.

Schevill: That's what Robert Brustein said just the other day.

Emigh: Maybe the political climate helped erode a sense of effectiveness in group collaboration. It's eroded the ability of those making theatre to have faith in their capacity to effect social and political thinking. One positive thing that happened was the re-emergence of the playwright—recreating and exposing contemporary speech and thought. I think that this new sensitivity to language started with the Black Theatre movement in America. Pinter's example probably provided an example and a goad, too. And then theatre turned back upon itself reflexively. The concerns of the more solitary artists—of the painters and lyric poets—crept into the theatre. This has gone beyond the Pirandellian or Brechtian sorts of play with the conventions of theatre to focus on the makers of theatre standing alone at the center of their work. So we got Richard Foreman's introverted use of Brecht's techniques, and Spalding Gray's theatrical play with the processes of autobiography, and Robert Wilson's playing with the way he perceives—and maybe we perceive—personal and political history, and Bob Carrol's cagey mixing of storytelling, stand-up comedy, "cheap mime," and self-exposure.[2]

Schevill: You remember that the early version of *Breakout*! focused largely on environmental theatre (see Schevill 1973). What do you think of environmental theatre today? Is it still influential?

Emigh: Certainly there is less aggressive activity, invading new spaces and theatricalizing them. But there has been a tendency to take old sites and convert them permanently into theatres without erasing their histories as pickle factories or churches or vaudeville houses or what have you. And the commercial theatre has swallowed whatever it could of the environmentalists' work. Eugene Lee's set for *Sweeney Todd* and the success of *Candide* come to mind.

Schevill: In the one-man performances you've been doing recently, haven't you found yourself playing in various unusual environments?

Emigh: I still like theatre popping up in unusual places and re-using old buildings, but in the work you're talking about, the stress has been more on unusual contexts than on the environments themselves. Working on your *Edison's Dream* in the factory-gymnasium-theatre that is Lyman Hall was a welcome return to that set of problems—but most of the time now, at least in my own performances, the focus of the work has moved away from the manipulation of space to a concern with the relationship of the performance to its immediate context. I've performed more or less the same stories at academic conferences, mental hospitals, nursing homes, university classrooms, public parks, and commercial theatres. Adjustments have to be made in the various spaces, but the essential audience-actor relationship doesn't change—not physically. There's always a curtain, a truncated oval or semicircle to perform in, and the audience gathered around watching a costumed performer dancing, portraying characters, telling stories and jokes. Essentially, it's the oldest physical arrangement for theatre that we know about, set down within whatever larger space is there. Certainly I have to be sensitive to the space around me, but, more importantly, each new audience and each new occasion calls for a rethinking and a reworking of the material, an addressing of the material to the people who are really there, and to the occasion that has brought them together.

Schevill: Can you describe how you developed these one-man performances?

Emigh: Mostly through a series of accidents. Although, just the other day, getting ready to talk to you, I looked back over the interview that we had several years ago and noticed to my amazement that the closing words were about the great market square of Marrakech, where storytellers and acrobats and people with trained animals perform and gather crowds (Schevill 1973: 257–65). So I guess the appeal of a more medieval sort of theatre, of a theatre that marks out its own space, draws a crowd, and addresses itself to the immediacy of performance is something that has been with me for a long time as an aesthetic model. But whatever tug this model had on me was unconscious. The conscious choice that I made was to try and find a way—as a director—to begin working with masks.

Schevill: Why masks?

Emigh: I realized that I had been avoiding them. And yet they appealed to me. As a student, I had loved Peter Schumann's work with Bread and Puppet Theater. I still do. I felt drawn to the pictures of masks—particularly from Indonesia and Oceania—that I occasionally saw in books, beginning with my grandmother's old *National Geographics*. I felt particularly fond of the Greek Theatre and the *commedia dell 'arte* among Western theatrical traditions. And still, my own training as an actor had been Stanislavsky-based (despite a predilection for Brecht and Beckett) and for me to put on a mask would be to throw away about 80 percent of what I knew how to do as an actor. And how could I coach someone else on how to use them? And Peter Schumann's work couldn't be mine; he was working on a bigger canvas. And the other uses of masks I'd seen seemed silly. Anyway, I had a year off from teaching and directing, so, with the help of a small grant from the unlikely direction of Brown's English Department, I decided to go to Bali and New Guinea, to put myself in contact with mask traditions that still seemed to have a great deal of power and expressive life.

Schevill: Why Bali in particular?

Emigh: Artaud's writings probably had something to do with my initial curiosity. Richard Schechner had—as a teacher of mine in New Orleans—deepened my interest in Artaud. This was before either of us had gone to Asia.[3] But it was a series of seemingly unrelated events that made me more and more conscious of Bali. I went into a secondhand shop in the Bronx one summer late in the sixties, looking for an oak chair, and I saw a mask I liked. The shop owner expressed surprise at my interest, said he thought the mask was from Africa somewhere; he called it Uncle Herman, it had been left there and never collected, and I could have it for ten dollars. It turned out to be a Rangda mask from Bali. That summer, I began to be attracted by wooden bowls, shadow puppets, weavings, all sorts of objects glimpsed around New York—and they all seemed to come from Indonesia. So I began to read mythologies and histories from that part of the world. It didn't have anything directly to do with theatre yet.

The next spring, I walked into a concert of what I thought was going to be Indian music. Sitting at what appeared to be a group of miniature benches, banging away like Santa's happy elves, were a group of musicians pounding out the happiest music I had ever heard. Brown had bought a Balinese *gamelan* from the World Fair. I'm a former saxophone player whose playing had lapsed, and I missed making music, so I decided to join the gamelan group. Every Wednesday, I would bang on a little set of cymbals as the music drifted over and around me.

Then there was an announcement about a summer program in Seattle, held by the American Society for Eastern Arts. I decided to go, play more music, and try to study the manipulation of Indonesian shadow puppets. I still wasn't thinking about applications in directing, just following curiosity. Once there, I enrolled in a class in Balinese dance, thinking that I could find out more about what Artaud had in mind. But that was naive. I had never studied any form of dance, my marriage was falling apart and I was unable to concentrate, and I dropped out of the class after a few weeks, having failed at Balinese dance worse than I had ever failed at anything I had ever tried to learn.

Still, I Nyoman Wenten, the teacher, had shown a set of masks one day that stayed in my mind and began to work on my imagination. So, when I had a chance to set out for somewhere, it occurred to me that such masks could be of use directing Brecht's *Caucasian Chalk Circle*, and I decided to go to Bali. I also hoped I might come up with some Balinese material that would be useful working with a local professional children's theatre some of my former students had joined, the work of which I admired. And Bali was as far away as I could go without coming back again. When I went, I was still thinking about masks somewhat naively as costume elements that could be grafted onto productions of texts that appealed to me.

Schevill: Then it became more psychological, more personal, right?

Emigh: It began to take on the dimensions of a quest—one I never meant to set out on. All I intended to do was to learn how to use masks as a director. But I learned in stages that I couldn't just take more or less appropriate masks, put them on actors' faces, and have them speak lines from a selected text. I ended up having to rethink the whole process of acting, and especially the relationship of self to character and of character to text. It became intensely personal in ways that I never would have predicted.

Schevill: How did this process of rethinking begin?

Emigh: On the way to Bali, I spent a couple of months in New Guinea and was struck by the power and extraordinary presence of the masks there. These masks were mostly used to call upon ancestral spirits and bring them into the social contexts of the present. Often the dancer was possessed, but there was usually a playfulness at work as well. That play between past and present began to fascinate me, along with the imaginative richness of the masks as objects and the powerfulness of their presence. And when I went on to Bali, I began to see performances that seemed to move between that whole tradition of using masks to restore an ancestral past and the topical theatre of *commedia dell' arte*, where masks were used to push human characteristics to their comic extremes—a tradition I was more familiar with from Theophrastus, Molière, Brecht, and Beckett (see fig. 84).

Schevill: What sort of studies did you pursue in Bali?

Emigh: I started asking around in Bali, looking for people who could tell me about masks and how to use them. It was slow going, since I was new at the language, but people kept encouraging me to go see I Nyoman Kakul, a master dancer, actor, and teacher. Finally, a friend who spoke some English brought me to Kakul's house, and I tried to explain to him what I wanted: that I was a theatre director interested in commissioning some masks and using them in producing plays. This made no sense at all to Kakul. The concept of theatre director had no Balinese equivalent, and anyone who wanted to learn how to use masks had to begin by studying dance. I had to become his dance student. I couldn't imagine a more unlikely metamorphosis: I had never intended to become any sort of dancer at all, let alone a Balinese dancer; my ineptness had already been proven in Seattle.

All I wanted to do was to "learn about masks." But my Indonesian was too inadequate to protest properly, and before I could finish saying that wasn't what I had in mind, Kakul and my friend were consulting an astrological calendar to see what day would be propitious to begin the dance lessons on. They announced that the next three days would be awful, and the next two weeks still unpropitious, and that I had to start lessons within the hour. I was told that I would live in Kakul's family compound and study with him daily. It all happened very quickly. My friend was congratulating me on my good fortune. I had no alternative plan to propose and was almost completely out of cash due to some shenanigans at the bank, and, suddenly, there I was, my body being forced through agonizing, odd, hypertense movements. So, for the next three months, I studied dance without putting on a mask, often wondering what I was doing and where it could take me.

One day, several weeks into the work, there was a breakthrough for me. I was trying to force myself through what was still an excruciating set of movements—holding elbows and legs in positions that I'd never held them in before, working in the hot sun with some mysterious tropical fever, trying to sweat my way through the simplest of choreographies used for a proud minister. As I sometimes will do when concentrating, I had my face screwed up and tongue grotesquely stuck out. Kakul stopped and laughed and said something like: "What in the world do you think you're doing?" And I said, "I'm just trying to get these movements right." And he said, "But your face—what are you doing with your face?" And I said, "Oh, that's going to be covered by a mask anyway." And Kakul suddenly looked very stern and said that, no, the mask was not a disguise. It hid nothing. If I didn't first learn to be a proud prime minister, then there was no point

Figure 84. Author as a roguish bondres character (Photo, Ernestina Koetting).

in putting on a mask at all. That it would just look silly, something lifeless stuck on my head. I think this was my first realization that what I was doing in Bali *did* have something to do with acting as I knew it after all. Kakul and Stanislavsky had closed ranks.

Schevill: But how far do these similarities go? Surely there are important differences.

Emigh: Sure. This is the way I now understand it. In the West, at least in Stanislavsky's teaching, the actor works from the self towards character. In Bali the process is reversed. That is, the character, as potentially present in the fixed appearance of the mask, is the actor's starting point. The performer has to work imaginatively, intuitively, in order to own the mask—to let the potential life it contains flow through the body. The process begins with respecting the potential for life in the mask. The performer (traditonally male in the form of theatre I was studying) recognizes the mask as a type of character or personality, correctly portraying, say, the type of the proud minister; but the process of negotiating the right to wear a specific mask engages him in a much more immediate, personal process, moving between self and other to form the amalgam that is a character in action. The performer may place a mask by his head as he sleeps, or otherwise imaginatively introduce the mask to his own life. He may imagine the mask embodied and in action. He searches out a meeting ground between the self and what begins as the other.

It sounds occult, but it is really the same process a Western actor goes through when approaching a new text, say (God help the actor) *Hamlet.* The actor has to negotiate a meeting ground between life as he or she has experienced it—or can imagine it as being—and the words of a particular text. Somehow, the actor has to own those words, and a knowledge of how-to-act-Shakespeare, or what-kind-of-person-Hamlet-is—melancholy prince, scholar, soldier, courtier, lover—will get that actor only so far. At first the words, because they sit there as something apart from the actor's own being, are the obstacle as well as the goal, no matter how much admiration the actor has for the potential theatrical life suggested in Shakespeare's writing. So the actor becomes familiar with the words, improvises around them, finds experiences in a real or imagined life that connects with them, finds a way of centering the body's energy that could most naturally give rise to these words and actions, imagines his or her body in an ancestral, Renaissance world of court intrigue and doublets and tights. It's essentially the same process. But in the West the character remains the most fluid, changeable construct in the process—the result of the struggle between self and text. In Bali, the character—as mask—is the most fixed element in the process, what everything else must flow from. It is the text that becomes changing and malleable.

The story-lines of *topeng* come from well-known chronicle tales that are the communal property of the Balinese people. Having found a way of moving and speaking that allows the potential life of the mask to work through him—a process where the actor finally has a great deal of personal freedom and one that calls for an intense personal involvement with that "other" life that begins in the mask—the actor improvises his way through the story. He recites archaic poetry, he makes jokes, he affirms and sometimes questions the principles of his ancestors, he comments on the problems of the community and on the problems of being an individual within that community, he moves back and forth between the ancestral past and the immediate present—all in character.

As I began to understand what was happening, what at first had looked rather external and foreign began to acquire for me a kind of extraordinary attractiveness. Here was a form of theatre—not so different, really—that was at once theatrically arresting and very personal; and in this theatre, drawing on a sense of the past that they both owned, the audience and the performer could share their experiences in a very immediate way.

Schevill: That sense of ancestral past in Bali must be extraordinary. You probably know this recent book on Bali, *Negara: The Theatre State in Nineteenth Century Bali,* in which Clifford Geertz, the anthropologist, points out that theatre and state in Bali were inseparable (1980). He writes, "the extravagance of state rituals was not just the measure of the king's divinity; it was also the measure of the realm's well-being." Is part of your interest in Balinese theatre this close relationship of theatre to society?

Emigh: Definitely. Geertz goes on to say that, as far as he can figure out, it was not so much that the theatre affirmed the glory of the state, but that the state existed in order to present the glory of the theatre—which is an inversion of the way historians and the rest of us usually think about these things. Part of the excitement involved in working with Balinese theatre comes from dealing with a place where theatre is acknowledged as a vital, necessary part of life. Although the ancestral past is very rich and very alive in Bali, and is brought forcefully into the present through ingenious and striking means in Balinese theatre, the real glory of the theatre, at least for me, is its ability to celebrate the present as it contains the past in theatrical play.

Schevill: So there are always comments on the present situation.

Emigh: Topical comments are woven all through the dialogue. And comments about the act of performing, too. It's the theatre's capacity to make something of the past that's at issue. So the immediacy of the theatrical present is as important as the power of the ancestral past.

Schevill: That's a marvelous combination between history and the present. Do you see such a relationship between theatre and society ever developing in this country, or are we condemned to the kind of isolation that theatre has always had?

Emigh: I don't know. I suppose that's one of the issues I've been trying to play with in my own way. Certainly, you have been concerned with it in your own plays, which tend to move back and forth between history and the immediate present. Of course, theatre can't be completely isolated. To accept or reject a theatrical image is to make a judgment as to how we can imagine our world. And to make theatre always involves grappling with our sense of both past and present. In a lot of the contemporary work being done, this has become a matter of dealing with the personal and immediate past of the performer, say in Spalding Gray's work. But one of the suppositions in that kind of work—correct when it's successful—is that the performer's personal experience has been in some way representative of our shared social past—that we are dealing with a significant anecdote.

Schevill: Speaking of Spalding Gray's work, what do you think of this recent phenomenon of solo performances? Is there a specific artistic reason for them as well as an economic one?

Emigh: I think there are both. Certainly there are economic advantages to solo acts right now. The cost is small; they can be traveled with easily; they usually don't take a lot of scenery, so they're easy to set up. But all that stripping away of scenery and exposing of the actor at work has its own importance. It refocuses the act of watching theatre. Part of the heritage from the experiments of the sixties is that the performer became more and more responsible for his or her work. The act of creation became central to the work itself. Kakul happened to be a master of the one-man performance form in Bali, and I became very attracted to this aspect of his work. Part of the appeal is in the virtuosic display. I found myself marveling at one man embodying a whole world, transforming himself from character to character, singing, dancing, telling jokes, weaving tales. But, because of the awareness of the virtuosity involved, it also becomes a celebration of the capacity of theatre to embrace the world. And, since our consciousness moves back and forth between accepting the characters as characters and realizing that it is one man, after all, wearing all of these masks, enjoying the performance becomes a way of recognizing the complexity and multiple possibilities within all individuals. So it's not only the monetary economy that is attractive here, but also the economy of theatrical means that tends to focus attention on the processes and capacities of the theatre itself, and on the ways it intersects with life.

Schevill: Much of the work you have done recently has been in this one-man style.

Emigh: Yes, though I've always used live music, and the presence of the musicians is important to the sense of form and spontaneity, I think. I've been very lucky having excellent musicians available to me—I Wayan Suweca, Amy Catlin whom I lived and performed with for several years, Jim Koetting, Andy Toth, Allan Robinson, Lisa Lawson, Dane Harwood, I Wayan Lendra, sometimes gamelan orchestras in residence at universities. We've worked out ways to permit audience members to provide the music in its skeletal form when necessary. I'd rather use pots and pans and cereal cartons than taped music. Maybe this has to do with my earlier experience as a would-be jazz musician. I know that working with topeng has allowed me to experience—for the first time as an actor—the same rush of connectedness and the same soaring feeling that I used to occasionally feel playing jazz.

Schevill: You're particularly interested in the merger of Eastern and Western theatrical styles. How do you see the theatrical possibilities of such a merger?

Emigh: Well, first it's important to point out that the drawing upon Eastern forms is nothing new within Western theatre. Putting aside the probable indebtedness to the East of commedia, and of Greek theatre, and of medieval theatre, if you go back within this century—to Yeats, and to Artaud, and to Brecht and to Meyerhold—almost every innovative movement in contemporary Western theatre has somehow or other drawn upon sources from the East. Not exclusively, but significantly. And that's now part of our ongoing "Western" tradition. So it's no longer a simple question of "our" tradition or "their" tradition, and it hasn't been for a long time.[4] But still, there are a great many stupid things that can be done taking elements of one tradition, grafting them onto another. I've done some of these myself.

Once one acquires a certain degree of skill from another tradition, there begins a bewildering set of problems to be solved—or at least acknowledged and played with—about one's identity as a performer. I look sometimes at the things that are done in a sort of ecumenical fervor these days—taking techniques from other theatrical traditions and pasting them onto Western work—and I experience a feeling of horror that I'm associated with helping to transmit and encourage such things. Because techniques get wrenched from the contexts that give them meaning. They simply get traded on for their exotic appeal, without respect or intelligence or even real playfulness: a sort interior decorator's theatre. But I do think there are a number of ways that Asian examples can be used vitally. It's not for me to prescribe what other people can find in them. It's always a tightrope to walk and one can fall off either side very easily—towards exoticism and pedantic self-consciousness on the one hand, and towards crass, insensitive, ineffective cultural blundering on the other.

Schevill: Talk a little more about how you developed your storytelling technique, because that's a very interesting example to me of merging Eastern and Western ways. Is it at all like what Paul Sills was trying to do in *Story Theatre?*

Emigh: Yes, a little. One of the things that happened in the sixties was that we devalued narrative. I felt energized by the sense of creativity and theatrical presence that came of that work, but I missed the stories. Maybe Paul Sills did, too. There was a lot of talk about dreams. I don't know about other people, but I usually dream in stories. Anyway, I think that the story form has a power of its own and that there is a need for narrative, for patterns of action that cohere.

Schevill: The process you've been describing is a deep one and seems to involve the roots of myth, in addition to just stories. How have you regarded the role of myth in your masked performances?

Emigh: I suppose that a myth is a story that has come to be shared by a society, probably a venerable story, and one that helps give that society its identity and that carries with it important assumptions about what it's like to be alive. The Balinese do have a keen sense of myth. I've been experimenting with material, sometimes using Balinese stories, sometimes well-known Western stories, playing back and forth between the foreign and the familiar, and seeing if myths can travel, or if old tales can be reinvested with meaning this way.

I had fallen in love with the way that the Balinese performers work with their stories, but I really hadn't a clue as to how I might apply what I was learning. Toward the end, Kakul let me wear some of his masks, and I had commissioned many masks myself, and I began doing more and more character work—which came much more quickly than the initial and necessary dance training. Being familiar with Michael Chekhov's psycho-physical techniques helped.[5] But still, I was a very rough, very unfinished performer.

By the time I came back to Providence, I Wayan Suweca had been teaching Balinese music at Brown for almost a year. That was a great stroke of luck for me! We may have even passed each other in the air the year before. And all that time, people had been asking both of us if we knew the other. By now, his half-learned English and my half-learned Indonesian fit together into a language we could enjoy. And Suweca had studied with Kakul, too. So, we started to work together.

The first piece we worked on was a children's play that I was directing with Looking Glass Theatre in Providence, *Tjupak* (see fig. 85). That was a

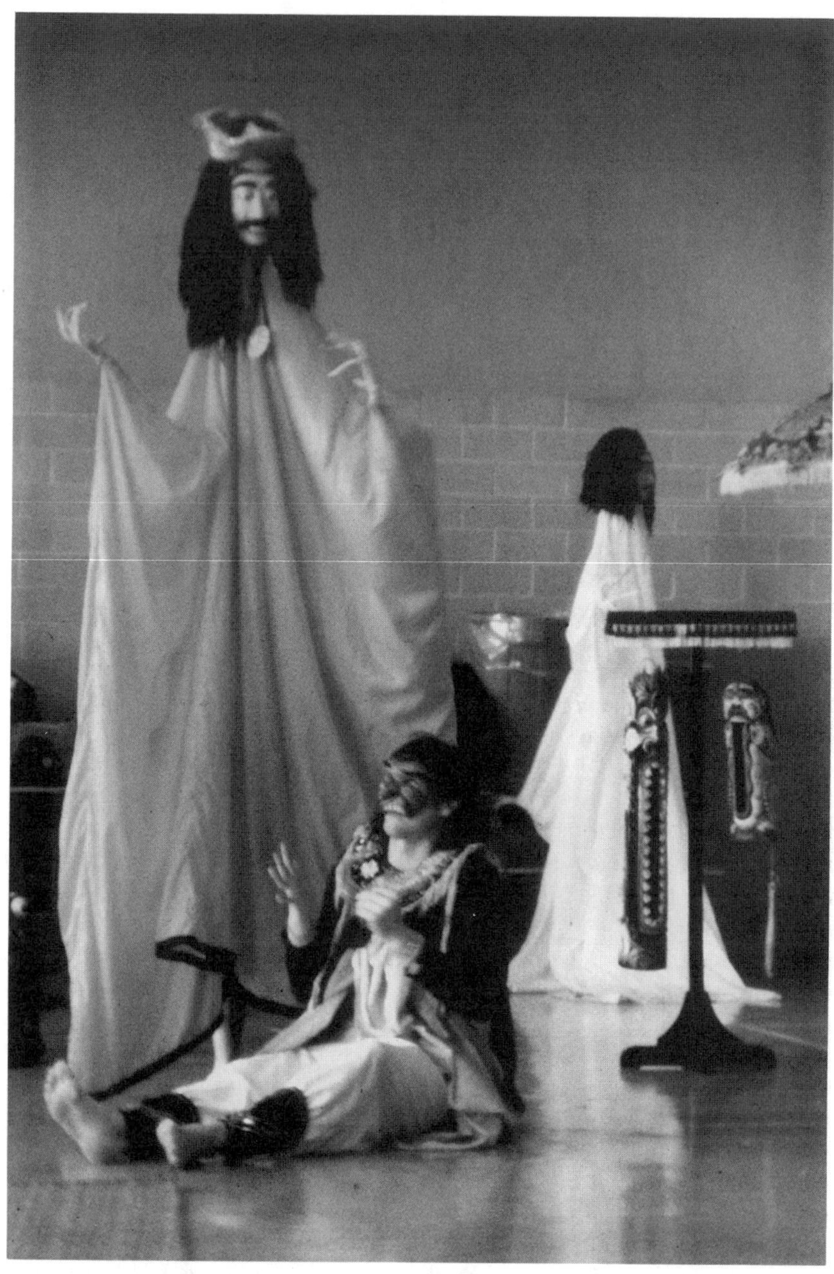

Figure 85. Puppets designed by Bernice Bronson for the Looking Glass Theatre Production of *Tjupak*. Providence, RI, 1976 (Photo, Joanne Kilkeen).

wonderful experience. Bunny Bronson, the Company's Artistic Director in those days, had been working for years on participatory techniques in children's theatre and had gotten it down to a fine art, and some of my favorite former students were now acting with the group. The story had to do with a braggart and glutton and bully who does worse and worse things because he is so jealous of his perfect little brother, until he is disgraced and then goes through a difficult regeneration. I had bought a set of masks for the project and had helped to translate an epic version of the story in Bali. And it seemed to me it could work as a sort of myth about sibling rivalry anywhere—certainly in America.

So I went through the epic with my son and daughter. My son Aaron, who was six, helped a lot to focus it for American kids. Bunny and I worked out a rough scenario and then I began to improvise through the story with the actors. Suweca arranged a scaled down version of Balinese music that could be played by the stage manager and by whatever actors were free—which became important as an example for our later work, and he taught one of the actresses a simplified version of *legong* to use as a princess and kept it all tolerably Balinese. And I worked on the storytelling and the character movements, and on using the masks. And Bunny made some wonderful god-puppets and worked out ways for the kids in the audience to participate in the story, though we didn't really divide the work up quite so neatly, of course.

Anyway, 25,000 saw *Tjupak* before it stopped touring. And I actually overheard one kid scold another in a supermarket by calling him a "Tjupak" because he had grabbed some grapes. So I guess it did begin to work mythically. I mean the characters did come to be reference points in the imaginations of the children who saw the play. And the masks proved to have a kind of mesmerizing appeal for the adults who saw the play as well as the kids. And, best of all, Suweca and I found out we enjoyed working together.

Schevill: How did you start performing topeng stories yourself?

Emigh: Well, I was playing in the gamelan that Suweca was leading, and he was helping me with my dancing, and I began helping him with some voice and character work in acting, and we would talk, and joke around, and we began to work with the masks I had brought back. Then, gradually, we began to add some dancing and rudimentary story telling to gamelan concerts. Suweca would dance the graceful parts, and I would play the demonic ones and do most of the storytelling. As his English and my dancing improved—I worked with I Nyoman Wenten again and studied some corporeal mime that next summer—we began to work up a version of one of the topeng chronicle tales—*The Death of Bedahulu* or, as we came to call it, *The Pig-Headed King* (fig. 86).

Figure 86. Author as Dalem Bedahulu. 1978 (Photo, Ernestina Koetting).

It's the story of a tyrant who is in the habit of demonstrating his powers by going into meditation and having a servant lop off his head. Every day this happens, and every day the head is put back in place and the tyrant brags about his control over the forces of life and death. Then, one day, the head rolls into the river and a panicked servant cuts off the head of a swine and sticks it on the king's neck. The king is so furious at being revealed as a pig-headed tyrant that he sets himself on a high tower and passes an edict that no one in Bali is allowed to look up from the ground. No one can see the sky or the stars or the sun or the sacred volcano, lest they look at his piggy face.

Now this was Watergate time, so it was easy to play back and forth between the Balinese myth and the American political situation with its abuses of power and obsessive denial. In the chronicle, the king consumes himself in his own self-hatred and anger, reducing himself to a pile of ashes under the gaze of Gajah Mada—the leader of an expeditionary force from Java. Gajah Mada conquered Bali in 1343, overthrowing a king known as "the different-headed one." That much is history. And Gajah Mada is regarded in Indonesia as a reincarnation of the god Vishnu. So, as Watergate receded and Jimmy Carter came to power, that allowed for a lot of jokes about born-again rulers and about Gajah Mada's fixed smile.

So we kept playing back and forth between America and Bali—and the play was mirrored in our own identities as performers—and the Balinese myth functioned as a kind of universal parable of political overreaching and tyranny, of what happened to people operating within the meshes of political power and to the people who are subject to that power. And about how our strengths can grow out of hand and become self-destructive. Swordfights and comic routines developed, and there were a lot of jokes and puns about prigs and pigs and pig-headedness, and the topical allusions kept changing as the headlines changed and we adjusted to the locales we were playing in. We began to tour the show around southern New England and brought it to the Theatre Project in Baltimore, using a gamelan that was in residence at UMBC there.

Schevill: Did you perform any other Balinese stories?

Emigh: Later. I Made Bandem came to Wesleyan University to earn his doctorate—he and his wife Suasti are both fine dancers—and Suweca came back to America to start up a gamelan group in San Francisco, and I Wayan Dibia and his wife Wiratini came to New York while he studied dance for a year, and Jim Brochin, Steve Samos, and Ron Jenkins, other Americans who had studied topeng in Bali, lived fairly nearby. So we occasionally were able to round up a troupe and perform other stories (see fig. 87). One was about the coming to Bali of a mysterious, menacing figure who had to be assimilated or else there would be famine and plague—a very sacred story

Figure 87. Left to right: Author, I Made Bandem, and I Wayan Suweca in a topeng production. Wesleyan University, 1979 (Photo, Amy Catlin).

in Bali. Another was an Indonesian version of the Frog Prince story, very rich in comedy and far more interesting than the one we know. In this version, there are several princesses involved, some of them quite unlikable; the frog has to defeat a demon army; and the youngest and best of the princesses falls in love with the frog and becomes very upset when he turns into a prince.[6] Then there was the story of Dalem Bungkut—an ancient ruler that no one can harm or defeat, who begins to do outrageous things to his people in the hope that someone can finally come and overthrow him. By this time Reagan was in power, so a lot of jokes about offerings requiring jelly beans and assassin-proof rulers and government programs being curtailed got woven into the dialogue.[7]

Schevill: How do you rehearse for such performances?

Emigh: You don't—not the way we tend to think of rehearsing. On the day of the performance, everyone gathers together. The storyline is gone over, the masks are selected, the introductory dances are set, and an order for entrances is established. Some fight sequences might have to be gone over. Comic *lazzi* and feed lines for topical jokes are thought up and traded. Everyone brings their own costumes, the entrance curtain defines the set, and the orchestra is told the sequence of tunes to be used. Since we were often working together for the first time and doing stories new to some of us, we would usually run through the entrances and exits and key bits of action with the orchestra once. But in Bali, that wouldn't be necessary. Though the stories mentioned are all very different from each other, the kinds of characters used and the order of entrances are more or less formulaic, and the comic masks and story-telling characters can be transferred from one story to another.

Then, immediately before the performance, while the gamelan is playing, a ceremony is held where water is sprinkled on the masks and the performers, *mantras* are spoken, and incense is inhaled. This helps concentration as well as imparting a sense of the sacred. The first lines hold for any story, then you improvise your way through the scenario that has been established, playing for two hours, sometimes more. And it all works, because preparation, training, and shared knowledge of tradition take the place of rehearsal. The jazz analogy works fairly well here. You know the basic tune and the sequence of chords that can be used, the patterns you like to run and the sounds you can contribute. You fix an order of entrances and exits, and, when it's working, the rest is inspiration and flying. When it isn't working, you fall back on technique, stay closer to safe territory, and get through it as painlessly and with as much grace as you can salvage.

Schevill: Lately, you've been working more with Western stories, such as *Little Red Riding Hood.* Why this change in direction?

Emigh: Partly because I began to get uncomfortable about my identity as a performer. As I got better at these things, people began to deal with me as a sort of pseudo-Balinese. I would be asked questions that can only legitimately be asked of a Balinese performer and, worse, I would sometimes answer them. So there had to be something warped in the identity I was assuming, since, even if I could master the skills that I'm using—which I hadn't done—I still could never claim membership as a Balinese performer. Perhaps it was all right while I was working with Suweca, and all right later, when Bandem and Dibia were around, because moving back and forth between those things that are Balinese and those things that are American was at the heart of those performances. The most important skill I could contribute was being able to maintain the semblance of Balinese form while moving the story along in English. But then, after two years of working together, Suweca was going away.

Although I had found a way to do *The Pig-Headed King* as a one-man show, I had begun to re-think what I was doing and wanted to de-emphasize the exotic elements (exotic for Western audiences) and work with stories as familiar to my audiences as the Balinese stories were to the Balinese. I wanted to work less with exposition and play more freely with the story values—in some ways be truer to the Balinese model—while exposing my own identity as an American performer more clearly.

Schevill: Why *Red Riding Hood*?

Emigh: Another set of accidents. I had promised to do a piece for Wastepaper Theatre—the itinerant poet's theatre in Providence which you founded and which pops up from time to time with and without your presence. The performance was to be on May 1st—May Day—1977. At the time, I had a friend who had what I considered to be some naive political ideas and we never talked about politics—probably because she and I both knew it wouldn't help either world politics or our relationship. But May Day seemed to be a good time to do a political piece. And so I set all of my masks out in front of me—an army of them made for *Caucasian Chalk Circle*, for *Tjupak*, for *The Pig-Headed King*, and for general topeng use. The full mask of a princess that I had gotten for display purposes happened to be placed on a red shawl (fig. 88), and near it was a jaw-snapping dog mask I had gotten for *Tjupak* but never used. It looked more like a wolf (fig 89). So *Red Riding Shawl* snapped into place, at first as a parable about political innocence, with the Wolf as Czar, and the Woodcutter—a red-faced, grim mask of great vigor but questionable heroism—being a sort of combined Lenin/Stalin figure. *Red Riding Shawl* herself was to be a comic figure of naive innocence caught between the two. I had a half-mask that could serve nicely for Grandmother (fig. 90); a photo I had bought in a New Hampshire junk shop of a beaming old lady holding up a cat provided a place

Figure 88. Red Riding Shawl (Photo, John Foraste).

Figure 89. The Wolf (Photo, Ernestina Koetting).

to begin with her, though it took me a long time to find her voice. And the storytellers I'd developed for the *Pig-Headed King*—one a braggart, the other one sly and cynical—lent themselves to approaching the story from different points of view. Suweca hadn't left yet, and the next morning he gave me a few quick lessons in Balinese female dance movement, and we rounded up a few more musicians, and *Red Riding Shawl* was born.

Schevill: It doesn't seem to be about Russian history anymore.

Emigh: No, it's evolved in different directions. The important thing was that I had found in the fairy tale something that was well enough known to any American audience, so that I could play around in the story a great deal—adding significance, questioning virtues, inverting values—without losing anyone. After that first time, I took off the Balinese topeng costume and replaced it with clothes that were unusual but had particular personal meanings for me—an embroidered vest made by my former wife, a shirt

Figure 90. Grandmother (Photo, John Foraste).

made by a friend—I was trying to work further away from the exotic, while still keeping up a play between East and West. I did it for parties and for schools, old-age homes, mental hospitals, at anthropological conferences and theatre conferences, at several universities and a mime school, in public parks, and, for a few weeks, at the Performing Garage in New York. It was also performed at the National School of Drama and the Tibetan School of Drama in India and the Conservatory of Dance and Music in Bali.

Schevill: That must have been a great thrill.

Emigh: Very thrilling, very scary, and very wonderful, because they were able to understand and appreciate what I was doing with their traditions. Anyway, as I kept performing the piece, it kept changing. Little Red Riding Shawl became less and less a transvestite joke and more and more an embodiment of whatever grace and lyricism I could find in myself. To find her in me somewhere became a very rewarding and welcome challenge. And at the same time, the cynical character became more and more crude and questioning about her innocence, insisting on a sexual interpretation of her attraction to the Wolf. What had started as a way of talking about political innocence metamorphosed into a parable about social and sexual innocence, about loving and separating and moving into and through adolescence. And, as the one person with real wisdom in the piece, Grandmother became the central character.

The political material didn't entirely disappear—it's still there, more in some performances than in others, in the treatment of the Woodcutter in the end, which might touch on Begin, or Sukarno and Suharto, or the U.S. in Vietnam, as well as Stalin. And, for example, when Red Riding Shawl tries to think who might be out there to rescue her, she considers the chances of a CIA agent snooping around in the woods, but realizes that to stabilize the situation he would supply the Wolf with 20,000 military advisors (Central America was on my mind).

Still, my most personal concerns and experiences began to find their way more and more into the piece. And so the masks of the Wolf and Red Riding Shawl and Grandmother and the various storytellers all became vessels for different feelings I had that coalesced around the problems of desire, innocence, connectedness, and separation in my own personal life. The personal, the political, and the theatrical all began to knit together in a rather complex web.

Schevill: How did the masks affect you psychologically? Were they a way of objectifying the personal experiences you're talking about?

Emigh: Yes, I suppose so. Each mask had such a specific, focused, clear way of approaching situations, wearing them all in turn gave me a great feeling of completeness and an ability to take each attitude and follow its logic as applied to the story, wherever that might lead me. I found myself being surprised by what my characters were saying quite often. One time—I was performing down in Baltimore—Grandmother came to the end of the story and offered up as the moral of the tale that "innocence is sometimes a lot more likable than it is helpful." Which is certainly true, but I had never thought of it before, and neither had she—which she immediately admitted to the audience. In another performance—in Boston—I had to go on after having just heard news that seemed about to turn my personal life inside out. The woman I had been loving and living with was going to leave me. I felt catatonic, couldn't say a word. But the wolf and the little girl could dance. And, in the performance, Grandmother amazed me by talking about it all in terms of the little girl and herself, and "she" made far more sense out of jealousy and the fear of separation, and the ways that love and selfishness tangle together, than I had been able to make "myself"; and she obviously touched other members of the audience with the clarity of her thoughts and feelings. There were laughs, tears, nods of recognition. But then, of course, grandmother *is* me, as are the wolf and the little girl, and the cynical observer—they all are me, and that makes this form of theatre a perpetual source of self-discovery. So Kakul was right. The masks are not costume elements; they are vehicles for a very direct sort of communication with whatever is happening—inside and outside of myself.

Schevill: What's unique about your performance, John, is this use of mask-spectacle that you've been discussing. How do you see the importance of masks and spectacle in theatre today?

Emigh: Well, they keep the process of transformation before us and they help keep the imagination awake and the body working. The masks have such clarity about them that they demand movements that are equally clear: the Balinese vocabulary of movement, while providing a great range within it for character expression that can be adjusted for each specific mask, also provides a rigorous sense of form to work with.

I have used masks in several productions by now. Usually, when working outside the frame of topeng, I try to apply the principles that I have learned, and not the Balinese vocabulary of movement itself. While in Bali, I got together a collection of about fifty masks specifically for use in *Caucasian Chalk Circle* (see color plate VIII). Occasionally, I would buy masks ready-made that I thought would fit the characters in the play, but more often I would sit with I Made Regug or I Wayan Tedun—both fine mask-carvers—and I would describe characters from the play, and we would exchange sketches or make faces at each other, and new masks would be commissioned and made. It was a couple of years before a production could finally be mounted, and then it wasn't entirely successful. My own associations with the masks were still so specifically Balinese, and sometimes bits of Balinese movement were imposed where they shouldn't have been, while at other times I had trouble getting the actors to arrive at movement patterns that matched the clarity of the masks; some of the actors were much better at this than others. Although I was determined not to repeat Brecht's own mistake of imposing masks as costume elements toward the end of the rehearsal process—Brecht ended up having to rework the whole play once he saw the masks on the actors—I hadn't as yet found reliable ways of introducing American actors to the process of working from the mask to meet its life.

The masks did serve, though, to create a grotesque human landscape through which Grusha and Simon and Azdak—all unmasked—had to negotiate their ways. I was looking for a figure-ground relationship with the vulnerability and changeableness of the human face highlighted against a sea of grotesque caricatures. The crowd scenes worked especially well this way, I thought—perhaps because I had to think more in terms of Breughel than in terms of the Balinese movement I had learned. And the villains and the cameo comic parts came off best. Too often, the work was neither fish nor fowl and either Balinese or Western elements stood out as imposed. The organic synthesis I was looking for kept slipping away. Still, it was an invaluable experience.

A few years later, I took on some of the same problems with *Volpone* (fig. 91). I think that production was much more successful. We had a student at the time named Larry Maslon—a fine caricaturist; together, Larry and I worked out a whole range of puppets, masks, partial masks, and makeup for the various characters, this time designing for specific actors: for their faces and for their particular capacities for voice and movement. The Venetian jury was essentially a huge nine-headed rod puppet worked by five puppeteers—a sort of parody of the Supreme Court, devised by caricaturing figures from Renaissance history and literature. So one figure hovered between an ancient pope and William Douglas and another somehow blended Othello and Thurgood Marshall, and the scribe looked something like Macchiavelli and a little like Truman Capote. Their rigid, semihuman grotesqueness was set off against the human faces of Bonario and Celia in the Court, while Corbaccio, Voltore, and Corvino—the stock villains—wore commedia-like half-masks, and Volpone and Mosca had partial masks that slightly disfigured the nose and brow but left them with relatively more human flexibility. Although I thought a lot about commedia traditions while preparing the play and working with the costumer, I was actually able to work more directly with the procedures for finding character and movement from the potential life of the mask that I had observed and practiced in Bali. I even began rehearsal with Balinese masks, but this time I intentionally worked with a movement coach, Gary Miller, who

Figure 91. Mosca and Voltore in *Volpone*. Brown University, 1981 (masks designed by Larry Maslon; costumes by Michael Hite; sets by John R. Lucas; photo, Michael Hite).

had no knowledge of Balinese theatre. I think that the theatrical world we ended up with had a sense of cohesiveness and completeness that wasn't quite there in *Chalk Circle.*

Sometimes the influences are less obvious. I was directing a production of *Henry IV Part I* recently and discovered that I had unconsciously cast the comic roles and blocked the battle scenes according to the convention of the Javanese shadow theatre. Once I was conscious of doing this, I could work with or against these conventions, understanding how they functioned, using them as a rough guide. The huge sponge-rubber Mother and Father masks that Erminio Pinque and I came up with for your *Edison's Dream* were inspired partly by some street theatre masks I'd used during the early 'seventies (in turn influenced by Bread and Puppet's Uncle Fatso), but mostly by the giant processional masks used in Bali and in parts of India. The use of the small Edison-as-a-child puppet in the same scene was inspired by Japanese *bunraku.* But the associations for the audience—valid, too—were probably with carnival grotesques and ventriloquists' dummies. So the scene had the quality of a very American nightmare. The Asian models had led me back to American equivalents, and these found their way into the play and allowed us to condense and concentrate the dialogue around an arresting set of visual images.

Schevill: It seems to me, in talking about spectacle, that your work is unusual, because the basic tendency in contemporary theatre seems to be back towards a kind of naturalism, reflecting television and film. And you're introducing this element of spectacle and masks again.[8]

Emigh: Sometimes. Though I'm certainly not the only one. I think that we're apt to end up with some surprising combinations. I recently directed *Curse of the Starving Class* and enjoyed it immensely. I think some of Shepard's most recent work is so strong because it combines naturalistic techniques with such startling visual images. The same is true with *Buried Child.*

Schevill: Particularly *Buried Child,* where you have that ritualistic image of draping the body with all those husks of corn.

Emigh: Yes. Of course, any good theatre has always had to find some way of working back and forth between the startling and the ordinary—between the audience's sense of life-as-it-is-usually-lived, unobserved, and the striking theatrical image that suddenly challenges or reveals or clarifies our sense of what it's like to be alive. It's at those moments that an imprint is left as a guide for understanding and imagining.

Schevill: What new directions do you see your performances taking?

Emigh: I really don't know. For the next year, I'll be in India, trying to better understand and document some forms of traditional theatre there. It will be the first time in a very long time that I won't be primarily acting or directing or teaching theatre, and I've got mixed feelings about this scholar's role I've stumbled into while trying to follow my curiosity and find some answers to what once seemed a rather practical and manageable set of questions. Most of the forms I'll be working with involve masks, of course, and some are deeply embedded in ritual and myth. But I also want to study street performers called *bahurupiyas.* [. . .] I know one man who claims to be able to perform over two hundred different characters. [. . .][10] His work fascinates me because so much of the theatre I've been dealing with has had to do with elaborate ritual and ceremony, often based on shamanistic practices. And it's refreshing to consider something which, as far as I can see, is a very old and essentially secular tradition—one that seems based on the same innate appeal attached to imitation and transformation that Aristotle insisted on. I don't know where all of this will take me—some place back into theatre, I hope. But, then, I didn't know where asking questions about Balinese masks would take me, either. I'm as surprised as anyone at where it *did* take me!

Schevill: Is there anything else you'd like to say about these borrowings back and forth between East and West?

Emigh: Of course they do flow both ways and they are not always successful. When I was in Bali, there was a very popular form of drama—*drama-gong*—that de-emphasized dance and music, but didn't seem to have the intensity or rigor of Western scripted drama, either. After a little while, the Balinese became bored with it and went back to their more traditional forms of theatre. But at the same time, other experiments were being made. For example, the *kecak,* or Monkey Chant—which has a crazy-quilt East-West history to begin with—was restaged by I Wayan Dibia, a young man who had studied with Balinese scholars and artists who had themselves studied in California. He used techniques ultimately derived from the Living Theatre, the Open Theatre, and Béjart's choreography, that stressed a very asymmetrical and athletic use of the human body. For me, his work was a startling success. All of these influences were recycled in strikingly Balinese ways. And the irony of it all was that the particular Western innovators being drawn upon were themselves greatly influenced by Antonin Artaud's writing, which in turn was partly inspired by his seeing a Balinese troupe perform in Paris! So we have a funny way of coming full circle, and practices, having been put through a Western sieve and interpreted according to Western needs, come back to Bali and are metamorphosed again.

A couple of years ago, I found myself in a situation where the ironies

Figure 92. Author as Penasar Cenikan.

involved in this sort of mutual exchange were impressed on me. I was in India, giving a paper at an anthropology conference, and was asked to conduct a series of master classes at the National School of Drama in India. There I was, an American giving classes on the use of Asian masks to Indian acting students, most of whom had never worn a mask, some of whom had come from places where masks were thought of as belonging to rather archaic and vestigial forms of theatre. I was coming to the school to impart a sense of the power and authority and appeal that masks can have in the theatre—a knowledge I had gained from Balinese practices. But, historically, Balinese practice had drawn extensively from Indian examples. So, again, there was this bizarre, cyclical movement happening. But always with a change at every turning; I suppose it's really more of a gyre I'm describing here.

In any case, it's bewilderingly one world now. The classes were well received and I was asked by Suresh Awasthi to do a TV interview and demonstration, which we taped for later presentation. Weeks later, I arrived late at Suresh's apartment complex to see the show. There was a bus strike, and I couldn't remember what apartment he lived in, so I knocked at the first apartment I saw with a light on. A distinguished Indian gentleman opened the door. He and his wife and three children were all watching television, and there I was on the screen demonstrating Balinese masks and performing bits of *Red Riding Shawl.* He looked at me, and pointed at the screen, and we both started to laugh until we could no longer stand.

We trade and we borrow and we change, we play and we work, and we try to maintain our sanity and sense of humor along with our ability to grow and our capacity for wonder.

Notes

1. The festival alluded to was the Rhode Island Festival: 71. It was held on the various college campuses of Rhode Island, was free to the public, and featured (among others) the Bread and Puppet Theatre, the Manhattan Project, the Performance Group, the Open Theatre, the National Black Theatre, the National Theatre of the Deaf, mime Michael Grando, and Burning City Theatre, as well as various symposia of playwrights and directors.

2. Bob Carrol is dead, Robert Wilson is in Stuttgart, probably, and Spalding Gray, bless him, is a star. The American experimental theatre still has no clear sense of direction. Meanwhile, the most joyous theatre of the 1980s was performed on the Berlin Wall, the most achingly tragic in Tienanmen square. For better and for worse, theatre and politics are more intimately linked than ever before.

3. I was a graduate student at Tulane University, where Schechner was teaching, from 1964 to 1967.

4. Snow (1986) discusses my own early work with Balinese traditions, along with work by Julie Taymor and Islene Pinder; Reeder (1979) has dealt with this work in semiological terms; Pitt (1982) discusses his own encounters with Balinese traditions and the role these traditions have played in his developing work; Brandon (1989) gives an excellent survey of the practice of Asian theatre in the West today. See Emigh and Brandon for a general survey of this subject (1995).

5. See Chekhov (1953: 85–93). I have found in my own work and in teaching acting that Chekhov's work with centers and imaginary bodies meshes particularly well with Balinese technique (not too surprisingly, since Chekhov was himself influenced by the theory and practice of yoga, particularly as it involves *chakras*, or concentrated centers of energy). Eugenio Barba also seems to have found Chekhov particularly useful in finding shared or translatable guiding principles in Asian and Western theatre practice (1995: 72–80). Kathy Foley (1990) has offered an intriguing report on a traditional variant to this approach used in Sunda, west Java, in a topeng tradition most often performed by women, and on its effect on her as a performer.

6. I have since staged more elaborate versions of this tale for the East-West Fusion Theatre of Sharon, Connecticut, working in collaboration with Teviot Pourchot, Hazel Chung, Gde Arsa Artha, and with companies of American and Balinese performers.

7. More recent performances have involved I Nyoman Catra, I Nyoman Sedana, I Nyoman Wenten, and myself, with the New York City Indonesian Consulate's gamelan, at New York's Summerfest '91 and the same group, with I Gusti Supartha and the Indonesian Embassy's gamelan, at Movement Theatre International's Clown Congress of 1991 in Philadelphia, as well as performances of a variant of *Calon Arang* in 1995, directed by Ron Jenkins and I Nyoman Catra, with Catra, I Gusti Windia, Desak Laksmi Suarti and the MIT gamelan, at Holy Cross College, Emerson College, and MIT.

8. Directing experiments have gone on, of course, since this interview. Erminio Pinque's puppets for *Edison's Dream* mutated and multiplied into a legion of grotesque giant adults used for the third act of a Brown University production of Wedekind's *Spring Awakening*; many of these same puppets, along with newer creations, now have an independent existence in Pinque's wonderful Big Nazo Puppet Bowling Alley Band and Theatre. The most recent collaboration with Pinque and his fellow artists was in a production of Anna Deavere Smith's *Piano*, in which the phantasms of Cuban-American history were represented by extraordinary grotesque puppets based on photos and cartoons of Teddy Roosevelt, Fulgencio Batista, Carmen Miranda, Nikita Khruschev, and Fidel Castro.

9. The performer referred to is Hajari Bhand. See the previous chapter.

Chapter 8
Conclusion

When a Balinese actor holds a new mask in his right hand, gazing upon it, turning it this way and that, making it move to a silent music, he is assessing the potential life of the mask and searching for the meeting place between himself and the life inherent in its otherness. If he is successful, then a bonding takes place that will allow him to let that potential life flow through his own body. If he finds that place of congruence between his physical and spiritual resources and the potential life of the mask, then a living amalgam is created: a character, a persona. This amalgam is at best unstable—based as it must be upon paradox, ambiguity, and illusion—but "it" moves, "it" speaks, "it" breathes, "it" is perceived—by the performer and by the audience—as having an organic integrity. If the performer fails to find such a meeting place within this field of paradox, ambiguity, and illusion, then the mask will retain its separateness: whatever its worth as an object, a "work" of art, it will at best function as a decoration, a costume element. The process begins with a respect for the mask's potential life as a separate entity and proceeds by narrowing the gap between self and other through a process of imaginative play.

The meeting place—the common ground found in this process—must be specific and precise. Ultimately, it must be located within the actor's own body, providing a locus of energy that will support and resonate with the mask's appearance in order to create a character—an *ethos* in Aristotle's suggestive terminology—that gives its fragile testament to yet one more way of being alive. In doing this, the mask does not hide or obscure; it is a revelatory device. As Peter Brook has noted in reference to the Balinese masks made for him by Ida Bagus Anom for (non-traditional) use in *The Conference of Birds,* "the traditional mask [. . .] is an image of the essential nature. In other words, a traditional mask is an image of a man without a mask [. . .] an outer casting that is a complete and sensitive reflection of the inner life" (1987: 218).

The coming to terms of actor and mask offers a paradigm through which we can draw closer to an understanding of how the alchemical procedures of theatre work—and how they sometimes fail. Summarizing a set of acting exercises I've developed in response to the encounters with masks and myth described above may help to indicate some of the connections between issues that are central to working and playing with masks and more general issues involved in theatrical performance and training. This set of exercises has several stages, and I usually draw these out over the first three weeks of an acting class, interspersed with other exercises designed to encourage spontaneity on the one hand, and a greater control over the placement of energy within the body on the other. The entire sequence is designed to open up student actors to a broader range of "characters," and, hopefully, a richer sense of "self."

In the first stage, the participants sit together in a circle. In random order, each tells two brief anecdotal stories as remembered from their own lives. In the second stage, each actor appropriates a story originally told by someone else: speaking in the first person, preserving the essential storyline, but changing details of time or place, of names, of secondary events, and, perhaps, changing the point of view from which the story is told in order to own more fully the adopted material. In the third stage, any of the collected stories may be retold—again in the first person, and again changes in point of view or supporting details may be made to help the telling—but this time the aim is to create a persona: to tell the adopted story "in character," trusting the logic and perspective of this persona to bring new meaning to a by now familiar story, perhaps somewhere along the way to becoming a myth.

A fourth stage can be added, in which an actual mask is made or selected; the mask is then approached through a process involving an exploration of its potential life, first by regarding it much as a Balinese actor regards a *topeng* mask, then by grounding its life—its movement, its voice, its spirit—in the specific body of a specific actor. In the process, the actor addresses the mask and eventually puts it on, sequentially closing the gaps from "it" to "he" or "she" to "you" to "I" as different centers of energy that sustain and shape voice and movement are found and are tested. The bond between mask and actor is finally checked in a mirror, adjustments are made, and the masked persona is then deployed to tell any of the collected stories now in circulation from his or her very specific vantage point. At each stage of the exercise, the problem is to find a meeting ground between the range of memories and possibilities experienced as the actor's self—the locus of "I"—and that which begins as outside the self—as "his" and "hers," as "it" and "you," as another person's story, another face, another way of talking and being. The addition of the final stage, involving mask work, serves to make this fundamental theatrical process more palpable, more visible (to the performer, to the audience), and to add a further demand for clarity (even if it is being clear about where the ambiguities lie) in the play between "self" and "other" that is involved.

This paradigm can be applied to theatrical procedures considered more broadly: the director's search for a way to embody and set in motion a playwright's script, the actor's attempt to give breath and body to the words and actions of a (fictional) other, the storyteller's resurrection of a memory, a myth, a fable. It may also be particularly apt in understanding the dynamics of "intercultural" productions. Many such productions have occurred and a spate of literature has been written about them since my interview with Jim Schevill (see, e.g., Pavis 1992; Marranca and Dasgupta 1991). At the time of that interview, I was not aware of the degree to which the mask provided a working model, as well as an obvious tool, for such ventures.

Intercultural projects follow the same procedural patterns that are at work when the topeng actor approaches a mask in Bali—a process that is represented and probably parodied on a vase which was painted in 340 BC in the Spartan colony of Taranto, in what is now Italy (see frontispiece). The vase painting depicts a paunchy, balding actor taking up a mask depicting a white-maned king—perhaps Sophocles' Tereus—from the literary, geographical, and historical past. Holding the mask in his right hand, the seemingly miscast provincial actor gazes intently upon that unlikely image of a self that he must lay claim to with voice and body. To project from my own experience, what actors in this situation seek—be they Balinese topeng dancers, superannuated Hellenic professionals, or American acting students—is what John Lutterman, in another context (and following a path laid down by Michel Foucault) has termed a "plane of similitude." While this phrase suggests an area of congruence between two circles representing the life of the self and the life of the other (however improbable finding such an area of congruence might be for the hapless Greek actor with his tragic mask), it is not—or not simply—a least common denominator that is at issue. Lutterman's model is best imagined as three dimensional: the circles overlap and the distances between them may be narrowed, but the work of bonding takes place in an active field of resonation and interaction established *between* the overlapping (but still separate) domains of "self" and "other." The initial distance between these domains may be great or small (and it will appear to be greater or smaller from some vantage points than from others); but, if the overlap found is significant, then the "plane of similitude" activated by their conflation will provide a locus for creativity and transformative play.

As Freud (1960 [1916]) and, following him, Koestler (1964) have pointed out, this is precisely the way in which jokes, dreams, poems, and scientific discoveries are generated—through the sudden and playful resonation between previously disparate informational fields.[1] It is worth noting the structural similarities between Freud and Koestler's heuristic model and the theoretical constructions of Winnicott, Turner, and Bateson outlined in the first chapter of this work: the active "plane of similitude" that allows for the resonation between two separate experiential domains and for the generation of new, syncretic behaviors—new ways of moving and talking and being—is (paradoxically perhaps) akin to Winnicott's notion of a "potential space" created by a gap in the seeming continuity of events; in both metaphoric constructions—the one based on a break in continuity, the other on a convergence of disparate fields—the locus for creative work in the mode of play is characterized by Turner's subjunctive "liminality," and the creative work done there is made possible precisely by the ambiguities noted in Bateson's discussion of the framing of "play." The masked actor provides an exemplary demonstration of this playful syncretic process, working within a "plane of similitude" to create the amalgam of self and other that may be experienced as character. Intercultural performances—and, it seems, cultures themselves—depend on similar strategies in order to acquire their dynamic form, significance, and vitality.

For me, one of the most successful intercultural performances of the past twenty years has been Suzuki Tadashi's adaptation of Euripides' *The Trojan Women.* The action of the play is set in an open field, shortly after the explosion of the atomic bombs at Hiroshima and Nagasaki. An old woman, played by the remarkable Shiraishi Kayoko, is lost in reverie, her world shattered. Shiraishi's character acts as a sort of shaman without the power to heal, letting the tragic lives of Hecuba and Andromache flow through her mind and her body while the traditional Japanese god of compassion and the hearth looks on impassively, helplessly. Euripides' words are translated into Japanese, of course, but, more significantly, the conventions of the Greek stage find a transforming resonance with Japanese performing traditions: the impassive masks of *noh,* the contorted faces of *kabuki,* the compulsive grounding of movement. These conventions are never employed literally, but their resonance across the "plane of similitude" Suzuki and his co-workers have found between Greek and Japanese performative traditions act to reshape the form and action of Euripides' drama, transforming the Greek masks, characters, and action.

The relatively static, passive, but supportive chorus behaves more like a chorus in noh drama than the traditional chorus of Greek tragedy. The "Greeks" are reconfigured through the cultural filters of the old woman's mind: their *samarai* costumes, guttural speech, and foot stomping movements are all deeply influenced by (though never imitative of) kabuki conventions. The old woman's psyche is seized by the characters of Hecuba and Andromache as she does verbal battle with these transformed assailants from myth, history, and an alien literature that have been called to mind by the devastation around her—a legacy of latter day militarism. In a shocking ending, a young woman in contemporary dress—perhaps the old woman's granddaughter—comes to bring the old woman home, and, finding her psyche broken, hurls the flowers she has brought into the face of the agonized but powerless god of compassion, triggering a burst of loud, banal rock music, blaring out a Japanese pop tune with a mangled English chorus: "I want love you tonight!" The piece acts simultaneously as both a brilliant example and a scathing critique of the phenomenon of interculturalism as it has been experienced in Japan.

In another recycling of Greek tragedy—this time in America—Lee Breuer and Bob Telson, in their *Gospel at Colonus*, redeployed the conventions of African-American Gospel music and church rhetoric to serve the text and themes of Sophocles' *Oedipus at Colonus*, hiring outstanding performers from these traditions to enact this syncretic work, and (less obviously, but very importantly) adapting principles of traditional Japanese scenography, audience-actor, and narrator-actor-chorus relationships (Breuer 1988, personal communication). Breuer says that the project developed, in part, out of a long search for an American performance idiom capable of handling classical verse; the gospel tradition suggested itself as an American mode already a part of his own cultural consciousness which possessed the necessary emotional depth and range, as well as a formal integrity that more "naturalistic" contemporary acting styles lacked. In this context, Sophocles' play could be read as a sermon delivered by the nonagenarian playwright to his sometimes wayward Attic community. The far more subtle connections with Japanese scenographic and staging techniques act catalytically, enabling the fusion of Greek text and African-American musical and rhetorical conventions to take a viable theatrical form (Breuer 1988 and 1990, personal communication). The well-honed skills of the African-American professional performers of the gospel tradition (and of Telson himself, who has clearly studied that tradition well), the multiple levels of narration suggested by the Japanese *bunraku* theatre but grounded in African-American church conventions, and Sophocles' translated and adapted text all resonate with each other to create a syncretic and organic whole.

Some have been troubled by Breuer's ability, as a white director/playwright, to co-opt black sacred traditions and the performers of these traditions for the purpose of resurrecting a Greek play: a secular cultural artifact. Yet, the minister who originally served as a consultant to Morgan Freeman eventually replaced him on tour; he became convinced after watching performances that *Gospel at Colonus* could lay claim to being a celebration of sacred values (Breuer 1990, personal communication). The balance of elements is such that it is difficult to say whether the piece has ultimately used the gospel idiom as a means for expressing Sophocles' arguably secular themes, or whether Sophocles' words have become the basis for an essentially sacred musical celebration within the Christian gospel tradition. Though the starting place is different (this was a project generated in and for the decidedly "liminoid" realm of the American commercial theatre), the intertwining of sacred and secular traditions and the ambiguities surrounding the relative strength of the container and the contained add power to the piece, just as they do to *Prahlada Nataka* or *Calon*

Arang presentations, and, perhaps, to Sophocles' original production at the Festival of Dionysus in war-torn Athens. The issues of cultural identity and authority are similarly complex; Breuer has noted that, growing up in urban Los Angeles, the black musical tradition was a dominant element in his own acculturation (1988, personal communication).

Similar issues of ownership, authority, and identity have emerged elsewhere in the world, as, for example, in regard to Habib Tenvir's remarkable productions using tribal performers from the Chatisgarh region of Madhya Pradesh to make urban theatre in Delhi and Calcutta. Are these performers simply used as expressive tools in Tenvir's hands, or do they themselves—and the communities they are drawn from—have a vital stake (beyond a modest material one) in adapting their skills to urban and modernist concerns? When I asked Tenvir about these issues, he talked of his own long struggle to find a form that would allow him to combine his boyhood memories of performances in Chatisgarh with the skills he had acquired at RADA in London and while working with professional actors in Delhi's modern theatre. He also talked of ways his actors have transformed work done with him and have brought elements of it back into their own village performances (1995, personal communication).

A recent production at England's National Theatre of *Tartuffe* further demonstrates some of the complexities of cultural identity involved in intercultural work. The director, Jatinder Verma, is of Maharastran ancestry, but grew up in Kenya prior to moving to England. His cast consisted of actors partially or wholly of Indian ancestry who now live in England. The premise for the production was inspired by an historical incident—the visit to Aurangazeb's court by a classmate of Molière's; Verma's production begins with the (fictional) notion that this visitor brought with him a copy of Molière's new play as a gift from one royal patron of the arts to another. As "Aurangazeb's Court" struggles to put on this play by a "contemporary" Frenchman—and to make sense of its surprising dramaturgy—the production alternately highlights and collapses cultural differences, at the same time giving powerful evidence of the existence of a new ethnic diversity within the population of Great Britain. When asked in 1991 at international conference in Barcelona about his own relationship to the complex play with cultural identities represented in and by his production, Verma asserted that his multi-layered ethnic identity as a person of Indian ancestry who grew up in East Africa and now lives as a citizen of Great Britain (engaged in helping to reshape that country's slowly emerging sense of ethnic pluralism) was only more obvious in its multiple identities and memberships than that of others in the room—that even as the world in general and Europe in particular seem to be rife with an undercurrent of resurgent tribalism, forces are a work—some benign and others much less so—that must inevitably destabilize exclusive notions of cultural (and personal) identity. Like Breuer, Suzuki, and Verma, we all have a shifting set of multiple cultural memberships—overlapping here but not there, creating creative possibilities as well as tension and conflict, and characterized by an array of masks adapted to our own psyches and situations. Because of its inherent play with identity that throws into doubt fixed ontological notions (and occasions the frequent ostracism of its practitioners), the theatre may be particularly well suited to sift through the complex interrelationships that emerge.

As Karl Weber points out (1991 [1989]), productions such as those cited above tend to be *trans*cultural as well as intercultural: they take elements embedded in one culture's performative traditions and adapt, recast, and/or recontextualize them to fit a new cultural context, as the Greeks may have done with Egyptian ritual and theatre (and, if Martin Bernal [1987] is right, with Egyptian culture more broadly considered), as Molière certainly did with the Italian *commedia dell'arte*, as the Group Theatre did with techniques learned from the Moscow Art Theatre, and as the Balinese did, long ago, with icons, stories, and ritual forms from India and are proceeding to do now with traditions that have (for the most part) been developed in the West. This syncretic process, this creolization, may be inspired or grotesque (or both), but it is, in any event, inevitable. For Bali, the alternative would be an existence as a sort of ossified Disneyland for cultural tourists.

Such transculturally generated performances can often cross back successfully to their point(s) of origin, reversing the flow of energy along the interactive plane. American audiences can understand and appreciate what Suzuki has done (though no doubt from different perspectives than Japanese audiences); both African-American and Greek audiences have enjoyed *Gospel at Colonus* (albeit not without the questions regarding the appropriateness of co-opting sacred Black traditions for a secular venture by White artists); and Indian audiences have admired Balinese treatments of the *Ramayana*. One production that has resisted such a return is Peter Brook and Jean Claude Carrière's much celebrated *Mahabharata* project—probably the most widely known intercultural project to date. It may be worth asking why.

Brook has been one of the most prominent directors of intercultural theatre. Lessons learned from Persian, Balinese, African, and Indian traditions have characterized his often brilliant directorial work since at least *A Midsummer Night's Dream*. His most ambitious production to date, though, his staging of the *Mahabharata*, has proved problematic in ways that are important to this discussion. Working with an international company housed at the International Centre for Theatre Research in Paris, Brook aspires to a more fully intercultural—and less transcultural—theatre. Thus he shares many of the interests that have guided Eugenio Barba's investigations at the Institute for the Study of Theatre Anthropology in Denmark and Jerzy Grotowski's recent Theatre of Sources workshops in California and Italy.

To varying degrees, and with varying agendas, all three have expressed the desire to get "beyond" specific cultural codings to universal theatrical principles, stripping away what is "accidental" or "superficial" to find shared approaches, techniques, and principles (see Barba 1979, 1995; Brook 1987; Grotowski 1980, 1991).

Barba's thesis that theatre—or at least "Eurasian theatre"—is itself a sort of culture, with its own deeply ingrained and shared understandings about the body and its theatrical presentation, is a daring and provocative one, and one that has already produced some fascinating exchanges among performers—bringing out, for example, shared principles in producing tension and suspense through the use of balance and imbalance in divergent dance traditions. Brook himself talks of the need to for actors to "shed the superficial traits" and "superficial mannerisms" of national cultures in order "to become true to themselves" (1987: 236–39). In the *Mahabharata* project, Brook, working closely with his adapter Jean-Claude Carrière, sought to avoid pastiche and the folkloric, to get beyond "culture imprisoned within a language or style." The problem with the *Mahabharata* that emerges, though, is that "the universal style" arrived at on the one hand lacks verbal power (the poetry is gone), and, on the other hand, looks remarkably like an (often very good) production of Shakespeare.

Quite legitimately, I believe, Brook and Carrière edited the *Mahabharata* to concentrate on certain themes—the relationship between illusion of reality, the fragility of values—that the *Mahabharata* shares with other influences on their work: Shakespeare, Gurdjieff and Buñuel. Sometimes with greater grace than others, parallels are suggested between the god-given magic weapon, *pashupati*, and the nuclear bomb. The result is an intriguing, uneven, somewhat prosaic, and quite often visually stunning piece of theatre—very Western in its look and feel—performed by an international company whose specific cultural and individual skills remain largely unused.

The negative side of this ledger was compounded by a singularly obnoxious advertising campaign that touted the production (for years before it appeared and throughout its run in Paris and New York) as being the first time, ever, that anyone had put the *whole Mahabharata* on the stage. The claim, of course, is preposterous twice over: (a) Brook and Carrière could not and did not render the whole *Mahabharata* story in their eight hour production; they even found it necessary to omit important narrative sections such the escape of the Pandavas from the House of Lac; (b) The claim ignores and insults the many Asian artists who have also framed composite versions of the *Mahabharata* (including a *kathakali* troupe that toured the United States and Europe) or have presented a sequence of stories from the *Mahabharata* back to back in festival format (as has been done in Jogjakarta, in the form of *wayang kulit*, over the period of a month). Across a potentially admirable venture in interculturalism and cultural pluralism was inscribed the clear message that only European theatre counts when theatrical history is tabulated.

I see nothing wrong with Brook and Carrière's focusing on certain themes within the *Mahabharata* to the exclusion of others (leading them to stage fascinating sections usually left unplayed in Asian productions, such as the vengeance of Aswattoman, even as they skipped portions far more commonly presented in South and Southeast Asian theatre): this is a freedom that Balinese or Javanese shadow puppeteers, for example, would regard as entirely within their rights, and even, perhaps, as their duty to assume; a similar refocusing of meaning and nuance characterized the recent serialization of the *Ramayana* and *Mahabharata* on Indian television. The opening sequence of Brook and Carrière's production, though, sets up a disturbing framework for the epic: playing Vyasa, an English actor establishes the telling of the story to an Indian boy as an act of giving him back "his" culture on the stages of Paris and New York. The narrative convention itself is lifted from the source, but the staging and casting of this framing device reveals an astonishing appropriation of cultural authority, as well as a remarkable neo-colonial obtuseness: as if India (as embodied in the child actor) had ever lost these stories in the fist place!

Small wonder then, that Indian critics reviewing the production have been far harsher than others. Daryl Chin summarizes their critiques: "Brook's approach does not account for the distinctiveness of the text, its non-linearity, and its multiplicity of meanings. Rather, he extracts from the outline of the *Mahabharata* the rudiments of the narrative, to which he then imposes an ethnocentric meaning" (1991 [1989]: 88; cf. Bharucha 1989; Dasgupta 1991[1987]). Indian (and Southeast Asian) performances "impose ethnocentric meanings," too. The continuous reformulation of the epics in South and Southeast Asia have both been prompted by and have generated changing perspectives and meanings; and that has been one measure of the vitality of these theatrical traditions. As Walter Benjamin noted, "every image of the past that is not recognized by the present as one of its own concerns threatens to disappear irretrievably" (1968 [1955]: 255). Artistic and ethical problems arise, though, when respect for the "other"—the first step in forging a new life with an old mask—is violated, and when transcultural appropriation is presented as a universal "poetical history of mankind."

Such thoroughgoing transcultural projects as Breuer and Telson's *Gospel at Colonus*, Verma's production of *Tartuffe*, and Suzuki's *The Trojan Women* are rare (although there have been all too many formulaic, mechanical and clichéd impositions of Asian styles upon Western texts—usually incompetently acted by performers who have not grasped the underlying logic of the "style" adapted, leaving form and content hopelessly estranged). Another tack has been to selectively draw inspiration from Asian forms and to apply lessons learned from these traditions in a transformed and non-literal manner, as both Breuer and Robert Wilson have done with principles of Japanese scenography. Thus, in a playful melding of texts and cultures, Andrei Serban and Julie Taymor drew upon traditions of mask and movement from (primarily) Java with great skill in refashioning Gozzi's *King Stag*, using borrowed and transformed elements to suggest the once-upon-a-time Kingdom of Serendippo. Ariadne Mnouchkine, in her staging of Shakespeare's history plays, the *Oresteia*, and (more ambitiously and problematically) the life of Norodom Sihanouk, has adapted costume and movement patterns from (among many other sources) kabuki, *kutiyattam*, topeng, *jing-xi* (Beijing Opera), Sikh sword dance, Balkan folk dance, and Javanese court dance.

When these borrowings work, it is because of a resonation along the "planes of similitude" between the potential life of the script and the conventions being adapted. The Javanese mask, movement, and shadow conventions adapted in the Serban/Taymor *King Stag* serve to expand and give more precise form to Gozzi's fanciful imaginative world—itself an extension of the possibilities inherent in the masked commedia dell'arte. If the project is an Orientalist one—as it surely is—at least the Orientalism began with Gozzi and declares itself as fantasy. The Java-based court etiquette in Mnouchkine's production of *Richard II* and the *kabuki*-inspired fights for her company's *Henry IV* provide a match for the intensity and precision of Shakespeare's poetry and provide models for behavior missing in our own daily lives and theatrical practice. In the *Libation Bearers*, the red and black costumes adapted from kutiyattam and the traces of Kali in the chorus makeup help to suggest male and female energies gone awry, out of alignment, out of control—a fascinating match with and challenge to playwright Hélène Cixous's feminist theoretical concerns. The danger in such productions (as, arguably, in any production) is that a borrowed technique or convention will stick out as a foreign element, as a bit of exotica. The result, at its worst, is theatre in the manner of interior decoration. Significantly, the more successful productions cited here do not use the borrowed conventions in their "pure" form, but have learned from and adapted these conventions in the process of creating an imaginative world that can (hopefully) be experienced as organic and whole.

Once adapted, conventions used in this manner may not appear "alien" or "exotic" at all. To draw from my own experience, a production I directed of Romulus Linney's *Childe Byron* in 1986 had its ground plan, physical textures, costuming, use of music, and basic blocking of the principal characters all influenced by the strategies and conventions of Japanese noh drama. The conventions adapted allowed (I hope) for an uncluttering of the stage and a clarification of lines of action, yet all of the actual elements used—dark, polished parquet floors, Chinese embroidery and capes, a desk in the *waki's* traditional corner down left, Hector Berlioz's music—carried immediate associations with nineteenth-century Romanticism; the elements drawn form noh practice were radically reworked and redeployed in relationship to this very different ethos. The influence of noh on the production began when I noticed a pattern in the play's dramaturgy that replicated the quintessential plot structuring of noh drama: a character from the past (Byron's daughter) is visited by a disturbing specter from the more distant past with unfinished affairs on earth (Byron himself); their confrontation, abetted by a chorus, serves to remove a weight from the past and to strengthen their bond. I later found out from Linney that he had once been fascinated by noh, had tried his hand at writing noh plays as a playwriting student, but had not noticed the noh-like structuring of this particular play (1986, personal communication). The patterning had become integral to his own artistic procedures.

This absorption and redeployment of Eastern influences may be happening increasingly in my own work, both in ways that I am conscious of and in ways I am oblivious to, and a similar process may be occurring in our broader cultural life, as well. What is interesting to me in these experiments has been the play between conscious and unconscious choices, and the sense that the less obvious the influence may be, the deeper it may sometimes be worked into the tapestry woven: that in the best of our work—East and West—it is finally not a matter of "ours" and "theirs," of choosing between the over-familiar and the exotic, but of finding better ways—more encompassing, more enlivening, and therefore "truer" ones—to interrogate human identity, to structure human exchange, and to channel and focus creative energy through the shifting and restless mechanisms of performance.

The starting point for this discussion—and the point I wish to return to—is that, when successful, the process involved in producing inter-cultural works is very much like that of adjusting to a new mask: approaching a performative tradition with respect, appreciating the potential life residing within a form, and finding a meeting ground between "self" and "other" that will allow a new theatrical life to flourish. When this works, the stylistic choices are felt and perceived as organic to the vision of life presented. As in the masked perfomances described in the previous chapters, a hardening of form may result, allowing for a clearer, less cluttered, and even, eventually, a more powerfully emotional connection with the nature of that world and the events within it than a more "naturalistic" approach would have permitted.

Such a forging of new identities out of contradictory tendencies is, it might be added, very much "like living" these days. James Clifford, in *The Predicament of Culture,* notes that "the complex process that generates cultural meanings (and) definitions of self and other" has come to be characterized by an ongoing "ironic play of similarity and difference, the familiar and the strange, the here and the elsewhere" (1988: 145–46; cf. Trinh 1989; Bhabha 1994). While Clifford discusses this process as one particularly germane to the formation and depiction of identity in an age of "global modernism," his description is also a particularly apt summary of the strategies of a Balinese topeng *pajegan* performance, as well as the work of certain solo performance artists who have either directly learned from topeng's play with persona and mask or have reinvented its strategies, driven by a similar need to theatricalize the individual as the container of disparate strands of a larger world. While there are no doubt economic factors at work in the re-emergence of the solo artist on an unadorned stage, there is also an aesthetic and metaphysical significance to the best of this work as it reconfigures and recreates something akin to the Upanishadic notion of *Tat Twam Asi*: "Thou Art That."

One such performer is Fred Curchack—best known for his solo show, *Stuff As Dreams Are Made On*—a sort of one-man *Tempest* or, more accurately, a theatricalization of his attempt to perform a one-man *Tempest.* Curchak has studied with a virtual who's who of theatre artists in the world: Jacques LeCoq, Joseph Chaikin, Zbigniew Cynkutis, Ryzard Cieslak and Jerzy Grotowski, Sam Shepard, Lee Hudson and Alwyn Nikolais, Kristin Linklatter, Peter Brook, Gene Frankel, Bertram Joseph, and members of the Living Theatre and Odin Teatrat from the West, as well as masters of noh, kabuki, kathakali, *hindustani* classical music, African dance, and *tai-chi chuan.* From this enormous, eclectic range of influences, he has been able to select out and synthesize elements and aesthetic principles that have allowed him to create his own highly individual and idiosyncratic performances. Of particular importance to his on-stage struggles with the *Tempest,* though, is the example of topeng pajegan.

Curchack had stepped in briefly as a percussionist in my own early attempts at adaptation, and went on to study the form with I Nyoman Wenten in California. He has taken the lessons of topeng and internalized them, enabling him to transform the *Tempest* into "something strange and wondrous." There is not a single bit of topeng technique used in the show (kathakali training and techniques of Tibetan chant are somewhat more in evidence, but even these have undergone a transformation and have been put to new use); as in topeng pajegan, however, the show proceeds through a succession of masks, each with its own particular point of view on the story at hand; as in topeng, the aim is not to validate any one point of view, any one mask or persona; rather, it is the clash of values, of ways of being in the world, that is at issue (cf. Keats's famous observations on Shakespeare's "negative capability"); as in topeng, there are sallies back and forth between past and present, the sacred and the profane, and the sublime and the ludicrous, criss-crossing boundaries of gender, age, ethnicity, and historicity; as in topeng, there is a range of meta-textual commentary, sometimes parodic, sometimes not, on the performance itself as performance and on the collision of old and new values that erupts as a revered text is taken up and looked at in new contexts. In *Stuff As Dreams*

Are Made On, this meta-textual play is abetted by the occasional presence of the unmasked performer himself—"Fred," a latter-day, would-be Prospero—harassing and being castigated by the ventriloquist's dummy that plays Miranda, getting tangled up in the play's thematic strands, and—in an extraordinary moment—becoming more literally trapped in the rubber mask of Caliban, as he tries desperately to pull it off. Flashing bic lighters and a huge shadow screen are used to create an unsettling and eerily beautiful tribute to illusion and magic, even as the text is being robbed of its inviolate sanctity, its mysterium. At the end of the play, the various masks—Caliban's, Ariel's, Ferdinand's, Prospero's—are stripped off one by one as the familiar epilogue is spoken, renouncing the play of illusion, until Curchack takes hold of his own face by the eye sockets and strains to remove this last, most resistant mask of all.

Anna Deavere Smith does not literally use masks and, so far as I know, has not studied or set out to use Asian techniques; yet her work, too, profoundly reaffirms a sense of the individual as the container of and microcosm for a larger range of experience. Her best-known works to date have been *Fires in the Mirror: Brooklyn, Crown Heights, and Other Identities,* performed at the New York Shakespeare Festival, and *Twilight: Los Angeles, 1992.* These are themselves part of a larger, ongoing project, *On the Road: A Search for American Character.* Unlike Curchack's work with Shakespeare's plays or Kakul's quoting and referencing of the Balinese babad and Indian epics, Smith does not rework received literary texts, teasing out meaning through a succession of masks; rather, she tape-records people involved in what Turner has called "social dramas" and replicates sections of the taped interviews—with their ellipses, starts and stops, diminutions and eruptions—using these tapes as verbal masks to be encountered, grappled with, and embodied.

Though Smith's work has been glowingly reviewed, it has a significance in the context of this inquiry into the power and value of the mask that has not yet been adequately stressed. Smith's work has too often been reviewed as a kind of cut-rate approach to documentary. She has been widely praised for her skills as a mimic and for her ability to capture so much of the human reality surrounding the events at Crown Heights—where a young boy, Gavin Cato, was run over and killed by an Hasidic van, and a visiting Jewish scholar from Australia, Yankel Rosenbaum, was killed in revenge—and in riot-torn Los Angeles. The praise is certainly well deserved; her performances provide moving and thought-provoking confrontations with American racial tensions. But *Fires in the Mirror* would not only be more expensive and less focused if it could be re-done through the usual collage of filmed interviews and commentary more frequently used to represent our emergent history, it would be a different piece altogether. What such an approach would miss—and what brings her work closer to topeng—would be the *embodiment* of one person's struggle (Smith's) to embrace and, in some profound sense, to own the voices of others with disparate and sometimes mutually exclusive points of view and cultural identities.

As she moves from interviews that tease out general principles about race, identity, and the physics of mirrors, through anecdotal histories, to the tragedy in Crown Heights and its aftermath of racial confrontation, Smith is not, finally, offering us impersonations of Al Sharpton, Letty Cottin Pogrebin, Gavin Cato's father, or his Jewish neighbors; she is offering us, instead, the results of her attempt to find a meeting ground in her own body for their various voices. Smith's skills as a mimic are impressive, but limited, and these limitations are themselves a part of the performance: in *Fires in the Mirror* she at one point plays an actual tape of Norman Rosenbaum addressing a rally for his dead brother; in a daring gesture, the tape underscores that gap that still remains between Smith's embodiment and Rosenbaum's pain and anger, making her own struggle for representation and containment all the more compelling.

Far more impressive than her skills at mimicry is Smith's generosity of spirit towards those whose words and speech patterns she struggles to embody: children and adults, men and women, black and Jewish, the anonymous and the famous. Particularly impressive is the understanding shown of the moments when the flow of conversation breaks down, when dislocations, wonder, humor, compassion, and the limits of understanding are revealed. By interviewing, editing, and taking on these various voices—very much as the masked dancer grapples with the alterity of the mask—Smith makes the implicit statement that she contains (or could imagine herself containing) the aspirations, hopes, wounds, and wonderment that have been given voice. It is not so much her skill as a mimic that is at issue then (though without that skill, the performance would be far less effective), but the philosophical and human consequences of her stepping into the words, rhythms, and ellipses of others. Like Kakul in his sacred performance, like Hajari Bhand in his secular ones, she must maintain her balance, sense of humor, and her compassion while moving from voice to voice, from mask to mask; like their performances, hers can be seen as an exemplary human action.

In a public-radio interview in 1994, Smith remarked that "one person can try to embody difference." This is, of course, a statement characterized by paradox. While explicitly recognizing difference, her performances, her "trying to embody difference," implicitly demonstrate that people contain multiple potentials; the result is a radical assault on the categorical stereotypes of race, class, and gender even as cultural differences and their social impact are being acknowledged and given a space within her own body. Her performances, like those of Kakul and Hajari Bhand, provide exemplary demonstrations that every human being contains within herself or himself the potential life of the cosmos.

Smith, of course, is working—most of the time—within a social, not a cosmological frame of reference; her performances are most likely influenced far more by Emerson, William James, Whitman, Martin Luther King and Homi Bhabha than by the *Upanishads*; still, the political, social, and aesthetic implications of her work extend well beyond its topicality. In her performances, she implicitly and profoundly confronts the issue of where the boundaries of self and other lie and how the categories of race, culture, and gender that, in Herbert Blau's words, constitute "the new doxology of cultural otherness" (1992: 138) can affect and obscure issues of personal and national identity: hence the work of her larger project, *A Search for American Character* is, as it must be, both outer and inner directed; it takes place in the "planes of similitude" she finds between her own voice, body, and thought processes and those she encounters in her interviews and in her audiences.

Smith is not alone in this work. As Blau has noted about a spectrum of performance artists, "What we have seen [. . .] in the theater is the reimagining of performance through the permutations of character actor person self [. . .] playing the nuances of behavior off against each other" (1992: 138). Kate Bornstein, for example, a post-operative transsexual lesbian, has used her considerable skills as an actor to construct works of "gender terrorism" with titles like *Hidden: A Gender, The Opposite Sex Is Neither* and, most recently, *Virtually Yours*—confronting the various masks in her own complex personal history and current struggle for a coherent identity, a struggle that places her in defiance of many of our most deeply held categorical assumptions (see Bornstein 1994). These are metaphorical masks, to be sure, but then, the gendered body itself is revealed as a mask in Bornstein's work.

Not surprisingly in this time of radical questioning about the nature of "self," the mask—both as metaphor and as object—is increasingly being looked to as a healing device, as a means of taking inventory of the various aspects of "self" that compete in an individual or communal psyche. Strategies for recovering and expanding human behavior, ranging from Assagioli's clinical work with "psychosynthesis" (1965) to Augusto Boal's paratheatrical sessions—isolating the "cops in the head," distinguishing the multi-faceted "person" from the more rigidly constructed "personality," and exploring "the rainbow of desire" through a strategy of dedicated play (1995: 35–39)—partake of the mask's strategies and underlying assumptions as they inventory potentials and personae. But this, of course, is a very old function of the mask and takes us back to its roots in Shamanism. In an apocalyptic vein, Foucault prophesied that "in our day, [. . .] new gods, the same gods, are already swelling the ocean; man will disappear. Rather than the death of God, [. . .] it is the explosion of man's face in laughter, and the return of masks" (1973 [1971]: 385). My own view is less apocalyptic and less anti-humanist. As I understand it, the masked performer, in moving from persona to persona, weaving narratives, find-

Figure 93. The brothers Mai retreat to their improvised "greenroom" after a performance. Mindimbit, Sepik River, 1974.

ing humor, generating new ways to put thoughts together, and maintaining balance in a sea of difference, exemplifies and, ultimately, celebrates a remarkable human capacity—one that is much needed for survival and sanity. If we can gain access to its truths, the mask may well be a powerful tool in reclaiming not only our theatre, but our lives.

Note

1. Koestler assumed there must be a neuronal basis for this work and coined the term "holon" for a cluster of neurons constituting a conceptual field. Gerald Edelman has recently set forth a model of perceptual categorization, recategorization, and concept formation in the brain based on the interactions of ever changing neuronal groups (involving neurons far more widely dispersed than Koestler may have imagined) that may provide a physical basis for this procedure (1992: 83–102, 147–54). A redefinition of categories, a rerouting of thought, the addition of new images and associations and the supplanting of old ones would, then, betoken an actually change in the biology of the self. Nurture, as cognitive scientist James McIlwain once pointed out to me, becomes nature (1994, personal communication): the casual phrase, "to change one's mind," may have a far more literal significance than has been apparent—a significance that is deeply connected to the need for performative play.

Appendix: A List of Basic Questions That Might Be Asked About Performances

Appendices are things a body can really do without. I suppose that is true of this one, too; but I include this list at the urging of a few colleagues and with the assurance of former students that it has sometimes come in handy. The list was born of exasperation and frustration—at myself, first of all. While in New Guinea and Bali in 1974–75, I had passed up the chance to ask questions that occurred to me later as obvious and necessary. Looking for models, I then began to consult the anthropological literature on performing traditions. It seemed that more often than not the anthropologists hadn't asked such questions, either. I drew up this list as a rough guide to the kinds of basic information necessary in the study of a performance—any performance, really—after a class discussion on February 2, 1977, the first day I had tried to teach a class on "Non-Western Performance." I was co-teaching that class with James Koetting, an ethnomusicologist, and the first discovery we had made while preparing was that we tended to favor and neglect different areas of performance as we looked at things in the field. The list was intended as a set of reminders that all the areas covered need attention before the topography of a tradition can be drawn. It has no pretense toward being exhaustive or definitive in any way, and with any given tradition the relative importance of the questions will vary greatly. I have never used it systematically as a questionnaire—for myself or for others—nor would I advise anyone else to do so. Still, I have found it a useful teaching tool, and it has occasionally reminded me to ask the obvious—sometimes with surprising results. Here it is, imperfect and arbitrary though it may be. It is offered as a goad to further thinking about the nature of studying performances: a field which has developed greatly in the years since I first drew up this list, but which is still in its early stages of development.

Who are the performers?

- Is there a distinction between performers and viewers during performance? If so, how are performers distinguished from other people present?
- Is there a distinction between performers and other people within the culture? If so, how is this distinction made?
- Who is eligible to perform? Is this determined by age, gender, caste or social status, economic level, religion, demonstrable skill, family connections, connections to other performers, or other discernible social means?
- Is anyone not eligible to perform due to age, gender, caste, religion, etc.?
- How are performance activities assigned? Who assigns them and how is leadership determined? Is there a tryout or casting process? If so, what criteria are used?
- Are there occasions or places where some performers may appear but not others?
- Is there a hierarchy of performers? If so, how is it determined? Are there functions or roles that some performers may take on but not others? Are some activities deemed more prestigious, enjoyable, difficult, or dangerous than others, and if, so, why?
- Are performers compensated for performing? If so, how, how much, and by whom?
- Is there a distinction between "amateur" and "professional" performers?
- Do performers ordinarily earn their livelihood through activities other than performing? If so, through what activities?
- What is the status of the performer within the society? Is the status determined by his or her skill or notoriety as a performer?
- Are performers expected to fulfill any special obligations other than performing within the society?
- Are there special privileges that performers enjoy because of their status as performers?
- Do performers undergo a formal training process? How else do performers learn performance skills?
- How do performers begin performing? Are there any special ceremonies marking this event?
- When do performers cease to perform? Are there any special circumstances marking this event?

Who is in the audience?

- Does there have to be anyone in attendance other than the performers for the event to be considered a performance?
- Are spiritual entities understood to be in attendance?
- Are any people forbidden to view the performance on the basis of sex, gender, status, religion, age, or other categorical distinction?
- Is anyone required to view the performance?
- Do audience members pay in order to view the performance? How much? To whom?
- Are there any other transactions that must take place in order to qualify as an audience member?
- Who are the patrons of the form? Are they members of the audience? Why do they support the form?
- Does the audience tend to be characterized by age, sex, caste or social status, regional background, economic wealth, education, family connections, geographical proximity, religious affiliation, or other recognizable designation?
- Do people tend to come to performances individually or in groups?
- Who sits or stands with whom during the performance?
- Can or must audience members become performers during the event?
- Do audience members share the skills being used in the performance?
- What training have audience members received?
- What general information is the audience expected to share?
- Is the audience given any special instructions or information regarding the performance?

How does the performer relate to the performance?

- What activities are involved in performing?
- What activities does the performer go through in preparation for the performance? Are there offerings to be made? Prayers to be said? Introductory remarks to be made?
- Are all of the performer's activities during the time of performance thought to be "performing?"
- Are there activities of the performer that are hidden from the audience?
- How do the activities of the "performance" relate to "non-performance" activities in the daily lives of the performers?
- Are special clothes worn during performance? If so, how are they chosen and when and how does the change occur?
- Do performers use atypical gestures in performances? Atypical words, syntax, or speech rhythms?

- Does the performer violate moral taboos or legal regulations of day-to-day life while performing?
- Does the performer assume a fictional role? If so, is the role fixed or mutable?
- Does the performer enter a state of trance or possession? If so, how and when is this state induced? How is it described and explained?
- Is there any other sense in which the performer effects a transformation in his or her state of being or character?
- Do performers and audience members share the same sense of the state of mind of the performer?
- Are there activities of the performer which have a different meaning for him or her than for the audience?
- How do performers view the function of their performance? Does this coincide with the audience members' and/or patrons' understandings?
- What criteria do performers use in evaluating their performance? Are these the same criteria used by the audience members and/or patrons?
- What is the performer's attitude towards his or her audience and patrons? How do performers talk about audiences and patrons?
- What vocabulary do performers use to describe the act of performing? Is it talked of in terms of work? play? specific skills? achieving certain effects?
- Are there activities the performer is forbidden to perform? If so, what are they? What are the sanctions? Who administers them?
- Who determines a performer's score or script?
- What elements of improvisation, if any, are permissible?
- What rehearsal processes, if any, is the performer involved in? Are other people present at rehearsals?
- Is there a noticeable carryover from performance activities to activities in day-to-day life? Are performers expected to have special ways of moving, talking, or responding in day-to-day life? Are these expectations changed after a performance?

How do audience members relate to the performance?

- Are the performer and audience members distinguishable? If so, how are they distinguished?
- Are the roles of performer and audience member fixed?
- What do the audience members expect of the performers?
- What do the audience members attend to while witnessing the performance? What do they not attend to?
- Do patrons in the audience have any special privileges or responsibilities toward the performance?
- What senses are considered relevant in appreciating and/or compre-

hending the performance? Is any one sensory mode understood to be dominant?

- What constitutes good and bad manners while watching a performance? Is this the same for all audience members?
- What are the criteria used in judging a performance? What is considered to be expressive? What is considered to be effective or affective?
- How is appreciation of a performance manifested?
- How is displeasure at a performance manifested?
- Are criteria other than "aesthetic" criteria used to judge a performance?
- How is a "good" performance praised? How is a "bad" performance criticized? Do performers use the same criteria in judging their own performances?
- Is the audience/performer relationship viewed in terms of confrontation? Community? Complementarity? Reciprocity?
- Does the audience's response during performance differ from patterns of response outside of a performance situation?
- Is the tradition a "popular" one and, if so, popular with whom?
- Is popularity considered to be a reliable sign of excellence?
- Do observers from "outside" the cultural base tend to respond to performances for different reasons or to assign different values to performative events?
- How do performers relate to the audience during performance?
- Do performers vary their performance plans depending on an anticipated audience response?
- How do performers adjust to the audience during performance?
- Is the audience aware of the performer as well as that which is performed?
- How are the actions of the performers understood to affect the interests of the audience members?
- Do audience members wear special clothing to the performance?

How is space used?

- What physical requirements are necessary for the performance?
- Does a special space or building need to exist? What are the requirements for such a space or building?
- Are there limited means of access and or viewing?
- Are performance spaces used for other activities besides performing?
- What maintenance is necessary so that the space can accommodate the performance? Who maintains the space?
- Are some performance spaces held to be better than others? What criteria are used?

- What functional units are built or prepared for performance? Who builds them? How are they used?
- What decorative elements are built or prepared for the performance? Who builds them? Who sees them? How important are they to the performance?
- How is the space divided between audience and performers? Are there fixed areas? How are they delineated?
- How is the audience arranged in the space? Are some viewing places more desirable than others, and why?
- Does the space change during a performance?
- Is the "illusion" of a fictional world established in the space?
- If so, how does the fictive world relate to the world outside of the performance space?
- What special preparations are necessary so that the space can accommodate the performance? Who makes these preparations?
- How do the performers related to the space in performance?
- How does the audience relate to the space during performance?
- What is the relationship of the space of performance to the landscape of the surrounding countryside? To other nearby spaces?

How is time used?

- When are performances held?
- Are they seasonal? Do they relate to specific events, such as illness, passage into adulthood, the celebration of a birth or a marriage, the acknowledgment of a death or burial?
- Do they occur regularly?
- Do they occur at times of crisis?
- Do they occur in relationship to agricultural or other work patterns?
- Are they determined by financial considerations?
- How frequent are performances?
- What time of day is the performance held?
- When does the performance "begin"? How is this determined? Who determines it?
- When does the performance end? How does the audience know?
- Are there periods of non-performance time interspersed with periods of performance? How does the audience know when these occur?
- How long is a performance expected to last? How fixed is this expectation?
- Is the illusion of a fictional time established? Does the audience understand themselves to be viewing events taking place in "the past" or "the future"? Is the illusion consistent?
- Do figures from another time period or cosmology visit the present time and everyday world?

- When are performances scheduled?
- Can performances occur spontaneously?
- What are the principles of temporal organization?
- Is time manipulated so as to create a mood or atmosphere? If so, how?
- Is there an element of "suspense"?
- Is there a "plot" or story? If so, is the story drawn from or form a part of a larger myth?
- If myths are used, can they be altered for performance? In what ways?

What is the history and present state of the performance tradition?

- What are the legendary and historical origins of the tradition?
- What defines "a performance" within the tradition? Within the culture?
- What is the relationship of the tradition to the religious and metaphysical beliefs of the culture? Has this changed?
- What is the relationship of the tradition to the political and economic structures of the culture? Has this changed?
- What is the relationship of the tradition to the sexual and social mores of the culture?
- What are the historical connections to other traditions of the same culture?
- What are the historical connections to traditions from other cultures, Western or non-Western?
- Are there significant parallels or discrepancies with performance practices in other cultures, non-Western or Western?
- Are there recognizable stylistic differences within the tradition? How are these categorized? Are the distinctions deliberately maintained?
- How have new forms or styles appeared? How is innovation encouraged and/or discouraged?
- Who is supporting change, who is discouraging it, and why?
- How have forms or styles died out?
- Who supports the tradition economically?
- Has the popularity of the tradition remained constant? Have audience changes taken place?
- Have any changes taken place as to who can perform in the tradition?
- Are there "folk" and professional forms?
- Are there city and village forms?
- Are there forms or styles that are recognized as being more "advanced" or "degenerate" or "reactionary" than others?
- Are there regional variations?
- Are new forms or styles still developing?
- How has innovation taken place within the tradition?
- How are various other performance media interrelated within the tra-

dition? Have the interrelationships changed during the history of the tradition?

- What are the purposes that the tradition serves?
- Is there a current attempt to preserve or revive older forms? If so, who is making this attempt? Why?
- Are there new pressures on the tradition? And if so, how are these being handled?

References

'Allami, Abu'l Fazl
1978 [1948] *The A'in-i Akbari.* Rev. 2nd ed. 4 vols. Sir Jadanath Sarkar, ed. Col. H.S. Jarrett, trans. New Delhi: Oriental Books Reprint Corporation [1st ed. of trans. 1894].

Anderson, Benedict R. O'G.
1965 *Mythology and Tolerance of the Javanese.* Ithaca, NY: Cornell Modern Indonesia Project, Monograph 37

Ardika, I Wayan and Peter Bellwood
1991 "Sembiran: The Beginnings of Indian Contact with Bali." *Antiquity* 65, 247: 221–31.

Aristotle
1961 *Aristotle's Poetics.* Francis Fergusson, ed. S. H. Butcher, trans. New York: Hill and Wang [Rev. 4th ed. of trans. 1st published 1932; 1st ed. of transl. 1894].

Artaud, Antonin
1958 The *Theatre and Its Double.* Mary Caroline Richards, trans. New York: Grove Press [1st French ed. 1938].

Aryan, K. C.
1980 *The Little Goddesses (Matrikas).* New Delhi: Rekha Prakashan.

Ashiya, Ranchor Singh
1983 "Mulakat Hajari Bhand se." *Rangayan* 16, 10: 13–19.

Assagioli, Roberto
1965 *Psychosynthesis: A Collection of Basic Writings.* New York: Penguin.

Avalon, Arthur (Sir John Woodroffe)
1978 *Shakti and Shakta.* 6th rev. ed. New York: Dover Publications [1st ed. 1918].

Awasthi, Suresh
1983 *Drama, The Gift of the Gods: Culture, Performance and Communication in India.* Tokyo: Institute for the Study of Languages and Cultures of Asia and Africa.

Ballinger, Rucina
1978 "The Tradition of Dance in Bali." MA thesis. University of Hawaii at Manoa.

Bandem, I Made and Fredrik Eugene deBoer
1981 *From Kaja to Kelod: Balinese Dance in Transition.* Kuala Lumpur: Oxford University Press.

Bandem, I Made and I Nyoman Rembang
1976 *Pertubangan Topeng-Bali Sebagai Seni Pertunjukan.* Denpasar: Proyek Penggalian, Penbinaan, Pengembangan Seni Klasik/Tradisionil dan Kesenian Baru.

Barba, Eugenio
1986 *Beyond the Floating Islands.* Judy Barba, Richard Fowler, Jerrold C. Rodesch, and Saul Shapiro, trans. New York: PAJ Publications.
1995 *The Paper Canoe: A Guide to Theatre Anthropology.* Richard Fowler, trans. London and New York: Routledge.

Barba, Eugenio and Nicolo Savarese, eds.
1991 *The Encyclopedia of Theatre Anthropology: The Secret Art of Acting.* London and New York: Routledge.

Barth, Fredrik
1993 *Balinese Worlds.* Chicago and London: University of Chicago Press.

Bates, Brian
1988 *The Way of the Actor: A Path to Knowledge and Power.* Boston: Shambhala.

Bateson, Gregory
1958 [1936] *Naven.* 2nd ed. Palo Alto, CA: Stanford University Press.
1970 [1937] "An Old Temple and a New Myth." In *Traditional Balinese Culture,* ed. Jane Belo. New York: Columbia University Press, pp. 110–36.
1972a [1949] "Bali: The Value System of a Steady State." In *Steps to an Ecology of the Mind.* San Francisco: Chandler, pp. 107–27.
1972b [1955] "A Theory of Play and Fantasy." In *Steps to an Ecology of the Mind.* San Francisco: Chandler, pp. 177–93.
1972c [1967] "Style, Grace, and Information in Primitive Art." In *Steps to an Ecology of the Mind.* San Francisco: Chandler, pp. 128–52.

Bateson, Gregory and Margaret Mead
1942 *Balinese Character: A Photographic Analysis.* New York: New York Academy of Sciences, Special Publication 2.

Barthes, Roland
1975 *The Pleasure of the Text.* Richard Miller trans. New York: Hill and Wang.
1977 *Image, Music, Text.* Stephen Heath, trans. New York: Hill and Wang.

Becker, Alton L.
1979 "Text-Building, Epistemology, and Aesthetics in Javanese Shadow Theatre." In *The Imagination of Reality: Essays in Southeast Asian Coherence Systems,* ed. A. Yengoyan and A. L. Becker. Norwood, NJ: Ablex, pp. 211–43.

Behera, Karuna Sagar
1993 "Ancient Orissa/Kalinga and Indonesia: The Maritime Contacts." *Utkal Historical Research Journal* 10: 122–29.

Behera, Sarat Chandra
1982 *Rise and Fall of the Sailodbhavas: History and Culture of Ancient Orissa from Ca. 550AD to 736AD.* Calcutta: Punthi Pustak.

Belo, Jane

1949 *Bali: Rangda and Barong.* Monographs of the American Ethnological Society 16. Seattle: University of Washington Press.

1960 *Trance in Bali.* New York: Columbia University Press.

1966 [1953] *Bali: Temple Festival.* Monographs of the American Ethnological Society 22. Seattle: University of Washington Press.

Benjamin, Walter

1968 *Illuminations.* Hannah Arendt, ed. Harry Zahn, trans. New York: Schocken Books [1st German ed. 1955].

Bernal, Martin

1987 *Black Athena: The Afroasiatic Roots of Classical Civilization.* Vol. 1: *The Fabrication of Ancient Greece 1785–1985.* New Brunswick, NJ: Rutgers University Press.

Berne, Eric

1972 *What Do You Do After You Say Hello?* New York: Grove Press.

Bhabha, Homi K.

1994 *The Location of Culture.* London and New York: Routledge.

Bhanawat, Mahendra

1974 "Nakal ko Bhand ki." *Rangayog: Journal of the Rajasthan Sangeet Natak Akademi.*

1979 "Overview of the Folk Theatre of Rajasthan." *Sangeet Natak: Journal of Sangeet Natak Akademi* 53–54: 26–32.

Bharata-Muni

1967 *The Natyasastra: A Treatise on Ancient Indian Dramaturgy and Histrionics.* Manomohan Ghosh, trans. Calcutta: Granthalaya [rev. 2nd ed. of transl.; 1st ed. of transl. 1951].

Bharucha, Rustam

1989 *Theatre and the World.* New Delhi: Manohar.

Bhattacharyya, N. N.

1992 *History of the Tantric Religion: A Historical, Ritualistic, and Philosophical Study.* New Delhi: Manohar.

Bihalji-Merin, Oto

1971 *Masks of the World.* London: Thames and Hudson, Ltd.

Blau, Herbert

1982 *Blooded Thought: Occasions of the Theatre.* New York: Performing Arts Journal Publications.

1992 *To All Appearances: Ideology and Performance.* London and New York: Routledge.

Bloch, Susana, Pedro Orthous, and Guy Santibañez-H.

1987 "Effector Patterns of Basic Emotions: A Psychophysical Method for Training Actors." *Journal of Social Biological Structures* 10: 1–19.

Boal, Augusto

1995 *The Rainbow of Desire: The Boal Method of Theatre and Therapy.* Adrian Jackson, trans. London and New York: Routledge.

Boon, James A.

1984 "Folly, Bali, and Anthropology, or Satire across Cultures." In *Text, Play, and Story: The Construction and Reconstruction of Self and Society,* Washington, DC: American Ethnological Society, pp. 156–77.

1986 "Symbols, Sylphs, and Siwa: Allegorical Machineries in the

Text of Balinese Culture." In *The Anthropology of Experience*, ed. Victor W. Turner and Edward M. Bruner. Urbana and Chicago: University of Illinois Press, pp. 239–60.

1990 *Affinities and Extremes.* Chicago: University of Chicago Press.

Bornstein, Kate
1994 *Gender Outlaw: On Men, Women, and the Rest of Us.* London and New York: Routledge.

Bosch, F. D. K.
1960 *The Golden Germ: An Introduction to Indian Symbolism.* The Hague: E. J. Nijhoff.

Bourgignon. Erika
1968 "World Distribution and Patterns of Possession States." In *Trance and Possession States*, ed. Raymond Prince. Montreal: R. M. Bucke Memorial Society.

1973 *Religion, Altered States of Consciousness and Social Change.* Columbus: Ohio University Press.

Brandon, James R.
1989 "A New World: Asian Theatre in the West Today." *Drama Review* 3,1: 25–50.

Brecht, Bertolt
1964 *Brecht on Theatre: The Development of an Aesthetic.* John Willett, ed. and trans. New York: Hill and Wang.

Breguet, G., R. Ney, et al.
1982 "Genetic Survey of an Isolated Community in Bali, Indonesia: I. Blood Groups, Serum Proteins and Hepatitis B Serology and II. Haemoglobin Types and Red Cell Isotomes." *Human Heredity* 32: 52–61, 308–17.

Brook, Peter
1987 *The Shifting Point: Theatre, Film, Opera 1946–1987.* New York: Harper and Row.

Burke, Kenneth
1962 [1945, 1950] *A Grammar of Motives and A Rhetoric of Motives.* Cleveland: World Publishing Company.

Byrski, Christopher
1981 "Sanskrit Drama As an Aggregate of Model Situations." In *Sanskrit Drama in Performance*, ed. Rachel Van M. Baumer and James R. Brandon. Honolulu: University Press of Hawaii, pp. 141–66.

Cairns, Grace E.
1992 *Man as Microcosm in Tantric Hinduism.* New Delhi: Manohar.

Campbell, Joseph
1988 *Historical Atlas of World Mythology.* Vol. I: *The Way of the Animal Powers* (2 Parts). New York: Harper and Row.

1989 *Historical Atlas of World Mythology.* Vol. II: *The Way of the Seeded Earth* (3 Parts). New York: Harper and Row.

Catra, I Nyoman
1989 "Sida Karya, The Brahman from Kling: A Balinese Topeng Pajegan." Fredrik E. deBoer and I Nyoman Sumandhi, trans. and ed. (unpublished MS).

Ceram, C. W.
1967 *Gods, Graves, and Scholars: The Story of Archeology.* 2nd rev. ed. E. B. Garside and Sophie Wilkins, trans. New York: Alfred A. Knopf.

Chekhov, Michael
1953 *To the Actor: On the Technique of Acting.* New York: Harper and Row.
1991 *On the Technique of Acting.* Mel Gordon, ed. New York: Harper Perennial.

Chin, Daryl
1991 [1989] "Interculturalism, Postmodernism, Pluralism." In *Interculturalism and Performance: Writings from PAJ,* ed. Bonnie Marranca and Gautam Dasgupta. New York: PAJ Publications, pp. 83–98.

Chockkalingam, K., G. Breguet, et al.
1982 "Glucose 6 Phosphate Dehydrogenate Variants of Bali Island (Indonesia)." *Human Genetics* 60: 60–62.

Clifford, James
1988 *The Predicament of Culture: Twentieth Century Ethnography, Literature, and Art.* Cambridge, MA: Harvard University Press.

Clifford, James and George E. Marcus, eds.
1986 *Writing Culture: The Poetics and Politics of Ethnography.* Berkeley: University of California Press.

Colaabavala, Capt. F. D.
1976 *Tantra: The Erotic Cult.* New Delhi: Orient Paperbacks.

Cole, Toby and Helen Kritch Chinoy, eds.
1970 [1949] *Actors on Acting: The Theories, Techniques, and Practices of the World's Great Actors, Told in their Own Words.* New York: Crown Publishers.

Coomaraswamy, Ananda K.
1985 [1927] *History of Indian and Indonesian Art.* New York: Dover Publications.

Connor, Linda, Patsy Asch, and Timothy Asch
1986 *Jero Tapakan, Balinese Healer: An Ethnographic Film Monograph.* Cambridge: Cambridge University Press.

Corbin, George A.
1979 "The Art of the Baining: New Britain." In *Exploring the Visual Art of Oceania,* ed. S. M. Mead. Honolulu: University Press of Hawaii.
1984 "The Central Baining Revisited: 'Salvage' Art History Among the Kairak and Uramot Baining of East New Britain, Papua New Guinea." *Res* 7/8: 44–69.

Covarrubias, Miguel
1974 [1937] *Island of Bali.* Kuala Lumpur: Oxford University Press.

Cravath, Paul
1986 "The Ritual Origins of the Classical Dance Drama of Cambodia." *Asian Theatre Journal* 3, 2: 179–203.

Cribb, Robert, ed.
1991 [1990] *The Indonesian Killings 1965–1966: Studies from Java and Bali.* Monash Papers on Southeast Asia 21. Clayton, Victoria: Centre of Southeast Asian Studies, Monash University.

Crooke, W.
1974 [1896] *Tribes and Castes of Northwestern India.* 4 vols. Delhi: Cosmo Publications.

Csikszentmihalyi, Mihaly
1975 "Play and Intrinsic Rewards." *Journal of Humanistic Psychology* 15, 3: 41–64.
1993 *The Evolving Self: A Psychology for the Third Millennium.* New York: HarperCollins.

Damasio, Antonio R.
1994 *Descartes' Error: Emotion, Reason, and the Human Brain.* New York: G. P. Putnam's Sons.

Daniel, Ana
1981 *Bali: Behind the Mask.* New York: A. A. Knopf.

Das, Ajay Kumar
1991 *Shaivism in Orissa (from 600 AD to 1200 AD).* Bhubaneswar: Privately printed.

Das, H. C.
1992 "Brahmanical Tantric Art in Orissa." In *Rangarekha,* special issue. Bhubaneswar: Orissa Lalit Kala Akademi, Silver Jubilee Publication, pp. 79–93.

Das, K. B. and L. K. Mahapatra
1979 *Folklore of Orissa.* New Delhi: National Book Trust, India.

Dasgupta, Gautam
1991 [1987] "The *Mahabharata*: Peter Brook's Orientalism." In *Interculturalism and Performance: Writings from PAJ,* ed. Bonnie Marranca and Gautam Dasgupta. New York: PAJ Publications, pp. 75–82.

Dash, Dhiren
n.d. *Danda Nata in Orissa.* Bhubaneswar: Orissa Sangeet Natak Akademi.
1979 "Jatra": People's Theatre of Orissa." *Sangeet Natak: Journal of the Sangeet Natak Akademi* 52: 11–26.

deBoer, Fredrik E.
1987 "Functions of the Comic Attendants (Panasar) in a Balinese Shadow Play." In *Humor and Comedy in Puppetry: Celebration in Popular Culture,* ed. Joel Sherzer and Dina Sherzer. Bowling Green, OH: Popular Press, pp. 79–105.

Derrida, Jacques
1978 *Writing and Difference.* Alan Bass, trans. Chicago: University of Chicago Press.

de Zoete, Beryl and Walter Spies
1973 [1938] *Dance and Drama in Bali.* Kuala Lumpur: Oxford University Press.

Dibia, I Wayan
1985 "Odalan of Hindu Bali: A Religious Festival, a Social Occasion, and a Theatrical Event." *Asian Theatre Journal* 2, 1: 61–66.

Duchartre, Pierre Louis
1966 [1929] *The Italian Comedy: The Improvisation, Scenarios, Lives, Attributes, Portraits, and Masks of the Illustrious Characters of the Commedia dell'Arte.* Randolph T. Weaver, trans. New York: Dover Publications.

Dukore, Bernard F., ed.
1974 *Dramatic Theory and Criticism: Greeks to Grotowski.* New York: Holt, Rinehart, and Winston.

Dunn, Deborah
1983 "Topeng Pajegan: The Mask Dance of Bali." PhD dissertation. Union Graduate School.

Edelman, Gerald M.
1992 *Bright Air, Brilliant Fire: On the Matter of the Mind.* New York: HarperCollins.

Eiseman, Fred B. Jr.(I Wayan Darsana) with Margaret Eiseman
1986 *Bali: Sekala (What You Can See) and Niskala (What You Can't).* Vol. 2. Scottsdale, AZ: privately printed.
1989 *Bali: Sekala and Niskala* Vol. 1. Berkeley, CA: Periplus Editions.
1990 *Bali: Sekala and Niskala* Vol. 2. Berkeley, CA: Periplus Editions.

Ekman, Paul and Wallace V. Friesen
1975 *Unmasking the Face: A Guide to Recognizing Emotions from Facial Expressions.* Englewood Cliffs, NJ: Prentice-Hall.

Ekman, Paul, R. W. Levenson, and W[allace]. V. Friesen
1983 "Autonomic Nervous System Activity Distinguishes Among Emotions." *Science* 221: 1208–10.

Eliade, Mircea
1959 *The Sacred and the Profane: The Nature of Religion.* New York: Harcourt, Brace and World.
1964 *Shamanism: Archaic Techniques of Ecstasy.* Willard R. Trask, trans. Bollingen Series 76. Princeton, NJ: Princeton University Press.
1965 *Rites and Symbols of Initiation.* New York: Harper Torchbooks. [Originally published as *Birth and Rebirth,* 1958].

Elliot, R. C.
1960 *The Power of Satire: Magic, Ritual, Art.* Princeton, NJ: Princeton University Press.

Else, Gerald
1965 *The Origin and Early Form of Greek Tragedy.* Cambridge, MA: Harvard University Press.

Emigh, John
1979 "Playing with the Past: Visitation and Illusion in the Mask Theatre of Bali." *Drama Review* 23, 2: 11–48.
1981 "Masking and Playing: Observations on Masked Performance in New Guinea." *World of Music* 3: 5–25.
1984 "Dealing with the Demonic: Strategies for Containment in Hindu Iconography and Performance." *Asian Theatre Journal* 1,1: 21–39.
1989 "The Domains of Topeng." In *Art and Politics in Southeast Asia: Six Perspectives; Papers from the Distinguished Scholars Series 1984–85,* ed. Robert Van Neil. Southeast Asia Paper 32, Honolulu: University of Hawaii Center for Southeast Asia Studies, pp. 65–96.

Emigh, John with Ulrike Emigh
1986 "Hajari Bhand of Rajasthan: A Joker in the Deck." *Drama Review* 30, 1: 101–30.

1993 "A Joker in the Deck: The Many Faces of Bahurupiya Hajari Bhand of Rajasthan." In *The Idea of Rajasthan: Explorations in Regional Identity*, Vol. I: *Constructions*, ed. Karine Schomer, Joan L. Erdman, Deryck O. Lodrick, and Lloyd I. Rudolph. Riverdale, MD: Riverdale Publications; New Delhi: Manohar.

Emigh, John and James Brandon
1995 "Asian Influences on Western Theatre." In *Cambridge Guide to Theatre*. New ed. Cambridge and New York: Cambridge University Press.

Emigh, John and Jamer Hunt
1992 "Gender Bending in Balinese Performance." In *Gender in Performance: The Presentation of Difference in the Performing Arts*, ed. Laurence Senelick. Hanover, NH: University Press of New England, pp. 195–222.

Erasmus, Desidirius
1941 *The Praise of Folly*. Hoyt Hopewell Hudson, trans. Princeton, NJ: Princeton University Press [1st Latin edition 1511].

Errington, Frederick Karl
1974 *Karavar: Masks and Power in a Melanesian Ritual*. Ithaca, NY: Cornell University Press.

Errington, Shelly
1979 "Some Comments on Style in the Meaning of the Past." *Journal of Asian Studies* 37, 2: 231–44.

Eschmann, Anncharlott
1978a "Hinduization of Tribal Deities in Orissa: The Formative Phase." In *The Cult of Jagannath and the Regional Tradition of Orissa*, ed. A. Eschmann, H. Kulke, and G. C. Tripathi. New Delhi: Manohar, pp. 61–78.
1978b "The Vaisnava Typology of Hinduization and the Origin of Jagannatha." In *The Cult of Jagannath and the Regional Tradition of Orissa*. A. Eschmann, H. Kulke, and G. C. Tripathi. New Delhi: Manohar, pp. 99–117.

Fabri, Charles
1974 *History of the Art of Orissa*. Bombay: Orient Longman.

Fischer, Eberhard, Sitakant Mahapatra, and Dinanath Pathy
1980 *Orissa: Kunst und Kulture in Nordöst-Indien*. Zurich: Museum Rietberg Zurich.

Foley, Kathy
1984 "The Clown in the Sundanese Wayang Golek: Democratization of a Feudal Ethos." *Scenarium* 9: 88–101.
1986 "At the Graves of the Ancestors: Chronicle Plays in the Wayang Cepak Puppet Theatre of Cirebon, Indonesia." *Historical Drama*, ed. James Redmond. Themes in Drama 8. Cambridge: Cambridge University Press, pp. 31–50.
1990 "My Bodies: The Performer in West Java." *Drama Review* 34, 2: 62–80.

Forge, Anthony
1978 *Balinese Traditional Paintings*. Sydney: Australian Museum.

Foster, Mary LeCron
1979 "Synthesis and Antithesis in Balinese Ritual." In *The Imagination of Reality: Essays in Southeast Asian Coherence Systems*, ed.

A. L. Becker and Aram A. Yengoyan. Norwood, NJ: Ablex, pp. 175–96.

Foucault, Michel
1973 [1971] *The Order of Things: An Archaeology of the Human Sciences.* New York: Random House.

Frasca, Richard Armando
1990 *The Theatre of the Mahabharata: Terukkuttu Performances in South India.* Honolulu: University of Hawaii Press.

Freud, Sigmund
1960 [1916] *Jokes and Their Relationship to the Unconscious.* James Strachey, trans. New York: W. W. Norton.

Fuchs, Elinor
1983 "Signs of Signs: The Death of Character and the Autopresentational Stage." Unpublished Paper Presented at the American Theatre Association Conference, Minneapolis, Minn. [A shorter version of this paper also appeared the same year in *Theatre Communications* 5, 3: 1–6. An expanded treatment of the subject will be included in *The Death of Character, Essays on Post-Modern Theatre: Theory and Practice.* Bloomington, IN: Indiana University Press, forthcoming.

Geertz, Clifford
1973 *The Interpretation of Cultures.* New York: Basic Books, Inc.
1980 *Negara: The Theatre State in Nineteenth-Century Bali.* Princeton, NJ: Princeton University Press.

Geertz, Hildred
1990 "A Theatre of Cruelty: The Contexts of a Topeng Performance." In *State and Society in Bali: Historical, Textual, and Anthropological Approaches,* ed. Hildred Geertz. Leiden: Verhandelingen van let Koninklijk Institut voor Taal-, Land-, en Volkenunde.
1995 *Images of Power: Balinese Paintings Made for Gregory Bateson and Margaret Mead.* Honolulu: University of Hawaii Press.

Geertz, Hildred and Clifford Geertz
1975 *Kinship in Bali.* Chicago: University of Chicago Press.

George, David E.R
1989 "The *Tempest* in Bali." *Performing Arts Journal* 34–35: 84–107.

Ghosh, Prodyot
1979 "Gambhira: Traditional Masked Dance of Bengal." *Sangeet Natak: Journal of the Sangeet Natak Akademi* 53–54: 14–25.

Goffman, Erving
1959 *The Presentation of Self in Everyday Life.* Garden City, NY: Doubleday/ Anchor.

Goodlad, J. S. R.
1971 *The Sociology of Popular Drama.* Totowa, NJ: Rowman and Littlefield.

Gourlay, K. A.
1975 "Sound Producing Instruments in Traditional Society: A Study of Ecstatic Instruments and their Role in Male-Female Relations." *New Guinea Research Bulletin* 60: 1–139.

Grotowski, Jerzy
1969 *Towards a Poor Theatre.* New York: Simon and Schuster.
1980 "Wandering Towards a Theatre of Sources." J. Kumiega,

trans. *Dialectics and Humanism* (Polish Academy of Sciences), Spring: 31–40.

1991 "Pragmatic Laws." In *The Encyclopedia of Theatre Anthropology: The Secret Art of Acting*, ed. Eugenio Barba, Eugenio Savarese, and Nicolo Savarese. London and New York: Routledge, pp. 236–37.

Gupt, Bharat
1994 *Dramatic Concepts, Greek and Indian: A Study of the* Poetics *and the Natyasastra.* New Delhi: D. K. Printworld.

Hagen, Uta with Haskel Frankel
1973 *Respect for Acting.* New York: Macmillan.

Halifax, Joan, ed.
1979 *Shamanic Voices: A Survey of Visionary Narratives.* New York: Dutton.

Halpin, Marjorie
1983 "The Mask of Tradition." In *The Power of Symbols: Masks and Masquerade in the Americas*, ed. N. Ross Crumine and Marjorie Halpin. Vancouver: University of British Columbia Press, pp. 219–26.

Harvey, David
1989 *The Condition of Postmodernity: An Inquiry into the Origins of Cultural Change.* Oxford and Cambridge, MA: Blackwell.

Hawley, John Stratton
1981 *At Play with Krishna.* Princeton, NJ: Princeton University Press.

Herrigel, Eugen
1964 [1953] *Zen.* New York: McGraw-Hill.

Hoff, Frank
1985 "Killing the Self: How the Narrator Acts." *Asian Theatre Journal* 2, 1: 1–27.

Holt, Claire
1967 *Art in Indonesia: Continuities and Change.* Ithaca, NY: Cornell University Press.

Hooykaas, C.
1973 *Religion in Bali.* Iconography of Religion Series 13, 10. Leiden: E. J. Brill.

Hornby, Richard
1977 *Script into Performance: A Structuralist View of Production.* Austin: University of Texas Press.

Horton, Robin
1963 "The Kalabari Ekine Society: A Borderland of Religion and Art." *Africa* 30, 2: 94–113.

Howe, L.E.A.
1984 "Gods, People, Spirits, and Witches," *Bijdragen tot do Taal-, Land- en Volkenkunde* 140, 2: 193–222.

Huizinga, Johan
1955 [1938] *Homo Ludens.* Boston: Beacon Press.

Innes, Christopher
1981 *Holy Theatre: Ritual and the Avant Garde.* New York: Cambridge University Press.

Jenkins, Ron
1978 "Topeng: Balinese Dance Drama." *Performing Arts Journal* 3: 39–52.

1979 "On Becoming a Clown in Bali." *Drama Review* 23, 2: 49–56.

1994 *Subversive Laughter: The Liberating Power of Comedy*. New York: Free Press.

Jones, Clifford R.

1963 "Bhagavata Mela Natakam, a Traditional Dance-Drama Form." *Journal of Asian Studies* 22, 2/3: 193–200.

Joosten, P. Leo

1992 *Samosir: The Old Batak Society*. E. M. Verrijt, trans. Pomotangiantar, Sumatra.

Kakul, I Nyoman

1979 "Jelantik Goes to Blambangan." I Made Bandem and John Emigh, trans. *The Drama Review* 23, 2: 37–48.

Kalweit, Holger

1992 *Shamans, Healers, and Medicine Men*. Michael H. Cohn, trans. Boston and London: Shambhala.

Kandel, Eric R., James H. Schwartz, and Thomas M. Jessell

1991 *Principles of Neural Science*, 3rd ed. Norwalk, CT: Appleton and Lange.

Kapferer, Bruce

1983 *A Celebration of Demons: Exorcism and the Aesthetics of Healing in Sri Lanka*. Bloomington: Indiana University Press.

1986 "Performance and the Structuring of Meaning and Experience." In *The Anthropology of Experience*, ed. Victor W. Turner and Edward M. Bruner. Urbana and Chicago: University of Illinois Press, pp. 188–206.

Keene, Donald

1966 *No: The Classical Theatre of Japan*. Tokyo: Kodansha International.

Kempers, A.J. Bernet

1991 *Monumental Bali: Introduction to Balinese Archeology and Guide to the Monuments*. Berkeley, CA. and Singapore: Periplus Editions.

Kenner, Hugh

1961 *Samuel Beckett: A Critical Study*. New York: Grove Press.

Kinsley, David R.

1975 *The Sword and the Flute: Kali and Krishna, Dark Visions of the Terrible and the Sublime in Hindu Mythology*. Berkeley: University of California Press.

Kirk, Malcolm

1993 [1981] *Man as Art: Photographs by Malcolm Kirk*. San Francisco: Chronicle Books.

Kitto, H.D.F.

1960 [1956] *Form and Meaning in Drama*. London and New York: University Paperbacks.

Koestler, Arthur

1964 *The Act of Creation*. New York: Macmillan.

Konishi, Masutoshi A.

1981 "Masks and Masked Performing Arts in South Asia with Special Reference to Chhau of Eastern India." In *Dance and Music in South Asian Drama: Chhau, Mahakali Pyakhan, and Yakshagana, Report of Asian Traditional Performing Arts* (ATPA) III. Tokyo: Japan Foundation, pp. 78–87.

Kris, Ernst
1952 *Psychoanalytic Explorations in Art.* New York: International Universities Press.

Langer, Susanne K.
1953 *Feeling and Form.* New York: Scribners.

Lannoy, Richard
1971 *The Speaking Tree.* London: Oxford University Press.

Lansing, J. Stephen
1974 *Evil in the Morning of the World.* Ann Arbor: University of Michigan Center for South and Southeast Asian Studies.
1983a *The Three Worlds of Bali.* New York: Praeger.
1983b "The Indianization of Bali," *South East Asian Studies* 14, 2: 409–21.

Lévi-Strauss, Claude
1966 [1952] *The Savage Mind.* Chicago: University of Chicago Press.
1969 *The Raw and the Cooked.* John Weightman and Doreen Weightman, trans. New York: Harper and Row.
1982 *The Way of Masks.* Sylvia Modeski, trans. Seattle: University of Washington Press.
1983 [1977] *L'identité seminaire interdisciplinaire a l'École des Hautes-Études dirigé par Claude Lévi-Strauss.* Paris: Presses Universitaires de France.

Lewis, I. M.
1971 *Ecstatic Possession: An Anthropological Study of Spirit Possession and Shamanism.* Harmondsworth: Penguin.

Lommel, Andreas
1967 *Shamanism: The Beginnings of Art.* Michael Bullock, trans. New York: McGraw Hill.
1972 *Masks: Their Meaning and Function.* Nadia Fowler, trans. London: Paul Elek Books.

Lovejoy, Arthur O.
1960 [1936] *The Great Chain of Being: The Study of the History of an Idea.* New York: Harper and Row.

Mabbett, I. W.
1977 "The Indianization of Southeast Asia: Reflections on the Prehistoric Sources." *Journal of Southeast Asian Studies* 8, 1: 2–14.

Mack, John, ed.
1994 *Masks and the Art of Expression.* New York: Harry N. Abrams.

Mahapatra, Sitakant
1986 "*Prahlada Nataka*: A Window on a Syncretic Performative Tradition." *National Center for Performing Arts Quarterly Journal* 14, 1: 15–25.

Majumdar, R. C.
1973 *Ancient Indian Colonies in the Far East.* Vol. 2: *Suvarnadvipa.* Calcutta: H. L. Mukhapadhyay.

Marranca, Bonnie and Gautam Dasgupta, eds.
1991 *Interculturalism and Performance: Writings from PAJ.* New York: PAJ Publications.

Mathur, V.B.
1969 *Ethnographic Atlas of Rajasthan with Reference to Scheduled Castes and Scheduled Tribes.* Jaipur: Rajasthan Census Operations.

McPhee, Colin
1966 *Music in Bali.* New Haven, CT: Yale University Press.

Mead, Margaret
1970 [1939] "The Strolling Players in the Mountains of Bali." In *Traditional Balinese Culture,* ed. Jane Belo. New York: Columbia University Press, pp. 137–45.

Mershon, Katherine
1971 *Seven Plus Seven.* New York: Vantage Press.

Miyao Jiryo
1987 "The Lion Dance in China: A Comparison of Northern and Southern Customs." In *Masked Performances in Asia: International Symposium on the Conservation and Restoration of Cultural Property.* Tokyo: National Research Institute of Cultural Properties, pp. 112–27.

Mookerjee, Ajit and Madhu Khanna
1977 *The Tantric Way: Art, Science, Ritual.* Boston: New York Graphic Society.

Naipal, V. S.
1979 [1977] *India: A Wounded Civilization.* Harmondsworth: Penguin.

Napier, A. David
1986 *Masks, Transformation, and Paradox.* Berkeley: University of California Press.

Newton, Douglas
1988 "Reflections in Bronze: Lapita and Dong-Son Art in the Western Pacific." In *Islands and Ancestors: Indigenous Styles of Southeast Asia,* ed. Jean Paul Barbier and Douglas Watson. Munich: Prestel-Verlag, pp. 10–23.

Nooy-Palm, Clementine H. M.
1988 "The Mamasa and Sa'dan Toraja of Sulawesi." In *Islands and Ancestors: Indigenous Styles of Southeast Asia,* ed. Jean Paul Barbier and Douglas Watson. Munich: Prestel-Verlag, pp. 86–105.

O'Neill, Roma Sisly
1978 "Spirit Possession and Healing Rites in a Balinese Village." MA thesis, University of Melbourne.

Oohashi Tsutomu
1987 "Shishi and Barong—A Humanbiological Approach on Trance-Inducing Animal Masks in Asia." In *Masked Performances in Asia: International Symposium on the Conservation and Restoration of Cultural Property.* Tokyo: National Research Institute of Cultural Properties, pp. 128–53.

Oreglia, Giacomo
1968 *The Commedia dell' Arte.* Lowell F. Edwards, trans. New York: Hill and Wang [1st Italian edition 1961].

Orissan Institute of Maritime and Southeast Asian Studies
[1993] Untitled anonymous brochure and account of early contacts. Bhubaneswar: DIPS.

Panda, Bhagaban
1973 Introduction to *Prahlada Nataka of Raja Rama Krushna Chhotaray* (in Oriya). Bhagaban Panda, ed. Bhubaneswar, Orissa: Directorate of Cultural Affairs.

Pani, Jiwan
1983 "*Prahlad-Natak*: A Theatre of Liberated Reality." *Indian Horizons* 32, 4: 24–33.
n.d. *Ravana Chhaya.* New Delhi: Sangeet Natak Akademi.

Park Mira
1987 "A Comparative Study of Lion Dances in Japan and Korea: The Urayhama Shishi-Mai and the Pukchong Sazamu." In *Masked Performances in Asia: International Symposium on the Conservation and Restoration of Cultural Property.* Tokyo: National Research Institute of Cultural Properties, pp. 101–11.

D. N. Patnaik
1992 "*Prahlad Natak.*" *Sangeet Natak: Journal of the Sangeet Natak Akademi* 104: 26–33

Pavis, Patrice, D.N.
1982 *Languages of the Stage: Essays in the Semiology of the Theatre.* New York: Performing Arts Journal.
1992 *Theatre at the Crossroads of Culture.* Loren Kruger, trans. London and New York: Routledge.

Penfield, W. and T. Rasmussen
1950 *The Cerebral Cortex of Man: A Clinical Study of Localization and Function.* New York: Macmillan.

Pernet, Henry
1992 *Ritual Masks: Deceptions and Revelations.* Laura Grillo, trans. Columbia: University of South Carolina Press.

Phalgunadi, I. G. P.
1984 "Hinduism in Bali." *South East Asian Perspectives* 1, 1: 37–56.

Picard, Michel
1990 " 'Cultural Tourism' in Bali: Cultural Performances as Tourist Attractions." *Indonesia,* 49.

Pickard-Cambridge, Sir Arthur
1927 *Dithyramb, Tragedy, and Comedy.* Oxford: Clarendon Press.

Pitt, Leonard
1982 "Leonard Pitt: Berkeley, California." *Mime Journal* 1980–82: 130–44.

Plato
1944 [1892] *The Republic.* In *The Dialogues of Plato,* Vol. 3. 3rd rev. ed. B. Jowett, trans. New York: Heritage Press [1st ed. of trans. 1871].

Pronko, Leonard
1967 *Theatre East and West.* Berkeley: University of California Press.

Raghavan, V.
1981 "Sanskrit Drama in Performance." In *Sanskrit Drama in Performance,* ed. Rachel Van M. Baumer and James R. Brandon. Honolulu: University Press of Hawaii, pp. 9–44.

Rajguru, S. N.
1968 *History of the Gangas.* Part I. Bhubaneswar: Orissa State Museum.

Ramseyer, Urs
1977 *The Art and Culture of Bali.* Eileen Walliser-Schwarzbach, trans. Oxford: Oxford University Press.

Reeder, Roberta
1979 "An Encounter of Codes: Little Red Riding Shawl and the Balinese Topeng." *Drama Review* 23, 4: 81–92.

Revel-MacDonald, Nicole
1988 "The Dayak of Borneo: On the Ancestors, The Dead, and The Living." In *Islands and Ancestors: Indigenous Styles of Southeast Asia*, ed. Jean Paul Barbier and Douglas Watson. Munich: Prestel-Verlag, pp. 66–85.

Reynaud, J. D.
1973 "La Personne et l'Évolution de la Societé Industrielle." In *Problèmes de la personne, colloque de recherches de psychologie comparative sous la direction d'Ignace Meyerson.* Paris: Mouton, pp. 213–24.

Richmond, Farley
1971 "Some Religious Aspects of Indian Traditional Theatre." *Drama Review* 15, 3: 123–51.

Ridgeway, William
1966 [1910] *The Origin of Tragedy, with Special Reference to the Greek Tragedians.* New York: Benjamin Blom.

Roach, Joseph R.
1993 [1985] *The Player's Passion: Studies in the Science of Acting.* Ann Arbor: University of Michigan Press.

Rouget, Gilbert
1985 *Music and Trance: A Study of the Relationship between Music and Possession.* Brunhilde Biebuyk trans. and rev. in collaboration with the author. Chicago: University of Chicago Press.

Rudlin, John
1994 *Commedia dell'Arte: An Actor's Handbook.* London and New York: Routledge.

Russell, R. V. and Rai Bahadur Hira Lal
1975 [1915] *Tribes and Castes of the Central Provinces of India.* 4 vols. Delhi: Rajdhani Book Centre.

Sahu, N. K.
1984 *Kharavela.* Bhubaneswar: Orissa State Museum.

Sahu, N. K., P. K. Misra and J. K. Sahu
1979 *History of Orissa.* Cuttack, Orissa: Nalanda Publishers.

Savran, David
1985 "The Wooster Group, Arthur Miller and *The Crucible.*" *Drama Review* 29, 2: 99–109.

Schechner, Richard
1973 "Drama, Script, Theatre, and Performance." *Drama Review* 17, 3: 5–36. [revised in Schechner 1977: 33–62; Schechner 1988: 68–105.]

1977 *Essays in Performance Theory 1970–1976.* New York: Drama Book Specialists.

1982 *The End of Humanism.* New York: PAJ Publications.

1985 *Between Theater and Anthropology.* Philadelphia: University of Pennsylvania Press.

1988 *Performance Theory.* New York and London: Routledge, Chapman and Hall [includes revised material from Schechner 1977].

Schevill, James
1973 "An Interview with John Emigh." In *BreakOut: In Search of New Theatrical Environments*, ed. James Schevill. Chicago: Swallow Press, pp. 257–65.

Schieffelin, Edward L.
1976 The *Sorrow of the Lonely and the Burning of the Dancers.* New York: St. Martin's Press.

Sharma, G. N.
1968 *Social Life in Medieval Rajasthan: 1500–1800 AD.* Agra: Laxmi Narain Agarwal.

Shattuck, Roger
1985 *The Innocent Eye: On Modern Literature and the Arts.* New York: Washington Square Press.

Shewey, Don
1985 *Sam Shepard.* New York: Dell Publishing.

Slattum, Judy
1992 *Masks of Bali: Spirits of an Ancient Drama.* San Francisco: Chronicle Books.

Snow, Stephen
1983 "Rangda: Archetype in Action." In *Drama and Religion*, ed. James Redmond. Themes in Drama 5. Cambridge: Cambridge University Press.
1986 "Intercultural Performance: The Balinese American Model." *Asian Theatre Journal* 3, 2: 204–32.

Soifer, Deborah A.
1991 *The Myths of Narasimha and Vamana: Two Avatars in Cosmological Perspective.* Albany: State University of New York Press.

Solheim, Wilhelm G.
1975 "Reflections on the New Data of Southeast Asian Prehistory: Austronesian Origin and Consequence." *Asian Perspectives* 18, 2: 146–60.

Staal, J. F.
1963 "Sanskrit and Sanskritization." *Journal of Asian Studies* 22, 2/3: 261–75.

Stanislavski, Constantin
1961 *Creating a Role.* Elizabeth Hapgood Reynolds, trans. New York: Theatre Arts Books [1st Russian edition 1933].

Strasberg, Lee
1987 *A Dream of Passion: The Development of the Method.* Evangeline Morphos, ed. Boston: Little Brown and Company.

Stutterheim, Willem F.
1935 *Indian Influences in Old Balinese Art.* London: India Society.

Suryani, Luh Ketut and Gordon D. Jensen
1993 *Trance and Possession in Bali: A Window on Western Multiple Personality, Possession Disorder, and Suicide.* Kuala Lumpur: Oxford University Press.

Swellengrebel, J. L.
1960 Introduction to *Bali: Studies in Life, Thought and Ritual*, ed. W. F. Wertheim et al. The Hague and Bandung: W. van Hoeve, pp. 1–76.

Teele, Rebecca
1984 *No/Kyogen Masks and Performance.* Claremont, CA: Mime Journal.

Tenzer, Michael
1991 *Balinese Music.* Berkeley, CA and Singapore: Periplus Editions.

Teyler, Timothy
1975 *A Primer in Psychobiology: Brain and Behavior.* San Francisco: W. H. Freeman.

Tillyard, E. M.
1943 *The Elizabethan World Picture.* London: Macmillan.

Trinh T. Minh-ha
1989 *Woman, Native, Other: Writing Postcoloniality and Feminism.* Bloomington: Indiana University Press.

Turner, Frederick
1991 "The Universal Solvent: Meditations on the Marriage of World Cultures." In *Interculturalism and Performance: Writings from PAJ,* ed. Bonnie Marranca and Gautam Dasgupta. New York: PAJ Publications, pp. 257–80.

Turner, Victor
1967 *The Forest of Symbols: Aspects of Ndembu Ritual.* Ithaca, NY and London: Cornell University Press.

1969 *The Ritual Process: Structure and Anti-Structure.* Ithaca, NY: Cornell University Press.

1982 *From Ritual to Theatre: The Seriousness of Human Play.* New York: Performing Arts Journal Press.

1986 *The Anthropology of Performance.* New York: PAJ Publications.

Valentine, C. S.
1961 *Masks and Men in a Melanesian Society: The Valuku or Tubuan of the Lakalai of New Britain.* Lawrence: University of Kansas Publications.

Van Gennep, Arnold
1960 *The Rites of Passage.* Monika B. Vizedom and Gabrielle L. Caffee, trans. Chicago: University of Chicago Press [1st French edition 1909].

Vatsyayan, Kapila
1980 *Traditional Indian Theatre: Multiple Streams.* New Delhi: National Book Trust.

Vickers, Adrian
1982 "When Is a Text Not a Text? The Malat and Philology." Unpublished paper presented at the 4th national conference, Asian Studies of Australia, Monash University.

1986 "The Desiring Prince: A Study of the Kidung Malat as Text." PhD dissertation. University of Sydney.

1989 *Bali: A Paradise Created.* Berkeley, CA and Singapore: Periplus Editions.

Volkman, Toby Alice
1979 *Feasts of Honor: Ritual and Change in the Toraja Highlands.* Illinois Studies in Anthropology 16. Urbana: University of Illinois Press.

von Steitencron, H.
1978 "The Advent of Vishnuism in Orissa: An Outline of Its History According to Archeological and Epigraphic Sources from the Gupta Period up to 1135 A.D." In *The Cult of Jagannath and the Regional Tradition of Orissa*, ed. A. Eschmann, H. Kulke, and G. C. Tripathi. New Delhi: Manohar, pp. 1–30.

Wallis, Richard
1979 "Balinese Theatre: Coping with Old and New." In *What Is Modern Indonesian Culture? Papers Presented to the Conference on Indonesian Studies, July 29-August 1, 1976*, ed. Gloria Davis. Studies Southeast Asia Series 52. Athens, OH: Ohio University Center for International Studies , pp. 37–45.
1980 "The Voice As a Mode of Cultural Expression in Bali." PhD dissertation. University of Michigan, Ann Arbor.

Weber, Carl
1991 [1989] "AC/TC: Currents of Theatrical Exchange." In *Interculturalism and Performance: Writings from PAJ*, ed. Bonnie Marranca and Gautam Dasgupta. New York: PAJ Publications, pp. 27–37.

Weiss, Peter
1966 *The Persecution and Assassination of Jean-Paul Marat As Performed by the Inmates of the Asylum of Charenton Under the Direction of the Marquis de Sade.* English verse adaptation by Adrian Mitchell. New York: Atheneum.

Welsford, Enid
1968 [1935] *The Fool: His Social and Literary History.* London: Faber and Faber.

Wiles, David
1991 *The Masks of Menander.* Cambridge and New York: Cambridge University Press.

Willeford, William
1969 *The Fool and His Scepter: A Study in Clowns and Jesters and Their Audience.* Evanston, IL: Northwestern University Press.

Wilshire, Bruce
1982 *Role Playing and Identity: The Limits of Theatre as Metaphor.* Bloomington: Indiana University Press.

Winnicott, D.W.
1989 [1971] *Playing and Reality.* London and New York: Tavistock/Routledge.

Worsley, P.J.
1972 *Babad Buleleng: A Balinese Dynastic Genealogy.* The Hague: Nijhoff.

Worthen, William
1984 *The Idea of the Actor.* Princeton, NJ: Princeton University Press.

Worthen, William et al.
1995 "Disciplines of the Text/Sites of Performance" with responses from Jill Dolan, Joseph Roach, Richard Schechner, Phillip B. Zarrilli, and Worthen himself. *Drama Review* 39, 1: 13–44.

Yeats, W. B.
1956 *The Collected Poems of W. B. Yeats.* New York: Macmillan.

Young, Elizabeth
1980 "Topeng in Bali: Change and Continuity in a Traditional Drama Genre." PhD dissertation. University of California.

Young, Elizabeth, trans. (performer not named)
1982 "The Tale of Erlangga: Text Translation of a Village Drama Performance in Bali." *Bijdragen tot do Taal-, Land- en Volkenkunde* 138, 4: 470–491.

Zarrilli, Phillip B.
1977 "De-Mystifying Kathakali." *Sangeet Natak: Journal of the Sangeet Natak Akademi* 43: 48–59.
1984 *The Kathakali Complex: Actor, Performer and Structure.* New Delhi: Abhinav Publications.
1987 "Structure and Subjunctivity: Putu Wijaya's Theatre of Surprise." *The Drama Review* 31, 3: 126–159.
1990 "What Does It Mean to 'Become the Character'? Power, Presence, and Transcendence in Asian In-Body Disciplines of Practice." In *By Means of Performance,* ed. Richard Schechner and Willa Appel. Cambridge and New York: Cambridge University Press.

Zide, Norman H.
1968 "Munda and Non-Munda Austro-Asiatic Languages." *Current Trends in Linguistics* 5: 411–30.

Zimmer, Heinrich
1972 [1946] *Myths and Symbols in Indian Art and Civilization.* Joseph Campbell, ed. Bollingen Series 6. Princeton, NJ: Princeton University Press.

Zoetmulder, P. J.
1974 *Kalangwan: A Survey of Old Javanese Literature.* The Hague: Nijhoff.

Zurbuchen, Mary
1987 *The Language of Balinese Shadow Theatre.* Princeton, NJ: Princeton University Press.

Index

actors: and caste, 147–48; dangers to, 196; exercises for, 276–77; female, 143, 205n.14, 210; as mediators between sacred and secular, 150–51, 188–89, 194, 196, 202, 222, 279–80, 286; role of, xix; sanctity accorded some, 186, 217–18, 222. *See also* Bhand, Hajari; character actors; Kakul, I Nyoman; masks
Ada, K. S., 211
Adrastus, 21
Aeschylus, 21, 175
"affective-memory," 25
Agama Hindu Bali, 74, 113
Agung, I Gusti Dauh (character), 123, 125
A'in-i Akbari ('Allami), 210, 211–12
Airlangga (Balinese prince), 79, 80–81, 103n.11
Alit, Ida Bagus, 205n.14
'Allami, Abu'l Fazl, 210
American Society for Eastern Arts, 248
ancestors: Balinese languages associated with, 129–31, 136, 147, 150–51, 199; embodiment of, in topeng pajegan, 150–51, 156n.13, 186; masks' association with, 7, 14, 20–21, 79, 113, 115–16, 153, 248; realm of, 184; and temple ceremonies, 120; worship of, 75, 79. *See also* visitation
Andhra Pradesh (India), 43, 77, 84, 85
androgyny (of Rangda figure), 102n.8
Angkor (Kampuchea), 37
animals (and humans in Balinese culture), 67–73, 79. *See also* lions; tigers
Anom, Ida Bagus, 205n.14, 275
apheterion (point of departure), 77–78
arak (liquor), 153
archaeology, 75–76, 78–79, 95
Archilochus, 222
Arctic, 7
Aristotle, 174, 175, 181, 271, 275
arja, 64, 156n.14, 167, 196, 205.14
Arjuna (hero), 143
Artaud, Antonin, 31, 172, 193–95, 200, 202, 247, 248, 254, 271
Artha, Gde Arsa, 273n.6
Arthur Rimbaud's in Town, xviii
Aryans, 93, 95
Ashiya, R. S., 213
Ashoka, 77
Assagioli, Robert, 289
Assam (India), 77
Attenborough, David, 75, 102n.8
audiences: actor's relationship with, 246; for *bahurupiyas*, 207–18, 221, 227–28; Balinese, 118, 120, 125, 127, 129, 131, 134, 136–37, 151, 153–54, 169–70, 181, 186–87, 197; Balinese, on stories cannibalized by ritual, 64, 66; for contemporary Western theatre, 174; effects of humor on, 140, 142–43; for intercultural plays, 281; space occupied by, 182–84, 189, 246; women in, 56
Australoid peoples, 93
Austro-Asian peoples, 91, 93, 95–96
L'Avant Garde (journal), 195
avant-garde theatre, 195, 198
Awasthi, Suresh, 273
Aztecs, 7

babad dalem (chronicles of the kings), 127, 131, 142, 148, 150, 175–77, 287
bahu (many), 207
bahurupiya (jester), 207–43, 271; artistry of, 225–42; characteristics of, 212; working conditions of, 211, 212–18, 220–25

Baining people (Papua New Guinea), 17, 19, 46
Bali (Indonesia): calendars in, 154n.2; cultural links of, to India, xx, 74–99, 129, 272, 281; films on, 98, 102n.8, 155n.3; funerary customs in, 41, 81, 107, 108, 151, 177; Hinduism in, 41; masked performance in, xxi, xxii, 60–74, 105–54, 247; origins of peoples in, 93; trance performances in, xx, 64, 84, 91, 98–99, 118, 198; Westernization in, 205n.13. See also *Calon Arang*; topeng; topeng pajegan
Bali: Mask of Rangda (film), 98, 102n.8
Bali Jatra ceremony, 90
Balinese language (contemporary), 134, 135–36. *See also* languages
Banaspati Raja, 41, 61, 75
Bandem, I Made, 61, 67, 96, 102n.8, 157, 203n.5, 259, 262
Bandem, Suasti, 259
Bania caste, 218, 227, 229. *See also* Oswali Bania caste
Banjara caste, 226, 228
Barba, Eugenio, 27, 281–82
baris gilak, 120, 123, 142, 166–67
barong (animalistic figures), 61
Barong (film), 102n.8
Barong Ket, 60–99, 113, 186, 197
barong landung masks, 91
Barthes, Roland, 180, 193, 198–99, 204n.7
Bassi (India), 214, 216
Batak funerary rites, 3, 5, 8, 20
Bateson, Gregory, 19, 277, 278; film on Bali by, 102n.8; on play, 1, 27; on use of skulls in performance, 7–8
Batuan village (Bali), 115, 185
Baturenggong, Dalem (King of Gelgel), 127, 148, 150; in *Jelantik Goes to Blambangan*, 130, 136, 137, 140, 156n.8, 158–60, 166, 176–77
Baulagaon village (Orissa, India), 41–60, 101n.6, 113
Bawurawah, Pedanda (character), 165
Becker, A. L., 131
Beckett, Samuel, 193, 202, 247, 249
bedi (theatrical competitions), 43, 56, 60
Begin, Menachem, 266
Behru Jogi, 217–18, 222, 228
Béjart, Maurice, 271
Bellin, Harvey, 98, 102n.8
Belo, Jane, 75, 80, 81
Benaru (giant character), 64, 66
Bengal, 77, 100n.7
Benjamin, Walter, 283
Berliner Ensemble, 24
Berlioz, Hector, 284
Bernal, Martin, 281
Berne, Eric, 22
berutuk masks, 113
Besakih temple, 148, 164, 168
Bhabha, Homi, 289
bhagavata mela, 84, 100n.3
bhakti (personal devotion), 80
Bhaliagara (India), 85
bhana (comic monodrama), 210
Bhand, Ambalalji, 218
Bhand, Babulal, 213
Bhand, Champalal, 216
Bhand, Hajari, xx, xxii, 207–43, 271, 288
Bhand, Janakilal (Hajari Bhand's son), 207, 221, 233, 236, 238–39
Bhand, Jhora, 214
Bhand, Kaluji (Hajari Bhand's father), 213, 214, 216
Bhand, Mohan (Hajari Bhand's brother), 213, 216, 217, 239
Bhand, Moraji (Hajari Bhand's grandfather), 214
Bhand, Onkarji, 224
bhanda (jester), 210
bhandai, 213, 221–25, 241
Bhandakakhera (India), 214
bhand pather, 210
Bhands: as beggars, 213; as caste, 207, 213, 241; history of, 210–16
Bharada, Mpu, 81
bharat (India; west), 99
Bharata-Muni, 27, 52
Bhartiya Lok Kala Mandal (Udaipur), 211, 213
bhavai theatre, 211
bhavas (states of feeling), 28
Bhils, 239
Bhilwara (India), 221
Bhoma (demon), 41, 75
bhuta kala, 60
bighas, 214
Big Nazo Puppet Bowling Alley Band and Theatre, 274n.8
bija (kernel), 175
black magic, 67, 80–81
Blambangan (Java), xx, 127, 137, 142, 176
Blambangan, Sri Dalem (King of), 137, 140, 143, 165, 199, 201
Blangsinga, Keyai (character), 159

Blau, Herbert, 289
blood types, 76, 79
Boal, Augusto, 289
boars, 75
bondres (clowns), 140–47, 187, 188, 194, 205n.14. *See also* humor
bone-setting, 215, 218, 222
Boon, James A., 80, 186, 195–96, 199
Bornstein, Kate, 289
Borokadanda village (India), 93
boundaries (between domains), 172–74
Brahma (god), 158, 164
Brahmana caste, 89, 127, 153, 167, 183, 185; *bahurupiyas* from, in India, 212, 215; Balinese actors from, 147, 148; priests among, 107, 108, 111, 150, 151, 177, 186
brain, 71–73, 102n.10
Brazil, 205n.13
Bread and Puppet Theater, 21, 247, 270, 273n.1
BreakOut! (ed. Schevill), 244, 245
Brecht, Bertolt, 23, 195; influence of, 172, 193, 247, 249; theatre of, 28, 30, 174, 245, 248, 254, 268. See also *Caucasian Chalk Circle*
Breuer, Lee, 173, 193, 279–80, 283, 284
bricolage, 177
Brochin, Jim, 259
Bronson, Bernice ("Bunny"), 257
bronze casting, 95
Brook, Peter, 155n.7, 193, 195, 275, 281–82, 286
Brown University, 21, 244, 247, 255, 274n.8
Brustein, Robert, 245
Buddhism: in Bali, 74–78, 80; carved-head decorations associated with, 35, 37; in India, 85; leonine figures associated with, 69; Rangda's counterparts in, 89–90. *See also* Tantrism
Budevi, 89
buffalos. *See* water buffalos
Buñuel, Luis, 282
Buried Child (Shepard), 270
Burke, Kenneth, 175
Burning City Theatre, 273n.1
Burstyn, Ellen, 21
buwana agung. See macrocosmos (divine)
buwana alit. See microcosmos (human)

Cage, John, 174
Calcutta (India), 280
Calderón de la Barca, Pedro, 223
Calingae. *See* Kalinga
Calon Arang, xx, 90, 91, 274n.7, 279; influence of, on politics, 98; intercultural influences on, 96; music associated with, 95; setting of, 79; widow/witch figure in, 66–67, 80–81, 85, 103n.11
Candide, 246
caritera (babad stories), 176, 177, 187. See also *babad dalem*
carnivalesque traditions, 24, 205n.13
Carpenter, Edmund, 11, 13
Carrière, Jean-Claude, 281–83
Carrol, Bob, 245
Carter, Jimmy, 259
caru (blood sacrifices), 60
castes: of *bahurupiya* performers, 211–12; in Balinese society, 130–31, 143, 147–48, 199; as basis for humor, 212, 225–41; Indian merchant, 216, 218, 221, 223–25; in *Jelantik Goes to Blambangan,* 147, 159, 183. *See also* names of specific castes
Catlin, Amy, 254
Cato, Gavin, 287, 288
Catra, I Nyoman, 102n.8, 156n.12, 205n.14, 274n.7
Catur Marga (film), 155n.3
The Caucasian Chalk Circle (Brecht), 248, 262, 267–68, 270
cemeteries. *See* graveyards
Cenikan, Penasar (character), 132–33, 136, 140, 143, 147, 160–66, 182, 184, 187, 189, 200
Chaikin, Joseph, 286
Chamunda, 89
Chandi (Indian goddess), 9, 55
character actors, 24–30, 255; in Indian performances, 51, 57, 59; in performance history, 105. *See also* characters
characters: in *bahurupiya,* 207, 209–10, 212, 217–41, 271; exercises for developing, 276–77; female, 143, 148, 161–67, 215, 233, 236, 238; order of appearance of, 126, 261; in topeng pajegan, 104, 116, 125, 182, 187, 201–2, 261. *See also* character actors; identity; specific actors
Chatisgarh region (India), 280
Chekhov, Michael, 25, 255
Chelitalo (India), 90
chhau (*chho*) (Hindu performance form), 28, 46, 85, 90
chho. See *chhau*
Childe Byron (Linney), 284–85
Chilika Lake, 78, 79

chimta, 229
Chin, Daryl, 283
China: and Bali, 76, 78, 95, 96; Indian influence on, 75; lions in, 69, 75
Chittorgarh (India), 207, 213–16, 218, 233, 236
Chodaganga, 77, 103n.13
Chottaray, Raja Rama Krishna Deva, 43
Chung, Hazel, 273n.6
Cieslak, Ryzard, 286
Cili, Diah Bima Cili (character), 159
Cirebon (Java), 197
Cixous, Hélène, 284
Clifford, James, xxii, 285–86
Clown Congress of 1991, 274n.7
Coast, John, 75
Coates, George, 22
Coleridge, Samuel Taylor, 27
commedia dell' arte, 28, 105, 155n.7, 247, 249, 254, 281, 284
The Conference of Birds, 275
Conservatory of Dance and Music (Bali), 266
Corneille, Pierre, 174
costume, 11. See also *vesh*
court jesters, xx. *See also* Bhand, Hajari
Covarrubias, Miguel, 130
cremations, 107, 108, 151, 177, 182. *See also* graveyards
"critical attitude," 195
Crooke, W., 210
The Crucible (Miller), 173
Csikszentmihalyi, Mihaly, 26, 28
Cucul (peasant character), 143, 147, 167, 184, 186, 189, 200
culture, 99. *See also* interculturalism
Cupak (tale), 64, 66
Curchack, Fred, 193, 286–87
Curse of the Starving Class (Shepard), 270
Cynkutis, Zbigniew, 286

Dabhai, Tulsinath, 211, 225
daksine (offering), 168
dalang (puppeteer), 197
Damasio, Antonio, 73
Dance and Drama in Bali (de Zoete and Spies), 176
dances: balance in topeng, 198; Emigh's experience with Balinese, 107, 116, 171, 248, 255, 257, 264; martial arts' influence on Balinese topeng, 111, 120, 137, 143; in Papua New Guinea, 11, 14, 19, 21, 29, 96, 129; in ritual, 151; in topeng pajegan, 116–26, 130, 136–40, 142, 181, 182; trance, performed by girls, 113, 116. See also *baris gilak*; *gambhira*
danda nata, 84–85, 90, 91
Daniel, Ana, 116–17, 153
Dantapura (capital of Kalinga), 77, 78, 90
darbar, 214
Darika, 85
daru (entrance songs), 52
Das, K. B., 95
Dasahara, 214
dasar (foundation), 134
death masks, 32n.4
The Death of Bedahulu. See *Pig-Headed King*
deBoer, Fredrik Eugene, 61, 67, 96, 185, 203n.5
"de-centered" works, 199–201
deconstruction, 199–200
Delhi (India), 280
Denpasar (Bali), 64, 98, 150
Depati, Sang Hyang Yama, 161
Derrida, Jacques, 193, 199
desia nata (mask theatre), 84, 90
Devanagri script, 79
de Zoete, Beryl, 176
dharamsala, 217
dharma, 184, 186, 240, 241
Dibia, I Wayan, 102n.8, 259, 262, 271
Dibia, Wiratini, 259
Diderot, Denis, 25–27
Dimade, Dalem, 204n.5
Dionysos, 32n.12
director, 173–75, 247, 284–85
disguise. See *vesh*
Divali (holiday), 218, 221, 224, 227
the divine (female aspect of), 37. *See also* names of specific deities
domains (of topeng), 171–206
Dong-Son culture (Vietnam), 76, 95
"drama" (as domain), 172–73, 175, 176–77, 181
drama-gong, 271
"Drama-Script-Theatre-Performance" (Schechner), 171–93
Dravidian peoples, 91, 93, 95, 96
dreams, 117, 255
Durga, 46, 67, 70, 75, 80–81, 84, 98
Dutch (in Bali), 98, 182–83, 185, 196, 197
Dutch Pavilion (Paris Exposition), 193
Dwari (doorman), 52

East-West Fusion Theatre (Sharon, Connecticut), 273n.6

Edison's Dream (Schevill), 246, 270, 274n.8
effigy figures. See *tau-tau*
Egyptian theatre, 281
Einstein, Albert, 24
Eiseman, Fred B., Jr., 84
Eliade, Mircea, 13
Elizabethan theatre, 204n.8. *See also* Shakespeare, William
Emerson, Ralph Waldo, 289
Emerson College, 274n.7
Emigh, Aaron, 72, 257
Emigh, John: as director, 284–85; effects of Asian performance on, xxi; *gamelan* experiences of, 247–48, 254, 257, 259, 261, 274n.7; interest of, in masks, 247–48, 267–68, 270; interview with, xxi, 244–74, 277; jazz experience of, 254, 261; study of masked dance by, 107, 116, 171, 248; translations by, 157–70; use of myth by, 255, 257, 259; as Western performer of Eastern material, 262
Emigh, Ulrike, 84, 207–43
environmental theatre, 174, 245–46
Erasmus, Desiderius, 241
Errington, Frederick, 17, 32n.7
Errington, Shelly, 156n.13
Eschmann, Anncharlott, 85, 95–96
Ethnographic Atlas of Rajasthan, 211
Euripides, 21, 175, 278
"everyday life": and art, 189–90, 194–97, 199; as domain, 172, 183–87, 189
"evil eye," 71
experimental theatre, 244–45

Fabri, Charles, 85
family life: in *Cupak*, 64; in *Jelantik Goes to Blambangan*, 162–63, 177; as portrayed by *bahurupiya*, 233, 236, 238, 239; in *Prahlada Nataka*, 55–56, 74; in *Tjupak*, 257
films (on Bali), 98, 102n.8, 155n.3
Fires in the Mirror: Brooklyn, Crown Heights, and Other Identities (Smith), 287–88
"flow episodes," 26, 28
Fo, Dario, 23, 155n.7
Foley, Kathy, 197
"Folly, Bali, and Anthropology, or Satire Across Cultures" (Boon), 186
fool. See *bahurupiya*
The Fool and His Scepter (Willeford), 207
Foreman, Richard, 28, 173, 174, 193, 245
Foucault, Michel, 277, 289
Frankel, Gene, 286
Frederick the Great, 24
Freeman, Morgan, 279
Freud, Sigmund, 24, 201–2, 277
From Ritual to Theatre (Turner), 191
Frye, Northrop, 186
Fuchs, Elinor, 199

Gaduliya characters, 215, 225–26, 228, 229, 236, 239
gahaka (principal narrator), 50, 56
Galungan holiday (Bali), 61
gambhira (Hindu performance form), 46, 85, 90
gambuh drama, 129, 160, 167, 176, 180
gamelan (orchestra), 177; as all-male, 143; in Balinese theatre, 64, 118, 120, 123, 129, 130, 148, 181, 198; Emigh's experiences with, 247–48, 254, 257, 259, 261, 274n.7; in *Jelantik Goes to Blambangan*, 157, 160, 161, 164, 166–67, 183, 187
Ganesha (son of Shiva), 50–51, 89, 129
Ganjam District (Orissa, India), 43, 46, 77, 78, 85, 90, 93
garamut (New Guinea drum), 20–21
gargoyles, 37
Garrick, David, 25–27
Gauri (India), 213
Geertz, Clifford, 101n.7, 147, 196, 198, 205n.15, 252
Geertz, Hildred, 185, 204n.11
Gegek, Ratu (character), 205n.14
Gelgel (ancient Balinese kingdom), 123, 125, 127, 130, 131, 136, 137, 140, 158, 161–62
Genet, Jean, 193
gestures, 193–94
gini (cymbals), 50
Giriputi (an aspect of Shakti), 61
Goa Gajah cave (Bedulu), 70–71, 90, 96
Goffman, Erving, 22
Gonello (Italian buffoon), 212
gorgons, 69–70
Gospel at Colonus (Breuer and Telson), 279, 281, 283
Gozzi, Carlo, 284
graciosos, 223
Grando, Michael, 273n.1
Grantang (character), 64, 66
graveyards, 98, 99, 103n.11. *See also* cremations
Gray, Spalding, 23, 174, 245, 253
Greek theatre, 254; conventions in, 175, 204nn.10, 11, 278–79; leonine figures in,

Greek theatre (*continued*) 68, 69–70; masks in, 34n.16, 105, 247; sources for, 21, 281
Grisgris, Pasung (character), 121, 123, 125
Grotowski, Jerzy, 29, 193, 281–82, 286, 1741
Group Theatre, 281
Gujarat (India), 211
Gunung Agung mountain, 90, 115, 148, 198
Gupta dynasty, 77
Gurdjieff, Georges Ivanovitch, 282
guru, 116, 213

Hagen, Uta, 31n.3
Halloween, 24
Halpin, Marjorie, 32n.11
halus, 140
Hanks, Tom, 26
Hanuman (deity), 218, 229
Harappa, 93
Hari, 55. *See also* Vishnu
Hariti, 89
Harvey, David, 199
Harwood, Dane, 254
Haryana (India), 210
haus tamboran (spirit house), 8–11
headhunting, 7
heads (carved), 35, 37, 41, 71. *See also* Kirtimukhas
Henry IV, Part I (Shakespeare), 270, 284
Herodotus, 21
Herrigel, Eugen, xix, 19
Hidden: A Gender, The Opposite Sex Is Neither (Bornstein), 289
high Balinese language, 130–31, 157, 168
high school graduations, 13, 14
hikayat (tenseless texts), 156n.13
Hinduism: in Bali, 74, 79–80, 111; iconography and performance in, 35, 41–74; among Rajasthani Bhands, 210, 212, 213, 241. *See also* Tantrism
hing, 228
Hiranyakashipu (Indian demon), 43, 52–53, 55–57, 59–60
Hiranyasimhi (Indian demon), 43
Hiroshima (Japan), 278
Hkaravela, 77
Hoff, Frank, 34n.18
Holi (holiday), 218, 221
Holy Cross College, 274n.7
Homer, 175
Homo Ludens (Huizinga), 19
homunculus, 71–73, 102n.10
Hooykaas, C., 60
Hudson, Lee, 286
Huizinga, Johan, 19
Humbaba (leonine apotropaic figure), 68
humor: in topeng, 127, 129–32, 134, 140–47, 183, 184–86, 188, 194, 205n.14. See also *bahurupiya*

Iatmul people, 7, 10, 14, 20–21, 24, 32n.6, 96
Ibsen, Henrik, 172, 174
Id (Muslim holiday), 218
identity: *bahurupiya*'s play with, xviii–xix, 207, 209–10, 212, 217–41; Emigh's, as Western performer of Eastern material, 262; and masks, 28, 29, 275; multiple, 23, 253, 271; national, 287–89; presentation of, in everyday life, 22–23. *See also* characters
illusion: "me" and "not-me" in, 22–30; in play, 2–3, 19; postmodern views of reality as, 199; in topeng pajegan, 130, 150; versus visitation (possession), 29, 99, 107, 136–37, 150, 187, 199. *See also* play
"imaginary body," 25
"imaginary center," 25
Incas, 7
incense, 113, 115, 120, 261
incest, 162–63
India: cultural links of, to Bali, xx, 74–99, 129, 272, 281; Emigh in, 271, 272; Independence of, 207, 212, 216; masked performance in, xxi, 24; trance performances in, xx, 41–60, 66, 73, 74, 84–85, 89–91. See also *bahurupiya*; Orissa (India); *Prahlada Nataka*; Rajasthan (India)
"indication," 23
Indonesia: Balinese ambivalence towards, 142, 166, 184, 185–86, 252; communist coup of 1965 in, 98, 198; Emigh's work in, 247–48; killings of 1966 in, 98, 196, 198; mass suicide in, 98; war for independence of, 185. *See also* Bali; Java; languages; specific villages and features
Indonesian Embassy, 274n.7
Indonesian language, 130, 131, 136, 142, 153, 157, 170, 189
inequality. *See* caste
Institute for the Study of Theatre (Denmark), 281

interculturalism, xx, xxi, 113, 244, 277; between Bali and East India, 74–99; between Western and Eastern theatre, 254–73, 278–85. *See also* sea trade
International Centre for Theatre Research (Paris), 281
Ireland, 222
Islam: in India, 210, 212, 217–18, 228–29; in Java, 79–80
Island of Bali (Covarrubias), 130
Iswara (god), 158
Italy. See *commedia dell' arte*; Gonello

jaba, 107
Jagannath temple (Puri), 103n.13
Jagidars, 211
jaguars, 69
Jaipur (India), 211, 218
Jalandhara (Titan), 37
Jalantara palace (India), 85
James, William, 289
Japan: and Bali, 196; *bunraku* in, 270, 279; dragons in, 75; *kabuki* in, 278, 286; *kyogen* comedies in, 204n.11; *noh* theatre in, 28, 34n.18, 105, 204n.11, 278, 284–86; *shi-shi* in, 69; *Trojan Women* set in, 278
Jataka stories, 77
Java, 74; connections of, with Bali, 76, 79–81; demons in, 37, 41; Indian influence on, 75, 76, 79, 85; rulers of, 79
Javanese language. *See* Middle Javanese language; Old Javanese language
Jayakusuna (King of Loripan), 61
Jelantik, I Gusti (Javanese hero), xx, 203n.5; in *Jelantik Goes to Blambangan*, 132–43, 147–48, 161–64, 166; Schechner's "domains" applied to performance about, 174–77, 183, 187, 199–201
Jelantik Goes to Blambangan, 157–70, 174–77, 183, 187, 199–201
Jenkins, Ron, 118, 184–85, 205n.14, 259, 274n.7
Jericho, 7
jester. See *bahurupiya*
Jimbaran, 103n.11
Joosten, P. Leo, 8
Joseph, Bertram, 286

Kakul, I Nyoman, 102n.8, 186, 205n.12, 288; caste of, 107, 108, 147, 151, 153; as Emigh's dance teacher, 107, 116, 249, 251, 255; notebook used by, 176, 177, 187, 189; origins of stories danced by, 80, 287; rival of, 156n.9; as solo performer, 107–54, 253; and text of *Jelantik Goes to Blambangan*, 157–70; topeng approach of, 171–72, 174, 187–92, 198, 199, 201, 241; topeng pajegan of, xx, xxii, 107–54, 196, 200
Kala, 37, 75
Kala, Batara (Indonesian demon), 37
Kalaratri (character), 85, 89
Kali, 46, 84, 85, 89, 93, 103n.13, 229, 230, 284
Kalidasa, 75, 78
Kalimantan, 75
Kalinga empire (India), 77–78, 91, 95, 150. *See also* Keling
Kalinganagara. *See* Kalinga
Kalinganagaram. *See* Kalinga
Kamasutra (Vatsyayana), 210
Kambeshvari, 96
El-Kanater, Ismail Abou, xviii
Kanjara caste, 233, 238, 239
Kantor, I Ketut, 205n.14
Kaprow, Allan, 174
Karangasam (Bali), 76
karma, 240–41
Karna, Prince (character), 159
karya (sacred work), 148
Karya, Sidha (character), 148–53, 167–70, 183, 186–89, 197
kasar, 140
Kashmir (India), 210
kathakali (Hindu performance form), 28, 46, 282, 286
kavat, 17, 19, 21, 22, 29, 46
Kawi. *See* Old Javanese language
Keats, John, 286
kecak (Monkey Chant), 271
Kediri, 159
kekawin poetry, 130, 134
Kelihan, Penasar (character), 127–36, 140, 143, 147, 148, 151, 157–60, 164–65, 182, 183, 187, 189
Keling, 79, 148, 150. *See also* Kalinga
Keling, Brahmana (character), 99, 148, 150
Kemmu, Motilal, 223
kepeng, 168
Kerala, 85
keras, 140
kerauhan (entered), 113
keris, 64, 67, 73, 84, 96, 98, 111
Keshava, 55. *See also* Vishnu
Kete village (Tanatoraja), 3–7
Khmer people, 93

Khond communities (Orissa, India), 96
kidung (romantic poetry), 129, 134, 177
Kidung Malat, 131, 134, 160, 164, 167, 180
Kidung Tantri, 129, 158
Kidung Wargasari (Song of Spiritual Essence), 113, 115
King, Martin Luther, Jr., 289
King Stag (Gozzi), 284
Kirk, Malcolm, 32n.13
Kirtimukhas ("Visages of Glory"—carved heads), 37, 41, 43, 61, 68, 70, 72, 74, 75, 81, 96, 148. *See also* heads (carved)
Klein, Melanie, 22
Kling. *See* Kalinga
Klungkung province (Bali), 127, 157, 158; dialect from, 130, 160, 161, 165, 177
Koestler, Arthur, 277
Koetting, Jim, 254
Kohut, 201
Kongoda, 78, 95
Koraput district (Orissa, India), 84
Korea, 69, 75
Kothari, Komal, 225
Krambitan (Bali), 98
Kris, Ernst, 32n.4
Krishna, 55, 80. *See also* Vishnu
Kruttika, 89
Kshatriya (Indian caste designation), xxi, 127, 215
Kubutambahan village (Bali), 81
kuchipudi, 84, 100n.3
kulkul (gongs), 108
kutiyattam, 284
Kutri village (Bali), 81

Lacan, Jacques, 200, 201
Lakahi of Nepal, 89
lakhs, 223
Lakshmi (goddess), 218, 224, 229
La Mama ETC (New York City), 244
Langer, Susanne K., 204n.8
languages: ancestral Balinese, 129–31, 136, 147, 150–51, 199; caste effects on, 130, 131; in *Jelantik Goes to Blambangan*, 157, 187, 189; tenseless, 136, 156n.13; in topeng theatre, 129, 131–32, 134–36, 142, 143, 147, 150, 153, 181, 199. *See also* Balinese language (contemporary); high Balinese language; Indonesian language; low Balinese language; median Balinese language; Middle Javanese language; Old Javanese language; Oriya language; Sanskrit language; Telegu language
Lansing, J. Steven, 91, 155n.3
Lawson, Lisa, 254
lazzi, 261
Lea, Lepan, 32n.9
LeCoq, Jacques, 286
Lee, Eugene, 246
leeches, 184
Lefrink, F. A., 96, 98
legong dance, 167, 257
Leila and Majnun (Persian story), 233
lek, 198
Lendra, I Wayan, 254
Lepang, I Gusti Ngurah, 118, 125
Lévi-Strauss, Claude, 31, 177, 200, 203n.4
Libation Bearers, 284
life. *See* everyday life
lila, 241
Lilavati (character in *Prahlada Nataka*), 55, 57
limid (penis covering), 17
"liminal occasions": dangers associated with, 41, 46, 57, 66; Turner on, 1–3, 10, 184, 190–91, 278; uses of masks in, 7, 13, 14, 107–8, 197
"liminoid" occasions, 184, 191–92, 279
Linklatter, Kristin, 286
Linney, Romulus, 284–85
lions, 41, 43, 64, 68–73, 85, 214
Little Red Riding Hood, 261–62, 264, 266
Living Theatre, 271, 286
lokadharmi, 27–28, 52
lontar (palm leaves), 127, 176
Looking Glass Theatre (Providence, Rhode Island), 255, 257
low Balinese language, 130–31, 157, 166
LSD (performance piece), 173
Ludlum, Charles, 28
Lutterman, John, 277
Lycambes (King), 222

Mabbet, I. W., 95
macrocosmos (divine), 67, 132, 184, 186, 187, 196, 201, 241, 286
Mada, Gajah (of Majapahit), 204n.5, 259
Madhya Pradesh (India), 280
madness, 29–30, 101n.7, 230, 233
Magendo (Papua New Guinea), 10–11, 13
magic, 67, 80–81
"magic if," 25
Mahabharata, 99, 103n.13; influence of, on

Balinese theatre, 129, 131, 132, 176, 196; in *Jelantik Goes to Blambangan*, 158, 159, 161, 162, 164, 168; project regarding, 281–83
Mahadevi, 89
Mahadewa (god), 140, 148, 150, 153, 168
Mahapatra, L. K., 95
Mahapatra, Laxmi Dhanu, 89
maharanas, 213–16, 241
Mahendradatta (Airlangga's mother), 80–81, 98, 103n.11
Mahendragiri mountains (near Orissa, India), 78, 90, 91, 95
Mahendratanaya River, 90
Maheshwari caste, 221, 225, 227
Mahisasura (buffalo-demon), 81
Mai, Mulai (character), 20–21, 24, 30
Mai, Mulinja (character), 20–21, 24, 30
Mai, Yembogai (character), 20–21, 24, 30
Mai, Yembogeja (character), 20–21, 24, 30
Majapahit courts (Java), 79–80, 113, 115, 127, 129, 132, 148, 150, 158, 165
Makehuku village (Papua New Guinea), 11, 13, 22, 24
Makutavangshavadhana, 80
malanggan masks (Papua New Guinea), 32n.4
Malda region (West Bengal), 46
Man as Art (Kirk), 32n.13
Manhattan Project, 273n.1
Manikapatna (India), 76, 78
mantras, 49, 111, 113, 151, 153, 176, 187, 261
Maori people, 71
mapajar (encounters), 74, 84, 103n.11
Maprik region (Sepik River basin), 95
Marat/Sade (Weiss), 195
Marrakech, 246
martial arts, 111, 120, 137, 143
Marwari caste, 227
Marx Brothers, 194
masalai spirit (Papua New Guinea), 30
masks, xxi; as cosmetic disguise, 7, 51, 116, 249, 251, 267; of demons, 137–38, 140, 247; effectiveness of, 27–29, 32n.4; Emigh's interest in, 247–48, 267–68, 270; honoring of, 43, 261; and interculturalism, 99; linking of past and present through, 7–8, 13, 19, 113, 153; man-sized puppet, 91, 93; in modern Western theatre, 7, 21, 22, 248, 262, 267–68, 270; in New Guinea, 3, 7–20; potential for life in, 251–52, 275, 276, 285; powers associated with, 43, 49, 204n.5; protective functions of, 46, 48, 61, 67, 68, 71, 84, 85, 101n.7, 103n.10; psychological effects of, 266–67; and self-and-other theme, xvii–xviii, xx, 23–24, 116–17, 248, 251–52, 275–78, 285, 289–90; spirit of, xviii, 101n.7, 113, 116; and spiritual visitation, 14–20, 29–31, 43, 46, 49, 57, 66, 96, 99, 107, 113, 115–16, 136, 150–51, 156n.13, 186, 194, 248; as "transitional objects," 7–14; use of, to contain disruptive forces, xx, 17, 35–74, 79, 81, 99, 147, 189, 197, 205n.14; wood for, 155n.7. *See also* actors; *Calon Arang*; character; identity; *Prahlada Nataka*; topeng pajegan
Maslon, Larry, 268
masquerade balls, 24
Massachusetts Institute of Technology, 274n.7
Mata, Si Mata, 140, 142–43, 147, 166, 184, 185–86, 189, 201
Mazzoni-Clementi, Carlo, 155n.7
mbwatnggowi figures, 8
Mead, Margaret, 102n.8
median Balinese language, 130–31, 157, 159, 166
medieval theatre, 254
Medusa, 69
Melanesia, 7, 93, 95, 96
mendaska, 17
Mewar (India), xx, 207, 210; courts of, 207, 210, 214
Meyerhold, Vsevolod Y., 174, 254
microcosmos (human), 67, 132, 201, 241, 286
Middle Javanese language, 129, 131, 136, 157, 158, 164, 176, 177
A Midsummer Night's Dream (Shakespeare), 156n.11, 281
Miller, Arthur, 173
Miller, Gary, 268, 270
mime, 257
mimesis, 35, 46, 48–49, 52, 57, 59, 66, 99, 116
mimicry, xx, 288
Mindimbit village (Papua New Guinea), xvii–xviii, 20–21
Miracle of Bali: Night (film), 75, 102n.8
mise-en-scène, xix, 172, 175
MIT gamelan, 274n.7

Mnouchkine, Ariadne, 21–22, 284
modern theatre (Western), xx; compared to topeng, 196, 198, 286; masks in, 7, 21, 22, 248, 262, 267–68, 270
Moem village (Papua New Guinea), 32n.6
Molière, 249, 280, 281
momboto, 14, 96
Mons people, 93
Monty Python's Flying Circus, 174, 193
Moscow Art Theatre, 281
Mount Meru, 91
Movement Theatre International, 274n.7
mrdala (drums), 50
MTV videos, 28
mudiettu, 85
"mudmen" (of Papua New Guinea), 11, 13, 22, 24
mudras (ritualized hand gestures), 49, 151
mukhavina (oboe-like instrument), 50
Munda culture, 93
music: African-American, 279; in Asian theatre, 50; in Balinese theatre, 64, 95, 136, 181, 182, 247–48; in Emigh's performances, 254, 255–57; in Papua New Guinea performances, 11, 19, 21; in plays directed by Emigh, 284. See also *gamelan*
mythos, 175
myths: Emigh's use of, 255, 257, 259; in Greek theatre, 21; of Iatmul creation, 20, 32n.6; meaning of, 203n.4; mimetic elaborations of, 46, 48–49; and "social drama," 56. See also *puranas*

Nagasaki (Japan), 278
Nakhti, 236, 238
Napier, David, 68–71, 79, 80
Naqqal caste, 213
Narasimha mask, 41–60, 68, 70, 73, 84, 85, 93, 95–96, 103nn.12, 13, 113
Narasimhi, 46, 85
Narayana, 55. *See also* Vishnu
National Black Theatre, 245, 273n.1
National Geographic magazine, 247
National School of Drama (India), 266, 272
National Theatre (England), 280
National Theatre of the Deaf, 273n.1
naturalism, 270, 279
natyadharmi, 27–28, 52
Natyasastra (Sanskrit manual on acting), 27, 71
Navaratri festivities, 214
Naxalite terrorists, 101n.7
Ndembu rituals, 1, 3
Negara: The Theatre State in Nineteenth Century Bali (C. Geertz), 252
Nehru, Jawaharlal, 225
Nepal, 69, 75, 89
New Britain (Papua New Guinea), 14, 17, 22, 96
New Guinea. *See* Papua New Guinea
New Ireland (Papua New Guinea), 13, 32n.4
New York City Indonesian Consulate, 274n.7
New York Shakespeare Festival, 287
Nikolais, Alwyn, 286
Nipang, Diah Gusti Ayu (character), 158–59
North Africa, 68
nyepi, 84

Ocean of Streams of Stories (*Katha-sarit-sagara*), 85
odalan, 107–8, 113, 182
Odin Teatrat, 286
Oedipus at Colonus (Sophocles), 279–80
offerings (Balinese), 60–61, 168, 189, 191
Old Javanese language (Kawi), 129, 131, 132, 136, 137, 150, 157, 158, 168
O'Neill, Eugene, 175
one-man shows. *See* solo performances
"On the Balinese Theatre" (Artaud), 193
On the Road: A Search for American Character (Smith), 287, 289
Oohashi Tsutomu, 71
"open rehearsals," 174
Open Theatre, 271, 273n.1
Oresteia, 175, 284
Orissa (India): *bahurupiya* as term in, 212; historical connections between Bali and, 74–99; icons in, 81, 96; trance performances in, xx, xxii, 35, 41–60, 66, 73, 74, 90, 91
Oriya language, 43, 78, 100n.3
Oswali Bania caste, 221, 243n.5
"other side": in Hinduism, 41, 67; masks' use in dealing with, 46

Pacific Northwest, 69
pagal, 230, 240
pageants, 24
paisa, 229
paling (balance), 198
Paloura, 77–78

pamurtian, 66, 67, 99
Pancholi, R. C., 236
Papua New Guinea, xvii–xviii, xx, xxi, xxii, 95; ceremonial performances in, 1, 3–20, 46, 197; Emigh's experiences in, 248–49; masks in, 7–14, 93, 113, 247; trance performances in, 17, 19, 22, 29–30, 107, 248
The Paradox of Acting (Diderot), 25
Paricha, Goura Hari, 100n.3
Paris Exposition, 193
Pasurahan kingdom, 159, 176, 177
Patali, King of, 158
patel, 213, 218
patih characters, 118, 120, 121, 123, 125, 126, 147, 151, 156n.8, 189
patih keras, 126
"pay-back" ceremonies (Papua New Guinea), 1, 11
pedanda (Brahmana priest), 186
Pejeng village (Bali), 76, 95
Penarukan village (Bali), 98
pengejukan, 153
pengelembar (introductory dances in topeng pajegan), 118–27, 136, 137, 147, 157, 182, 187
"pentad," 175
"performance" (as domain), 172, 176, 181–84, 186–88
performance artists, 174
Performance Group, 273n.1
performance traditions: ceremonial, 1, 3; intercultural background of, 74–99; masks in modern Western, 7, 21, 22, 248, 262, 267–68, 270; of postmodern Western theatre, xx, 28, 174, 193, 198–202; questions about, for researchers, xxi, 293–300; and real politics, 98, 185, 196, 204n.5, 245, 252, 259, 261, 262, 264, 266, 274n.8, 287–88; sources for, 21; for tourists, 99; use of masked, to contain disruptive forces, xx, 17, 35–74, 79, 81, 99, 147, 189, 197, 205n.14; variety of modes in, 22–31. *See also* actors; *bedi*; characters; illusion; masks; play; rituals; solo performances; trance performances; specific performance forms and traditions
Performing Arts Journal, 244
Performing Garage (New York City), 266
Periplus Exo Thelasses, 78
persasti, 127
Persia, 210
persona, xix. *See also* identity
Phaedrus (Plato), 240
Phalundi, I. G. P., 90
Piano (Smith), 274n.8
The Pig-Headed King, 259, 262, 264
Pinjari character, 215, 233, 238
Pinque, Erminio, 270, 274n.8
Pinter, Harold, 245
Pirandello, Luigi, 245
Pithunda (India), 90
"plane of similitude," 277–78, 284
Plato, 28, 193–94, 240
play: as apt word for theatre, 13, 22; Bateson on, 1, 278; mimetic, 35, 46, 48–49, 52, 57, 59, 66, 99, 116; "potential space" for, 2, 13; in theatre, xviii, xxi. *See also* illusion
"play-back" singers, 50, 56
playwrights, 245
Pliny, 77
Portuguese (in Bali), 197
possession. *See* trance performances; visitation
postmodern theatre (Western), xx, 28, 174, 193, 198–202
"potential space," 154n.3, 278; in dramatic performance, 21, 107, 108, 174; in funerary customs, 7; for play, 2, 13
Pourchot, Teviot, 273n.6
Prahlada Nataka, xx, xxii, 43, 48–60, 66, 74, 77, 84–91, 129, 279; intercultural influences on, 96
The Praise of Folly (Erasmus), 241
prasanna (arriving), 46
prasjengan (offering), 168
praxis, 175
The Predicament of Culture (Clifford), 285
prembon, 205n.14
pretending, 23. *See also* illusion; mimesis; play
Prince, Harold, 174
Prithivi (Balinese goddess), 41
"psychological gesture," 25
"psychosynthesis," 289
Ptolemy, 77, 78
Pugra, I, 156n.9
puja (ceremony of welcome), 43, 49, 51, 57, 67, 113
Punjab (India), 210, 212
Punjab Census Report of 1881, 212
puppets: in Batak funerary rites, 8; in Java, 197; man-sized, 91, 93; Sudanese rod, 197. *See also* shadow puppets

puputan (mass suicide), 98
pura dalem, 61, 67
puranas, 24, 37, 46, 56
Pura Penataran Topeng, 203n.5
Puri, 103n.13

RADA (London), 280
Rahu (Indian demon), 37, 43
Rai, Desak Made (character), 143, 148, 166–67, 183, 189
Rai, I Ketut (character), 134, 160–61
Rajas, 211, 213, 215, 223, 224, 241
Rajasthan (India), 207, 209–12, 227, 228, 240, 241
Rajput caste, 222–24
Rajput courts, 211, 214–16
raksasa ("demon"), 215, 230
Rama, 55, 143, 229. *See also* Vishnu
ramai (busy and beautiful), 107, 108
Ramayana, 24, 75, 89, 281, 283; desia nata version of, 84; influence of, on Balinese theatre, 129, 130, 132, 176; in *Jelantik Goes to Blambangan*, 158, 168
Ramchandra (*bahurupiya*), 215, 216
ramlila performances (India), 24, 229
Ramseyer, Urs, 75
Rangda (Balinese demon), 61, 64, 66–68, 70–73, 186, 197, 198; mask of, 247; origins of, 74–99, 113; sexual identity of, 102n.8
Rarong (character), 81
raslila performances (India), 24
Rathors, 221–22
Ratu Dalem, 67
rauh (coming), 107
Ravana (character), 84
Rawal caste, 212
"reactualization," 13
Reagan, Ronald, 261
Red Riding Shawl, 262, 264, 266
Regug, I Made, 267
rehearsals (lack of, in topeng pajegan), 177–78, 261
reincarnation, 80
Reinhardt, Max, 172
religious processions, 24
Rembang, I Nyoman, 203n.5
Rendra, W. S., 117, 118
The Republic (Plato), 240
Respect for Acting (Hagen), 31n.3
Reynaud, J. D., 200, 201
Rhode Island Festival: 71, 273n.1
Richard II (Shakespeare), 284
Ridgeway, William, 32n.12
Rimbaud, Arthur, xviii
rites of passage, 1
rituals: dances associated with, 90–91, 151; for ending topeng ceremonies, 176, 183, 186; and exorcism, 46, 74; in masked theatre, xx, 74, 188–89; masks associated with, 19, 29–31, 35; for masks' powers, 43, 49, 111, 113, 151, 153, 186, 187; past and present in, 7–8, 10–11, 13, 19, 20–21; theatrical stories cannibalized by, 66. See also *Calon Arang*; *Prahlada Nataka*; topeng pajegan
Robinson, Allan, 254
Role Playing and Identity (Wilshire), 201
Rome, 78
Rosenbaum, Norman, 288
Rosenbaum, Yankel, 287
rupa (form), 207

sacred performances. *See* actors, as mediators between sacred and secular; *Calon Arang*; *Prahlada Nataka*; rituals; topeng; trance performances
sadhu caste, 228–29
Sailendra dynasty, 79
sakti, xxi, 81
salvars, 228
samkranti, 84
Samos, Steve, 259
Samwantiga, Ni Gusti Ayu (Jelantik's wife), 161–66
Samyaktva (Taruna Prabha Suri), 210, 213
sang (comic routine), 209–10, 215, 238–40
sanghyang dedari, 113, 116
"Sanskritization," 95
Sanskrit language, 49, 50, 56, 76, 107, 127, 129, 150, 157, 202, 207, 209, 210; Archipelago version of, 131, 189; Javanized, 111, 113, 176
Saraswati (goddess of learning), 50, 164
Sartre, Jean-Paul, 175
Satapathy, Shri Arjun, 43, 57, 59
satire, 229–30, 238
Satria (Balinese caste designation), xxi, 127, 130, 147, 148, 150, 159, 183
Satyanarayan (god), 224
Schechner, Richard, 21, 24; on "domains," xx, 171–93; on experimental theatre, 244, 247
Schevill, James, xxi, 244–74, 277

Schieffelin, Edward L., 32n.11
Schumann, Peter, 21, 193, 247
"script" (as domain), 172, 173, 175–77, 180–82, 198
sea trade (in South Asia), 75–80, 85, 90, 95–96, 197
Seattle (Washington), 248
sebel (unclean), 66
"Second Coming" (Yeats), 200
secular stories (in sacred plays), 151
Sedana, I Nyoman, 274n.7
self-and-other theme (and masks), xvii–xviii, xx, 23–24, 116–17, 248, 251–52, 275–78, 285, 289–90
self-stabbing, 84, 98–99
Sembiran (Bali), 76, 78
Sepik River (Papua New Guinea), 7, 20
Seraya, Gatutkaca (character), 159
Serban, Andrei, 284
sexual energy, 37, 41, 80
sexual politics (in Papua New Guinea), 10–11
shadow puppets, 164, 248, 270, 283; early references to, 79, 91; humor with, 185; in India, 90; language used with, 158. See also *wayang kulit*
Shailodbhava Kings (of Kongoda), 95
Shakespeare, William, 156n.11, 172, 204n.11, 223, 270, 282, 284, 286–87
Shaktawat, Mohan Singh, 225
Shakti ("feminine" energy), xxi, 37, 46, 61, 71, 75, 80; ambivalence toward, 81, 84–85, 89–90; masks associated with, 91, 93; performance traditions arising from worship of, 96, 103n.12, 193; rituals of, appropriated by terrorists, 101n.7. *See also* Durga; Kali
shamanism: and *bahurupiyas*, 222; and masks, 289; performances associated with, 14, 29, 31
Sharma, G. N., 210
Shaw, George Bernard, 244
Shepard, Sam, 172, 202, 270, 286
shikar, 214
Shiraishi Kayoko, 278
shi-shi (Japanese apotropaic figure), 69
Shiva (Indian god), 37, 67, 78, 80, 85, 89, 218, 221, 228, 229–30. *See also* Shakti; Siwa
sibling rivalry, 64, 257
siddhi (spiritual powers), 217, 222
Sideman village (Bali), 61
sidha (successful), 148
si galegale puppets, 8
Sihanouk, Norodom, 284
Sills, Paul, 255
Singh, Maharana Bhagat, 216, 242n.3
Singh, Maharana Bhupal, 215, 216, 225, 227, 233, 238, 242n.3
Singh, Maharana Fateh, 214
Singh, Maharana Hamir (King Hamir), 224
Singh, Kalyan (Thakur of Orli), 216, 221–22
Singh, Rawat Kesari, 211, 216, 223, 233
Singh, Maharana Sajan (of Udaipur), 214
Singh, Maharana Svarup, 214
sing nawang basa, 130
"sing-sings" (Papua New Guinea), 1, 10, 11, 24
Sita (wife of Rama), 229
Siwa, 67, 113, 115. *See also* Shiva
skulls (human), 7–8, 14. *See also* heads (carved); masks
slokas, 50, 56
Smith, Anna Deavere, 274n.8, 287–89
Snow Lion (of Nepal and Tibet), 69, 75
social drama, xx–xxi, 42, 56, 98, 205n.13, 287
societas, 184
solo performances, 253, 286–87; Anna Deavere Smith's, 287–89; Emigh's, xviii, 246, 254; Hajari Bhand's, xx, xxii, 207–43, 271; Kakul's, 107–54, 253
Sophocles, 21, 175, 279–80
South Asia: cultural mix in, 91; leonine apotropaic figures in, 68; trade in, 96, 197. *See also* sea trade; specific countries and regions
Southeast Asia: cultural mix in, 91, 95; leonine apotropaic figures in, 68; peoples in, 93; trade in, 78, 96. *See also* sea trade; specific countries
spectacle, 267–68, 270
Spenser, Edmund, 191
Spies, Walter, 176
Spring Awakening (Wedekind), 274n.8
Srikakulam District (Andhra Pradesh, India), 43, 77
Staal, J. F., 95
stage, 182
Stalin, Joseph, 24
Stanislavski, Constantin, 25, 174, 247, 251
status. *See* caste

Stendhal, 27, 28
sthayibhavas, 34n.14, 71
Story of Phalabuti, 85, 89
storytelling: Emigh's, 255, 257, 259, 261; in Papua New Guinea performances, 11; in topeng, 108, 127–31, 151, 181, 194, 252
Story Theatre (Sills), 255
Strasberg, Lee, 25
street performers. *See* Bhand, Hajari
Stuff As Dreams Are Made On (Curchack), 286–87
Suarti, Desak Laksmi, 274n.7
suci (offering), 168
Sudan, 197
Sudra caste: character depicted as from, 143; Kakul as belonging to, 107, 108, 147, 151, 153
Suharto, General, 204n.5, 266
suicides (Balinese mass public), 98. *See also* self-stabbing
Sukarno, 266
Sukawati, 204n.12
Sulawesi (Indonesia), 3
Sumandhi, I Nyoman, 102n.8
Sumatra, 8, 79. *See also* Batak funerary rites
Sumerta village (Bali), 64, 66
Summerfest '91 (New York City), 274n.7
Supartha, I Gusti, 274n.7
Suri, Taruna Prabha, 210
sutri dance, 167
Suweca, I Wayan, 102n.8, 254, 255, 257, 259, 262, 264
Suzuki Tadashi, 175, 278, 280, 281, 283
svanga, 209
swaihwe masks, 69
swang. See *sang*
Sweeney Todd (Sondheim), 246

tabasan durmanggala (offering), 168
tableaux vivants, 24
taksu, 30, 115–16, 118, 153, 186, 202
The Tale of Erlangga, 204n.12
Tamburlaine, 210
Tamil Nadu (India), 76–77, 84, 103n.12
Tanatoraja, 81
Tantrism, 37, 41, 43, 46, 73, 80–81, 84, 85, 89, 96, 193, 197
Taranto vase painting, 277
Tartuffe (Molière), 280, 283
Tat Twam Asi (maxim), 202, 286
tau-tau (Indonesian effigy figures), 3–7, 14
Tawney, C. H., 85
Taymor, Julie, 284
tebasan (offering), 168
Tedun, I Wayan, 267
Telegu language, 43, 77, 78, 90, 100n.3
Telson, Bob, 279, 283
The Tempest (Shakespeare), 286–87
Tendulkar, V. J., 101n.7
Tenganan village (Bali), 76, 79, 90
Tenvir, Habib, 280
terukkuttu, 84
"texts," xix, 180, 198–99
Thakur of Bhatyankakhera, 214–15, 218
Thakur of Orli (Kalyan Singh), 216, 221–22
"theatre" (as domain), 172, 176, 180–81, 187, 188. *See also* performance traditions
Théâtre du Soleil, 22
Theatre of Sources workshops, 281
Theatre Project (Baltimore), 259
Theophrastus, 249
"The Way(s) of How" (Coates), 22
"threat displays," 71–73
Three Worlds of Bali (film), 155n.3
Tibet, 69, 75
Tibetan School of Drama (India), 266
tigers, 93
Timur-leng (Tamburlaine), 210
Tjupak (children's play), 255, 257, 262
Tolai people (Papua New Guinea), 14, 19, 129
Tomlin, Lily, 24
tooth-filing ceremonies (Bali), 107, 108, 182
topeng, 105, 127; company forms of, 132, 147; domains of, 171–206; humor in, 127, 129–32, 134, 140–47, 183, 184–86, 188, 194, 205n.14; inclusiveness of, 186, 187, 197, 198, 202; Kakul's approach to, 171–72, 174, 187–92, 198, 199, 201, 241; literal meaning of, 203n.5; masks characteristic of, 181, 203n.5, 207; as satire, 186. *See also* masks; topeng pajegan
topeng arya, 126
topeng munyer, 156n.9
topeng pajegan, 28, 105–56, 192, 286; actor's preparation for, 111–18, 176–77; costumes associated with, 111; early references to, 79, 80, 91; ending ceremony of, 150–51, 153, 167, 176, 183, 186, 188–89; human and contemporary themes in, 147, 189, 195; introductory dances in, 118–27, 136, 137, 147, 157, 182, 187; masks worn by dancers of, 79, 105; occa-

sions for, 107–8, 182; origins of, 176; past and present in, xx, 104, 111, 113, 115, 125–27, 129–32, 134–37, 156n.13, 197, 199, 248, 252–53, 286; postmodern similarities with, 174, 193, 198–202; principals' dances in, 136–40; use of historical chronicles in, 99, 127, 131, 140, 142, 148, 150, 175–77, 252; visitation in, 34n.18, 107, 113, 115–16, 136, 150–51, 156n.13. *See also* masks; topeng
topeng panca, 132, 147
topeng wali (ritual topeng), 151. *See also* topeng pajegan
Torajan effigy figures, 3–7, 14, 20
Toth, Andy, 254
Trance and Dance in Bali (film), 102n.8
trance performances, 34n.17; in Bali, xx, 64, 84, 91, 118, 198; Hindu, in India, xx, 46, 48, 50–60, 84–85, 89–90; in Papua New Guinea, 17, 19, 22, 29–30, 107, 248; self-stabbing in, 84, 98–99. *See also* visitation
transculturalism, 281, 283
"transitional objects and events": death masks as, 32n.4; New Guinean masks as, 7–14, 20; in play, 2–3, 17, 19–20, 26; Torajan tau-tau as, 3–7
triwangsa (upper three castes), 143
The Trojan Women (Euripides), 278, 283
Trunyan village (Bali), 93, 113
tua (old man character), 123, 125, 126, 147, 156nn.8, 9, 189
tubuan dance (Papua New Guinea), 14, 19, 29, 96, 129
Turner, Victor, xx–xxi, 13, 33n.10, 183–84, 277, 287; on liminal occasions, 1–3, 10, 184, 190–91, 278
Tusan village (Bali), 107–54, 157, 172, 174–77, 183, 192
Twilight: Los Angeles, 1992 (Smith), 287

ucapan gambuh, 129
Udaipur Palace (India), 225
Udayana, 80, 103n.11
ugra, 85
Ularan, Patih (character), 177
UMBC (Baltimore), 259
Unda River (Batu Kerotok), 162–63
U.S. Supreme Court, 268
Upanishads, 289
Uramot Baining people (Papua New Guinea), 17, 19
Uttar Pradesh (India), 210

Valmiki, 75
Van Gennep, Arnold, 1, 204n.8
Varahi, 89
Vatsyayana, 210
Verma, Jatinder, 280, 283
vesa (clothing), 209
vesh (disguise), xx, 209–10, 216–18, 225, 228, 233, 238–40
via negativa, 29
Vickers, Adrian, 180
Victoria (Queen of England), 24
vidusakas, 210
Virtually Yours (Bornstein), 289
"Visages of Glory." *See* Kirtimukhas
Vishnu (Indian god), xxi, 41, 49, 89; avatars of, 43, 52, 259; devotees of, 50, 85; forbidden worship of, 52, 55, 56; names associated with, 55. *See also* Wisnu (Balinese god)
visitation (possession): dramatic representations of, 125–26; versus illusion, 29, 99, 107, 136–37, 150, 187, 199; spiritual, in performance, 14–20, 29–31, 43, 46, 49, 57, 66, 96, 99, 107, 113, 115–16, 136, 150–51, 156n.13, 186, 194, 248. *See also* ancestors; "other side"; trance performances
Volpone (Jonson), 268
von Steitencron, H., 103n.13

Wallis, Richard, 196–97
Wastepaper Theatre (Providence, Rhode Island), 262
water buffalos, 6, 14; demons based on, 81, 137
Watergate, 259
Waturenggong, Dalem, 167
wayang cepak puppet theatre, 197
wayang kulit (shadow puppet theatre), 131, 185, 282
Weber, Karl, 281
weddings: Balinese, 107, 108, 182; Indian, 224–25
Wedekind, Frank, 274n.8
Weiss, Peter, 193, 195
Welsford, Enid, 212
Wenten, I Nyoman, 102n.8, 248, 257, 274n.7, 286
Wesleyan University, 259
Wessing, Robert, 30
West Bengal, 46, 85
Westernization, 197, 205n.14
wet rice culture, 93

white magic, 67
Whitman, Walt, 289
widows, 80; in *Calon Arang*, 66–67, 80–81, 85, 103n.11
Wijaya, Putu, 200
Willeford, William, 207
Wilshire, Bruce, 201
Wilson, Robert, 24, 173, 193, 245, 284
Windia, I Gusti, 102n.8, 134, 140, 156n.12, 205n.14, 274n.7
Winnicott, D. W., 1–3, 13, 17, 19–20, 22, 24–26, 28, 33n.10, 277, 278
Wisnu (Balinese god), xxi, 67, 113, 158, 159. *See also* Vishnu (Indian god)
witches, 66–67, 71, 80–81, 84–85, 89, 96. *See also* Rangda
wives, 134, 143, 161–67, 184, 236, 238, 239
Wooster Group, 173, 193

xwexwe masks, 69

yakshagana (Hindu performance form), 46
Yali, 103n.12
Yeats, William Butler, 200, 254
Yet, Penget (character), 159
Young, Elizabeth, 185, 204n.12

zamindars, 214
Zarrilli, Phillip, 28
Zen, xix, 19
Zimmer, Heinrich, 41, 61